Chief Wahunsonacock Powhatan
Some Shawnee Descendants

by JD Weeks

Lulu Press
2012
The United States of America

Copyright

Copyright © 2012 by J D Weeks.

All rights reserved. No part of this book shall be reproduced, stored in a retrieval system, or transmitted by any means, electronic, mechanical, photocopying, recording, or otherwise, without prior written permission from J D Weeks.

ISBN: 978-1-105-54443-9

Printed in The United States of America.

Preface

26 January 2012

This publication contains some Shawnee descendants of Chief Wahunsonacock Powhatan from my genealogy database. I use this information as a working piece and it will already be out of date by the time this is read. As with all genealogy research, there will be errors and omissions. Some of this may lack the documentation desired by many, so use this as you see fit. Any corrections or additions would be appreciated very much.

Email jd@jdweeks.com
Personal Web Page www.jdweeks.com
Lulu Store Front www.lulu.com/jdweeks
Amazon Author Site www.amazon.com/author/jdweeks
Face Book Page www.facebook.com/jdweeks

Virtually all the early Shawnee research is far beyond my resources and capabilities, and all the credit for that goes to Don Friend Spirit Wolf Greene, Principal Chief of the Appalachian Shawnee Tribe. He has kindly agreed to speak toward that effort and for that I am very appreciative. Several of his books can be found at www.amazon.com and www.lulu.com. The titles are Shawnee Heritage I, ISBN No. 978-1-4357-1573-8 and Shawnee Heritage II, ISBN No. 978-0-557-03605-9.

Don Friend Spirit Wolf Greene

My works; "Shawnee Heritage" and "Shawnee Heritage II" were compiled to allow those of Shawnee descent, including those classified as members of the three Federal Shawnee Tribes, those holding membership in other Federal Indian tribes and in many non-Federal groups, the chance to trace their ancestry to their Colonial Period origins.

My Great Work began innocently enough in an effort to identify all the 1,000+ warriors fighting for Chief Cornstalk's Northern Confederacy at Point Pleasant WV in 1774. As I witnessed the connection between those warriors and so many "white" names that we know today I saw a subject that begged to be brought to the attention of their descendants. Over the years I came to the conclusion that the Northern Confederacy of some 22 tribes led by Cornstalk and the Southern Confederacy led by Dragging Canoe, that are known today as Algonquian- speaking tribes were no more than a reunion of the remnants of a major society that had existed in 1492 when the non-North Americans had arrived.

So my research expanded to address any blood connections to all current or seemingly extinct Algonquian-speaking tribes, from Canada to the Gulf States and from the Atlantic coast to the Rocky Mountains. For anyone to imagine that it is a completed work would be erroneous and invalid for it is clear that today there are quite literally millions of people that can claim such ancestry and heritage.

Even a cursory glance will reveal that the listings in my books go beyond simple genealogy for much of the history of their times is reflected in the listings, written in a format I developed over the years instead of a canned genealogy program. My opinion is that in order to fully understand and appreciate who and what your ancestors really were, you must know what was happening in the world they lived it. So my multiple-decade research will likely continue long after I have left this world. Since 2004 I have been blessed with the growth of the Appalachian Shawnee Tribe, founded by a handful of us that, despite being of Native descent, understood that we are not and cannot ever be Federal Indians and did not find satisfaction or completeness participating on the pow-wow circuit. Now there are nearly 1,000 of us, many contributing to our collective knowledge of who our ancestors were, what occurred in their world, what factors led them to not end up as Federal Indians today but rather to become part of the original melting pot of America.

A by-product of my work is that many "historical facts" have been seen in a new light; like the fallacy of the Delaware being the ancestral "grandfathers" of our Shawnee, the British-inspired origin of the Cherokee in 1693, the "emptiness" of this continent and the "heathens" that lived here. Good Lord willing, I will produce a third book of similar listings followed by a fourth book containing a narrative history of our people, from as early as I can find any information until the Removal in the 1830's. Works of such members as J D Great Eagle Weeks focus on their individual families and compliment my humble efforts and are greatly appreciated.

Descendants of Chief Wahunsonacock Powhatan

26 January 2012

First Generation

1. **Chief Wahunsonacock POWHATAN** was born in 1545 in James River, VA. He died in 1618 at the age of 73 in VA.

Chief Wahunsonacock POWHATAN and Bear Clan Shawano AMOPOTUSKEE were married in 1590 in Central VA. **Bear Clan Shawano AMOPOTUSKEE** was born in 1576 in Shenandoah Valley, VA.

Wahunsonacock POWHATAN and Bear Clan Shawano AMOPOTUSKEE had the following children:

- i. **Tatacoope the Shawano POWHATAN** was born in 1590 in VA. He died after 1610 at the age of 20.
- ii. **Taux the Shawano POWHATAN** was born in 1592 in VA. He died after 1610 at the age of 18 in VA.
- iii. **Pochins the Shawano POWHATAN** was born in 1594 in VA. He died after 1614 at the age of 20.
- iv. **Nantaquas the Shawano POWHATAN** was born in 1596 in VA. She died after 1614 at the age of 18.
- v. **Parahunt the Shawano POWHATAN** was born in 1598 in VA. He died in 1618 at the age of 20 in VA.
- 2 vi. **Cleopatra the Shawano POWHATAN**, born 1602, near Jamestown colony, VA; married Opechan STREAM, 1618, near Jamestown colony, VA; died 1680, VA.

Chief Wahunsonacock POWHATAN and Matatiske WINGANUSKE were married in 1586 in VA. **Matatiske WINGANUSKE** was born in 1571 in VA. She died after 1603 at the age of 32.

Chief Wahunsonacock POWHATAN and Nonoma WINGANUSKE were married in 1589 in VA. **Nonoma WINGANUSKE** died after 1600. She was born about 1774 in VA.

Wahunsonacock POWHATAN and Nonoma WINGANUSKE had the following child:

- 3 i. **Matoaka-Pocahontas POWHATAN**, born 17 Sep 1595, VA; married John ROLFE, 1614, VA; died 21 Mar 1616, Gravesend, England.

Chief Wahunsonacock POWHATAN and Quiquocohannock PONNOISKE were married in 1564 in VA. **Quiquocohannock PONNOISKE** was born in 1551 in Surry Co., VA. She died after 1600 at the age of 49.

Chief Wahunsonacock POWHATAN and Ottachugh OTTERMISKE were married in 1570 in VA. **Ottachugh OTTERMISKE** was born in 1556 in Lancaster Co., VA. She died after 1591 at the age of 35.

Chief Wahunsonacock POWHATAN and Pamukey APPOMOSISCUT were married in 1571 in VA. **Pamukey APPOMOSISCUT** was born in 1557 in King William Co., VA. She died after 1600 at the age of 43.

Chief Wahunsonacock POWHATAN and Tauxenent APPIMMONOISKE were married in 1572. **Tauxenent**

Descendants of Chief Wahunsonacock Powhatan

APPIMMONOISKE was born about 1558 in Fairfax Co, VA. She died after 1573 at the age of 15.

Chief Wahunsonacock POWHATAN and Sockobeck ATTOSSOCOMISKE were married in 1574 in VA. **Sockobeck ATTOSSOCOMISKE** was born in 1560 in King George Co., VA. She died after 1575 at the age of 15.

Chief Wahunsonacock POWHATAN and Werawahon OWEROUGHWOUGH were married in 1574 in VA. **Werawahon OWEROUGHWOUGH** was born about 1561 in New Kent Co., VA. She died after 1575 at the age of 14.

Chief Wahunsonacock POWHATAN and Nonoma CORNSTALK were married in 1576 in VA. **Nonoma CORNSTALK** was born in 1562 in Central VA. She died after 1580 at the age of 18.

Chief Wahunsonacock POWHATAN and Potomac OTTOPOMTACKE were married in 1578 in VA. **Potomac OTTOPOMTACKE** was born in 1564 in Stafford Co., VA. She died after 1579 at the age of 15.

Chief Wahunsonacock POWHATAN and ORTOUGHNOISKE were married in 1579 in VA. **ORTOUGHNOISKE** was born about 1565 in VA. She died after 1580 at the age of 15.

Chief Wahunsonacock POWHATAN and Uttamussamacoma UTTOPOMTACKE were married in 1581 in VA. **Uttamussamacoma UTTOPOMTACKE** was born in 1566 in Uttamussamacoma, Westmoreland Co., VA. She died after 1581 at the age of 15.

Chief Wahunsonacock POWHATAN and Amopotoiske SHAWANO were married in 1582 in VA. **Amopotoiske SHAWANO** was born in 1568 in VA. She died after 1583 at the age of 15.

Chief Wahunsonacock POWHATAN and ARTOUGHNOISKE were married in 1583 in VA. **ARTOUGHNOISKE** was born about 1569 in VA. She died after 1584 at the age of 15.

Chief Wahunsonacock POWHATAN and Secacawoni WAHUNSEEACAWH were married in 1584 in VA. **Secacawoni WAHUNSEEACAWH** was born about 1570 in Secacawoni, Northumberland Co., VA. She died after 1585 at the age of 15.

Descendants of Chief Wahunsonacock Powhatan

Chief Wahunsonacock POWHATAN and ITOYATIN were married in 1585 in VA. **ITOYATIN** was born in 1570 in VA. She died after 1586 at the age of 16.

Chief Wahunsonacock POWHATAN and Itoyah-Sasawpen OPIRHAPAN were married in 1587 in VA. **Itoyah-Sasawpen OPIRHAPAN** was born about 1572 in Sasawpen, VA. She died after 1590 at the age of 18.

Chief Wahunsonacock POWHATAN and ASHETOISKE were married in 1588 in VA. **ASHETOISKE** was born about 1574 in VA. She died after 1589 at the age of 15.

Chief Wahunsonacock POWHATAN and Queen WINGANUSKE were married in 1591 in VA. **Queen WINGANUSKE** was born about 1576 in VA. She died after 1622 at the age of 46 in VA.

Chief Wahunsonacock POWHATAN and Nonoma OPECHAN were married in 1590 in VA. **Nonoma OPECHAN** was born in 1576. She died after 1596 at the age of 20.

Chief Wahunsonacock POWHATAN and Nonoma MANGOPEESOMON were married in 1593 in VA. **Nonoma MANGOPEESOMON** was born in 1579 in VA. She died after 1592 at the age of 13.

Chief Wahunsonacock POWHATAN and Quiquocohannock OHOLASE were married in 1594 in VA. **Quiquocohannock OHOLASE** was born about 1580 in Quiquocohannock, Surry Co., VA. She died after 1595 at the age of 15.

Chief Wahunsonacock POWHATAN and Nonoma WOWINCHO were married in 1595 in VA. **Nonoma WOWINCHO** was born in 1580 in VA. She died after 1606 at the age of 26.

Descendants of Chief Wahunsonacock Powhatan

Second Generation

2. **Cleopatra the Shawano POWHATAN** (Wahunsonacock-1) was born in 1602 in near Jamestown colony, VA. She died in 1680 at the age of 78 in VA.

Cleopatra the Shawano POWHATAN and Opechan STREAM were married in 1618 in near Jamestown colony, VA. **Opechan STREAM**, son of Running STREAM and Morning FLOWER, was born in 1556 in VA. He died in 1644 at the age of 88 in VA.

Opechan STREAM and Cleopatra the Shawano POWHATAN had the following children:

- 4   i. **Nicketti OPECHAN**, born 1624, near Jamestown colony, VA; married John Rice HUGHES, abt 1640, near Jamestown colony, VA; died aft 1680, VA.
- 5   ii. **Hokolesqua Opechan CORNSTALK**, born 1628, VA; married Nonoma , 1648, VA; died 1696, Southwest VA.

3. **Matoaka-Pocahontas POWHATAN** (Wahunsonacock-1) was born on 17 Sep 1595 in VA. She died on 21 Mar 1616 at the age of 20 in Gravesend, England.

Matoaka-Pocahontas POWHATAN and John ROLFE were married in 1614 in VA. **John ROLFE**, son of John ROLFE and Dorthea MASON, was born in 1585. He died in 1622 at the age of 37 in VA.

John ROLFE and Matoaka-Pocahontas POWHATAN had the following child:

- 6   i. **Thomas ROLFE**, born 30 Jan 1613, VA.

Descendants of Chief Wahunsonacock Powhatan

Third Generation

4. Nicketti OPECHAN (Cleopatra the Shawano Powhatan-2, Wahunsonacock-1) was born in 1624 in near Jamestown colony, VA. She died after 1680 at the age of 56 in VA.

Nicketti OPECHAN and John Rice HUGHES were married about 1640 in near Jamestown colony, VA. **John Rice HUGHES** was born in 1610.

5. Hokolesqua Opechan CORNSTALK (Cleopatra the Shawano Powhatan-2, Wahunsonacock-1) was born in 1628 in VA. He died in 1696 at the age of 68 in Southwest VA.

Hokolesqua Opechan CORNSTALK and Nonoma were married in 1648 in VA. **Nonoma** was born in 1630 in Shawnee Nation, VA. She died in 1679 at the age of 49 in Running Water, TN.

Hokolesqua Opechan CORNSTALK and Nonoma had the following children:

- 7   i. **Big Turkey Hop CORNSTALK**, born abt 1660, TN/VA; married Chalakatha Woman ; died 1694, Southwest VA.
-   ii. **Little Turkey CORNSTALK** was born about 1662 in VA. He died in 1698 at the age of 36 in Southwest VA.
- 8   iii. **Nancy Turkey CORNSTALK**, born 1664, Running Water, TN; married Trader Tom CARPENTER, 1678, Running Water, TN; died 1732, England.
- 9   iv. **Sister Turkey CORNSTALK**, born 1666; married Muskrat OSHASQUA, 1682, TN.

6. Thomas ROLFE (Matoaka-Pocahontas Powhatan-2, Wahunsonacock-1) was born on 30 Jan 1613 in VA.

Jane POYTHRESS, daughter of Francis POYTHRESS and Mary Frances SLOMAN, was born about 1630 in Jamestown, VA. She died in Jan 1679 at the age of 49 in Charles City, VA.

Thomas ROLFE and Jane POYTHRESS had the following child:

- 10   i. **Jane ROLFE**, born 10 Oct 1650, VA; died 1676, VA.

Descendants of Chief Wahunsonacock Powhatan

Fourth Generation

7. Big Turkey Hop CORNSTALK (Hokolesqua Opechan-3, Cleopatra the Shawano Powhatan-2, Wahunsonacock-1) was born about 1660 in TN/VA. He died in 1694 at the age of 34 in Southwest VA.

Big Turkey Hop CORNSTALK and Chalakatha Woman were married. **Chalakatha Woman** was born in 1664. She died in 1694 at the age of 30.

Big Turkey Hop CORNSTALK and Chalakatha Woman had the following children:

- 11   i. **Raven Moytoy TURKEY**, born 1680, Upper Hiwassee, TN; married CHEROKEE WOMAN; died 1756, Chewohe, TN.
- 12   ii. **Quatsis Hop TURKEY**, born 1682, Great Tellico, TN; married John BEAMER, 1697, Great Tellico, TN; married Smallpox Conjurer TSULA FOX, 1705, Settico, TN; married William WEBBER, 1709, Chota, TN; died 1758, Telllico Plains, TN.
- 13   iii. **Aganunitsi-Wild Potato Hop TURKEY**, born 1684, Upper Hiwassee, TA; married YOUNG RAINMAKER, 1700, TN; died aft 1741, TN.
- 14   iv. **Swan-Wapehti Hop TURKEY**, born 1686, Upper Hiwassee, TN; married Oshaqua MUSKRAT, 1703, Running Water, TN; died 1754, Chota, TN.
- 15   v. **Standing Old Hop TURKEY**, born 1688, Chota, TN; married Sugi RAINMAKER, 1708, Chota, TN; died 1761, Chota, TN.
- 16   vi. **April-Tkikami Hop TURKEY**, born 1690, Chota, TN; married Richard BARNES, 1718, Chota, TN; died 1744, Upper Hiwassee, TN.
- 17   vii. **Oolootah-Ulutse Hop TURKEY**, born 1692, Chota, TN; married Blue Holly CHEROKEE, 1705, Chota, TN; married John BOWLES, 1722, Settico, TN; died aft 1756, TN.
- 18   viii. **Ghigoneli Hop TURKEY**, born 1694, Chota, TN; married Blue Holly CHEROKEE, 1707, TN; died 1724, Chota, TN.

8. Nancy Turkey CORNSTALK (Hokolesqua Opechan-3, Cleopatra the Shawano Powhatan-2, Wahunsonacock-1) was born in 1664 in Running Water, TN. She died in 1732 at the age of 68 in England.

Nancy Turkey CORNSTALK and Trader Tom CARPENTER were married in 1678 in Running Water, TN. **Trader Tom CARPENTER** was born in 1660 in Chota, TN.

Trader Tom CARPENTER and Nancy Turkey CORNSTALK had the following child:

- i. **Savannah Tom CARPENTER** was born in 1680 in Chota, TN. He died in 1710 at the age of 30 in Oconee, SC.

9. Sister Turkey CORNSTALK (Hokolesqua Opechan-3, Cleopatra the Shawano Powhatan-2, Wahunsonacock-1) was born in 1666.

Sister Turkey CORNSTALK and Muskrat OSHASQUA were married in 1682 in TN. **Muskrat OSHASQUA** was born (date unknown).

10. **Jane ROLFE** (Thomas-3, Matoaka-Pocahontas Powhatan-2, Wahunsonacock-1) was born on 10 Oct 1650 in VA. She died in 1676 at the age of 26 in VA.

Robert BOLLING was born (date unknown).

Descendants of Chief Wahunsonacock Powhatan

Fifth Generation

11. **Raven Moytoy TURKEY** (Big Turkey Hop-4, Hokolesqua Opechan-3, Cleopatra the Shawano Powhatan-2, Wahunsonacock-1) was born in 1680 in Upper Hiwassee, TN. He died in 1756 at the age of 76 in Chewohe, TN.

Raven Moytoy TURKEY and CHEROKEE WOMAN were married. **CHEROKEE WOMAN** was born (date unknown).

12. **Quatsis Hop TURKEY** (Big Turkey Hop-4, Hokolesqua Opechan-3, Cleopatra the Shawano Powhatan-2, Wahunsonacock-1) was born in 1682 in Great Tellico, TN. She died in 1758 at the age of 76 in Telllico Plains, TN.

Quatsis Hop TURKEY and John BEAMER were married in 1697 in Great Tellico, TN. **John BEAMER** was born (date unknown).

Quatsis Hop TURKEY and Smallpox Conjurer TSULA FOX were married in 1705 in Settico, TN. **Smallpox Conjurer TSULA FOX** was born (date unknown).

Quatsis Hop TURKEY and William WEBBER were married in 1709 in Chota, TN. **William WEBBER** was born (date unknown).

13. **Aganunitsi-Wild Potato Hop TURKEY** (Big Turkey Hop-4, Hokolesqua Opechan-3, Cleopatra the Shawano Powhatan-2, Wahunsonacock-1) was born in 1684 in Upper Hiwassee, TA. She died after 1741 at the age of 57 in TN.

Aganunitsi-Wild Potato Hop TURKEY and YOUNG RAINMAKER were married in 1700 in TN. **YOUNG RAINMAKER** was born (date unknown).

14. **Swan-Wapehti Hop TURKEY** (Big Turkey Hop-4, Hokolesqua Opechan-3, Cleopatra the Shawano Powhatan-2, Wahunsonacock-1) was born in 1686 in Upper Hiwassee, TN. She died in 1754 at the age of 68 in Chota, TN.

Swan-Wapehti Hop TURKEY and Oshaqua MUSKRAT were married in 1703 in Running Water, TN. **Oshaqua MUSKRAT** was born (date unknown).

15. **Standing Old Hop TURKEY** (Big Turkey Hop-4, Hokolesqua Opechan-3, Cleopatra the Shawano Powhatan-2,

Descendants of Chief Wahunsonacock Powhatan

Wahunsonacock-1) was born in 1688 in Chota, TN. He died in 1761 at the age of 73 in Chota, TN.

Standing Old Hop TURKEY and Sugi RAINMAKER were married in 1708 in Chota, TN. **Sugi RAINMAKER** was born in 1690.

16. **April-Tkikami Hop TURKEY** (Big Turkey Hop-4, Hokolesqua Opechan-3, Cleopatra the Shawano Powhatan-2, Wahunsonacock-1) was born in 1690 in Chota, TN. She died in 1744 at the age of 54 in Upper Hiwassee, TN.

April-Tkikami Hop TURKEY and Richard BARNES were married in 1718 in Chota, TN. **Richard BARNES** was born in 1695. He died in 1750 at the age of 55.

Richard BARNES and April-Tkikami Hop TURKEY had the following children:

- 19   i. **Mary Lewis BARNES**, born 1720, Chota, TN; married Edward Ned VANN, 1738, Chowan Co., NC; died 1744, Davidson Co., NC (TN).
- 20   ii. **Charity BARNES**, born 1726; married Edward Ned VANN.

17. **Oolootah-Ulutse Hop TURKEY** (Big Turkey Hop-4, Hokolesqua Opechan-3, Cleopatra the Shawano Powhatan-2, Wahunsonacock-1) was born in 1692 in Chota, TN. She died after 1756 at the age of 64 in TN.

Oolootah-Ulutse Hop TURKEY and Blue Holly CHEROKEE were married in 1705 in Chota, TN. **Blue Holly CHEROKEE** was born in 1685.

Oolootah-Ulutse Hop TURKEY and John BOWLES were married in 1722 in Settico, TN. **John BOWLES** was born in 1688.

John BOWLES and Oolootah-Ulutse Hop TURKEY had the following child:

- i. **Ghigoneli BOWLES** was born in 1723.

18. **Ghigoneli Hop TURKEY** (Big Turkey Hop-4, Hokolesqua Opechan-3, Cleopatra the Shawano Powhatan-2, Wahunsonacock-1) was born in 1694 in Chota, TN. She died in 1724 at the age of 30 in Chota, TN.

Ghigoneli Hop TURKEY and Blue Holly CHEROKEE were married in 1707 in TN. **Blue Holly CHEROKEE** was born in 1685.

Descendants of Chief Wahunsonacock Powhatan

26 January 2012

Sixth Generation

19. **Mary Lewis BARNES** (April-Tkikami Hop Turkey-5, Big Turkey Hop-4, Hokolesqua Opechan-3, Cleopatra the Shawano Powhatan-2, Wahunsonacock-1) was born in 1720 in Chota, TN. She died in 1744 at the age of 24 in Davidson Co., NC (TN).

Mary Lewis BARNES and Edward Ned VANN were married in 1738 in Chowan Co., NC. **Edward Ned VANN**, son of John B. Trader VANN and ANIKAWI (CHEROKEE), was born in 1720 in VA. He died in 1773 at the age of 53 in Overhills, Great Tellico, VA.

Edward Ned VANN and Mary Lewis BARNES had the following children:

- 21   i. **John Joseph VANN**, born 1738, VA; married WAH-LI-OTTERLIFTER; died 1800, Cherokee Nation, NC.
- 22   ii. **Jenny VANN**, born 1740; married James BROWN; died 1820.
- 23   iii. **James Clement VANN**, born 3 Apr 1742, VA; married Mary SCOTT; married Jennie FOSTER; married Peggy ; married Nancy Ann BROWN; married Elizabeth SCOTT; married DAWNEE; died 21 Feb 1809, Wilkes Co., GA.
-   iv. **Thomas VANN** was born in 1746.
- 24   v. **Edward Ned VANN Jr.**, born 1744, Ninety Six Dist., Edgefield, SC; married Mary KING, 1762, SC; died 23 Feb 1833, Horn's Creek, Edgefield Co., SC.

20. **Charity BARNES** (April-Tkikami Hop Turkey-5, Big Turkey Hop-4, Hokolesqua Opechan-3, Cleopatra the Shawano Powhatan-2, Wahunsonacock-1) was born in 1726.

Charity BARNES and Edward Ned VANN were married. **Edward Ned VANN**, son of John B. Trader VANN and ANIKAWI (CHEROKEE), was born in 1720 in VA. He died in 1773 at the age of 53 in Overhills, Great Tellico, VA.

Edward Ned VANN and Charity BARNES had the following children:

- i. **Avery VANN** was born in 1748.
- ii. **Edith VANN** was born in 1750.
- iii. **Susanna VANN** was born in 1752.

Descendants of Chief Wahunsonacock Powhatan

Seventh Generation

21. **John Joseph VANN** (Mary Lewis Barnes-6, April-Tkikami Hop Turkey-5, Big Turkey Hop-4, Hokolesqua Opechan-3, Cleopatra the Shawano Powhatan-2, Wahunsonacock-1) was born in 1738 in VA. He died in 1800 at the age of 62 in Cherokee Nation, NC.

John Joseph VANN and WAH-LI-OTTERLIFTER were married. **WAH-LI-OTTERLIFTER** was born in 1735 in Cherokee Nation, NC. She died in OK.

John Joseph VANN and WAH-LI-OTTERLIFTER had the following child:

    i. **James VANN** was born in 1766. He died in 1809 at the age of 43.

22. **Jenny VANN** (Mary Lewis Barnes-6, April-Tkikami Hop Turkey-5, Big Turkey Hop-4, Hokolesqua Opechan-3, Cleopatra the Shawano Powhatan-2, Wahunsonacock-1) was born in 1740. She died in 1820 at the age of 80.

Jenny VANN and James BROWN were married. **James BROWN** was born (date unknown).

23. **James Clement VANN** (Mary Lewis Barnes-6, April-Tkikami Hop Turkey-5, Big Turkey Hop-4, Hokolesqua Opechan-3, Cleopatra the Shawano Powhatan-2, Wahunsonacock-1) was born on 3 Apr 1742 in VA. He died on 21 Feb 1809 at the age of 66 in Wilkes Co., GA.

James Clement VANN and Mary SCOTT were married. **Mary SCOTT** was born (date unknown).

James Clement VANN and Mary SCOTT had the following child:

    25   i. **Robert B. VANN**, married Catherine MYERS, 1803.

James Clement VANN and Jennie FOSTER were married. **Jennie FOSTER** was born (date unknown).

James Clement VANN and Jennie FOSTER had the following child:

    26   i. **Sally VANN**, married Evan NICHOLSON; married James LAMAR.

James Clement VANN and Peggy were married. **Peggy** was born (date unknown).

James Clement VANN and Peggy had the following child:

    27   i. **John VANN**, married Martha DENTON.

James Clement VANN and Nancy Ann BROWN were married. **Nancy Ann BROWN** was born (date unknown).

James Clement VANN and Nancy Ann BROWN had the following children:

- 28   i. **Mary VANN**, born 1793; married FOX-TAYLOR; married Alexander NAVE; married John STIDHAM.
- 29   ii. **Joseph VANN**, born 1795; married Mary BLACKWOOD; married Gennie SPRINGSTON; died 1844, Louisville, Jefferson Co., KY.

James Clement VANN and Elizabeth SCOTT were married. **Elizabeth SCOTT** was born (date unknown).

James Clement VANN and Elizabeth SCOTT had the following child:

- 30   i. **Delilah Amelia VANN**, born 1798; married Captain David MCNAIR.

James Clement VANN and DAWNEE were married. **DAWNEE** was born (date unknown).

James Clement VANN and DAWNEE had the following child:

- 31   i. **Jesse VANN**, married Annawake FOSTER.

24. **Edward Ned VANN Jr.** (Mary Lewis Barnes-6, April-Tkikami Hop Turkey-5, Big Turkey Hop-4, Hokolesqua Opechan-3, Cleopatra the Shawano Powhatan-2, Wahunsonacock-1) was born in 1744 in Ninety Six Dist., Edgefield, SC. He died on 23 Feb 1833 at the age of 89 in Horn's Creek, Edgefield Co., SC. He held the title of Jr..

Edward Ned VANN Jr. and Mary KING were married in 1762 in SC. **Mary KING**, daughter of Squirrel KING and Thawakilla Shawnee Woman, was born in 1743 in Ninety Six Dist., Edgefield, SC. She died in 1786 at the age of 43 in MS.

Edward Ned VANN and Mary KING had the following children:

- 32   i. **Margaret VANN**, born 1767, Edgefield Co., SC; married Robert D. MOSELEY Sr., 1782, Edgefield Co., SC; died 10 Oct 1849, Montgomery Co., AL.
- 33   ii. **Edward VANN III**, born 24 Mar 1768, Horn's Creek, Edgefield Co., SC; married Elizabeth WALLS, 15 Dec 1790, Edgefield Co., SC; died 26 Jun 1854, Abbeville Dist., SC.
-       iii. **William VANN** was born in 1770.
- 34   iv. **Edith B. VANN**, born 1775, Edgefield Co., SC; married Martin CLOUD; died 1799, FL.
- 35   v. **Vashti VANN**, born 1776, Edgefield Co., SC; married Benjamin JERNIGAN; died 1821, Santa Rosa Co., FL.
- 36   vi. **Mason M. VANN**, born 1777, Edgefield Co., SC; married Elizabeth Marthina SIMMONS, 3 Mar 1846, Shelby Co., TX; married Jane SHAW; died 1860, Nacogdoches, Milam Co., TX.

Descendants of Chief Wahunsonacock Powhatan

Eighth Generation

25. **Robert B. VANN** (James Clement-7, Mary Lewis Barnes-6, April-Tkikami Hop Turkey-5, Big Turkey Hop-4, Hokolesqua Opechan-3, Cleopatra the Shawano Powhatan-2, Wahunsonacock-1) was born (date unknown).

Robert B. VANN and Catherine MYERS were married in 1803. **Catherine MYERS** was born (date unknown).

26. **Sally VANN** (James Clement-7, Mary Lewis Barnes-6, April-Tkikami Hop Turkey-5, Big Turkey Hop-4, Hokolesqua Opechan-3, Cleopatra the Shawano Powhatan-2, Wahunsonacock-1) was born (date unknown).

Sally VANN and Evan NICHOLSON were married. **Evan NICHOLSON** was born (date unknown).

Sally VANN and James LAMAR were married. **James LAMAR** was born (date unknown).

27. **John VANN** (James Clement-7, Mary Lewis Barnes-6, April-Tkikami Hop Turkey-5, Big Turkey Hop-4, Hokolesqua Opechan-3, Cleopatra the Shawano Powhatan-2, Wahunsonacock-1) was born (date unknown).

John VANN and Martha DENTON were married. **Martha DENTON** was born (date unknown).

28. **Mary VANN** (James Clement-7, Mary Lewis Barnes-6, April-Tkikami Hop Turkey-5, Big Turkey Hop-4, Hokolesqua Opechan-3, Cleopatra the Shawano Powhatan-2, Wahunsonacock-1) was born in 1793.

Mary VANN and FOX-TAYLOR were married. **FOX-TAYLOR** was born (date unknown).

Mary VANN and Alexander NAVE were married. **Alexander NAVE** was born (date unknown).

Mary VANN and John STIDHAM were married. **John STIDHAM** was born (date unknown).

29. **Joseph VANN** (James Clement-7, Mary Lewis Barnes-6, April-Tkikami Hop Turkey-5, Big Turkey Hop-4, Hokolesqua Opechan-3, Cleopatra the Shawano Powhatan-2, Wahunsonacock-1) was born in 1795. He died in 1844 at the age of 49 in

Descendants of Chief Wahunsonacock Powhatan

26 January 2012

Louisville, Jefferson Co., KY.

Joseph VANN and Mary BLACKWOOD were married. **Mary BLACKWOOD** was born (date unknown).

Joseph VANN and Gennie SPRINGSTON were married. **Gennie SPRINGSTON** was born (date unknown).

30. **Delilah Amelia VANN** (James Clement-7, Mary Lewis Barnes-6, April-Tkikami Hop Turkey-5, Big Turkey Hop-4, Hokolesqua Opechan-3, Cleopatra the Shawano Powhatan-2, Wahunsonacock-1) was born in 1798.

Delilah Amelia VANN and Captain David MCNAIR were married. **Captain David MCNAIR** was born (date unknown).

31. **Jesse VANN** (James Clement-7, Mary Lewis Barnes-6, April-Tkikami Hop Turkey-5, Big Turkey Hop-4, Hokolesqua Opechan-3, Cleopatra the Shawano Powhatan-2, Wahunsonacock-1) was born (date unknown).

Jesse VANN and Annawake FOSTER were married. **Annawake FOSTER** was born (date unknown).

32. **Margaret VANN** (Edward Ned-7, Mary Lewis Barnes-6, April-Tkikami Hop Turkey-5, Big Turkey Hop-4, Hokolesqua Opechan-3, Cleopatra the Shawano Powhatan-2, Wahunsonacock-1) was born in 1767 in Edgefield Co., SC. She died on 10 Oct 1849 at the age of 82 in Montgomery Co., AL.

Margaret VANN and Robert D. MOSELEY Sr. were married in 1782 in Edgefield Co., SC. **Robert D. MOSELEY Sr.**, son of William MOSELEY and Sarah MASON, was born in 1755 in Edgefield Co., SC. He died on 8 Dec 1831 at the age of 76 in Pintlala, Montgomery Co., AL. He held the title of Sr..

Robert D. MOSELEY and Margaret VANN had the following children:

37	i.	**Daniel MOSELEY**, born 15 Jul 1783, Edgefield Co., SC; married Mary CLEVELAND, 5 Jul 1810, SC; died aft 1833, TX.
38	ii.	**Elisha MOSELEY Sr.**, born 15 Jul 1783, Edgefield Co., SC; married Lydia MOSELEY, 1806, Edgefield Co., SC; died 1833, Montgomery Co., AL.
39	iii.	**Robert "Robin" MOSELEY Jr.**, born 1785, Edgefield Co., SC; died 1852, Montgomery Co., AL.
40	iv.	**Margaret Vann MOSELEY**, born 1786, Edgefield Co., SC.
41	v.	**Mary Ann MOSELEY**, born 11 Sep 1788, Edgefield Co., SC; died 13 Oct 1845, Montgomery Co., AL.
42	vi.	**Nancy Naomi MOSELEY**, born 1790, Edgefield Co., SC; married Thomas POLAND; died 1852, Montgomery Co., AL.
43	vii.	**Joseph MOSELEY Sr.**, born 1791, Edgefield Co., SC; died 1853, Montgomery Co., AL.
44	viii.	**Zelphia MOSELEY**, born 1793, Edgefield Co., SC; died 1850, TX.
45	ix.	**Benjamin MOSELEY**, born 1796, Edgefield Co., SC; died aft 1833.
46	x.	**George MOSELEY**, born 1797, Edgefield Co., SC; married Adra HOWARD, 30 Jan 1823, Montgomery Co., AL; died 1844, Ramer, Montgomery Co., AL.

Descendants of Chief Wahunsonacock Powhatan

	xi.	**Clement T. MOSELEY** was born in 1798 in Edgefield Co., SC. He died on 3 Nov 1858 at the age of 60.
47	xii.	**William Brantley MOSELEY Sr.**, born 1799, Edgefield Co., SC; died 1853, Upshur Co., TX.
48	xiii.	**Hannah MOSELEY**, born 1799, Edgefield Co., SC; married Nelson POLAND, 1820; died bef 1836.
49	xiv.	**Mason MOSELEY**, born 1805, Edgefield Co., SC; died 1870, TX.
50	xv.	**Mahulda Hulda MOSELEY**, born 27 Mar 1805, SC; married Edward Moody BUSSEY, 26 Sep 1824, Montgomery Co., AL; died 15 Jan 1856.

33. **Edward VANN III** (Edward Ned-7, Mary Lewis Barnes-6, April-Tkikami Hop Turkey-5, Big Turkey Hop-4, Hokolesqua Opechan-3, Cleopatra the Shawano Powhatan-2, Wahunsonacock-1) was born on 24 Mar 1768 in Horn's Creek, Edgefield Co., SC. He died on 26 Jun 1854 at the age of 86 in Abbeville Dist., SC. He held the title of III.

Edward VANN III and Elizabeth WALLS were married on 15 Dec 1790 in Edgefield Co., SC. **Elizabeth WALLS** was born in 1770. She died on 12 Dec 1863 at the age of 93.

Edward VANN and Elizabeth WALLS had the following child:

51	i.	**Edward VANN**, born 10 Mar 1797, Abbeville Dist., SC; married Rebecca HINTON, 1820; died 5 May 1877, Madison Co., FL.

34. **Edith B. VANN** (Edward Ned-7, Mary Lewis Barnes-6, April-Tkikami Hop Turkey-5, Big Turkey Hop-4, Hokolesqua Opechan-3, Cleopatra the Shawano Powhatan-2, Wahunsonacock-1) was born in 1775 in Edgefield Co., SC. She died in 1799 at the age of 24 in FL.

Edith B. VANN and Martin CLOUD were married. **Martin CLOUD** was born in 1775. He died in 1806 at the age of 31.

35. **Vashti VANN** (Edward Ned-7, Mary Lewis Barnes-6, April-Tkikami Hop Turkey-5, Big Turkey Hop-4, Hokolesqua Opechan-3, Cleopatra the Shawano Powhatan-2, Wahunsonacock-1) was born in 1776 in Edgefield Co., SC. She died in 1821 at the age of 45 in Santa Rosa Co., FL.

Vashti VANN and Benjamin JERNIGAN were married. **Benjamin JERNIGAN**, son of Benjamin JERNIGAN and Nancy , was born in 1778 in Wayne Co., NC. He died on 20 Apr 1847 at the age of 69 in FL.

Benjamin JERNIGAN and Vashti VANN had the following children:

52	i.	**Edith JERNIGAN**, born 1796; married COTTON; died 1853.
53	ii.	**William JERNIGAN**, born 14 May 1800, Edgefield Co., SC; married Winna DANIELS; died 1883.
54	iii.	**Cary JERNIGAN**, born 1802, SC; married Lucy Ann SNOWDEN, 12 Apr 1838, Covington Co., AL; died Sep 1855, Santa Rosa Co., FL.
55	iv.	**Mary JERNIGAN**, born 1803, Brewton, Conecuh Co., AL; married William WHITMIRE, 1818; died 1857, Milton, Santa Rosa Co., FL.
56	v.	**Nancy JERNIGAN**, born 1806; married MORRIS.
	vi.	**Joseph Jefferson JERNIGAN** was born in 1808. He died in 1889 at the age of 81.
57	vii.	**Susan JERNIGAN**, born 1810; married LONG.
	viii.	**Edward JERNIGAN** was born in 1813.
	ix.	**Benjamin W. JERNIGAN** was born in 1816. He died in 1898 at the age of 82.

36. **Mason M. VANN** (Edward Ned-7, Mary Lewis Barnes-6, April-Tkikami Hop Turkey-5, Big Turkey Hop-4, Hokolesqua Opechan-3, Cleopatra the Shawano Powhatan-2, Wahunsonacock-1) was born in 1777 in Edgefield Co., SC. He died in 1860 at the age of 83 in Nacogdoches, Milam Co., TX.

Mason M. VANN and Elizabeth Marthina SIMMONS were married on 3 Mar 1846 in Shelby Co., TX. **Elizabeth Marthina SIMMONS** was born in 1826 in AL.

Mason M. VANN and Elizabeth Marthina SIMMONS had the following children:

    i. **Joseph VANN** was born in 1843.
    ii. **Martha M. VANN** was born in 1845.
    iii. **Cynthia VANN** was born in 1847.

Mason M. VANN and Jane SHAW were married. **Jane SHAW** was born in 1790 in Edgefield Co., SC. She died in 1845 at the age of 55 in TX.

Mason M. VANN and Jane SHAW had the following children:

    i. **William VANN** was born in 1822 in Cherokee Nation, Republic of Mexico (TX).
    ii. **Mary Ann VANN** was born in 1824 in Cherokee Nation, Republic of Mexico (TX).
58   iii. **Mason M. VANN**, born 1827, Cherokee Nation, Republic of Mexico (TX); married Sophia MCMILLEN, 2 Mar 1846, DeSota Parish, LA; died 1860, Nacogdoches, Milam Co., TX.
59   iv. **Lavica Jane VANN**, born 10 Jul 1832, Cherokee Nation, Republic of Mexico (TX); married Andrew Jackson COTHERN, 1863, TX/LA; married James MCMILLEN, 1848; died 25 Jun 1899, Poteau, Le Flore Co., OK.
    v. **Robert VANN** was born in 1834 in Cherokee Nation, Republic of Mexico (TX).
60   vi. **Elizabeth Jane VANN**, born 1840, Cherokee Nation, Republic of Mexico (TX); married William I. SIMMONS.

Descendants of Chief Wahunsonacock Powhatan

Ninth Generation

37. Daniel MOSELEY (Margaret Vann-8, Edward Ned-7, Mary Lewis Barnes-6, April-Tkikami Hop Turkey-5, Big Turkey Hop-4, Hokolesqua Opechan-3, Cleopatra the Shawano Powhatan-2, Wahunsonacock-1) was born on 15 Jul 1783 in Edgefield Co., SC. He died after 1833 at the age of 50 in TX.

Daniel MOSELEY and Mary CLEVELAND were married on 5 Jul 1810 in SC. **Mary CLEVELAND** was born on 12 Nov 1792 in GA/SC.

Daniel MOSELEY and Mary CLEVELAND had the following children:

- 61   i. **Margaret Salena MOSELEY**, born abt 1805; married Abraham FANNIN, 10 Jan 1831, Montgomery Co., AL.
- 62   ii. **Robert MOSELEY**, born 1813, Edgefield Co., SC; married Martha A. ROBERTSON; died 1877, Clark Co., AL.
-    iii. **Jesse MOSELEY** was born about 1824.
-    iv. **Mary MOSELEY** was born about 1826.
-    v. **Daniel MOSELEY** was born about 1828.
- 63   vi. **George Washington MOSELEY**, born abt 1830; married Lucinda .
- 64   vii. **Lucinda E. MOSELEY**, born abt 1836; married William Henry MOSELEY, 3 Oct 1870, Montgomery Co., AL.

38. Elisha MOSELEY Sr. (Margaret Vann-8, Edward Ned-7, Mary Lewis Barnes-6, April-Tkikami Hop Turkey-5, Big Turkey Hop-4, Hokolesqua Opechan-3, Cleopatra the Shawano Powhatan-2, Wahunsonacock-1) was born on 15 Jul 1783 in Edgefield Co., SC. He died in 1833 at the age of 50 in Montgomery Co., AL. He held the title of Sr..

Elisha MOSELEY Sr. and Lydia MOSELEY were married in 1806 in Edgefield Co., SC. **Lydia MOSELEY**, daughter of Robert MOSELEY and Penelope TALLEY, was born on 22 Jan 1780 in Edgefield Co., SC. She died on 23 Dec 1843 at the age of 63 in Montgomery Co., AL.

Elisha MOSELEY and Lydia MOSELEY had the following children:

- 65   i. **Elisha MOSELEY Jr.**, born abt 1810; married Terraso DEAN, 8 Apr 1837, Lowndes Co., AL; died 1838, AL.
- 66   ii. **Mildred MOSELEY**, born abt 1812; married William GOODSON, 9 Oct 1830, Montgomery Co., AL.
- 67   iii. **Robert MOSELEY**, born abt 1814; married Sarah WALTERS, 15 Jan 1840, Montgomery Co., AL.
- 68   iv. **Tabitha MOSELEY**, born abt 1816, GA; married Stepehn C. GAFFORD, 11 Feb 1833, Montgomery Co., AL; died AL.
- 69   v. **Albert P. MOSELEY**, born 25 Sep 1818, Montgomery Co., AL; married Adeline COTTONHAM, 29 Aug 1844, Lowndes Co., AL; married Mary Matilda BUSSEY, 10 Sep 1865, Montgomery Co., AL; died 17 Apr 1899, Montgomery Co., AL.
- 70   vi. **Lydia MOSELEY**, born abt 1820; married John MATHEWS, 12 Jan 1837, Montgomery Co., AL.

39. Robert "Robin" MOSELEY Jr. (Margaret Vann-8, Edward Ned-7, Mary Lewis Barnes-6, April-Tkikami Hop Turkey-5, Big Turkey Hop-4, Hokolesqua Opechan-3, Cleopatra the Shawano Powhatan-2, Wahunsonacock-1) was born in 1785 in Edgefield Co., SC. He died in 1852 at the age of 67 in Montgomery Co., AL. He held the title of Jr..

Descendants of Chief Wahunsonacock Powhatan

26 January 2012

Sarah WATERS was born (date unknown).

40. Margaret Vann MOSELEY (Margaret Vann-8, Edward Ned-7, Mary Lewis Barnes-6, April-Tkikami Hop Turkey-5, Big Turkey Hop-4, Hokolesqua Opechan-3, Cleopatra the Shawano Powhatan-2, Wahunsonacock-1) was born in 1786 in Edgefield Co., SC.

Thomas BOYD died after 1833.

41. Mary Ann MOSELEY (Margaret Vann-8, Edward Ned-7, Mary Lewis Barnes-6, April-Tkikami Hop Turkey-5, Big Turkey Hop-4, Hokolesqua Opechan-3, Cleopatra the Shawano Powhatan-2, Wahunsonacock-1) was born on 11 Sep 1788 in Edgefield Co., SC. She died on 13 Oct 1845 at the age of 57 in Montgomery Co., AL.

Josiah PARMER died after 1833.

42. Nancy Naomi MOSELEY (Margaret Vann-8, Edward Ned-7, Mary Lewis Barnes-6, April-Tkikami Hop Turkey-5, Big Turkey Hop-4, Hokolesqua Opechan-3, Cleopatra the Shawano Powhatan-2, Wahunsonacock-1) was born in 1790 in Edgefield Co., SC. She died in 1852 at the age of 62 in Montgomery Co., AL.

Nancy Naomi MOSELEY and Thomas POLAND were married. **Thomas POLAND**, son of POLAND, died before 1838.

Thomas POLAND and Nancy Naomi MOSELEY had the following children:

- 71   i. **Sarah Ann POLAND**, born 1808; married John Kittle ARMSTRONG, 5 Feb 1830, AL; died 1851, Gladewater, TX.
- 72   ii. **Elvira POLAND**, born 1809; married James MONCRIEF, 18 Dec 1828.
- 73   iii. **John Stratton POLAND**, born 21 Dec 1812; married Lenora STACEY, 10 Aug 1837; married Caroline GRAY, 20 Jul 1856, Rusk Co., TX; died 12 Jul 1882.
- 74   iv. **Thomas POLAND**, born 22 Aug 1816; married Sarah Ann ; died 8 Mar 1869.

43. Joseph MOSELEY Sr. (Margaret Vann-8, Edward Ned-7, Mary Lewis Barnes-6, April-Tkikami Hop Turkey-5, Big Turkey Hop-4, Hokolesqua Opechan-3, Cleopatra the Shawano Powhatan-2, Wahunsonacock-1) was born in 1791 in Edgefield Co., SC. He died in 1853 at the age of 62 in Montgomery Co., AL. He held the title of Sr..

Mary UNK was born (date unknown).

44. Zelphia MOSELEY (Margaret Vann-8, Edward Ned-7, Mary Lewis Barnes-6, April-Tkikami Hop Turkey-5, Big

Descendants of Chief Wahunsonacock Powhatan

Turkey Hop-4, Hokolesqua Opechan-3, Cleopatra the Shawano Powhatan-2, Wahunsonacock-1) was born in 1793 in Edgefield Co., SC. She died in 1850 at the age of 57 in TX.

John BELEW died after 1833.

45. Benjamin MOSELEY (Margaret Vann-8, Edward Ned-7, Mary Lewis Barnes-6, April-Tkikami Hop Turkey-5, Big Turkey Hop-4, Hokolesqua Opechan-3, Cleopatra the Shawano Powhatan-2, Wahunsonacock-1) was born in 1796 in Edgefield Co., SC. He died after 1833 at the age of 37.

Nancy HOLMES was born (date unknown).

Frances R. UNK was born (date unknown).

46. George MOSELEY (Margaret Vann-8, Edward Ned-7, Mary Lewis Barnes-6, April-Tkikami Hop Turkey-5, Big Turkey Hop-4, Hokolesqua Opechan-3, Cleopatra the Shawano Powhatan-2, Wahunsonacock-1) was born in 1797 in Edgefield Co., SC. He died in 1844 at the age of 47 in Ramer, Montgomery Co., AL.

George MOSELEY and Adra HOWARD were married on 30 Jan 1823 in Montgomery Co., AL. **Adra HOWARD**, daughter of Enos HOWARD and Sarah GREEN, was born on 9 Jan 1799 in SC. She died in 1868 at the age of 69 in Ramer, Montgomery Co., AL.

George MOSELEY and Adra HOWARD had the following children:

	i.	**Huldah Lewis MOSELEY** was born in 1828 in AL.
	ii.	**Elizabeth MOSELEY** was born about 1838.
75	iii.	**George Benjamin Alexander MOSLEY**, born 31 Jan 1825, Montgomery Co., AL; married Rebecca CARR, 21 Mar 1850, Montgomery Co., AL; married Joanna FREEMAN; died 7 May 1894, Arkadelphia, Cullman Co., AL.
76	iv.	**Martha (Malinda) MOSELEY**, born 7 Feb 1827, Montgomery Co., AL; married Benjamin Harmon (Harm) BUSSEY Sr., 11 Aug 1847; died 4 Feb 1920, Lamar Co., AL.
	v.	**Adam MOSELEY** was born about 1834.
	vi.	**Adra Howard MOSELEY** was born in 1835 in Montgomery Co., AL. He/she died in 1869 at the age of 34. He/she was buried in 1869 in Sharp Cemetery, Montgomery Co., AL.
	vii.	**Hiram MOSELEY** was born about 1836.
77	viii.	**William Lafayette MOSLEY**, born 1 Jun 1840, Montgomery Co., AL; married B.B. TAYLOR, 12 Apr 1866, Montgomery, Montgomery Co., AL; married Mary TAYLOR, 20 Sep 1869, Montgomery, Montgomery Co., AL; married Mary Susanna JONES, 15 Jan 1874, Arkadelphia, Cullman Co., AL; died 26 Mar 1923, Morris, Jefferson Co., AL.

47. William Brantley MOSELEY Sr. (Margaret Vann-8, Edward Ned-7, Mary Lewis Barnes-6, April-Tkikami Hop Turkey-5, Big Turkey Hop-4, Hokolesqua Opechan-3, Cleopatra the Shawano Powhatan-2, Wahunsonacock-1) was born in

Descendants of Chief Wahunsonacock Powhatan

26 January 2012

1799 in Edgefield Co., SC. He died in 1853 at the age of 54 in Upshur Co., TX. He held the title of Sr..

Ann Thompson HICKMAN was born (date unknown).

48. **Hannah MOSELEY** (Margaret Vann-8, Edward Ned-7, Mary Lewis Barnes-6, April-Tkikami Hop Turkey-5, Big Turkey Hop-4, Hokolesqua Opechan-3, Cleopatra the Shawano Powhatan-2, Wahunsonacock-1) was born in 1799 in Edgefield Co., SC. She died before 1836 at the age of 37.

Hannah MOSELEY and Nelson POLAND were married in 1820. **Nelson POLAND**, son of POLAND, died after 1833.

Nelson POLAND and Hannah MOSELEY had the following children:

- 78   i. **William Henry POLAND**, born 8 Aug 1827, AL; married Kezzie PYTCHLYNN, abt 1852; died 10 Apr 1891.
-      ii. **Sarah Ann E. POLAND** was born on 24 Mar 1830. She was buried in Sep 1896 in Concord Cemetery, near Jonesville, TX. She died on 14 Sep 1896 at the age of 66.

49. **Mason MOSELEY** (Margaret Vann-8, Edward Ned-7, Mary Lewis Barnes-6, April-Tkikami Hop Turkey-5, Big Turkey Hop-4, Hokolesqua Opechan-3, Cleopatra the Shawano Powhatan-2, Wahunsonacock-1) was born in 1805 in Edgefield Co., SC. He died in 1870 at the age of 65 in TX.

Levinia Mildred SHEPPARD was born in 1810 in GA. She died in 1849 at the age of 39 in TX.

Mason MOSELEY and Levinia Mildred SHEPPARD had the following child:

- 79   i. **Margaret E. MOSELEY**, born abt 1830; married J. Walter BOYD, 19 Aug 1848, TX; died aft 1881, Gilmer, Upshur Co., TX.

Mary Ann SLATER was born (date unknown).

50. **Mahulda Hulda MOSELEY** (Margaret Vann-8, Edward Ned-7, Mary Lewis Barnes-6, April-Tkikami Hop Turkey-5, Big Turkey Hop-4, Hokolesqua Opechan-3, Cleopatra the Shawano Powhatan-2, Wahunsonacock-1) was born on 27 Mar 1805 in SC. She died on 15 Jan 1856 at the age of 50.

Mahulda Hulda MOSELEY and Edward Moody BUSSEY were married on 26 Sep 1824 in Montgomery Co., AL. **Edward Moody BUSSEY**, son of Dempsey L. BUSSEY and Mary (Sarah) LYON, was born on 17 Jan 1805 in Edgefield Co., SC. He died on 31 May 1884 at the age of 79 in Harrison Co., TX (near Longview).

Edward Moody BUSSEY and Mahulda Hulda MOSELEY had the following children:

-      i. **Mary BUSSEY** was born on 27 Aug 1826 in Montgomery Co., AL.
- 80   ii. **Benjamin Harmon (Harm) BUSSEY Sr.**, born 3 Jun 1828, Montgomery Co., AL; married Martha

Descendants of Chief Wahunsonacock Powhatan

26 January 2012

(Malinda) MOSELEY, 11 Aug 1847; died 7 Jun 1908, Carbon Hill, Walker Co., AL.

    iii. **Edward Moody, Jr. BUSSEY** was born on 20 Nov 1829 in AL. He died on 19 Feb 1873 at the age of 43 in TX. He was buried on 21 Feb 1873 in Concord Cemetery, near Jonesville, TX.

81   iv. **Dempsey C. BUSSEY**, born 14 May 1831, AL.

82   v. **Hezekiah BUSSEY**, born 10 Sep 1833, AL; married Mary Jane ALEXANDER, 21 Jan 1854, Pine Tree, Upsher Co. (now Gregg), TX; married ZOULA, abt 1906; died 14 Mar 1892, Upshur Co., TX.

    vi. **Robert BUSSEY** was born on 5 Jul 1833 in AL. He died on 7 Oct 1837 at the age of 4 in AL.

83   vii. **Sarah Ann BUSSEY**, born 2 Apr 1835, AL.

84   viii. **Joseph BUSSEY**, born 11 Jan 1837, AL; died TX.

    ix. **Letitia BUSSEY** was born on 8 Sep 1839 in AL. She died in TX.

85   x. **Mary Lou Tassie BUSSEY**, born 1841, AL; married Thomas Abney KILLINGSWORTH; married Hezekiah BOYD.

86   xi. **William J. BUSSEY**, born 17 Jul 1842, Montgomery Co., AL; married Sarah Ann DAVIS, 26 May 1863, Harrison Co., TX; died 10 May 1910, Tarrant Co., TX.

87   xii. **John L. BUSSEY**, born 22 May 1844, AL; married Anna E. ; died 1916, Longview, Harrison Co., TX.

---

51. Edward VANN (Edward-8, Edward Ned-7, Mary Lewis Barnes-6, April-Tkikami Hop Turkey-5, Big Turkey Hop-4, Hokolesqua Opechan-3, Cleopatra the Shawano Powhatan-2, Wahunsonacock-1) was born on 10 Mar 1797 in Abbeville Dist., SC. He died on 5 May 1877 at the age of 80 in Madison Co., FL.

Edward VANN and Rebecca HINTON were married in 1820. **Rebecca HINTON** was born (date unknown).

52. Edith JERNIGAN (Vashti Vann-8, Edward Ned-7, Mary Lewis Barnes-6, April-Tkikami Hop Turkey-5, Big Turkey Hop-4, Hokolesqua Opechan-3, Cleopatra the Shawano Powhatan-2, Wahunsonacock-1) was born in 1796. She died in 1853 at the age of 57.

Edith JERNIGAN and COTTON were married. **COTTON** was born (date unknown).

53. William JERNIGAN (Vashti Vann-8, Edward Ned-7, Mary Lewis Barnes-6, April-Tkikami Hop Turkey-5, Big Turkey Hop-4, Hokolesqua Opechan-3, Cleopatra the Shawano Powhatan-2, Wahunsonacock-1) was born on 14 May 1800 in Edgefield Co., SC. He died in 1883 at the age of 83.

William JERNIGAN and Winna DANIELS were married. **Winna DANIELS** was born about 1804 in AL.

William JERNIGAN and Winna DANIELS had the following child:

88   i. **Thomas Jefferson JERNIGAN**, born 3 Sep 1824, Conecuh Co., AL; married Martha Jane TRAVIS.

54. Cary JERNIGAN (Vashti Vann-8, Edward Ned-7, Mary Lewis Barnes-6, April-Tkikami Hop Turkey-5, Big Turkey Hop-4, Hokolesqua Opechan-3, Cleopatra the Shawano Powhatan-2, Wahunsonacock-1) was born in 1802 in SC. He died in Sep 1855 at the age of 53 in Santa Rosa Co., FL.

Descendants of Chief Wahunsonacock Powhatan

26 January 2012

Cary JERNIGAN and Lucy Ann SNOWDEN were married on 12 Apr 1838 in Covington Co., AL. **Lucy Ann SNOWDEN**, daughter of Aaron SNOWDEN and Esther WEBSTER, was born on 22 Feb 1812 in GA. She died after 1870 at the age of 58 in DeWitt Co., TX.

Cary JERNIGAN and Lucy Ann SNOWDEN had the following children:

      i. **Nancy V. JERNIGAN** was born in 1837 in AL.
     ii. **Josephine M. JERNIGAN** was born in 1839 in AL.
    iii. **Richard Call JERNIGAN** was born in 1841 in AL.
    iv. **Laura A. JERNIGAN** was born in 1843 in AL.
     v. **James W. JERNIGAN** was born in 1845 in AL.
    vi. **William JERNIGAN** was born in 1847 in FL.
89   vii. **George Washington JERNIGAN**, born Feb 1850, Milton, Santa Rosa Co., FL; married Diza M. CARR, 20 Jan 1876, Jackson Co., TX; died 1 Jul 1928, Eddy Co., NM.
   viii. **Fennig JERNIGAN** was born about 1850 in FL.
    ix. **Henry JERNIGAN** was born in 1852 in FL.

55. **Mary JERNIGAN** (Vashti Vann-8, Edward Ned-7, Mary Lewis Barnes-6, April-Tkikami Hop Turkey-5, Big Turkey Hop-4, Hokolesqua Opechan-3, Cleopatra the Shawano Powhatan-2, Wahunsonacock-1) was born in 1803 in Brewton, Conecuh Co., AL. She died in 1857 at the age of 54 in Milton, Santa Rosa Co., FL. She was buried in 1857 in Milton Cemetery, Milton, Santa Rosa Co., FL.

Mary JERNIGAN and William WHITMIRE were married in 1818. **William WHITMIRE** was born in 1790 in Pendleton Co., SC. He died on 18 Jun 1830 at the age of 40 in Santa Rosa Co., FL. He was buried on 19 Jun 1830 in Milton Cemetery, Milton, Santa Rosa Co., FL.

56. **Nancy JERNIGAN** (Vashti Vann-8, Edward Ned-7, Mary Lewis Barnes-6, April-Tkikami Hop Turkey-5, Big Turkey Hop-4, Hokolesqua Opechan-3, Cleopatra the Shawano Powhatan-2, Wahunsonacock-1) was born in 1806.

Nancy JERNIGAN and MORRIS were married. **MORRIS** was born (date unknown).

57. **Susan JERNIGAN** (Vashti Vann-8, Edward Ned-7, Mary Lewis Barnes-6, April-Tkikami Hop Turkey-5, Big Turkey Hop-4, Hokolesqua Opechan-3, Cleopatra the Shawano Powhatan-2, Wahunsonacock-1) was born in 1810.

Susan JERNIGAN and LONG were married. **LONG** was born (date unknown).

58. **Mason M. VANN** (Mason M.-8, Edward Ned-7, Mary Lewis Barnes-6, April-Tkikami Hop Turkey-5, Big Turkey Hop-4, Hokolesqua Opechan-3, Cleopatra the Shawano Powhatan-2, Wahunsonacock-1) was born in 1827 in Cherokee Nation, Republic of Mexico (TX). He died in 1860 at the age of 33 in Nacogdoches, Milam Co., TX.

Descendants of Chief Wahunsonacock Powhatan

26 January 2012

Mason M. VANN and Sophia MCMILLEN were married on 2 Mar 1846 in DeSota Parish, LA. **Sophia MCMILLEN**, daughter of Abasalom MCMILLEN and Anna , was born in 1827 in Bibb Co., AL. She died in 1860 at the age of 33 in Nacogdoches, Milam Co., TX.

Mason M. VANN and Sophia MCMILLEN had the following children:

- 90   i.   **James Mason VANN**, born 8 Dec 1846, Shelby Co., TX; married Luvicie Luice EZELL, 20 Aug 1870, Freestone Co., TX; died 12 Dec 1912, Luna, Freestone Co., TX.
-     ii.   **Anna VANN** was born in 1848.
-     iii.   **Nancy VANN** was born in 1850.

59. Lavica Jane VANN (Mason M.-8, Edward Ned-7, Mary Lewis Barnes-6, April-Tkikami Hop Turkey-5, Big Turkey Hop-4, Hokolesqua Opechan-3, Cleopatra the Shawano Powhatan-2, Wahunsonacock-1) was born on 10 Jul 1832 in Cherokee Nation, Republic of Mexico (TX). She died on 25 Jun 1899 at the age of 66 in Poteau, Le Flore Co., OK. She was buried on 27 Jun 1899 in Old Hall Cemetery, Poteau, Le Flore Co., OK.

Lavica Jane VANN and Andrew Jackson COTHERN were married in 1863 in TX/LA. **Andrew Jackson COTHERN**, son of William COTHERN and Nancy GATES, was born on 5 Jan 1826 in Pike Co., MS. He died on 24 Jan 1892 at the age of 66 in Brownwood, Coleman Co., TX. He was buried on 26 Jan 1892 in Trickham, Cemetery, Brownwood, Coleman Co., TX.

Andrew Jackson COTHERN and Lavica Jane VANN had the following children:

- 91   i.   **Mary Lavisa COTHERN**, born 19 Sep 1865, OK; married Andrew Jackson RILEY Sr., 27 Oct 1881, OK; died 7 Sep 1934, Hartshorne, Pittsburg Co., OK.
- 92   ii.   **Nancy Carlida COTHERN**, born 12 May 1867, OK; married Christopher Cornelius SADLER, 4 Nov 1883, OK; died 5 Apr 1947, Hartshorne, Pittsburg Co., OK.
-     iii.   **William COTHERN** was born on 30 Jan 1871 in OK. He died in 1897 at the age of 26 in Hartshorne, Pittsburg Co., OK.
- 93   iv.   **Walter COTHERN**, born 20 Oct 1873, Summerfield, Le Flore Co., OK; married Mary Jane WILLIAMS, 16 Sep 1900, Richert, Poteau Co., OK; married Mollie RAINES, 18 Nov 1894, Poteau, Le Flore Co., OK; died 15 Jun 1970, Sardis, Pushmataha Co., OK.
- 94   v.   **Vevi Vann COTHERN**, born 17 Dec 1876, Sallisaw, OK; married Sallie Emma KNOX, 27 May 1906, Whon, Coleman Co., TX; married Nannie LAYMAN, 25 Jun 1901, Northern District, Indian Territory, OK; died 27 Aug 1935, Stamford, Jones Co., TX.
-     vi.   **Emma Hawkins COTHERN** was born (date unknown).
- 95   vii.   **Edd Pickens COTHERN**, married Mamie LOGAN, 27 Feb 1904, Phillips, OK.

Lavica Jane VANN and James MCMILLEN were married in 1848. **James MCMILLEN**, son of Abasalom MCMILLEN and Anna , was born in 1828 in AL. He died in 1863 at the age of 35.

James MCMILLEN and Lavica Jane VANN had the following children:

- 96   i.   **John H. MCMILLEN**, born 1849, TX; married Elizabeth .
- 97   ii.   **Bettie H. MCMILLEN**, born 1854, TX; married ALEXANDER.
-     iii.   **Mahalia MCMILLEN** was born in 1857 in TX.

60. **Elizabeth Jane VANN** (Mason M.-8, Edward Ned-7, Mary Lewis Barnes-6, April-Tkikami Hop Turkey-5, Big Turkey Hop-4, Hokolesqua Opechan-3, Cleopatra the Shawano Powhatan-2, Wahunsonacock-1) was born in 1840 in Cherokee Nation, Republic of Mexico (TX).

Elizabeth Jane VANN and William I. SIMMONS were married. **William I. SIMMONS** was born (date unknown).

Descendants of Chief Wahunsonacock Powhatan

Tenth Generation

61. **Margaret Salena MOSELEY** (Daniel-9, Margaret Vann-8, Edward Ned-7, Mary Lewis Barnes-6, April-Tkikami Hop Turkey-5, Big Turkey Hop-4, Hokolesqua Opechan-3, Cleopatra the Shawano Powhatan-2, Wahunsonacock-1) was born about 1805.

Margaret Salena MOSELEY and Abraham FANNIN were married on 10 Jan 1831 in Montgomery Co., AL. **Abraham FANNIN** was born (date unknown).

62. **Robert MOSELEY** (Daniel-9, Margaret Vann-8, Edward Ned-7, Mary Lewis Barnes-6, April-Tkikami Hop Turkey-5, Big Turkey Hop-4, Hokolesqua Opechan-3, Cleopatra the Shawano Powhatan-2, Wahunsonacock-1) was born in 1813 in Edgefield Co., SC. He died in 1877 at the age of 64 in Clark Co., AL.

Robert MOSELEY and Martha A. ROBERTSON were married. **Martha A. ROBERTSON** was born (date unknown).

63. **George Washington MOSELEY** (Daniel-9, Margaret Vann-8, Edward Ned-7, Mary Lewis Barnes-6, April-Tkikami Hop Turkey-5, Big Turkey Hop-4, Hokolesqua Opechan-3, Cleopatra the Shawano Powhatan-2, Wahunsonacock-1) was born about 1830.

George Washington MOSELEY and Lucinda were married. **Lucinda** was born (date unknown).

64. **Lucinda E. MOSELEY** (Daniel-9, Margaret Vann-8, Edward Ned-7, Mary Lewis Barnes-6, April-Tkikami Hop Turkey-5, Big Turkey Hop-4, Hokolesqua Opechan-3, Cleopatra the Shawano Powhatan-2, Wahunsonacock-1) was born about 1836.

Lucinda E. MOSELEY and William Henry MOSELEY were married on 3 Oct 1870 in Montgomery Co., AL. **William Henry MOSELEY** was born (date unknown).

65. **Elisha MOSELEY Jr.** (Elisha-9, Margaret Vann-8, Edward Ned-7, Mary Lewis Barnes-6, April-Tkikami Hop Turkey-5, Big Turkey Hop-4, Hokolesqua Opechan-3, Cleopatra the Shawano Powhatan-2, Wahunsonacock-1) was born about 1810. He died in 1838 at the age of 28 in AL. He held the title of Jr..

Elisha MOSELEY Jr. and Terraso DEAN were married on 8 Apr 1837 in Lowndes Co., AL. **Terraso DEAN** was born (date unknown).

Elisha MOSELEY and Terraso DEAN had the following child:

98   i. **Eliaha Anne MOSELEY**, born 1838; married Marew INGRAM, 28 Jul 1854, Montgomery Co., AL.

66. Mildred MOSELEY (Elisha-9, Margaret Vann-8, Edward Ned-7, Mary Lewis Barnes-6, April-Tkikami Hop Turkey-5, Big Turkey Hop-4, Hokolesqua Opechan-3, Cleopatra the Shawano Powhatan-2, Wahunsonacock-1) was born about 1812.

Mildred MOSELEY and William GOODSON were married on 9 Oct 1830 in Montgomery Co., AL. **William GOODSON** was born (date unknown).

67. Robert MOSELEY (Elisha-9, Margaret Vann-8, Edward Ned-7, Mary Lewis Barnes-6, April-Tkikami Hop Turkey-5, Big Turkey Hop-4, Hokolesqua Opechan-3, Cleopatra the Shawano Powhatan-2, Wahunsonacock-1) was born about 1814.

Robert MOSELEY and Sarah WALTERS were married on 15 Jan 1840 in Montgomery Co., AL. **Sarah WALTERS** was born (date unknown).

68. Tabitha MOSELEY (Elisha-9, Margaret Vann-8, Edward Ned-7, Mary Lewis Barnes-6, April-Tkikami Hop Turkey-5, Big Turkey Hop-4, Hokolesqua Opechan-3, Cleopatra the Shawano Powhatan-2, Wahunsonacock-1) was born about 1816 in GA. She died in AL.

Tabitha MOSELEY and Stepehn C. GAFFORD were married on 11 Feb 1833 in Montgomery Co., AL. **Stepehn C. GAFFORD** was born (date unknown).

69. Albert P. MOSELEY (Elisha-9, Margaret Vann-8, Edward Ned-7, Mary Lewis Barnes-6, April-Tkikami Hop Turkey-5, Big Turkey Hop-4, Hokolesqua Opechan-3, Cleopatra the Shawano Powhatan-2, Wahunsonacock-1) was born on 25 Sep 1818 in Montgomery Co., AL. He died on 17 Apr 1899 at the age of 80 in Montgomery Co., AL. He was buried on 19 Apr 1899 in Old Rehoboth Church Cemetery, Mt. Carmel, Montgomery Co., AL.

Albert P. MOSELEY and Adeline COTTONHAM were married on 29 Aug 1844 in Lowndes Co., AL. **Adeline COTTONHAM** was born (date unknown).

Albert P. MOSELEY and Adeline COTTONHAM had the following children:

     i. **John Albert MOSELEY** was born on 23 Dec 1846 in Lowndes Co., AL. He died on 1 Oct 1917 at the age of 70 in Montgomery, Montgomery Co., AL.
     ii. **Lydia F. MOSELEY** was born in 1848.
     iii. **Texaner MOSELEY** was born in Sep 1849.

Albert P. MOSELEY and Mary Matilda BUSSEY were married on 10 Sep 1865 in Montgomery Co., AL. **Mary Matilda BUSSEY**, daughter of Zadock BUSSEY and Sarah HAGENS, was born (date unknown).

Descendants of Chief Wahunsonacock Powhatan

70. **Lydia MOSELEY** (Elisha-9, Margaret Vann-8, Edward Ned-7, Mary Lewis Barnes-6, April-Tkikami Hop Turkey-5, Big Turkey Hop-4, Hokolesqua Opechan-3, Cleopatra the Shawano Powhatan-2, Wahunsonacock-1) was born about 1820.

Lydia MOSELEY and John MATHEWS were married on 12 Jan 1837 in Montgomery Co., AL. **John MATHEWS** was born (date unknown).

71. **Sarah Ann POLAND** (Nancy Naomi Moseley-9, Margaret Vann-8, Edward Ned-7, Mary Lewis Barnes-6, April-Tkikami Hop Turkey-5, Big Turkey Hop-4, Hokolesqua Opechan-3, Cleopatra the Shawano Powhatan-2, Wahunsonacock-1) was born in 1808. She died in 1851 at the age of 43 in Gladewater, TX.

Sarah Ann POLAND and John Kittle ARMSTRONG were married on 5 Feb 1830 in AL. **John Kittle ARMSTRONG**, son of John ARMSTRONG and Nancy KITTLE, was born about 1806 in GA. He died in Gladewater, Gregg Co., TX.

John Kittle ARMSTRONG and Sarah Ann POLAND had the following child:

    99   i. **Monroe Griffin ARMSTRONG**, born 1851, Gladewater, Gregg Co., TX; married Ella Virginia SMITH; died 1925.

72. **Elvira POLAND** (Nancy Naomi Moseley-9, Margaret Vann-8, Edward Ned-7, Mary Lewis Barnes-6, April-Tkikami Hop Turkey-5, Big Turkey Hop-4, Hokolesqua Opechan-3, Cleopatra the Shawano Powhatan-2, Wahunsonacock-1) was born in 1809.

Elvira POLAND and James MONCRIEF were married on 18 Dec 1828. **James MONCRIEF** was born (date unknown).

James MONCRIEF and Elvira POLAND had the following child:

    100   i. **Peneloupe "Penny" MONCRIEF**, born 28 Sep 1834; died 1935.

73. **John Stratton POLAND** (Nancy Naomi Moseley-9, Margaret Vann-8, Edward Ned-7, Mary Lewis Barnes-6, April-Tkikami Hop Turkey-5, Big Turkey Hop-4, Hokolesqua Opechan-3, Cleopatra the Shawano Powhatan-2, Wahunsonacock-1) was born on 21 Dec 1812. He was buried in Jul 1882 in Oak Hill Cemetery, Jefferson, TX. He died on 12 Jul 1882 at the age of 69.

John Stratton POLAND and Lenora STACEY were married on 10 Aug 1837. **Lenora STACEY** was born in 1822.

John Stratton POLAND and Lenora STACEY had the following children:

        i. **Virginia "Jenny" POLAND** was born in 1840.
    101   ii. **Lenora Lee POLAND**, born 26 Aug 1857; married John Guthrie LATTA, 6 Dec 1882; died 22 Mar

Descendants of Chief Wahunsonacock Powhatan

26 January 2012

1951, Dyersburg, TN.

John Stratton POLAND and Caroline GRAY were married on 20 Jul 1856 in Rusk Co., TX. **Caroline GRAY** died in 1897 in Dyersburg, TN.

74. Thomas POLAND (Nancy Naomi Moseley-9, Margaret Vann-8, Edward Ned-7, Mary Lewis Barnes-6, April-Tkikami Hop Turkey-5, Big Turkey Hop-4, Hokolesqua Opechan-3, Cleopatra the Shawano Powhatan-2, Wahunsonacock-1) was born on 22 Aug 1816. He was buried in Mar 1869 in Concord Cemetery, near Jonesville, TX. He died on 8 Mar 1869 at the age of 52.

Thomas POLAND and Sarah Ann were married. **Sarah Ann** was born on 22 Jul 1815. She was buried in Apr 1887 in Concord Cemetery, near Jonesville, TX. She died on 11 Apr 1887 at the age of 71.

Thomas POLAND and Sarah Ann had the following child:

102   i. **Mary A. POLAND**, born 21 Mar 1839; married Daniel K SMITH, 15 Feb 1855; died 4 Feb 1864.

75. George Benjamin Alexander MOSLEY (George-9, Margaret Vann-8, Edward Ned-7, Mary Lewis Barnes-6, April-Tkikami Hop Turkey-5, Big Turkey Hop-4, Hokolesqua Opechan-3, Cleopatra the Shawano Powhatan-2, Wahunsonacock-1) was born on 31 Jan 1825 in Montgomery Co., AL. He died on 7 May 1894 at the age of 69 in Arkadelphia, Cullman Co., AL. He was buried on 9 May 1894 in Arkadelphia Cemetery, Cullman Co., AL.

George Benjamin Alexander MOSLEY and Rebecca CARR were married on 21 Mar 1850 in Montgomery Co., AL. **Rebecca CARR** was born in 1830 in AL. She died after 1880 at the age of 50.

George Benjamin Alexander MOSLEY and Rebecca CARR had the following children:

    i. **George MOSLEY** was born in 1854 in AL.
    ii. **Alabama MOSLEY** was born in 1858 in AL.
103   iii. **William Alexander Newton MOSLEY**, born 15 Nov 1863, Troy, Pike Co., AL; married Malinda Irene BURRELL; married Susan Emoley (Lee) (Sudie) ROLLO, 6 Sep 1883, Blount Co., AL; died 7 Jun 1907, Brimingham, Jefferson Co., AL.
    iv. **Lousana MOSLEY** was born in 1867 in AL.
    v. **Ann MOSLEY** was born in 1870 in AL.
    vi. **Hiram A. MOSLEY** was born in 1871 in AL.

George Benjamin Alexander MOSLEY and Joanna FREEMAN were married. **Joanna FREEMAN**, daughter of Ira FREEMAN, was born (date unknown).

George Benjamin Alexander MOSLEY and Joanna FREEMAN had the following child:

104   i. **Virginia MOSELEY**, born bef 1850, AL; married Curby Brack CRAUSWELL.

Descendants of Chief Wahunsonacock Powhatan

26 January 2012

76. Martha (Malinda) MOSELEY (George-9, Margaret Vann-8, Edward Ned-7, Mary Lewis Barnes-6, April-Tkikami Hop Turkey-5, Big Turkey Hop-4, Hokolesqua Opechan-3, Cleopatra the Shawano Powhatan-2, Wahunsonacock-1) was born on 7 Feb 1827 in Montgomery Co., AL. She died on 4 Feb 1920 at the age of 92 in Lamar Co., AL. She was buried on 6 Feb 1920 in Crews Cemetery, Beaverton, Lamar Co., AL.

Martha (Malinda) MOSELEY and Benjamin Harmon (Harm) BUSSEY Sr. were married on 11 Aug 1847. **Benjamin Harmon (Harm) BUSSEY Sr.**, son of Edward Moody BUSSEY and Mahulda Hulda MOSELEY, was born on 3 Jun 1828 in Montgomery Co., AL. He died on 7 Jun 1908 at the age of 80 in Carbon Hill, Walker Co., AL. He was buried on 9 Jun 1908 in Crews Cemetery, Beaverton, Lamar Co., AL. Benjamin held the title of Sr..

Benjamin Harmon (Harm) BUSSEY and Martha (Malinda) MOSELEY had the following children:

	i.	**Susan BUSSEY** was born about 1848. She died after 1860 at the age of 12.
105	ii.	**Benjamin Harm BUSSEY Jr.**, born 19 Sep 1850, Marion Co., AL; married Martha Ellen HUFFMAN, 22 Jul 1875, Arkadelphia, Cullman Co., AL; died 14 Jun 1934, Winfield, Marion Co., AL.
	iii.	**Mary BUSSEY** was born about 1852. She died after 1860 at the age of 8.
106	iv.	**Martha BUSSEY**, born abt 1854; died aft 1860.
107	v.	**Edmund Moody BUSSEY**, born 17 Apr 1856, Pine Level, Montgomery Co. Alabama; married Mary Frances "Missy" ROLLO, 18 Dec 1879, Blount Co., AL; married Eula Mae GUYTON, 28 Jan 1904; died 1934, Cockran Bridge, MS.
108	vi.	**Adra "Addie" BUSSEY**, born 1858; died aft 1920.
109	vii.	**Dempsey (Demcey) BUSSEY**, born 1865; married Martha A. (Mattie R.) SUGGS, 7 Jan 1883, Blount Co., AL.
110	viii.	**William M. (Will) BUSSEY**, born 24 Aug 1868, Montgomery Co., AL; married Sarah Jane PARKER, 6 Jan 1887, Blount Co., AL; died 26 Jan 1940, Ft. Worth, Tarrant Co., TX.

77. William Lafayette MOSLEY (George-9, Margaret Vann-8, Edward Ned-7, Mary Lewis Barnes-6, April-Tkikami Hop Turkey-5, Big Turkey Hop-4, Hokolesqua Opechan-3, Cleopatra the Shawano Powhatan-2, Wahunsonacock-1) was born on 1 Jun 1840 in Montgomery Co., AL. He died on 26 Mar 1923 at the age of 82 in Morris, Jefferson Co., AL. He was buried on 28 Mar 1923 in Liberty Minter Cemetery, Morris, Jefferson Co., AL.

William Lafayette MOSLEY and B.B. TAYLOR were married on 12 Apr 1866 in Montgomery, Montgomery Co., AL. **B.B. TAYLOR** died after 16 Jan 1867 in Montgomery, Montgomery Co., AL.

William Lafayette MOSLEY and B.B. TAYLOR had the following child:

111	i.	**Hiram Mace MOSLEY**, born 16 Jan 1867, Montgomery Co., AL; married Lena Deloys SUDDETH, Jan 1892; died 29 Mar 1931, Kimberly, Jefferson Co., AL.

William Lafayette MOSLEY and Mary TAYLOR were married on 20 Sep 1869 in Montgomery, Montgomery Co., AL. **Mary TAYLOR** was born (date unknown).

William Lafayette MOSLEY and Mary TAYLOR had the following child:

112	i.	**Adrin Bethiah MOSLEY**, born 20 Sep 1870; married William Jackson EATON.

William Lafayette MOSLEY and Mary Susanna JONES were married on 15 Jan 1874 in Arkadelphia, Cullman Co., AL.

Descendants of Chief Wahunsonacock Powhatan

Mary Susanna JONES was born in 1848 in AL. She died on 25 Oct 1942 at the age of 94 in Inglenook, Jefferson Co., AL. She was buried on 27 Oct 1942 in Liberty Minter Cemetery, Morris, Jefferson Co., AL.

William Lafayette MOSLEY and Mary Susanna JONES had the following children:

113	i.	**James Augusta MOSLEY**, born 11 Mar 1875; married Nora Josephine HARDING; died Nov 1968, Escondido, San Diego Co., CA.
114	ii.	**William Lee MOSLEY**, born 30 Jul 1879, Morris, Jefferson Co., AL; married Mildred Rosa BEVILS; married Cora M. DAY; died 27 Sep 1955, Morris, Jefferson Co., AL.
115	iii.	**Robert Elisha MOSLEY**, born 20 Sep 1882, AL; married Stella WHISENANT, 19 Dec 1904, Warrior, Jefferson Co., AL; died 17 Dec 1958, Springville, St. Clair Co., AL.
116	iv.	**Myrtle Addie MOSLEY**, born 16 Apr 1888, AL; married Adolphus WHISENANT, 21 Dec 1904, Jefferson Co., AL; died 26 Apr 1925, Jefferson Co., AL.
	v.	**George W. MOSLEY** was born on 16 Aug 1888. He died on 22 Aug 1902 at the age of 14 in Jefferson Co., AL. He was buried on 24 Aug 1902 in Liberty Baptist Church Cemetery, Morris, Jefferson Co., AL.
117	vi.	**Benjamin Milton MOSLEY**, born 17 Oct 1891, Jefferson Co., AL; married Addie M. BLANTON; married Nell Hortnese KYKER, 23 Jun 1919, Athens, TN; died 5 Nov 1986, Holly Hill, Volusaia Co., FL.

78. **William Henry POLAND** (Hannah Moseley-9, Margaret Vann-8, Edward Ned-7, Mary Lewis Barnes-6, April-Tkikami Hop Turkey-5, Big Turkey Hop-4, Hokolesqua Opechan-3, Cleopatra the Shawano Powhatan-2, Wahunsonacock-1) was born on 8 Aug 1827 in AL. He died on 10 Apr 1891 at the age of 63.

William Henry POLAND and Kezzie PYTCHLYNN were married about 1852. **Kezzie PYTCHLYNN**, daughter of John PYTCHLYNN, was born in 1824. She died in 1858 at the age of 34.

William Henry POLAND and Kezzie PYTCHLYNN had the following children:

118	i.	**William Pytchlynn POLAND**, born 1855; married Emma Lucy AGRRETT, 12 Sep 1878.
119	ii.	**Walter Henry POLAND**, born 26 Dec 1860; married Florence CARTER, 16 Feb 1887; died 5 Feb 1945.
	iii.	**C.L. POLAND** was born in 1857 in Indian Nation.

Sophia FOLSOM, daughter of Ebenezer FOLSOM, was born (date unknown).

Nitka was born (date unknown).

79. **Margaret E. MOSELEY** (Mason-9, Margaret Vann-8, Edward Ned-7, Mary Lewis Barnes-6, April-Tkikami Hop Turkey-5, Big Turkey Hop-4, Hokolesqua Opechan-3, Cleopatra the Shawano Powhatan-2, Wahunsonacock-1) was born about 1830. She died after 1881 at the age of 51 in Gilmer, Upshur Co., TX.

Margaret E. MOSELEY and J. Walter BOYD were married on 19 Aug 1848 in TX. **J. Walter BOYD**, son of Walter BOYD and Letitia BUSSEY, was born on 1 Nov 1827. He died on 18 Dec 1907 at the age of 80 in Gilmer, Upshur Co., TX.

Descendants of Chief Wahunsonacock Powhatan

26 January 2012

J. Walter BOYD and Margaret E. MOSELEY had the following children:

	i.	**Levina Pamelia BOYD** was born on 30 Jun 1849 in Smith Co., TX. She died on 8 Jan 1933 at the age of 83 in Gilmer, Upshur Co., TX.
	ii.	**Letitia Jane BOYD** was born on 5 Mar 1851 in Smith Co., TX. She died in TX.
	iii.	**Mary Virginia BOYD** was born on 14 Nov 1853 in Smith Co., TX.
	iv.	**James Watson BOYD** was born (date unknown).
	v.	**Anna T. BOYD** was born about 1857 in Gilmer, Upshur Co., TX.
	vi.	**Alabama Texana BOYD** was born on 18 Mar 1858 in Gilmer, Upshur Co., TX. She died about 1910 at the age of 52 in TX.
	vii.	**Walter BOYD Jr.** was born on 27 May 1860 in Gilmer, Upshur Co., TX. He held the title of Jr..
120	viii.	**Margaret "Maggie" BOYD**, born 19 Dec 1866, Gilmer, Upshur Co., TX; married James W. BUSSEY, 8 Nov 1884, Pine, Upshur Co., TX; died 24 Oct 1898, Pine, Upshur Co., TX.
	ix.	**Mae (May) BOYD** was born on 1 Apr 1869 in Gilmer, Upshur Co., TX. She died about 1910 at the age of 41 in TX.
	x.	**Martha BOYD** was born on 29 Nov 1871 in Gilmer, Upshur Co., TX. She died about 1910 at the age of 39 in TX.
	xi.	**Emma BOYD** was born on 3 Jan 1875 in Gilmer, Upshur Co., TX. She died in TX.
	xii.	**Bessie BOYD** was born on 21 Jan 1879 in Gilmer, Upshur Co., TX.
	xiii.	**Infant BOYD** was born on 10 Sep 1881 in Smith Co., TX. He/she died on 3 Oct 1881 at the age of 0 in Smith Co., TX.

80. **Benjamin Harmon (Harm) BUSSEY Sr.** (Mahulda Hulda Moseley-9, Margaret Vann-8, Edward Ned-7, Mary Lewis Barnes-6, April-Tkikami Hop Turkey-5, Big Turkey Hop-4, Hokolesqua Opechan-3, Cleopatra the Shawano Powhatan-2, Wahunsonacock-1) was born on 3 Jun 1828 in Montgomery Co., AL. He died on 7 Jun 1908 at the age of 80 in Carbon Hill, Walker Co., AL. He was buried on 9 Jun 1908 in Crews Cemetery, Beaverton, Lamar Co., AL. Benjamin held the title of Sr..

Benjamin Harmon (Harm) BUSSEY Sr. and Martha (Malinda) MOSELEY were married on 11 Aug 1847. **Martha (Malinda) MOSELEY**, daughter of George MOSELEY and Adra HOWARD, was born on 7 Feb 1827 in Montgomery Co., AL. She died on 4 Feb 1920 at the age of 92 in Lamar Co., AL. She was buried on 6 Feb 1920 in Crews Cemetery, Beaverton, Lamar Co., AL.

Benjamin Harmon (Harm) BUSSEY and Martha (Malinda) MOSELEY had the following children:

	i.	**Susan BUSSEY** was born about 1848. She died after 1860 at the age of 12.
105	ii.	**Benjamin Harm BUSSEY Jr.**, born 19 Sep 1850, Marion Co., AL; married Martha Ellen HUFFMAN, 22 Jul 1875, Arkadelphia, Cullman Co., AL; died 14 Jun 1934, Winfield, Marion Co., AL.
	iii.	**Mary BUSSEY** was born about 1852. She died after 1860 at the age of 8.
106	iv.	**Martha BUSSEY**, born abt 1854; died aft 1860.
107	v.	**Edmund Moody BUSSEY**, born 17 Apr 1856, Pine Level, Montgomery Co. Alabama; married Mary Frances "Missy" ROLLO, 18 Dec 1879, Blount Co., AL; married Eula Mae GUYTON, 28 Jan 1904; died 1934, Cockran Bridge, MS.
108	vi.	**Adra "Addie" BUSSEY**, born 1858; died aft 1920.
109	vii.	**Dempsey (Demcey) BUSSEY**, born 1865; married Martha A. (Mattie R.) SUGGS, 7 Jan 1883, Blount Co., AL.
110	viii.	**William M. (Will) BUSSEY**, born 24 Aug 1868, Montgomery Co., AL; married Sarah Jane PARKER, 6 Jan 1887, Blount Co., AL; died 26 Jan 1940, Ft. Worth, Tarrant Co., TX.

81. **Dempsey C. BUSSEY** (Mahulda Hulda Moseley-9, Margaret Vann-8, Edward Ned-7, Mary Lewis Barnes-6, April-

Descendants of Chief Wahunsonacock Powhatan

Tkikami Hop Turkey-5, Big Turkey Hop-4, Hokolesqua Opechan-3, Cleopatra the Shawano Powhatan-2, Wahunsonacock-1) was born on 14 May 1831 in AL.

UNK was born (date unknown).

Dempsey C. BUSSEY and UNK had the following child:

    121   i. **Leo R. BUSSEY**.

82. Hezekiah BUSSEY (Mahulda Hulda Moseley-9, Margaret Vann-8, Edward Ned-7, Mary Lewis Barnes-6, April-Tkikami Hop Turkey-5, Big Turkey Hop-4, Hokolesqua Opechan-3, Cleopatra the Shawano Powhatan-2, Wahunsonacock-1) was born on 10 Sep 1833 in AL. He was buried in Mar 1892 in Old City Cemetery, Gilmer, TX. He died on 14 Mar 1892 at the age of 58 in Upshur Co., TX.

Hezekiah BUSSEY and Mary Jane ALEXANDER were married on 21 Jan 1854 in Pine Tree, Upsher Co. (now Gregg), TX. **Mary Jane ALEXANDER**, daughter of James Lindsey ALEXANDER and Clarissa Ann CRAIN, was born on 2 Dec 1837 in Meridian, Lauderdale Co., MS. She was buried in Feb 1897 in Old City Cemetery, Gilmer, TX. She died on 22 Feb 1897 at the age of 59 in Upshur Co., TX.

Hezekiah BUSSEY and Mary Jane ALEXANDER had the following children:

    122   i. **Clary BUSSEY**, born abt 1856, Upshur Co., TX; married Robert M. GEE, abt 1876; died bef 1880.
    123   ii. **Mary Elizabeth (Eliza) BUSSEY**, born abt 1858, Upshur Co., TX; married James W. BONHAM, 20 Aug 1874, Pine, Upshur Co., TX.
    124   iii. **James W. BUSSEY**, born 1866, Pine, Upshur Co., TX; married Margaret "Maggie" BOYD, 8 Nov 1884, Pine, Upshur Co., TX.
    125   iv. **Edward "Eddie" H. BUSSEY**, born Jan 1870, Upshur Co., TX; married Minnie E. JACOBS, 27 Aug 1893, Gregg Co., TX.
            v. **Mai BUSSEY** was born in 1878 in Upshur Co., TX.

Hezekiah BUSSEY and ZOULA were married about 1906. **ZOULA** was born about 1872 in TX.

Hezekiah BUSSEY and ZOULA had the following child:

        i. **Lela BUSSEY** was born about 1907.

83. Sarah Ann BUSSEY (Mahulda Hulda Moseley-9, Margaret Vann-8, Edward Ned-7, Mary Lewis Barnes-6, April-Tkikami Hop Turkey-5, Big Turkey Hop-4, Hokolesqua Opechan-3, Cleopatra the Shawano Powhatan-2, Wahunsonacock-1) was born on 2 Apr 1835 in AL.

H. Augustus BOWLES was born in 1833 in Attala Co., MS. He died after 1871 at the age of 38 in TX.

H. Augustus BOWLES and Sarah Ann BUSSEY had the following children:

        i. **Samuel BOWLES** was born in 1856 in Upshur Co., TX.
    126   ii. **Sarah "Sally" Mahulda BOWLES**, born Aug 1861, Upshur Co., TX; married John Molton MOORE,

1880, Harrison Co., TX; died 1940.
- iii. **Maticia J. "Mattie" BOWLES** was born in 1862 in TX.
- 127 iv. **Edward Augustus "Gus" BOWLES**, born 1866, TX; married Annie Mae RICHARDSON, 1885, Harrison Co., TX; died 1938, Harrison Co., TX.
- v. **William BOWLES** was born in 1867 in TX.
- vi. **Anna BOWLES** was born in 1869 in Hopkins Co., TX.
- 128 vii. **John Thomas BOWLES**, born Sep 1870, TX; married Maude Lillie COLE, 1892, TX; died aft 1930, TX.

84. **Joseph BUSSEY** (Mahulda Hulda Moseley-9, Margaret Vann-8, Edward Ned-7, Mary Lewis Barnes-6, April-Tkikami Hop Turkey-5, Big Turkey Hop-4, Hokolesqua Opechan-3, Cleopatra the Shawano Powhatan-2, Wahunsonacock-1) was born on 11 Jan 1837 in AL. He died in TX.

Sarah DAVIS was born (date unknown).

85. **Mary Lou Tassie BUSSEY** (Mahulda Hulda Moseley-9, Margaret Vann-8, Edward Ned-7, Mary Lewis Barnes-6, April-Tkikami Hop Turkey-5, Big Turkey Hop-4, Hokolesqua Opechan-3, Cleopatra the Shawano Powhatan-2, Wahunsonacock-1) was born in 1841 in AL.

Mary Lou Tassie BUSSEY and Thomas Abney KILLINGSWORTH were married. **Thomas Abney KILLINGSWORTH** was born (date unknown).

Thomas Abney KILLINGSWORTH and Mary Lou Tassie BUSSEY had the following children:

- 129 i. **James KILLINGSWORTH**, born 30 May 1859; married Annie ZIEGLER; married Tracy DAVIS; died 13 Jan 1928, Freeport, TX.
- 130 ii. **Lee Levy R. KILLINGSWORTH**, born 1861; married Martha E. Mattie NOWELL; died 13 Feb 1913, Austin, Travis Co., TX.
- 131 iii. **Mary Mollie Antoniette KILLINGSWORTH**, born 4 Feb 1865, Caddo Mills, Hunt Co., TX; married James William MCFARLAND; died 23 Oct 1950, Duncan, Stephers Co., OK.
- iv. **Mattie KILLINGSWORTH** was born on 18 Sep 1866. She died on 27 Jan 1943 at the age of 76 in Tyler, Smith Co., TX.

Mary Lou Tassie BUSSEY and Hezekiah BOYD were married. **Hezekiah BOYD** was born (date unknown).

Hezekiah BOYD and Mary Lou Tassie BUSSEY had the following child:

- i. **Hezekiah BOYD Jr.** held the title of Jr..

86. **William J. BUSSEY** (Mahulda Hulda Moseley-9, Margaret Vann-8, Edward Ned-7, Mary Lewis Barnes-6, April-Tkikami Hop Turkey-5, Big Turkey Hop-4, Hokolesqua Opechan-3, Cleopatra the Shawano Powhatan-2, Wahunsonacock-1) was born on 17 Jul 1842 in Montgomery Co., AL. He died on 10 May 1910 at the age of 67 in Tarrant Co., TX. He was buried on 11 May 1910 in Rehobeth Cemetery, Fannin Co., TX.

Descendants of Chief Wahunsonacock Powhatan

William J. BUSSEY and Sarah Ann DAVIS were married on 26 May 1863 in Harrison Co., TX. **Sarah Ann DAVIS**, daughter of Henry Clay DAVIS and Frances "Fannie" BOAZ, was born in 1845 in AL.

William J. BUSSEY and Sarah Ann DAVIS had the following children:

132	i.	**Mary Leonah "Molly" BUSSEY**, born 1865, TX; married John K. Clinton PATRICK, 12 Sep 1882, Gregg Co., TX.
133	ii.	**Elizabeth M. "Lizzie" BUSSEY**, born 1867, TX; married John K. Clinton PATRICK, 14 Jan 1888, Gregg Co., TX.
134	iii.	**Frances Maud BUSSEY**, born aft 1870.

87. John L. BUSSEY (Mahulda Hulda Moseley-9, Margaret Vann-8, Edward Ned-7, Mary Lewis Barnes-6, April-Tkikami Hop Turkey-5, Big Turkey Hop-4, Hokolesqua Opechan-3, Cleopatra the Shawano Powhatan-2, Wahunsonacock-1) was born on 22 May 1844 in AL. He died in 1916 at the age of 72 in Longview, Harrison Co., TX. He was buried in 1916 in Elmira Chapel Cemetery, Gregg Co., TX.

John L. BUSSEY and Anna E. were married. **Anna E.** was born in 1840 in NC. She died in 1914 at the age of 74 in TX. She was buried in 1914 in Old Summerfield Cemetery, Longview, Gregg Co., TX.

John L. BUSSEY and Anna E. had the following children:

	i.	**Anna BUSSEY** was born in 1867 in TX.
135	ii.	**William Lafayette "Willie" BUSSEY**, born 23 Apr 1869, TX; married Hannah Suttizie (Tizie) BARTON, 10 Sep 1892, Gregg Co., TX; died 13 Dec 1945, Longview, Gregg Co., TX.
	iii.	**Julia BUSSEY** was born in 1875.
	iv.	**Eula BUSSEY** was born in 1878. She died in 1956 at the age of 78.

88. Thomas Jefferson JERNIGAN (William-9, Vashti Vann-8, Edward Ned-7, Mary Lewis Barnes-6, April-Tkikami Hop Turkey-5, Big Turkey Hop-4, Hokolesqua Opechan-3, Cleopatra the Shawano Powhatan-2, Wahunsonacock-1) was born on 3 Sep 1824 in Conecuh Co., AL.

Thomas Jefferson JERNIGAN and Martha Jane TRAVIS were married. **Martha Jane TRAVIS**, daughter of Nicholas Stallworth TRAVIS and Mary WILSON, was born in 1830 in AL.

Thomas Jefferson JERNIGAN and Martha Jane TRAVIS had the following children:

	i.	**Van Stallworth JERNIGAN** was born on 8 Mar 1858 in AL. He died on 6 May 1915 at the age of 57 in Brewton, Escambia Co., AL.
	ii.	**Benjamin Lomax JERNIGAN** was born on 25 Aug 1862 in Pollard, Escambia Co., AL. He died on 29 Jun 1940 at the age of 77 in Brewton, Escambia Co., AL.
136	iii.	**Martha Lulu JERNIGAN**, born 18 Sep 1865, AL; married Walker Isaiah COBB, bef 1880; died 11 Dec 1945, Wiggins, Stone Co., MS.

89. George Washington JERNIGAN (Cary-9, Vashti Vann-8, Edward Ned-7, Mary Lewis Barnes-6, April-Tkikami Hop Turkey-5, Big Turkey Hop-4, Hokolesqua Opechan-3, Cleopatra the Shawano Powhatan-2, Wahunsonacock-1) was born in

Feb 1850 in Milton, Santa Rosa Co., FL. He died on 1 Jul 1928 at the age of 78 in Eddy Co., NM.

George Washington JERNIGAN and Diza M. CARR were married on 20 Jan 1876 in Jackson Co., TX. **Diza M. CARR**, daughter of Wiley CARR and Esther , was born in 1849 in Carroll Co., MS.

George Washington JERNIGAN and Diza M. CARR had the following children:

    i. **William Wiley JERNIGAN** was born on 22 Nov 1877 in Llano Co., TX. He died in Mexico.
    ii. **Robert Henry JERNIGAN** was born on 5 Jan 1880 in Llano Co., TX. He died on 6 Jul 1967 at the age of 87 in Pinion, NM.
    iii. **Ernest Edwin JERNIGAN** was born on 5 Sep 1882 in Llano Co., TX. He died on 11 Jul 1952 at the age of 69 in Eddy Co., NM.
    iv. **Curtis LeRoy JERNIGAN** was born (date unknown).
    v. **Ida Evelyn JERNIGAN** was born (date unknown).
    vi. **Dizzy M. JERNIGAN** was born (date unknown).

90. **James Mason VANN** (Mason M.-9, Mason M.-8, Edward Ned-7, Mary Lewis Barnes-6, April-Tkikami Hop Turkey-5, Big Turkey Hop-4, Hokolesqua Opechan-3, Cleopatra the Shawano Powhatan-2, Wahunsonacock-1) was born on 8 Dec 1846 in Shelby Co., TX. He died on 12 Dec 1912 at the age of 66 in Luna, Freestone Co., TX.

James Mason VANN and Luvicie Luice EZELL were married on 20 Aug 1870 in Freestone Co., TX. **Luvicie Luice EZELL** was born on 4 Nov 1851 in Hardin Co., TN. She died on 1 Jan 1929 at the age of 77 in Franklin, TX. She was buried on 3 Jan 1929 in Henry Prairie Cemetery.

James Mason VANN and Luvicie Luice EZELL had the following children:

    i. **Maggie VANN** was born in 1875 in DeSota Parish, LA.
    ii. **John David VANN** was born on 1 Jan 1877 in DeSota Parish, LA.
    iii. **Sarah VANN** was born on 1 Jan 1877 in DeSota Parish, LA.
137   iv. **William Green VANN**, born 17 Dec 1881, Luna, Freestone Co., TX; married Mary Appie HODGES.
138   v. **James Albert VANN**, born 17 Oct 1844, Teague, Freestone Co., TX; married Addie Mae HODGES; died 12 Dec 1958.
    vi. **Katie VANN** was born on 6 Nov 1886 in Nacogdoches, Milam Co., TX.
    vii. **Robert VANN** was born on 6 Dec 1888 in Smith Co., TX.
    viii. **Eva Lou VANN** was born in 1894 in Smith Co., TX.
    ix. **Thomas VANN** was born in Mar 1896 in Freestone Co., TX.
    x. **Mary Ann VANN** was born in 1898 in Freestone Co., TX.

91. **Mary Lavisa COTHERN** (Lavica Jane Vann-9, Mason M.-8, Edward Ned-7, Mary Lewis Barnes-6, April-Tkikami Hop Turkey-5, Big Turkey Hop-4, Hokolesqua Opechan-3, Cleopatra the Shawano Powhatan-2, Wahunsonacock-1) was born on 19 Sep 1865 in OK. She died on 7 Sep 1934 at the age of 68 in Hartshorne, Pittsburg Co., OK. She was buried on 9 Sep 1934 in Mountain Station Cemetery, Higgins, Latimer Co., OK.

Mary Lavisa COTHERN and Andrew Jackson RILEY Sr. were married on 27 Oct 1881 in OK. **Andrew Jackson RILEY Sr.**, son of Alfred Barry RILEY, was born on 25 Jan 1856. He died on 10 Dec 1939 at the age of 83 in Higgins, Latimer Co., OK. He was buried on 12 Dec 1939 in Mountain Station Cemetery, Higgins, Latimer Co., OK. Andrew held the title of Sr..

Andrew Jackson RILEY and Mary Lavisa COTHERN had the following children:

139	i.	**Levi Lavan RILEY**, born 23 Sep 1882, Indian Territory, OK; married Ann CHESTER; died 12 Jun 1919, Kiowi, OK.
140	ii.	**Letty Annety RILEY**, born 20 Sep 1884, Indian Territory, OK; married John Sheridan MCCASLIN, 28 Oct 1911, Wilburton, Latimer Co., OK; died 17 Jul 1957, Hardshorne Co., OK.
141	iii.	**Willey Price RILEY**, born 5 Apr 1887, TX; married Gus MITCHELL; died 6 Feb 1926, Higgins, Latimer Co., OK.
	iv.	**Sidney Alfred RILEY** was born on 6 Feb 1889 in TX. He died on 16 Jan 1961 at the age of 71 in Higgins, Latimer Co., OK.
	v.	**Carrie Velma RILEY** was born on 15 Jun 1892 in TX. She died on 20 Mar 1908 at the age of 15 in Higgins, Latimer Co., OK.
142	vi.	**Andrew Leonard RILEY**, born 7 Jul 1895, Indian Territory, OK; married Thelma COSTEN, 9 Dec 1917, OK; died 22 Jul 1966, Hartshorne, Pittsburg Co., OK.
	vii.	**Joseph Arthur RILEY** was born on 24 Oct 1898 in Indian Territory, OK. He died on 29 Apr 1899 at the age of 0 in Poteau, Le Flore Co., OK.
143	viii.	**Chessie Grace RILEY**, born 8 Dec 1900, Indian Territory, OK; married Guy HOLMES; died 31 Mar 1995, Hartshorne, Pittsburg Co., OK.
	ix.	**Charles Robert RILEY** was born on 20 Aug 1903 in Indian Territory, OK. He died on 31 Aug 1995 at the age of 92 in Hartshorne, Pittsburg Co., OK.
144	x.	**Virgil Guy RILEY**, born 26 Jun 1906, Indian Territory, OK; married Ann BASDEN; died 15 Jun 1992, OR.

92. **Nancy Carlida COTHERN** (Lavica Jane Vann-9, Mason M.-8, Edward Ned-7, Mary Lewis Barnes-6, April-Tkikami Hop Turkey-5, Big Turkey Hop-4, Hokolesqua Opechan-3, Cleopatra the Shawano Powhatan-2, Wahunsonacock-1) was born on 12 May 1867 in OK. She died on 5 Apr 1947 at the age of 79 in Hartshorne, Pittsburg Co., OK.

Nancy Carlida COTHERN and Christopher Cornelius SADLER were married on 4 Nov 1883 in OK. **Christopher Cornelius SADLER**, son of John Armstrong SADLER and Louisa JANE, was born on 1 Oct 1858. He died on 2 Oct 1929 at the age of 71 in Kern Co., CA.

Christopher Cornelius SADLER and Nancy Carlida COTHERN had the following children:

	i.	**Lizzie SADLER** was born on 24 Sep 1884.
	ii.	**Lulu SADLER** was born on 11 Oct 1886.
	iii.	**Limmie SADLER** was born on 28 Nov 1889.
	iv.	**Ethel SADLER** was born on 11 Mar 1892.
	v.	**Earl SADLER** was born on 18 Jul 1895.
	vi.	**Bertha SADLER** was born (date unknown).
145	vii.	**Minnie Myrtle SADLER**, born 12 May 1902, Hartshorne, Pittsburg Co., OK; married William Bruce DEAR; married Jess MORROW; died 18 Sep 1938, Hartshorne, Pittsburg Co., OK.
146	viii.	**Ira Melbert SADLER**, born 4 May 1905, Hartshorne, Pittsburg Co., OK; married Eva Mae DEAR; died Feb 1987, Tuolurnne, Sonora Co., CA.
	ix.	**Ed SADLER** was born (date unknown).
	x.	**Melvin SADLER** was born (date unknown).

93. **Walter COTHERN** (Lavica Jane Vann-9, Mason M.-8, Edward Ned-7, Mary Lewis Barnes-6, April-Tkikami Hop Turkey-5, Big Turkey Hop-4, Hokolesqua Opechan-3, Cleopatra the Shawano Powhatan-2, Wahunsonacock-1) was born on 20 Oct 1873 in Summerfield, Le Flore Co., OK. He died on 15 Jun 1970 at the age of 96 in Sardis, Pushmataha Co., OK. He was buried on 17 Jun 1970 in Sardis Cemetery, Sardis, Pushmataha Co., OK.

Descendants of Chief Wahunsonacock Powhatan

Walter COTHERN and Mary Jane WILLIAMS were married on 16 Sep 1900 in Richert, Poteau Co., OK. **Mary Jane WILLIAMS**, daughter of Pete WILLIAMS and Nancy SHUCK, was born on 10 Apr 1872 in Johnson, Sharp Co., AR. She died on 6 Feb 1968 at the age of 95 in Sardis, Pushmataha Co., OK. She was buried on 8 Feb 1968 in Sardis Cemetery, Pushmataha Co., OK.

Walter COTHERN and Mary Jane WILLIAMS had the following children:

147	i.	**Letha Lovie COTHERN**, born 6 Aug 1902; married Thomas CAREY, 22 Dec 1920.
	ii.	**Nannie COTHERN** was born in Jan 1905 in OK. She died in Jan 1907 at the age of 2 in Le Flore Co., OK.
148	iii.	**Willie Jewell COTHERN**, born 18 Sep 1907, Le Flore Co., OK; married Coy LEMONS, 20 Sep 1927, Waurika, Jefferson Co., OK; married Henry BRANCH, 20 Jun 1949, Marietta, TX; married Gomer FARRIS, 16 Jun 1923, Clarksville, AR.
149	iv.	**Farrie COTHERN**, born 3 Oct 1909, Le Flore Co., OK; married Earl Monroe LYONS, 1925, Waurika, Jefferson Co., OK; died 13 Aug 1961.
	v.	**Walter James COTHERN** was born on 21 Oct 1911 in OK. He died on 27 Apr 1956 at the age of 44 in OK.

Walter COTHERN and Mollie RAINES were married on 18 Nov 1894 in Poteau, Le Flore Co., OK. **Mollie RAINES** was born in 1877.

Walter COTHERN and Mollie RAINES had the following child:

i. **John Emery COTHERN** was born (date unknown).

94. Vevi Vann COTHERN (Lavica Jane Vann-9, Mason M.-8, Edward Ned-7, Mary Lewis Barnes-6, April-Tkikami Hop Turkey-5, Big Turkey Hop-4, Hokolesqua Opechan-3, Cleopatra the Shawano Powhatan-2, Wahunsonacock-1) was born on 17 Dec 1876 in Sallisaw, OK. He died on 27 Aug 1935 at the age of 58 in Stamford, Jones Co., TX. He was buried on 29 Aug 1935 in Bethel Cemetery, Funston, Jones Co., TX.

Vevi Vann COTHERN and Sallie Emma KNOX were married on 27 May 1906 in Whon, Coleman Co., TX. **Sallie Emma KNOX**, daughter of William Gaw KNOX and Laura Cordell JONES, was born on 28 May 1889 in Mangum, Indian Territory. She died on 27 Feb 1955 at the age of 65 in Hamlin, Jones Co., TX. She was buried 29 Feb 1955 in Bethel Cemetery, Funston, Jones Co., TX.

Vevi Vann COTHERN and Sallie Emma KNOX had the following children:

150	i.	**Willa Augusta COTHERN**, born 21 Nov 1907, Charlie, Clay Co., TX; married John Charles GOODMAN, 8 Dec 1935, Lueders, Jones Co., TX; died 3 Oct 1993, Bedford, Tarrant Co., TX.
151	ii.	**Bobby Nell COTHERN**, born 21 Apr 1910, Charlie, Clay Co., TX; married John Edward WRIGHT, 4 Sep 1933, Whon, Coleman Co., TX.
152	iii.	**Ruby Gayle COTHERN**, born 31 Jul 1912, Charlie, Clay Co., TX; married Troy Lee WRIGHT, 17 Dec 1933, Whon, Coleman Co., TX.
153	iv.	**Filo Knox COTHERN**, born 5 Sep 1914, Charlie, Clay Co., TX; married Frances COTHERN; married Mrytle NEWCOMBE, Jun 1941; married Beth JONES, AZ; died Oct 1987, AZ.
154	v.	**Murriel COTHERN**, born 7 Apr 1917, Vernon, Wilbarger Co., TX; married George Washington COLE, 3 Sep 1934, Anson, Jones Co., TX.
155	vi.	**Doris Loraine COTHERN**, born 27 Jun 1926, Whon, Coleman Co., TX; married John Wesley BEACH Jr., 8 Mar 1946, Prescott, Yavapai Co., AZ.

Vevi Vann COTHERN and Nannie LAYMAN were married on 25 Jun 1901 in Northern District, Indian Territory, OK. **Nannie LAYMAN** was born in 1871 in Sallisaw, OK. She died in Sallisaw, OK.

95. **Edd Pickens COTHERN** (Lavica Jane Vann-9, Mason M.-8, Edward Ned-7, Mary Lewis Barnes-6, April-Tkikami Hop Turkey-5, Big Turkey Hop-4, Hokolesqua Opechan-3, Cleopatra the Shawano Powhatan-2, Wahunsonacock-1) was born (date unknown).

Edd Pickens COTHERN and Mamie LOGAN were married on 27 Feb 1904 in Phillips, OK. **Mamie LOGAN** was born (date unknown).

96. **John H. MCMILLEN** (Lavica Jane Vann-9, Mason M.-8, Edward Ned-7, Mary Lewis Barnes-6, April-Tkikami Hop Turkey-5, Big Turkey Hop-4, Hokolesqua Opechan-3, Cleopatra the Shawano Powhatan-2, Wahunsonacock-1) was born in 1849 in TX.

John H. MCMILLEN and Elizabeth were married. **Elizabeth** was born (date unknown).

97. **Bettie H. MCMILLEN** (Lavica Jane Vann-9, Mason M.-8, Edward Ned-7, Mary Lewis Barnes-6, April-Tkikami Hop Turkey-5, Big Turkey Hop-4, Hokolesqua Opechan-3, Cleopatra the Shawano Powhatan-2, Wahunsonacock-1) was born in 1854 in TX.

Bettie H. MCMILLEN and ALEXANDER were married. **ALEXANDER** was born (date unknown).

Descendants of Chief Wahunsonacock Powhatan

Eleventh Generation

98. **Eliaha Anne MOSELEY** (Elisha-10, Elisha-9, Margaret Vann-8, Edward Ned-7, Mary Lewis Barnes-6, April-Tkikami Hop Turkey-5, Big Turkey Hop-4, Hokolesqua Opechan-3, Cleopatra the Shawano Powhatan-2, Wahunsonacock-1) was born in 1838.

Eliaha Anne MOSELEY and Marew INGRAM were married on 28 Jul 1854 in Montgomery Co., AL. **Marew INGRAM** was born (date unknown).

99. **Monroe Griffin ARMSTRONG** (Sarah Ann Poland-10, Nancy Naomi Moseley-9, Margaret Vann-8, Edward Ned-7, Mary Lewis Barnes-6, April-Tkikami Hop Turkey-5, Big Turkey Hop-4, Hokolesqua Opechan-3, Cleopatra the Shawano Powhatan-2, Wahunsonacock-1) was born in 1851 in Gladewater, Gregg Co., TX. He died in 1925 at the age of 74.

Monroe Griffin ARMSTRONG and Ella Virginia "Dubba" SMITH were married. **Ella Virginia "Dubba" SMITH**, daughter of Daniel K SMITH and Mary A. POLAND, was born in 1856. She was buried in 1856 at Scottsville Cemetery in Scottsville, TX. She died in 1943 at the age of 87 in Scottsville, TX.

Monroe Griffin ARMSTRONG and Ella Virginia SMITH had the following child:

- 156 i. **Sallie ARMSTRONG**, born 1879, Jonesville, TX; married John William ROGERS; died 1928.

100. **Peneloupe "Penny" MONCRIEF** (Elvira Poland-10, Nancy Naomi Moseley-9, Margaret Vann-8, Edward Ned-7, Mary Lewis Barnes-6, April-Tkikami Hop Turkey-5, Big Turkey Hop-4, Hokolesqua Opechan-3, Cleopatra the Shawano Powhatan-2, Wahunsonacock-1) was born on 28 Sep 1834. She died in 1935 at the age of 101.

OFFETT was born (date unknown).

OFFETT and Peneloupe "Penny" MONCRIEF had the following child:

- 157 i. **Nell OFFETT**.

101. **Lenora Lee POLAND** (John Stratton-10, Nancy Naomi Moseley-9, Margaret Vann-8, Edward Ned-7, Mary Lewis Barnes-6, April-Tkikami Hop Turkey-5, Big Turkey Hop-4, Hokolesqua Opechan-3, Cleopatra the Shawano Powhatan-2, Wahunsonacock-1) was born on 26 Aug 1857. She died on 22 Mar 1951 at the age of 93 in Dyersburg, TN.

Lenora Lee POLAND and John Guthrie LATTA were married on 6 Dec 1882. **John Guthrie LATTA** was born on 21 Jun 1857 in Dyersburg, TN. He died on 27 Dec 1925 at the age of 68 in Dyersburg, TN.

John Guthrie LATTA and Lenora Lee POLAND had the following child:

- 158 i. **Leslie Virginia LATTA**.

102. Mary A. POLAND (Thomas-10, Nancy Naomi Moseley-9, Margaret Vann-8, Edward Ned-7, Mary Lewis Barnes-6, April-Tkikami Hop Turkey-5, Big Turkey Hop-4, Hokolesqua Opechan-3, Cleopatra the Shawano Powhatan-2, Wahunsonacock-1) was born on 21 Mar 1839. She died on 4 Feb 1864 at the age of 24.

Mary A. POLAND and Daniel K SMITH were married on 15 Feb 1855. **Daniel K SMITH** was born on 4 Mar 1830 in Autauga Co., AL. He was buried in Jan 1873 in Concord Cemetery, near Jonesville, TX. He died on 8 Jan 1873 at the age of 42 in Shreveport, LA.

Daniel K SMITH and Mary A. POLAND had the following children:

159	i.	**Thomas Poland SMITH**.
160	ii.	**Ella Virginia "Dubba" SMITH**, born 1856; married Monroe Griffin ARMSTRONG; died 1943, Scottsville, TX.
	iii.	**Infant SMITH** was born on 28 May 1858. She was buried in Jun 1858 in Concord Cemetery, near Jonesville, TX. She died on 7 Jun 1858 at the age of 0.
	iv.	**Infant SMITH** was born on 30 May 1859. He was buried in Jun 1859 in Concord Cemetery, near Jonesville, TX. He died on 5 Jun 1859 at the age of 0.
	v.	**Infnat SMITH** was buried in Feb 1861 in Concord Cemetery, near Jonesville, TX. He was born on 14 Feb 1861. He died on 15 Feb 1861 at the age of 0.

103. William Alexander Newton MOSLEY (George Benjamin Alexander-10, George-9, Margaret Vann-8, Edward Ned-7, Mary Lewis Barnes-6, April-Tkikami Hop Turkey-5, Big Turkey Hop-4, Hokolesqua Opechan-3, Cleopatra the Shawano Powhatan-2, Wahunsonacock-1) was born on 15 Nov 1863 in Troy, Pike Co., AL. He died on 7 Jun 1907 at the age of 43 in Brimingham, Jefferson Co., AL.

William Alexander Newton MOSLEY and Malinda Irene BURRELL were married. **Malinda Irene BURRELL**, daughter of BURRELL and Matilda , was born in Feb 1875. She was buried on 11 Jun 1904 in Union Hill Cemetery, Birmingham, Jefferson Co., AL.

William Alexander Newton MOSLEY and Malinda Irene BURRELL had the following child:

161	i.	**John Erskine MOSLEY**, married Blanche Eloise TAYLOR.

William Alexander Newton MOSLEY and Susan Emoley (Lee) (Sudie) ROLLO were married on 6 Sep 1883 in Blount Co., AL. **Susan Emoley (Lee) (Sudie) ROLLO**, daughter of William Alexander ROLLO and Elizabeth Ann STONE, was born on 8 Mar 1857 in Pike Co., AL. She died in Blount Co., AL.

William Alexander Newton MOSLEY and Susan Emoley (Lee) (Sudie) ROLLO had the following children:

162	i.	**William Alexander (Oscar) MOSLEY**, born 8 Dec 1886, Arkadelphia, Cullman Co., AL; married Louise HATCHER, abt 1917, Bessemer, Jefferson Co., AL; died 23 Apr 1952, Florala, Covington Co., AL.
	ii.	**Earnest MOSLEY** was born on 1 Apr 1889. He died in Dec 1906 at the age of 17.
163	iii.	**Thomas Samuel MOSLEY**, born 16 Mar 1891; married Mattie MONKUS, 1907, Bessemer, Jefferson Co., AL; died 16 May 1958, Jefferson Co., AL.

104. Virginia MOSELEY (George Benjamin Alexander-10, George-9, Margaret Vann-8, Edward Ned-7, Mary Lewis Barnes-6, April-Tkikami Hop Turkey-5, Big Turkey Hop-4, Hokolesqua Opechan-3, Cleopatra the Shawano Powhatan-2, Wahunsonacock-1) was born before 1850 in AL.

Virginia MOSELEY and Curby Brack CRAUSWELL were married. **Curby Brack CRAUSWELL**, son of Burrell Perry (Burl) CRAUSWELL and Martha Laura (Mattie) ROLLO, was born on 19 Jun 1882 in Arkadelphia, Cullman Co., AL. He died on 5 Mar 1973 at the age of 90 in Warrior, Jefferson Co., AL.

Curby Brack CRAUSWELL and Virginia MOSELEY had the following children:

164	i.	**Amy CRAUSWELL**, married William A. O'NEAL.
165	ii.	**Spencer Avis "Skinny" CRAUSWELL**, died Feb 1935, AL.
166	iii.	**Trixie Ethelyn CRAUSWELL**, born 1 Nov 1914, Arkadelphia, Cullman Co., AL; married Louie Edgar FREEMAN; married Fletcher T. RUSSELL; died 27 Jun 2004, Birmingham, Jefferson Co., AL.

105. Benjamin Harm BUSSEY Jr. (Martha (Malinda) Moseley-10, George-9, Margaret Vann-8, Edward Ned-7, Mary Lewis Barnes-6, April-Tkikami Hop Turkey-5, Big Turkey Hop-4, Hokolesqua Opechan-3, Cleopatra the Shawano Powhatan-2, Wahunsonacock-1) was born on 19 Sep 1850 in Marion Co., AL. He was buried in Jun 1934 in Goodwater Cemetery, Winfield, Marion Co., AL. He died on 14 Jun 1934 at the age of 83 in Winfield, Marion Co., AL. Benjamin held the title of Jr..

Benjamin Harm BUSSEY Jr. and Martha Ellen HUFFMAN were married on 22 Jul 1875 in Arkadelphia, Cullman Co., AL. **Martha Ellen HUFFMAN** was born on 16 Apr 1848 in Montgomery Co., AL. She was buried in Jan 1940 in Goodwater Cemetery, Winfield, Marion Co., AL. She died on 17 Jan 1940 at the age of 91 in Winfield, Marion Co., AL.

Benjamin Harm BUSSEY and Martha Ellen HUFFMAN had the following children:

167	i.	**Charles Drennen BUSSEY**, born 24 May 1876, Marion Co., AL; married Redora Vianna CHANDLER, 28 Nov 1897; died 22 Aug 1915, Winfield, Marion Co., AL.
168	ii.	**Sallie Levert BUSSEY**, born 15 Feb 1878; died 19 Dec 1906, Crews, Lamar Co., AL.
169	iii.	**Walter BUSSEY**, born 11 Jan 1880; died Nov 1941.
170	iv.	**James "Jimmy" David BUSSEY**, born 14 Oct 1881, Arkadelphia, Cullman Co., AL; married Mattie Lula ROSE, 30 Nov 1905; died 4 Aug 1971, Crews, Lamar Co., AL.
171	v.	**Lula BUSSEY**, born 29 Jun 1883; married Stanford KNOX, 5 Mar 1906; died 29 Jul 1974.
172	vi.	**George Washington BUSSEY**, born 24 Jun 1885, Arkadelphia, Cullman Co., AL; married Ola BAIRD, 31 Aug 1907, Carbon Hill, Walker Co., AL; died 11 Feb 1946, Hitchita, McIntosh Co., OK.
173	vii.	**Oscar BUSSEY**, born 24 Oct 1887; died 29 Jul 1966.
174	viii.	**Mary Ellen BUSSEY**, born 20 Jun 1889; died 1951.
175	ix.	**Alma Eudora BUSSEY**, born 27 Jun 1892; married William Lee BOWLING, 15 Dec 1912; died 7 Dec 1975.

106. Martha BUSSEY (Martha (Malinda) Moseley-10, George-9, Margaret Vann-8, Edward Ned-7, Mary Lewis Barnes-6, April-Tkikami Hop Turkey-5, Big Turkey Hop-4, Hokolesqua Opechan-3, Cleopatra the Shawano Powhatan-2, Wahunsonacock-1) was born about 1854. She died after 1860 at the age of 6.

HAYGOOD was born (date unknown).

107. Edmund Moody BUSSEY (Martha (Malinda) Moseley-10, George-9, Margaret Vann-8, Edward Ned-7, Mary Lewis Barnes-6, April-Tkikami Hop Turkey-5, Big Turkey Hop-4, Hokolesqua Opechan-3, Cleopatra the Shawano Powhatan-2, Wahunsonacock-1) was born on 17 Apr 1856 in Pine Level, Montgomery Co. Alabama. He died in 1934 at the age of 78 in Cockran Bridge, MS. He was buried in 1934 in East Dora Cemetery, Dora, Walker Co., AL.

Edmund Moody BUSSEY and Mary Frances "Missy" ROLLO were married on 18 Dec 1879 in Blount Co., AL. **Mary Frances "Missy" ROLLO**, daughter of William Alexander ROLLO and Elizabeth Ann STONE, was born on 11 Feb 1863 in Pike Co., AL. She was buried in May 1901 in Crews Cemetery, Beaverton, Lamar Co., AL. She died on 18 May 1901 at the age of 38 in Lamar Co, AL.

Edmund Moody BUSSEY and Mary Frances "Missy" ROLLO had the following children:

176	i.	**Emma Ollie BUSSEY**, born 5 Dec 1880; died 19 Dec 1972.
177	ii.	**Lon A. BUSSEY**, born 11 May 1883; married Annie L. .
178	iii.	**Luanna BUSSEY**, born 6 Jun 1886; married Lonnie Alonzo GUYTON, 9 Jun 1904, Lamar Co, AL; died 12 Aug 1912.
179	iv.	**Rufus Thomas BUSSEY**, born 3 Mar 1886, Arkadelphia, Cullman Co., AL; married Luried Navada CLARK, 23 Dec 1908, Dora, Walker Co., AL; died 23 Oct 1947, Prestonburg, KY.
180	v.	**Milton Travis BUSSEY**, born 12 Feb 1889; died 6 May 1945.
181	vi.	**Elizabeth "Lizzie Beth" BUSSEY**, born 5 Apr 1892, Arkadelphia, Cullman Co., AL; married James Martin WEEKS, 16 Jan 1908; died 21 Apr 1974, Graysville, Jefferson Co., AL.
	vii.	**Pearly BUSSEY** was born on 15 Apr 1894. She died on 20 May 1897 at the age of 3 in AL. She was buried on 22 May 1897 in Crews Cemetery, Beaverton, Lamar Co., AL.
182	viii.	**Minnie Malinda BUSSEY**, born 12 Feb 1895.
183	ix.	**Willie Benjamin "Will" BUSSEY**, born 12 Feb 1895; married Ruby WARD.
184	x.	**Mattie Marie "Sweetie" BUSSEY**, born May 1898; married Charlie E. HOLLIS; died 9 Dec 1971.
	xi.	**Baby Girl #1 BUSSEY** was born on 11 May 1901 in Arkadelphia, Cullman Co., AL. She died on 11 May 1901 at the age of 0 in Arkadelphia, Cullman Co., AL.
	xii.	**Baby Girl #2 BUSSEY** was born on 11 May 1901 in Arkadelphia, Cullman Co., AL. She died on 11 May 1901 at the age of 0 in Arkadelphia, Cullman Co., AL.

Edmund Moody BUSSEY and Eula Mae GUYTON were married on 28 Jan 1904. **Eula Mae GUYTON**, daughter of Aaron P. GUYTON and Sarah Kathryn (Sally) HARRIS, was born on 5 Jun 1883 in AL. She was buried in Jun 1961 in East Dora Cemetery, Dora, Walker Co., AL. She died on 18 Jun 1961 at the age of 78.

Edmund Moody BUSSEY and Eula Mae GUYTON had the following children:

185	i.	**Edward "Ed" BUSSEY**, born 18 Jan 1905; married Marion GRIFFITH; died 4 Jun 1967.
186	ii.	**Richmond Hobson Pearson BUSSEY**, born 1905; died 1948.
	iii.	**Alice BUSSEY** was born in 1909. She died in 1925 at the age of 16. She was buried in 1925.
187	iv.	**Charlie BUSSEY**, born 1912; died 1968.
188	v.	**Ruby Lee BUSSEY**, born 11 Jan 1915; married Thomas Clarence PARR, 9 Jun 1936; died 19 Aug 2008, Empire, Walker Co., AL.
189	vi.	**Euell BUSSEY**, born 1917.
190	vii.	**Frank BUSSEY**, born 1919; married Lillian Tolbert ROBINSON, 18 Nov 1942; died Feb 1999, Walker Co., AL.
191	viii.	**Johnny BUSSEY**, born 22 Jul 1922, Walker Co., AL; married Edith BOX, 2 Jan 1941, Dora, Walker Co., AL; died 18 Nov 2008, Dora, Walker Co., AL.
192	ix.	**Gertrude BUSSEY**, born Dec 1926, Lamar Co, AL; married Mabrie STYLES, 22 Feb 1946.

108. **Adra "Addie" BUSSEY** (Martha (Malinda) Moseley-10, George-9, Margaret Vann-8, Edward Ned-7, Mary Lewis Barnes-6, April-Tkikami Hop Turkey-5, Big Turkey Hop-4, Hokolesqua Opechan-3, Cleopatra the Shawano Powhatan-2, Wahunsonacock-1) was born in 1858. She died after 1920 at the age of 62.

George ABBOTT was born (date unknown).

George ABBOTT and Adra "Addie" BUSSEY had the following child:

    193   i. **Ludie ABBOTT**.

ABBOTT was born (date unknown).

109. **Dempsey (Demcey) BUSSEY** (Martha (Malinda) Moseley-10, George-9, Margaret Vann-8, Edward Ned-7, Mary Lewis Barnes-6, April-Tkikami Hop Turkey-5, Big Turkey Hop-4, Hokolesqua Opechan-3, Cleopatra the Shawano Powhatan-2, Wahunsonacock-1) was born in 1865.

Dempsey (Demcey) BUSSEY and Martha A. (Mattie R.) SUGGS were married on 7 Jan 1883 in Blount Co., AL. **Martha A. (Mattie R.) SUGGS** was born (date unknown).

110. **William M. (Will) BUSSEY** (Martha (Malinda) Moseley-10, George-9, Margaret Vann-8, Edward Ned-7, Mary Lewis Barnes-6, April-Tkikami Hop Turkey-5, Big Turkey Hop-4, Hokolesqua Opechan-3, Cleopatra the Shawano Powhatan-2, Wahunsonacock-1) was born on 24 Aug 1868 in Montgomery Co., AL. He died on 26 Jan 1940 at the age of 71 in Ft. Worth, Tarrant Co., TX. He was buried on 29 Jan 1940 in Greenwood Cemetery, Ft. Worth, Tarrant Co., TX.

William M. (Will) BUSSEY and Sarah Jane PARKER were married on 6 Jan 1887 in Blount Co., AL. **Sarah Jane PARKER**, daughter of Davis PARKER and Mary Adeline SANDLIN, was born in Mar 1867. She died after 1940 at the age of 73.

William M. (Will) BUSSEY and Sarah Jane PARKER had the following children:

           i. **William "Willie" BUSSEY** was born in 1884. He died in 1910 at the age of 26. He was buried in 1910 in Coleman Cemetery, Coleman, TX.
          ii. **Mell BUSSEY** was born (date unknown).
         iii. **Mack BUSSEY** was born in 1891. He died in 1919 at the age of 28. He died before 1940 at the age of 49.
         iv. **Clifford BUSSEY** died before 1940.
    194   v. **Lillian (Lillie) Chester BUSSEY**, born 1894; married William Newton NASH, 1910, Coleman, TX; died 1986.
    195 vi. **Myrtle Katherine BUSSEY**, born 1897; married HENDERSON; married James Elbert BUSE; died 1981.
         vii. **Amanda BUSSEY** was born (date unknown).
        viii. **Clovus Alvon Alvin BUSSEY** was born in 1900.

Descendants of Chief Wahunsonacock Powhatan

26 January 2012

    196   ix. **Addie BUSSEY**, born 1903; married Fred NUNCIO; died 1980.

111. **Hiram Mace MOSLEY** (William Lafayette-10, George-9, Margaret Vann-8, Edward Ned-7, Mary Lewis Barnes-6, April-Tkikami Hop Turkey-5, Big Turkey Hop-4, Hokolesqua Opechan-3, Cleopatra the Shawano Powhatan-2, Wahunsonacock-1) was born on 16 Jan 1867 in Montgomery Co., AL. He died on 29 Mar 1931 at the age of 64 in Kimberly, Jefferson Co., AL.

Hiram Mace MOSLEY and Lena Deloys SUDDETH were married in Jan 1892. **Lena Deloys SUDDETH**, daughter of Pete F. SUDDETH and Lizzie FREEMAN, was born on 11 Jan 1872 in GA. She died on 14 Dec 1935 at the age of 63 in Kimberly, Jefferson Co., AL. She was buried on 16 Dec 1935 in Liberty Minter Cemetery, Morris, Jefferson Co., AL.

Hiram Mace MOSLEY and Lena Deloys SUDDETH had the following children:

    197   i. **Lizzie Irene MOSLEY**, born 24 Nov 1892, AL; married Tommie Pierce OGLETREE; died 3 May 1983, Addison, Winston Co., AL.

    198   ii. **Alice Mae MOSLEY**, born 31 Oct 1893, Jefferson Co., AL; married Lonnie WINNETT; married Arthur Jackson BRADY Sr., 6 Sep 1917, Hamilton Co., TN; died 3 Aug 1955, Birmingham, Jefferson Co., AL.

    199   iii. **Travis Forrest MOSLEY Sr.**, born 9 Apr 1895, AL; married Gertrude Lenora REED, 20 Jul 1913; died 15 Nov 1979, Morris, Jefferson Co., AL.

    200   iv. **Annie MOSLEY**, born 27 Aug 1896, AL; married Ranzy DOSS; died 8 Mar 1965, AL.

    201   v. **Bessie MOSLEY**, born 10 Jul 1900, Kimberly, Jefferson Co., AL; married William McKinley BYRD, 3 Feb 1923; married Hobart Garet BYRD, 4 Jun 1962; died 13 Oct 1980, Birmingham, Jefferson Co., AL.

    202   vi. **Matilda MOSLEY**, born 21 Sep 1901, Kimberly, Jefferson Co., AL; married Dennis HUGHES, 12 Dec 1923; died 19 Apr 1964, AL.

    203   vii. **Robert Herman MOSLEY**, born 29 Apr 1904, Kimberly, Jefferson Co., AL; married Mary Amy Bell CHRESTMAN, 23 Jan 1926; died 2 Dec 1981, Morris, Jefferson Co., AL.

                  viii. **John M. MOSLEY** was born on 2 Mar 1907 in Kimberly, Jefferson Co., AL. He died on 26 Nov 1915 at the age of 8 in Kimberly, Jefferson Co., AL. He was buried on 28 Nov 1915 in Liberty Baptist Church Cemetery, Morris, Jefferson Co., AL.

    204   ix. **S.E. MOSLEY**, born 21 Apr 1908, Kimberly, Jefferson Co., AL; married James Ernest SELF; married George Melvin CRANE; died 9 Aug 1971, AL.

112. **Adrin Bethiah MOSLEY** (William Lafayette-10, George-9, Margaret Vann-8, Edward Ned-7, Mary Lewis Barnes-6, April-Tkikami Hop Turkey-5, Big Turkey Hop-4, Hokolesqua Opechan-3, Cleopatra the Shawano Powhatan-2, Wahunsonacock-1) was born on 20 Sep 1870. She was buried in Lebanon, Morgan Co., AL.

Adrin Bethiah MOSLEY and William Jackson EATON were married. **William Jackson EATON** was born on 6 Apr 1860. He was buried in Lebanon, Morgan Co., AL.

William Jackson EATON and Adrin Bethiah MOSLEY had the following children:

    205   i. **Stella EATON**, born 26 Sep 1888, Morris, Jefferson Co., AL; married John REEVES; married Henry OWENS.

    206   ii. **Will EATON**, born 21 Mar 1891, Jefferson Co., AL; married Minnie .

    207   iii. **Grover EATON**, born 26 Feb 1893, Jefferson Co., AL; married BYARS.

    208   iv. **Mary Lou EATON**, born 20 Apr 1894, Jefferson Co., AL; married Dan REEVES; died 8 Nov 1979, Gardendale, Jefferson Co., AL.

    209   v. **Eula EATON**, born 31 Dec 1895, Jefferson Co., AL; married BRONFIELD.

                  vi. **Infant EATON** was born on 17 Mar 1901 in Jefferson Co., AL. He/she died on 17 Mar 1901 at the age

of 0 in Jefferson Co., AL.
- 210   vii. **George EATON**, born 23 Mar 1903, Jefferson Co., AL; married Bertie TUCKER.

113. **James Augusta MOSLEY** (William Lafayette-10, George-9, Margaret Vann-8, Edward Ned-7, Mary Lewis Barnes-6, April-Tkikami Hop Turkey-5, Big Turkey Hop-4, Hokolesqua Opechan-3, Cleopatra the Shawano Powhatan-2, Wahunsonacock-1) was born on 11 Mar 1875. He died in Nov 1968 at the age of 93 in Escondido, San Diego Co., CA. He was buried in Nov 1968 in CA.

James Augusta MOSLEY and Nora Josephine HARDING were married. **Nora Josephine HARDING** was born on 5 Oct 1883. She died on 27 Apr 1941 at the age of 57. She was buried on 29 Apr 1941 in Liberty Minter Cemetery, Morris, Jefferson Co., AL.

James Augusta MOSLEY and Nora Josephine HARDING had the following children:

-      i. **George Sylvester MOSLEY** was born (date unknown).
-      ii. **Celeste MOSLEY** was born (date unknown).
- 211   iii. **Jeffery Terence MOSLEY**.
-      iv. **Willie MOSLEY** was born (date unknown).
- 212   v. **Grover Cecil MOSLEY**, married Frances .
- 213   vi. **Etta MOSLEY**, married Norman THEEL.
-      vii. **Beaulta MOSLEY** was born in Feb 1912. She died in Feb 1912 at the age of 0.
- 214   viii. **Eleanora MOSLEY**, married MCNEICE.
- 215   ix. **Bethia MOSLEY**, married WINSTANLEY.

114. **William Lee MOSLEY** (William Lafayette-10, George-9, Margaret Vann-8, Edward Ned-7, Mary Lewis Barnes-6, April-Tkikami Hop Turkey-5, Big Turkey Hop-4, Hokolesqua Opechan-3, Cleopatra the Shawano Powhatan-2, Wahunsonacock-1) was born on 30 Jul 1879 in Morris, Jefferson Co., AL. He died on 27 Sep 1955 at the age of 76 in Morris, Jefferson Co., AL. He was buried on 29 Sep 1955 in Morris Cemetery, Morris, Jefferson Co., AL.

William Lee MOSLEY and Mildred Rosa BEVILS were married. **Mildred Rosa BEVILS** was born on 9 Apr 1894 in AL. She died on 16 Mar 1959 at the age of 64 in Jefferson Co., AL. She was buried on 18 Mar 1959 in Morris Cemetery, Morris, Jefferson Co., AL.

William Lee MOSLEY and Mildred Rosa BEVILS had the following children:

- 216   i. **Colleen MOSLEY**, born 18 Mar 1924, Jefferson Co., AL; married Arthur Leonard DANIEL.
- 217   ii. **Daphne MOSLEY**, born 1 Feb 1926; married Vernon WATSON.
- 218   iii. **Royce George MOSLEY**, born 14 Nov 1927, Morris, Jefferson Co., AL; married Martha Nan GOODWIN, 30 Jul 1950, Morris, Jefferson Co., AL; died 16 Sep 1987, Warrior, Jefferson Co., AL.
- 219   iv. **J.D. MOSLEY**, born 25 Sep 1929, Village Springs, Jefferson Co., AL; married Jackie MCCOMBS.
- 220   v. **Gerald Olaf MOSLEY**, born 16 Feb 1931, Morris, Jefferson Co., AL; married Billie MCCOMBS; died 7 Jan 2000, Morris, Jefferson Co., AL.

William Lee MOSLEY and Cora M. DAY were married. **Cora M. DAY** was born on 19 May 1880 in AL. She died on 9 May 1922 at the age of 41.

William Lee MOSLEY and Cora M. DAY had the following children:

Descendants of Chief Wahunsonacock Powhatan

26 January 2012

221	i.	**Thelma Mae MOSLEY**, born 2 May 1904, Winston Co., AL; married George JOHNSON, 17 Feb 1923, Guntersville, Marshall Co., AL; died 25 Aug 1975, Bessemer, Jefferson Co., AL.
222	ii.	**Clarence Lee MOSLEY**, born 17 Jan 1906, AL; married Helen GUTHERIE; died 26 Mar 1989, Jefferson Co., AL.
223	iii.	**Fannie Sue MOSLEY**, born 19 Jan 1908, AL; married David PICKETT, 1926; died 22 Dec 1999, West Blockton, Bibb Co., AL.
224	iv.	**Myrtle Lucile MOSLEY**, born 1 Nov 1909, AL; married Wiley Mason MCCOMBS; died 7 Nov 1997, Pinson, Jefferson Co., AL.
	v.	**Savannah MOSLEY** was born on 18 Jan 1912.

115. **Robert Elisha MOSLEY** (William Lafayette-10, George-9, Margaret Vann-8, Edward Ned-7, Mary Lewis Barnes-6, April-Tkikami Hop Turkey-5, Big Turkey Hop-4, Hokolesqua Opechan-3, Cleopatra the Shawano Powhatan-2, Wahunsonacock-1) was born on 20 Sep 1882 in AL. He died on 17 Dec 1958 at the age of 76 in Springville, St. Clair Co., AL. He was buried on 19 Dec 1958 in Morris Cemetery, Morris, Jefferson Co., AL.

Robert Elisha MOSLEY and Stella WHISENANT were married on 19 Dec 1904 in Warrior, Jefferson Co., AL. **Stella WHISENANT**, daughter of John WHISENANT and Zillia SMITH, was born on 6 Jul 1887 in Jefferson Co., AL. She died on 13 Dec 1964 at the age of 77 in Oneonta, Blount Co., AL.

Robert Elisha MOSLEY and Stella WHISENANT had the following children:

225	i.	**Ruby Estelle MOSLEY**, born 12 Sep 1906, Jefferson Co., AL; married Ollie Lee MCCURRY; died 25 Sep 1966, Kimberly, Jefferson Co., AL.
	ii.	**Earsie MOSLEY** was born on 31 Oct 1908 in Jefferson Co., AL. He/she died on 14 Nov 1937 at the age of 29 in Jefferson Co., AL. He/she was buried on 16 Nov 1937 in Morris Cemetery, Morris, Jefferson Co., AL.
	iii.	**Opal Mae MOSLEY** was born on 16 Apr 1912 in Jefferson Co., AL. She died on 2 Dec 1985 at the age of 73 in Cropwell, St. Clair Co., AL.
226	iv.	**Minnie Pearl MOSLEY**, born 11 Jan 1914, Jefferson Co., AL; married Clayton BURTRAM.
	v.	**Dovie Lorene MOSLEY** was born on 12 Mar 1917 in Jefferson Co., AL.
	vi.	**Kathleen MOSLEY** was born on 18 Oct 1919 in Jefferson Co., AL. She died on 29 Apr 1987 at the age of 67 in Jacksonville, Calhoun Co., AL.
	vii.	**Christine MOSLEY** was born on 26 Sep 1922 in Jefferson Co., AL.
	viii.	**James Earl MOSLEY** was born (date unknown).

116. **Myrtle Addie MOSLEY** (William Lafayette-10, George-9, Margaret Vann-8, Edward Ned-7, Mary Lewis Barnes-6, April-Tkikami Hop Turkey-5, Big Turkey Hop-4, Hokolesqua Opechan-3, Cleopatra the Shawano Powhatan-2, Wahunsonacock-1) was born on 16 Apr 1888 in AL. She died on 26 Apr 1925 at the age of 37 in Jefferson Co., AL. She was buried on 28 Apr 1925 in Morris Cemetery, Morris, Jefferson Co., AL.

Myrtle Addie MOSLEY and Adolphus WHISENANT were married on 21 Dec 1904 in Jefferson Co., AL. **Adolphus WHISENANT**, son of John WHISENANT and Zillia SMITH, was born on 18 Dec 1883 in Jefferson Co., AL. He died on 14 Jul 1924 at the age of 40 in Jefferson Co., AL. He was buried on 15 Jul 1924 in Morris Cemetery, Morris, Jefferson Co., AL.

Adolphus WHISENANT and Myrtle Addie MOSLEY had the following children:

227	i.	**Trudy Sylvia WHISENANT**, born 3 Oct 1906, Jefferson Co., AL; married JACKS; died 1 Jun 1990, Gardendale, Jefferson Co., AL.

Descendants of Chief Wahunsonacock Powhatan

26 January 2012

    228   ii. **Clyde Earl WHISENANT**, born 21 Dec 1907, Jefferson Co., AL; married Lilly Mae ; died 25 Jun 1979, Gardendale, Jefferson Co., AL.

    229   iii. **Olive Inez WHISENANT**, born 15 Jan 1910, Jefferson Co., AL; married BLAIKIE; died 28 Nov 1995, Warrior, Jefferson Co., AL.

    230   iv. **Nightie Mae WHISENANT**, born Jefferson Co., AL; married CASSIDY.

    231   v. **Mary Louise WHISENANT**, born Kimberly, Jefferson Co., AL; married RASCO.

              vi. **Roland Johnnie WHISENANT** was born on 19 May 1924 in Morris, Jefferson Co., AL. He died on 28 Nov 1975 at the age of 51 in Birmingham, Jefferson Co., AL.

117. **Benjamin Milton MOSLEY** (William Lafayette-10, George-9, Margaret Vann-8, Edward Ned-7, Mary Lewis Barnes-6, April-Tkikami Hop Turkey-5, Big Turkey Hop-4, Hokolesqua Opechan-3, Cleopatra the Shawano Powhatan-2, Wahunsonacock-1) was born on 17 Oct 1891 in Jefferson Co., AL. He died on 5 Nov 1986 at the age of 95 in Holly Hill, Volusaia Co., FL. He was buried on 7 Nov 1986 in Holly Hill Cemetery, Holly Hill, Volusia Co., FL.

Benjamin Milton MOSLEY and Addie M. BLANTON were married. **Addie M. BLANTON** was born (date unknown).

Benjamin Milton MOSLEY and Nell Hortnese KYKER were married on 23 Jun 1919 in Athens, TN. **Nell Hortnese KYKER**, daughter of Samuel KYKER and Mary STONE, was born on 24 Aug 1898 in Sweetwater, TN. She died on 4 Mar 1975 at the age of 76 in Holly Hill, Volusaia Co., FL. She was buried on 6 Mar 1975 in Holly Hill Cemetery, Holly Hill, Volusia Co., FL.

Benjamin Milton MOSLEY and Nell Hortnese KYKER had the following children:

              i. **Benjamin Milton MOSLEY Jr.** was born on 31 Jul 1920 in Birmingham, Jefferson Co., AL. He died on 27 Apr 1995 at the age of 74 in Birmingham, Jefferson Co., AL. He held the title of Jr..

              ii. **Ruth Stone MOSLEY** was born on 5 Sep 1921 in Birmingham, Jefferson Co., AL.

118. **William Pytchlynn POLAND** (William Henry-10, Hannah Moseley-9, Margaret Vann-8, Edward Ned-7, Mary Lewis Barnes-6, April-Tkikami Hop Turkey-5, Big Turkey Hop-4, Hokolesqua Opechan-3, Cleopatra the Shawano Powhatan-2, Wahunsonacock-1) was born in 1855.

William Pytchlynn POLAND and Emma Lucy AGRRETT were married on 12 Sep 1878. **Emma Lucy AGRRETT**, daughter of Robert C. AGRRETT and Lucy Jane LONG, was born in 1860.

William Pytchlynn POLAND and Emma Lucy AGRRETT had the following children:

    232   i. **Robert Pytchlynn POLAND**, born Sep 1879.

              ii. **Raymond POLAND** was born (date unknown).

    233   iii. **Lucy POLAND**.

119. **Walter Henry POLAND** (William Henry-10, Hannah Moseley-9, Margaret Vann-8, Edward Ned-7, Mary Lewis Barnes-6, April-Tkikami Hop Turkey-5, Big Turkey Hop-4, Hokolesqua Opechan-3, Cleopatra the Shawano Powhatan-2, Wahunsonacock-1) was born on 26 Dec 1860. He died on 5 Feb 1945 at the age of 84.

Walter Henry POLAND and Florence CARTER were married on 16 Feb 1887. **Florence CARTER** was born on 3 Nov 1868. She died on 17 Apr 1961 at the age of 92.

120. **Margaret "Maggie" BOYD** (Margaret E. Moseley-10, Mason-9, Margaret Vann-8, Edward Ned-7, Mary Lewis Barnes-6, April-Tkikami Hop Turkey-5, Big Turkey Hop-4, Hokolesqua Opechan-3, Cleopatra the Shawano Powhatan-2, Wahunsonacock-1) was born on 19 Dec 1866 in Gilmer, Upshur Co., TX. She was buried in Oct 1898 in Old City Cemetery, Gilmer, Upshur Co., TX. She died on 24 Oct 1898 at the age of 31 in Pine, Upshur Co., TX.

Margaret "Maggie" BOYD and James W. BUSSEY were married on 8 Nov 1884 in Pine, Upshur Co., TX. **James W. BUSSEY**, son of Hezekiah BUSSEY and Mary Jane ALEXANDER, was born in 1866 in Pine, Upshur Co., TX.

James W. BUSSEY and Margaret "Maggie" BOYD had the following children:

- 234   i. **Donnis BUSSEY**, born abt 1885, Upshur Co., TX; married J.P. FORD, 22 Dec 1911, Gregg Co., TX; married HORTON.
- ii. **Louis BUSSEY** was born about 1889 in Upshur Co., TX.
- iii. **Mary Elizabeth BUSSEY** was born on 10 Jun 1897 in Upshur Co., TX. She was buried in Aug 1900 in Old City Cemetery, Gilmer, TX. She died on 27 Aug 1900 at the age of 3 in Upshur Co., TX.

121. **Leo R. BUSSEY** (Dempsey C.-10, Mahulda Hulda Moseley-9, Margaret Vann-8, Edward Ned-7, Mary Lewis Barnes-6, April-Tkikami Hop Turkey-5, Big Turkey Hop-4, Hokolesqua Opechan-3, Cleopatra the Shawano Powhatan-2, Wahunsonacock-1) was born (date unknown).

UNK was born (date unknown).

Leo R. BUSSEY and UNK had the following child:

- i. **Charles BUSSEY** was born (date unknown).

122. **Clary BUSSEY** (Hezekiah-10, Mahulda Hulda Moseley-9, Margaret Vann-8, Edward Ned-7, Mary Lewis Barnes-6, April-Tkikami Hop Turkey-5, Big Turkey Hop-4, Hokolesqua Opechan-3, Cleopatra the Shawano Powhatan-2, Wahunsonacock-1) was born about 1856 in Upshur Co., TX. She died before 1880 at the age of 24. She was buried before 1880 in King's Grave Yard/Maroney Cemetery, Nacogdoches, Nacogdoches Co., TX.

Clary BUSSEY and Robert M. GEE were married about 1876. **Robert M. GEE**, son of Philip GEE and Hulda COOK, was born in 1852 in AL. He died in 1933 at the age of 81. He was buried in 1933 in Old Kings Grave Yard, Nacogdoches, TX.

Robert M. GEE and Clary BUSSEY had the following children:

- 235   i. **Elbert J. GEE**, born Feb 1877, Upshur Co., TX; married Fannie , 1897; married Josephine N. , 1928.
- ii. **Lucille GEE** was born in Jul 1899.

Descendants of Chief Wahunsonacock Powhatan

26 January 2012

123. **Mary Elizabeth (Eliza) BUSSEY** (Hezekiah-10, Mahulda Hulda Moseley-9, Margaret Vann-8, Edward Ned-7, Mary Lewis Barnes-6, April-Tkikami Hop Turkey-5, Big Turkey Hop-4, Hokolesqua Opechan-3, Cleopatra the Shawano Powhatan-2, Wahunsonacock-1) was born about 1858 in Upshur Co., TX.

Mary Elizabeth (Eliza) BUSSEY and James W. BONHAM were married on 20 Aug 1874 in Pine, Upshur Co., TX. **James W. BONHAM** was born in 1859 in AL. He died after 1930 at the age of 71.

James W. BONHAM and Mary Elizabeth (Eliza) BUSSEY had the following child:

    i. **J.H. I/L? BONHAM** was born in 1877 in Upshur Co., TX.

124. **James W. BUSSEY** (Hezekiah-10, Mahulda Hulda Moseley-9, Margaret Vann-8, Edward Ned-7, Mary Lewis Barnes-6, April-Tkikami Hop Turkey-5, Big Turkey Hop-4, Hokolesqua Opechan-3, Cleopatra the Shawano Powhatan-2, Wahunsonacock-1) was born in 1866 in Pine, Upshur Co., TX.

James W. BUSSEY and Margaret "Maggie" BOYD were married on 8 Nov 1884 in Pine, Upshur Co., TX. **Margaret "Maggie" BOYD**, daughter of J. Walter BOYD and Margaret E. MOSELEY, was born on 19 Dec 1866 in Gilmer, Upshur Co., TX. She was buried in Oct 1898 in Old City Cemetery, Gilmer, Upshur Co., TX. She died on 24 Oct 1898 at the age of 31 in Pine, Upshur Co., TX.

James W. BUSSEY and Margaret "Maggie" BOYD had the following children:

234   i. **Donnis BUSSEY**, born abt 1885, Upshur Co., TX; married J.P. FORD, 22 Dec 1911, Gregg Co., TX; married HORTON.
    ii. **Louis BUSSEY** was born about 1889 in Upshur Co., TX.
    iii. **Mary Elizabeth BUSSEY** was born on 10 Jun 1897 in Upshur Co., TX. She was buried in Aug 1900 in Old City Cemetery, Gilmer, TX. She died on 27 Aug 1900 at the age of 3 in Upshur Co., TX.

125. **Edward "Eddie" H. BUSSEY** (Hezekiah-10, Mahulda Hulda Moseley-9, Margaret Vann-8, Edward Ned-7, Mary Lewis Barnes-6, April-Tkikami Hop Turkey-5, Big Turkey Hop-4, Hokolesqua Opechan-3, Cleopatra the Shawano Powhatan-2, Wahunsonacock-1) was born in Jan 1870 in Upshur Co., TX.

Edward "Eddie" H. BUSSEY and Minnie E. JACOBS were married on 27 Aug 1893 in Gregg Co., TX. **Minnie E. JACOBS** was born about 1878 in TX.

Edward "Eddie" H. BUSSEY and Minnie E. JACOBS had the following child:

236   i. **Dr. J. Everette BUSSEY**, born 1898, TX; married Vivian .

126. **Sarah "Sally" Mahulda BOWLES** (Sarah Ann BUSSEY-10, Mahulda Hulda Moseley-9, Margaret Vann-8, Edward Ned-7, Mary Lewis Barnes-6, April-Tkikami Hop Turkey-5, Big Turkey Hop-4, Hokolesqua Opechan-3, Cleopatra the Shawano Powhatan-2, Wahunsonacock-1) was born in Aug 1861 in Upshur Co., TX. She died in 1940 at the age of 79.

Sarah "Sally" Mahulda BOWLES and John Molton MOORE were married in 1880 in Harrison Co., TX. **John Molton**

MOORE, son of Lewis MOORE and Sarah Ann LAVARIA, was born in Dec 1852 in TX. He died after May 1910 at the age of 57 in Harrison Co., TX.

John Molton MOORE and Sarah "Sally" Mahulda BOWLES had the following children:

237	i.	**Drue Milton MOORE**, born 21 Dec 1881, Harrison Co., TX; married Dallvore "Dolly" Frances HARRIS, 1904, Harrison Co., TX.
238	ii.	**Annie Louvenia Lou MOORE**, born May 1883, Harrison Co., TX; married Jesse Monroe MOORE, 1900, Harrison Co., TX.
239	iii.	**Gus Lewis MOORE**, born Dec 1884, Harrison Co., TX; married Lorena S. "Lola" SMITH, 1909, Harrison Co., TX.
240	iv.	**Johnnie MOORE**, born Aug 1889, Harrison Co., TX; married Ross PITTS.
241	v.	**Lillie Mande MOORE**, born 9 Apr 1893, Harrison Co., TX; married Leon Hill DICKARD.
242	vi.	**Guy Ellis MOORE**, born Dec 1894, Hallsville, Harrison Co., TX; married Clara Lucile ONEY; married UNK.

127. Edward Augustus "Gus" BOWLES (Sarah Ann BUSSEY-10, Mahulda Hulda Moseley-9, Margaret Vann-8, Edward Ned-7, Mary Lewis Barnes-6, April-Tkikami Hop Turkey-5, Big Turkey Hop-4, Hokolesqua Opechan-3, Cleopatra the Shawano Powhatan-2, Wahunsonacock-1) was born in 1866 in TX. He died in 1938 at the age of 72 in Harrison Co., TX.

Edward Augustus "Gus" BOWLES and Annie Mae RICHARDSON were married in 1885 in Harrison Co., TX. **Annie Mae RICHARDSON**, daughter of William Edward RICHARDSON and Mary Isadora TINCHER, was born in 1868 in TX. She died in 1960 at the age of 92 in TX. She was buried in 1960 in Forest Hill Cemetery, Harrison Co., TX.

Edward Augustus "Gus" BOWLES and Annie Mae RICHARDSON had the following children:

	i.	**Gussie Olive BOWLES** was born on 20 Mar 1887 in Harrison Co., TX. She died on 11 Sep 1899 at the age of 12 in Harrison Co., TX.
	ii.	**Willie A. BOWLES** was born on 17 Jul 1890 in Harrison Co., TX. He died on 16 Sep 1906 at the age of 16.
243	iii.	**Grace BOWLES**, born 25 Apr 1895; married Marton SMITH; died 22 Jul 1976.
	iv.	**Annie E. BOWLES** was born in 1900 in Harrison Co., TX.
244	v.	**Perry H. BOWLES**, born 1903, Harrison Co., TX; married Alma , 1923, Harrison Co., TX.
	vi.	**Ina Ruth BOWLES** was born in 1905 in Harrison Co., TX. She died on 16 Oct 1993 at the age of 88.
	vii.	**Ethel BOWLES** was born (date unknown).
	viii.	**Pearl BOWLES** was born (date unknown).

128. John Thomas BOWLES (Sarah Ann BUSSEY-10, Mahulda Hulda Moseley-9, Margaret Vann-8, Edward Ned-7, Mary Lewis Barnes-6, April-Tkikami Hop Turkey-5, Big Turkey Hop-4, Hokolesqua Opechan-3, Cleopatra the Shawano Powhatan-2, Wahunsonacock-1) was born in Sep 1870 in TX. He died after 1930 at the age of 60 in TX.

John Thomas BOWLES and Maude Lillie COLE were married in 1892 in TX. **Maude Lillie COLE**, daughter of Willis Franklin COLE, was born in Feb 1870 in TX. She died after 1920 at the age of 50 in Harrison Co., TX.

John Thomas BOWLES and Maude Lillie COLE had the following children:

	i.	**Edward R. "Eddie" BOWLES** was born in Feb 1894 in Harrison Co., TX.
	ii.	**Ethel M. BOWLES** was born in Aug 1897 in Harrison Co., TX.

- iii. **Eva M. BOWLES** was born in 1901 in Harrison Co., TX.
- iv. **Maybelle BOWLES** was born in 1906 in Harrison Co., TX.
- v. **Mary Christine BOWLES** was born in 1908 in Harrison Co., TX.
- vi. **Richard Bassett BOWLES** was born in 1910 in Harrison Co., TX.

129. **James KILLINGSWORTH** (Mary Lou Tassie BUSSEY-10, Mahulda Hulda Moseley-9, Margaret Vann-8, Edward Ned-7, Mary Lewis Barnes-6, April-Tkikami Hop Turkey-5, Big Turkey Hop-4, Hokolesqua Opechan-3, Cleopatra the Shawano Powhatan-2, Wahunsonacock-1) was born on 30 May 1859. He died on 13 Jan 1928 at the age of 68 in Freeport, TX.

James KILLINGSWORTH and Annie ZIEGLER were married. **Annie ZIEGLER** was born (date unknown).

James KILLINGSWORTH and Tracy DAVIS were married. **Tracy DAVIS** was born (date unknown).

130. **Lee Levy R. KILLINGSWORTH** (Mary Lou Tassie BUSSEY-10, Mahulda Hulda Moseley-9, Margaret Vann-8, Edward Ned-7, Mary Lewis Barnes-6, April-Tkikami Hop Turkey-5, Big Turkey Hop-4, Hokolesqua Opechan-3, Cleopatra the Shawano Powhatan-2, Wahunsonacock-1) was born in 1861. He died on 13 Feb 1913 at the age of 52 in Austin, Travis Co., TX.

Lee Levy R. KILLINGSWORTH and Martha E. Mattie NOWELL were married. **Martha E. Mattie NOWELL**, daughter of Robert Adolphus NOWELL and Susan SHADDOCK, was born (date unknown).

131. **Mary Mollie Antoniette KILLINGSWORTH** (Mary Lou Tassie BUSSEY-10, Mahulda Hulda Moseley-9, Margaret Vann-8, Edward Ned-7, Mary Lewis Barnes-6, April-Tkikami Hop Turkey-5, Big Turkey Hop-4, Hokolesqua Opechan-3, Cleopatra the Shawano Powhatan-2, Wahunsonacock-1) was born on 4 Feb 1865 in Caddo Mills, Hunt Co., TX. She died on 23 Oct 1950 at the age of 85 in Duncan, Stephers Co., OK.

Mary Mollie Antoniette KILLINGSWORTH and James William MCFARLAND were married. **James William MCFARLAND**, son of J. Daniel MCFARLAND and Elizabeth SHADDOCK, was born on 6 Feb 1863.

James William MCFARLAND and Mary Mollie Antoniette KILLINGSWORTH had the following children:

- 245   i. **Albert MCFARLAND**, married Dorothy PATTERSON.
- ii. **Thomas Leo MCFARLAND** was born (date unknown).
- iii. **Tessie MCFARLAND** was born (date unknown).
- iv. **Myrtle MCFARLAND** was born (date unknown).
- v. **Lottie MCFARLAND** was born (date unknown).
- vi. **Ruth Mae MCFARLAND** was born (date unknown).
- vii. **James Alford MCFARLAND** was born (date unknown).
- viii. **Fred MCFARLAND** was born (date unknown).
- ix. **Fannie Antoniette MCFARLAND** was born (date unknown).

Descendants of Chief Wahunsonacock Powhatan

26 January 2012

132. Mary Leonah "Molly" BUSSEY (William J.-10, Mahulda Hulda Moseley-9, Margaret Vann-8, Edward Ned-7, Mary Lewis Barnes-6, April-Tkikami Hop Turkey-5, Big Turkey Hop-4, Hokolesqua Opechan-3, Cleopatra the Shawano Powhatan-2, Wahunsonacock-1) was born in 1865 in TX.

Mary Leonah "Molly" BUSSEY and John K. Clinton PATRICK were married on 12 Sep 1882 in Gregg Co., TX. **John K. Clinton PATRICK** was born (date unknown).

133. Elizabeth M. "Lizzie" BUSSEY (William J.-10, Mahulda Hulda Moseley-9, Margaret Vann-8, Edward Ned-7, Mary Lewis Barnes-6, April-Tkikami Hop Turkey-5, Big Turkey Hop-4, Hokolesqua Opechan-3, Cleopatra the Shawano Powhatan-2, Wahunsonacock-1) was born in 1867 in TX.

Elizabeth M. "Lizzie" BUSSEY and John K. Clinton PATRICK were married on 14 Jan 1888 in Gregg Co., TX. **John K. Clinton PATRICK** was born (date unknown).

134. Frances Maud BUSSEY (William J.-10, Mahulda Hulda Moseley-9, Margaret Vann-8, Edward Ned-7, Mary Lewis Barnes-6, April-Tkikami Hop Turkey-5, Big Turkey Hop-4, Hokolesqua Opechan-3, Cleopatra the Shawano Powhatan-2, Wahunsonacock-1) was born after 1870.

James William BRADLEY was born (date unknown).

James William BRADLEY and Frances Maud BUSSEY had the following children:

            i. **Horace Grady BRADLEY** was born (date unknown).
           ii. **Dennis Houghton BRADLEY** was born (date unknown).
          iii. **James Thurman BRADLEY** was born (date unknown).
246   iv. **Myrtis Edith BRADLEY**, married COLLARD.
247   v. **Maud BRADLEY**, married ARTHUR.

135. William Lafayette "Willie" BUSSEY (John L.-10, Mahulda Hulda Moseley-9, Margaret Vann-8, Edward Ned-7, Mary Lewis Barnes-6, April-Tkikami Hop Turkey-5, Big Turkey Hop-4, Hokolesqua Opechan-3, Cleopatra the Shawano Powhatan-2, Wahunsonacock-1) was born on 23 Apr 1869 in TX. He died on 13 Dec 1945 at the age of 76 in Longview, Gregg Co., TX. He was buried on 15 Dec 1945 in Elmira Chapel Cemetery, Gregg Co., TX.

William Lafayette "Willie" BUSSEY and Hannah Suttizie (Tizie) BARTON were married on 10 Sep 1892 in Gregg Co., TX. **Hannah Suttizie (Tizie) BARTON** was born on 11 Nov 1873. She died on 2 Jan 1957 at the age of 83 in TX. She was buried on 4 Jan 1957 in Elmira Chapel Cemetery, Gregg Co., TX.

William Lafayette "Willie" BUSSEY and Hannah Suttizie (Tizie) BARTON had the following children:

            i. **Lillian B. BUSSEY** was born in Nov 1893 in TX.

Descendants of Chief Wahunsonacock Powhatan

  ii. **Annie BUSSEY** was born in Sep 1895 in TX.
  iii. **Clyde BUSSEY** was born in Aug 1898 in TX. She died in 1902 at the age of 4 in TX. She was buried in 1902 in Summerfield Cemetery, Longview, Gregg Co., TX.
  iv. **William BUSSEY** was born in 1902 in TX.

136. **Martha Lulu JERNIGAN** (Thomas Jefferson-10, William-9, Vashti Vann-8, Edward Ned-7, Mary Lewis Barnes-6, April-Tkikami Hop Turkey-5, Big Turkey Hop-4, Hokolesqua Opechan-3, Cleopatra the Shawano Powhatan-2, Wahunsonacock-1) was born on 18 Sep 1865 in AL. She died on 11 Dec 1945 at the age of 80 in Wiggins, Stone Co., MS.

Martha Lulu JERNIGAN and Walker Isaiah COBB were married before 1880. **Walker Isaiah COBB**, son of William Stephen Riley COBB and Mary Jane MAINE, was born in Aug 1861 in Santa Rosa Co., FL. He died on 18 Feb 1904 at the age of 42 in Wiggins, Stone Co., MS.

137. **William Green VANN** (James Mason-10, Mason M.-9, Mason M.-8, Edward Ned-7, Mary Lewis Barnes-6, April-Tkikami Hop Turkey-5, Big Turkey Hop-4, Hokolesqua Opechan-3, Cleopatra the Shawano Powhatan-2, Wahunsonacock-1) was born on 17 Dec 1881 in Luna, Freestone Co., TX.

William Green VANN and Mary Appie HODGES were married. **Mary Appie HODGES** was born in Mar 1890.

William Green VANN and Mary Appie HODGES had the following children:

  i. **VANN** was born (date unknown).
  ii. **Joseph VANN** was born (date unknown).
  iii. **Vernon VANN** was born (date unknown).
  iv. **Howard VANN** was born (date unknown).
  v. **Luther VANN** was born (date unknown).
  vi. **William Green VANN Jr.** held the title of Jr..

138. **James Albert VANN** (James Mason-10, Mason M.-9, Mason M.-8, Edward Ned-7, Mary Lewis Barnes-6, April-Tkikami Hop Turkey-5, Big Turkey Hop-4, Hokolesqua Opechan-3, Cleopatra the Shawano Powhatan-2, Wahunsonacock-1) was born on 17 Oct 1844 in Teague, Freestone Co., TX. He died on 12 Dec 1958 at the age of 114.

James Albert VANN and Addie Mae HODGES were married. **Addie Mae HODGES** was born on 17 Nov 1892. She died on 12 Jan 1959 at the age of 66.

James Albert VANN and Addie Mae HODGES had the following children:

  i. **Homer VANN** was born (date unknown).
  ii. **Melvin VANN** was born (date unknown).
  iii. **Pauline VANN** was born (date unknown).
  iv. **Harvey VANN** was born (date unknown).
248 v. **Lois Mae VANN**, born 3 Mar 1920; married James Franklin MORGAN; died 12 Mar 1985.

Descendants of Chief Wahunsonacock Powhatan

26 January 2012

139. Levi Lavan RILEY (Mary Lavisa Cothern-10, Lavica Jane Vann-9, Mason M.-8, Edward Ned-7, Mary Lewis Barnes-6, April-Tkikami Hop Turkey-5, Big Turkey Hop-4, Hokolesqua Opechan-3, Cleopatra the Shawano Powhatan-2, Wahunsonacock-1) was born on 23 Sep 1882 in Indian Territory, OK. He died on 12 Jun 1919 at the age of 36 in Kiowi, OK. He was buried on 14 Jun 1919 in Kiowa Cemetery, Kiowa, Pittsburg Co., OK.

Levi Lavan RILEY and Ann CHESTER were married. **Ann CHESTER** was born (date unknown).

Levi Lavan RILEY and Ann CHESTER had the following children:

- i. **Lewis RILEY** was born on 26 Mar 1911.
- ii. **Dora RILEY** was born in 1913.
- iii. **Clarence RILEY** was born on 30 May 1914.

140. Letty Annety RILEY (Mary Lavisa Cothern-10, Lavica Jane Vann-9, Mason M.-8, Edward Ned-7, Mary Lewis Barnes-6, April-Tkikami Hop Turkey-5, Big Turkey Hop-4, Hokolesqua Opechan-3, Cleopatra the Shawano Powhatan-2, Wahunsonacock-1) was born on 20 Sep 1884 in Indian Territory, OK. She died on 17 Jul 1957 at the age of 72 in Hardshorne Co., OK. She was buried on 19 Jul 1957 in Elmwood Cemetery, Hartshorne, Pittsburg Co., OK.

Letty Annety RILEY and John Sheridan MCCASLIN were married on 28 Oct 1911 in Wilburton, Latimer Co., OK. **John Sheridan MCCASLIN** was born on 13 Sep 1889 in Webber Falls, Muskogee Co., OK. He died on 27 Jul 1940 at the age of 50 in Hartshorne, Pittsburg Co., OK.

John Sheridan MCCASLIN and Letty Annety RILEY had the following children:

- i. **Ron Lee MCCASLIN** was born on 22 Nov 1908 in Wild Horse, Lattimer Co., OK.
- ii. **Kenneth Van MCCASLIN** was born on 21 Oct 1914 in Hartshorne, Pittsburg Co., OK. He died on 1 Jan 1977 at the age of 62 in Los Angeles, Monrovia Co., CA.
- 249 iii. **Grace Loyce MCCASLIN**, born 24 Nov 1916, Hartshorne, Pittsburg Co., OK; married Leslie Eugene SAVAGE, 6 Jul 1948, Greenwood, Sebastian Co., AR; died 4 Mar 1989, Tulsa, Tulsa Co., OK.
- iv. **Florence Maggie MCCASLIN** was born on 6 Jun 1921 in Hartshorne, Pittsburg Co., OK. She died on 12 Aug 1979 at the age of 58 in Midwest City, OK.
- v. **John Sheridan MCCASLIN** was born on 8 Jun 1926 in Hartshorne, Pittsburg Co., OK. He died on 15 Feb 2001 at the age of 74 in McAlester, Pittsburg Co., OK.

141. Willey Price RILEY (Mary Lavisa Cothern-10, Lavica Jane Vann-9, Mason M.-8, Edward Ned-7, Mary Lewis Barnes-6, April-Tkikami Hop Turkey-5, Big Turkey Hop-4, Hokolesqua Opechan-3, Cleopatra the Shawano Powhatan-2, Wahunsonacock-1) was born on 5 Apr 1887 in TX. She died on 6 Feb 1926 at the age of 38 in Higgins, Latimer Co., OK. She was buried on 8 Feb 1926 in Mountain Station Cemetery, Higgins, Latimer Co., OK.

Willey Price RILEY and Gus MITCHELL were married. **Gus MITCHELL** was born (date unknown).

Gus MITCHELL and Willey Price RILEY had the following children:

- i. **Fay MITCHELL** was born (date unknown).
- ii. **Rebedda MITCHELL** was born (date unknown).
- iii. **Gladys MITCHELL** was born (date unknown).
- iv. **Ray MITCHELL** was born (date unknown).

- v. **Edith MITCHELL** was born (date unknown).
- vi. **Bonnie Grace MITCHELL** was born (date unknown).

142. **Andrew Leonard RILEY** (Mary Lavisa Cothern-10, Lavica Jane Vann-9, Mason M.-8, Edward Ned-7, Mary Lewis Barnes-6, April-Tkikami Hop Turkey-5, Big Turkey Hop-4, Hokolesqua Opechan-3, Cleopatra the Shawano Powhatan-2, Wahunsonacock-1) was born on 7 Jul 1895 in Indian Territory, OK. He died on 22 Jul 1966 at the age of 71 in Hartshorne, Pittsburg Co., OK. He was buried on 24 Jul 1966 in Elmwood Cemetery, Hartshorne, Pittsburg Co., OK.

Andrew Leonard RILEY and Thelma COSTEN were married on 9 Dec 1917 in OK. **Thelma COSTEN**, daughter of Thomas Jefferson COSTEN, was born on 10 May 1902.

Andrew Leonard RILEY and Thelma COSTEN had the following children:

250	i.	**Arthur Leonard RILEY**, born 25 Nov 1918, OK; married Winnie BRITTON, 7 Feb 1941, OK.
251	ii.	**William Leon RILEY**, born 31 Jan 1921, OK; married Mavis WOLFORD, 16 Nov 1940, OK.
252	iii.	**Mary Louise RILEY**, born 10 Jan 1923, OK; married Howard STOTTS, 6 Sep 1942, OK.
253	iv.	**Andrew Lawrence RILEY**, born 29 Jul 1925, OK; married Sue LOVELACE, OK; died 23 Aug 1947, OK.
	v.	**Thomas Jefferson RILEY** was born on 8 Dec 1927 in OK.

143. **Chessie Grace RILEY** (Mary Lavisa Cothern-10, Lavica Jane Vann-9, Mason M.-8, Edward Ned-7, Mary Lewis Barnes-6, April-Tkikami Hop Turkey-5, Big Turkey Hop-4, Hokolesqua Opechan-3, Cleopatra the Shawano Powhatan-2, Wahunsonacock-1) was born on 8 Dec 1900 in Indian Territory, OK. She died on 31 Mar 1995 at the age of 94 in Hartshorne, Pittsburg Co., OK.

Chessie Grace RILEY and Guy HOLMES were married. **Guy HOLMES** was born (date unknown).

Guy HOLMES and Chessie Grace RILEY had the following children:

- i. **Lois HOLMES** was born (date unknown).
- ii. **Guy HOLMES** was born (date unknown).
- iii. **Lilac HOLMES** was born (date unknown).
- iv. **Ned Evans HOLMES** was born (date unknown).

144. **Virgil Guy RILEY** (Mary Lavisa Cothern-10, Lavica Jane Vann-9, Mason M.-8, Edward Ned-7, Mary Lewis Barnes-6, April-Tkikami Hop Turkey-5, Big Turkey Hop-4, Hokolesqua Opechan-3, Cleopatra the Shawano Powhatan-2, Wahunsonacock-1) was born on 26 Jun 1906 in Indian Territory, OK. He died on 15 Jun 1992 at the age of 85 in OR.

Virgil Guy RILEY and Ann BASDEN were married. **Ann BASDEN** was born (date unknown).

145. **Minnie Myrtle SADLER** (Nancy Carlida Cothern-10, Lavica Jane Vann-9, Mason M.-8, Edward Ned-7, Mary Lewis Barnes-6, April-Tkikami Hop Turkey-5, Big Turkey Hop-4, Hokolesqua Opechan-3, Cleopatra the Shawano Powhatan-2,

Descendants of Chief Wahunsonacock Powhatan

Wahunsonacock-1) was born on 12 May 1902 in Hartshorne, Pittsburg Co., OK. She died on 18 Sep 1938 at the age of 36 in Hartshorne, Pittsburg Co., OK.

Minnie Myrtle SADLER and William Bruce DEAR were married. **William Bruce DEAR** was born (date unknown).

Minnie Myrtle SADLER and Jess MORROW were married. **Jess MORROW** was born (date unknown).

146. **Ira Melbert SADLER** (Nancy Carlida Cothern-10, Lavica Jane Vann-9, Mason M.-8, Edward Ned-7, Mary Lewis Barnes-6, April-Tkikami Hop Turkey-5, Big Turkey Hop-4, Hokolesqua Opechan-3, Cleopatra the Shawano Powhatan-2, Wahunsonacock-1) was born on 4 May 1905 in Hartshorne, Pittsburg Co., OK. He died in Feb 1987 at the age of 81 in Tuolurnne, Sonora Co., CA.

Ira Melbert SADLER and Eva Mae DEAR were married. **Eva Mae DEAR** was born (date unknown).

147. **Letha Lovie COTHERN** (Walter-10, Lavica Jane Vann-9, Mason M.-8, Edward Ned-7, Mary Lewis Barnes-6, April-Tkikami Hop Turkey-5, Big Turkey Hop-4, Hokolesqua Opechan-3, Cleopatra the Shawano Powhatan-2, Wahunsonacock-1) was born on 6 Aug 1902.

Letha Lovie COTHERN and Thomas CAREY were married on 22 Dec 1920. **Thomas CAREY** died on 17 Jan 1935 in Wesley, OK. He was buried on 19 Jan 1935 in Coffeyville, KS.

Thomas CAREY and Letha Lovie COTHERN had the following child:

    i. **Esther CAREY** was born (date unknown).

148. **Willie Jewell COTHERN** (Walter-10, Lavica Jane Vann-9, Mason M.-8, Edward Ned-7, Mary Lewis Barnes-6, April-Tkikami Hop Turkey-5, Big Turkey Hop-4, Hokolesqua Opechan-3, Cleopatra the Shawano Powhatan-2, Wahunsonacock-1) was born on 18 Sep 1907 in Le Flore Co., OK.

Willie Jewell COTHERN and Coy LEMONS were married on 20 Sep 1927 in Waurika, Jefferson Co., OK. **Coy LEMONS** was born (date unknown).

Willie Jewell COTHERN and Henry BRANCH were married on 20 Jun 1949 in Marietta, TX. **Henry BRANCH** died on 30 Jun 1960 in San Bernadino Co., CA.

Willie Jewell COTHERN and Gomer FARRIS were married on 16 Jun 1923 in Clarksville, AR. **Gomer FARRIS** was born

Descendants of Chief Wahunsonacock Powhatan

(date unknown).

149. **Farrie COTHERN** (Walter-10, Lavica Jane Vann-9, Mason M.-8, Edward Ned-7, Mary Lewis Barnes-6, April-Tkikami Hop Turkey-5, Big Turkey Hop-4, Hokolesqua Opechan-3, Cleopatra the Shawano Powhatan-2, Wahunsonacock-1) was born on 3 Oct 1909 in Le Flore Co., OK. She died on 13 Aug 1961 at the age of 51.

Farrie COTHERN and Earl Monroe LYONS were married in 1925 in Waurika, Jefferson Co., OK. **Earl Monroe LYONS** died in Jun 1967 in Loco, OK.

Earl Monroe LYONS and Farrie COTHERN had the following child:

    254   i. **Annie Mae LYONS**, married BURNETT; married Gill GILBREATH.

150. **Willa Augusta COTHERN** (Vevi Vann-10, Lavica Jane Vann-9, Mason M.-8, Edward Ned-7, Mary Lewis Barnes-6, April-Tkikami Hop Turkey-5, Big Turkey Hop-4, Hokolesqua Opechan-3, Cleopatra the Shawano Powhatan-2, Wahunsonacock-1) was born on 21 Nov 1907 in Charlie, Clay Co., TX. She died on 3 Oct 1993 at the age of 85 in Bedford, Tarrant Co., TX. She was buried on 5 Oct 1993 in Bethel Cemetery, Funston, Jones Co., TX.

Willa Augusta COTHERN and John Charles GOODMAN were married on 8 Dec 1935 in Lueders, Jones Co., TX. **John Charles GOODMAN** was born on 19 Jul 1910. He died in Dec 1978 at the age of 68.

151. **Bobby Nell COTHERN** (Vevi Vann-10, Lavica Jane Vann-9, Mason M.-8, Edward Ned-7, Mary Lewis Barnes-6, April-Tkikami Hop Turkey-5, Big Turkey Hop-4, Hokolesqua Opechan-3, Cleopatra the Shawano Powhatan-2, Wahunsonacock-1) was born on 21 Apr 1910 in Charlie, Clay Co., TX.

Bobby Nell COTHERN and John Edward WRIGHT were married on 4 Sep 1933 in Whon, Coleman Co., TX. **John Edward WRIGHT** was born on 11 Jan 1911. He died on 18 Apr 1996 at the age of 85.

152. **Ruby Gayle COTHERN** (Vevi Vann-10, Lavica Jane Vann-9, Mason M.-8, Edward Ned-7, Mary Lewis Barnes-6, April-Tkikami Hop Turkey-5, Big Turkey Hop-4, Hokolesqua Opechan-3, Cleopatra the Shawano Powhatan-2, Wahunsonacock-1) was born on 31 Jul 1912 in Charlie, Clay Co., TX.

Ruby Gayle COTHERN and Troy Lee WRIGHT were married on 17 Dec 1933 in Whon, Coleman Co., TX. **Troy Lee WRIGHT** was born on 18 Sep 1914. He died on 13 Sep 1974 at the age of 59.

153. **Filo Knox COTHERN** (Vevi Vann-10, Lavica Jane Vann-9, Mason M.-8, Edward Ned-7, Mary Lewis Barnes-6,

April-Tkikami Hop Turkey-5, Big Turkey Hop-4, Hokolesqua Opechan-3, Cleopatra the Shawano Powhatan-2, Wahunsonacock-1) was born on 5 Sep 1914 in Charlie, Clay Co., TX. He died in Oct 1987 at the age of 73 in AZ.

Filo Knox COTHERN and Frances COTHERN were married. **Frances COTHERN** was born (date unknown).

Filo Knox COTHERN and Mrytle NEWCOMBE were married in Jun 1941. **Mrytle NEWCOMBE** died in Jul 1976 in AZ.

Filo Knox COTHERN and Beth JONES were married in AZ. **Beth JONES** was born on 17 Jan 1927.

154. **Murriel COTHERN** (Vevi Vann-10, Lavica Jane Vann-9, Mason M.-8, Edward Ned-7, Mary Lewis Barnes-6, April-Tkikami Hop Turkey-5, Big Turkey Hop-4, Hokolesqua Opechan-3, Cleopatra the Shawano Powhatan-2, Wahunsonacock-1) was born on 7 Apr 1917 in Vernon, Wilbarger Co., TX.

Murriel COTHERN and George Washington COLE were married on 3 Sep 1934 in Anson, Jones Co., TX. **George Washington COLE** was born on 30 Aug 1913 in Whon, Coleman Co., TX. He died on 25 May 1996 at the age of 82.

155. **Doris Loraine COTHERN** (Vevi Vann-10, Lavica Jane Vann-9, Mason M.-8, Edward Ned-7, Mary Lewis Barnes-6, April-Tkikami Hop Turkey-5, Big Turkey Hop-4, Hokolesqua Opechan-3, Cleopatra the Shawano Powhatan-2, Wahunsonacock-1) was born on 27 Jun 1926 in Whon, Coleman Co., TX.

Doris Loraine COTHERN and John Wesley BEACH Jr. were married on 8 Mar 1946 in Prescott, Yavapai Co., AZ. **John Wesley BEACH Jr.** was born on 14 Aug 1924. He died in Jul 1987 at the age of 62. He held the title of Jr..

Descendants of Chief Wahunsonacock Powhatan

Twelfth Generation

156. Sallie ARMSTRONG (Monroe Griffin-11, Sarah Ann Poland-10, Nancy Naomi Moseley-9, Margaret Vann-8, Edward Ned-7, Mary Lewis Barnes-6, April-Tkikami Hop Turkey-5, Big Turkey Hop-4, Hokolesqua Opechan-3, Cleopatra the Shawano Powhatan-2, Wahunsonacock-1) was born in 1879 in Jonesville, TX. She died in 1928 at the age of 49.

Sallie ARMSTRONG and John William ROGERS were married. **John William ROGERS**, son of William J. ROGERS, was born in 1873 in Jonesville, TX. He died in 1917 at the age of 44.

John William ROGERS and Sallie ARMSTRONG had the following child:

 255 i. **Ella Mae ROGERS**, born Aug 1900, Jonesville, Harrison Co., TX; married Alda W. HINCHMAN M.D.; died 1989.

157. Nell OFFETT (Peneloupe "Penny" Moncrief-11, Elvira Poland-10, Nancy Naomi Moseley-9, Margaret Vann-8, Edward Ned-7, Mary Lewis Barnes-6, April-Tkikami Hop Turkey-5, Big Turkey Hop-4, Hokolesqua Opechan-3, Cleopatra the Shawano Powhatan-2, Wahunsonacock-1) was born (date unknown).

Albert R. ERSKINE was born (date unknown).

Fenton CRAIG was born (date unknown).

158. Leslie Virginia LATTA (Lenora Lee Poland-11, John Stratton-10, Nancy Naomi Moseley-9, Margaret Vann-8, Edward Ned-7, Mary Lewis Barnes-6, April-Tkikami Hop Turkey-5, Big Turkey Hop-4, Hokolesqua Opechan-3, Cleopatra the Shawano Powhatan-2, Wahunsonacock-1) was born.

Harry Beaumont WATKINS was born (date unknown).

Harry Beaumont WATKINS and Leslie Virginia LATTA had the following children:

 256 i. **Nelle WATKINS**.
 257 ii. **Flay Latta WATKINS**, born 6 May 1892, Dyersburg, TN; died 27 Dec 1911, Dyersburg, TN.

159. Thomas Poland SMITH (Mary A. Poland-11, Thomas-10, Nancy Naomi Moseley-9, Margaret Vann-8, Edward Ned-7, Mary Lewis Barnes-6, April-Tkikami Hop Turkey-5, Big Turkey Hop-4, Hokolesqua Opechan-3, Cleopatra the Shawano Powhatan-2, Wahunsonacock-1) was born (date unknown).

WASKOM was born (date unknown).

Thomas Poland SMITH and WASKOM had the following children:

258   i. **Louella SMITH**.
       ii. **Thomas Pollard, Jr. SMITH** was born (date unknown).
       iii. **Asbury Waskom SMITH** was born (date unknown).

160. **Ella Virginia "Dubba" SMITH** (Mary A. Poland-11, Thomas-10, Nancy Naomi Moseley-9, Margaret Vann-8, Edward Ned-7, Mary Lewis Barnes-6, April-Tkikami Hop Turkey-5, Big Turkey Hop-4, Hokolesqua Opechan-3, Cleopatra the Shawano Powhatan-2, Wahunsonacock-1) was born in 1856. She was buried in 1856 at Scottsville Cemetery in Scottsville, TX. She died in 1943 at the age of 87 in Scottsville, TX.

Monroe Griffin ARMSTRONG was born (date unknown).

Ella Virginia "Dubba" SMITH and Monroe Griffin ARMSTRONG were married. **Monroe Griffin ARMSTRONG**, son of John Kittle ARMSTRONG and Sarah Ann POLAND, was born in 1851 in Gladewater, Gregg Co., TX. He died in 1925 at the age of 74.

Monroe Griffin ARMSTRONG and Ella Virginia SMITH had the following child:

156   i. **Sallie ARMSTRONG**, born 1879, Jonesville, TX; married John William ROGERS; died 1928.

161. **John Erskine MOSLEY** (William Alexander Newton-11, George Benjamin Alexander-10, George-9, Margaret Vann-8, Edward Ned-7, Mary Lewis Barnes-6, April-Tkikami Hop Turkey-5, Big Turkey Hop-4, Hokolesqua Opechan-3, Cleopatra the Shawano Powhatan-2, Wahunsonacock-1) was born (date unknown).

John Erskine MOSLEY and Blanche Eloise TAYLOR were married. **Blanche Eloise TAYLOR** was born (date unknown).

John Erskine MOSLEY and Blanche Eloise TAYLOR had the following child:

       i. **Betty MOSLEY** was born (date unknown).

162. **William Alexander (Oscar) MOSLEY** (William Alexander Newton-11, George Benjamin Alexander-10, George-9, Margaret Vann-8, Edward Ned-7, Mary Lewis Barnes-6, April-Tkikami Hop Turkey-5, Big Turkey Hop-4, Hokolesqua Opechan-3, Cleopatra the Shawano Powhatan-2, Wahunsonacock-1) was born on 8 Dec 1886 in Arkadelphia, Cullman Co., AL. He died on 23 Apr 1952 at the age of 65 in Florala, Covington Co., AL.

William Alexander (Oscar) MOSLEY and Louise HATCHER were married about 1917 in Bessemer, Jefferson Co., AL. **Louise HATCHER**, daughter of Jack HATCHER and Paralee STEWART, was born on 10 Nov 1889 in Birmingham, Jefferson Co., AL. She died on 17 Dec 1978 at the age of 89 in Jonesboro, Clayton Co., GA.

William Alexander (Oscar) MOSLEY and Louise HATCHER had the following children:

259   i. **Oscar Newton "Junior" MOSLEY**, born 1916, Florala, Covington Co., AL; married Ruby Lee WARREN; died 1995, Pensacola, Escambia Co., FL.

260	ii.	**Sudie "Sue" MOSLEY**, born 1918, Covington Co., AL; married Dale TWITCHELL; died 1968, Florala, Covington Co., AL.
261	iii.	**Ferrolyn MOSLEY**, born 1 Aug 1921, Lockhart, Covington Co., AL; married Walter Lafayette STINSON Jr., Florala, Covington Co., AL.
262	iv.	**Martha Louise MOSLEY**, born 7 Apr 1924, Lockhart, Covington Co., AL; married John M. RAY; died 23 Jan 2001, Florala, Covington Co., AL.
263	v.	**John Edythe "Edie" MOSLEY**, born Florala, Covington Co., AL; married Roak TITTLE.

163. **Thomas Samuel MOSLEY** (William Alexander Newton-11, George Benjamin Alexander-10, George-9, Margaret Vann-8, Edward Ned-7, Mary Lewis Barnes-6, April-Tkikami Hop Turkey-5, Big Turkey Hop-4, Hokolesqua Opechan-3, Cleopatra the Shawano Powhatan-2, Wahunsonacock-1) was born on 16 Mar 1891. He died on 16 May 1958 at the age of 67 in Jefferson Co., AL.

Thomas Samuel MOSLEY and Mattie MONKUS were married in 1907 in Bessemer, Jefferson Co., AL. **Mattie MONKUS** was born on 30 Jan 1882. She died on 15 Oct 1963 at the age of 81 in Jefferson Co., AL.

164. **Amy CRAUSWELL** (Virginia Moseley-11, George Benjamin Alexander-10, George-9, Margaret Vann-8, Edward Ned-7, Mary Lewis Barnes-6, April-Tkikami Hop Turkey-5, Big Turkey Hop-4, Hokolesqua Opechan-3, Cleopatra the Shawano Powhatan-2, Wahunsonacock-1) was born (date unknown).

Amy CRAUSWELL and William A. O'NEAL were married. **William A. O'NEAL** was born (date unknown).

165. **Spencer Avis "Skinny" CRAUSWELL** (Virginia Moseley-11, George Benjamin Alexander-10, George-9, Margaret Vann-8, Edward Ned-7, Mary Lewis Barnes-6, April-Tkikami Hop Turkey-5, Big Turkey Hop-4, Hokolesqua Opechan-3, Cleopatra the Shawano Powhatan-2, Wahunsonacock-1) died in Feb 1935 in AL.

Octavia SANFORD, daughter of William Oliver SANFORD and Lillie Perry Lou Ada HAYNES, died in Apr 1936 in Paintsville, KY. She was buried in Apr 1936 in Dora, AL.

Spencer Avis "Skinny" CRAUSWELL and Octavia SANFORD had the following children:

264	i.	**Betty CRAUSWELL**.
	ii.	**Dorothy CRAUSWELL** was born (date unknown).
	iii.	**Jack CRAUSWELL** was born (date unknown).

166. **Trixie Ethelyn CRAUSWELL** (Virginia Moseley-11, George Benjamin Alexander-10, George-9, Margaret Vann-8, Edward Ned-7, Mary Lewis Barnes-6, April-Tkikami Hop Turkey-5, Big Turkey Hop-4, Hokolesqua Opechan-3, Cleopatra the Shawano Powhatan-2, Wahunsonacock-1) was born on 1 Nov 1914 in Arkadelphia, Cullman Co., AL. She died on 27 Jun 2004 at the age of 89 in Birmingham, Jefferson Co., AL. She was buried on 29 Jun 2004 in Walker Memorial Gardens, Jasper, Walker Co., AL.

Descendants of Chief Wahunsonacock Powhatan

Trixie Ethelyn CRAUSWELL and Louie Edgar FREEMAN were married. **Louie Edgar FREEMAN**, son of Dennie Asberry FREEMAN and Bertha Ann WILLIAMS, was born on 21 Mar 1926 in Anderson, Lauderdale Co., AL. He died on 3 Sep 2003 at the age of 77 in Birmingham, Jefferson Co., AL. He was buried on 5 Sep 2003 in Walker Memorial Gardens, Jasper, Walker Co., AL.

Louie Edgar FREEMAN and Trixie Ethelyn CRAUSWELL had the following children:

- 265   i. **Betty J. FREEMAN**, married Frank SELLERS.
-       ii. **Cora Lee FREEMAN** was born (date unknown).
-       iii. **Peggy FREEMAN** was born (date unknown).

Trixie Ethelyn CRAUSWELL and Fletcher T. RUSSELL were married. **Fletcher T. RUSSELL** was born (date unknown).

Fletcher T. RUSSELL and Trixie Ethelyn CRAUSWELL had the following children:

- 266   i. **L.C. RUSSELL**, married Elizabeth .
- 267   ii. **Thomas S. RUSSELL**, married Pat .

167. **Charles Drennen BUSSEY** (Benjamin Harm-11, Martha (Malinda) Moseley-10, George-9, Margaret Vann-8, Edward Ned-7, Mary Lewis Barnes-6, April-Tkikami Hop Turkey-5, Big Turkey Hop-4, Hokolesqua Opechan-3, Cleopatra the Shawano Powhatan-2, Wahunsonacock-1) was born on 24 May 1876 in Marion Co., AL. He was buried in Aug 1915 in Goodwater Cemetery, Winfield, Marion Co., AL. He died on 22 Aug 1915 at the age of 39 in Winfield, Marion Co., AL.

Charles Drennen BUSSEY and Redora Vianna CHANDLER were married on 28 Nov 1897. **Redora Vianna CHANDLER**, daughter of John Calhoun CHANDLER and Judy Abigail "Abbie" HILL, was born on 21 Sep 1875 in Winfield, Marion Co., AL. She died on 31 Jul 1965 at the age of 89. She was buried in Aug 1965 in Magnolia Cemetery, Bristow, OK.

Charles Drennen BUSSEY and Redora Vianna CHANDLER had the following children:

- 268   i. **Gladys Lula BUSSEY**, born 6 Mar 1899, Lamar Co, AL; married James Allen SMITH, abt 1918; died 7 Dec 1980.
- 269   ii. **Velma Leona BUSSEY**, born 18 Jan 1901; died 19 Dec 1988.
- 270   iii. **Felix Hobson BUSSEY**, born 4 Sep 1903; died 1979.
- 271   iv. **Delora BUSSEY**, born 26 Jun 1906; died 1960.
- 272   v. **Flora BUSSEY**, born 7 Feb 1909; died 13 Nov 1999.
- 273   vi. **Charles Marshall BUSSEY**, born 10 Apr 1912, Winfield, Marion Co., AL; married Louise JEFFERIES, 1937, Watsonville, CA; married Esther M. BYINGTON, 26 Jul 1946.
-       vii. **Mary Ellen BUSSEY** was born on 16 Dec 1914 in Winfield, Marion Co., AL.

168. **Sallie Levert BUSSEY** (Benjamin Harm-11, Martha (Malinda) Moseley-10, George-9, Margaret Vann-8, Edward Ned-7, Mary Lewis Barnes-6, April-Tkikami Hop Turkey-5, Big Turkey Hop-4, Hokolesqua Opechan-3, Cleopatra the Shawano Powhatan-2, Wahunsonacock-1) was born on 15 Feb 1878. She died on 19 Dec 1906 at the age of 28 in Crews, Lamar Co., AL. She was buried on 21 Dec 1906 at Crews Methodist Cemetery in Lamar Co., AL.

Sr. Frank Alexander ROSE was born on 4 Jul 1858 in Switzerland. He died on 29 Apr 1916 at the age of 57. He was buried on 1 May 1916 at Crews Methodist Cemetery in Lamar Co., AL.

Descendants of Chief Wahunsonacock Powhatan

26 January 2012

169. Walter BUSSEY (Benjamin Harm-11, Martha (Malinda) Moseley-10, George-9, Margaret Vann-8, Edward Ned-7, Mary Lewis Barnes-6, April-Tkikami Hop Turkey-5, Big Turkey Hop-4, Hokolesqua Opechan-3, Cleopatra the Shawano Powhatan-2, Wahunsonacock-1) was born on 11 Jan 1880. He died in Nov 1941 at the age of 61. He was buried in Nov 1941 in Goodwater Cemetery, Winfield, Marion Co., AL.

Mattie Sue SMITH was born in 1883. She died in 1976 at the age of 93. She was buried in 1976 in Goodwater Cemetery, Winfield, Marion Co., AL.

Walter BUSSEY and Mattie Sue SMITH had the following children:

274	i.	**Oral Lee BUSSEY**, born Jul 1902.
275	ii.	**Blanche Mae BUSSEY**, born 1910.
	iii.	**Lucy BUSSEY** was born on 18 Jun 1913. She was buried in Oct 1917 in Goodwater Cemetery, Winfield, Marion Co., AL. She died on 28 Oct 1917 at the age of 4.
276	iv.	**Catherine BUSSEY**, born 1915.
277	v.	**Hazel BUSSEY**, born 1917.
278	vi.	**Daisy BUSSEY**, born 1917.
	vii.	**Virginia BUSSEY** was born on 4 Jun 1921. She was buried in Jun 1923 in Goodwater Cemetery, Winfield, Marion Co., AL. She died on 24 Jun 1923 at the age of 2.
279	viii.	**Walter Edwin BUSSEY**, born 1924.
280	ix.	**Bennie Lucas BUSSEY**.

170. James "Jimmy" David BUSSEY (Benjamin Harm-11, Martha (Malinda) Moseley-10, George-9, Margaret Vann-8, Edward Ned-7, Mary Lewis Barnes-6, April-Tkikami Hop Turkey-5, Big Turkey Hop-4, Hokolesqua Opechan-3, Cleopatra the Shawano Powhatan-2, Wahunsonacock-1) was born on 14 Oct 1881 in Arkadelphia, Cullman Co., AL. He died on 4 Aug 1971 at the age of 89 in Crews, Lamar Co., AL.

James "Jimmy" David BUSSEY and Mattie Lula ROSE were married on 30 Nov 1905. **Mattie Lula ROSE**, daughter of Frank Alexander ROSE and Ann Elizabeth "Lulu" POSTON, was born on 12 May 1884 in Wilmington, TN. She died on 6 Apr 1952 at the age of 67 in Crews, Lamar Co., AL.

James "Jimmy" David BUSSEY and Mattie Lula ROSE had the following children:

281	i.	**Mattie Marie BUSSEY**, born 6 Sep 1906, Carbon Hill, Walker Co., AL; married Frank Julius FALGOUT, 19 Aug 1929.
	ii.	**David Clarence BUSSEY** was born on 20 Jun 1908 in Carbon Hill, Walker Co., AL. He died in Jan 1956 at the age of 47.
282	iii.	**Mable Ellen BUSSEY**, born 31 Jan 1911, Winfield, Marion Co., AL.
283	iv.	**Ruby Elizabeth BUSSEY**, born 3 Oct 1912, Winfield, Marion Co., AL; married Merico Cesare "Mike Chester" MANDOLINI, 18 Dec 1929.

171. Lula BUSSEY (Benjamin Harm-11, Martha (Malinda) Moseley-10, George-9, Margaret Vann-8, Edward Ned-7, Mary Lewis Barnes-6, April-Tkikami Hop Turkey-5, Big Turkey Hop-4, Hokolesqua Opechan-3, Cleopatra the Shawano Powhatan-2, Wahunsonacock-1) was born on 29 Jun 1883. She died on 29 Jul 1974 at the age of 91.

Descendants of Chief Wahunsonacock Powhatan

26 January 2012

Lula BUSSEY and Stanford KNOX were married on 5 Mar 1906. **Stanford KNOX** was born (date unknown).

John Thomas BOYETTE was born (date unknown).

John Thomas BOYETTE and Lula BUSSEY had the following children:

    i. **Troy BOYETTE** was born (date unknown).
    ii. **Grady BOYETTE** was born (date unknown).
    iii. **Unk BOYETTE** was born (date unknown).

John W. COUCH, son of Meredith Jacob "Jake" COUCH and Susan BERRYHILL, was born in 1867. He died on 23 Apr 1946 at the age of 79 in Purcell, OK.

John W. COUCH and Lula BUSSEY had the following children:

    i. **Johnnie Lou COUCH** was born (date unknown).
    ii. **Myrtle COUCH** was born (date unknown).
    iii. **Anita COUCH** was born (date unknown).
    iv. **Dawson COUCH** was born (date unknown).
    v. **Betty Jo COUCH** was born (date unknown).

172. **George Washington BUSSEY** (Benjamin Harm-11, Martha (Malinda) Moseley-10, George-9, Margaret Vann-8, Edward Ned-7, Mary Lewis Barnes-6, April-Tkikami Hop Turkey-5, Big Turkey Hop-4, Hokolesqua Opechan-3, Cleopatra the Shawano Powhatan-2, Wahunsonacock-1) was born on 24 Jun 1885 in Arkadelphia, Cullman Co., AL. He was buried in Feb 1946 in Hitchita, McIntosh Co., OK. He died on 11 Feb 1946 at the age of 60 in Hitchita, McIntosh Co., OK.

George Washington BUSSEY and Ola BAIRD were married on 31 Aug 1907 in Carbon Hill, Walker Co., AL. **Ola BAIRD**, daughter of Joe Calls BAIRD and Lavania Isabelle TOWNLEY, was born on 16 Jul 1893 in Walker Co., AL. She was buried in Dec 1967 in Hitchita, McIntosh Co., OK. She died on 13 Dec 1967 at the age of 74 in Henryetta, McIntosh Co., OK.

George Washington BUSSEY and Ola BAIRD had the following children:

284	i.	**Christina BUSSEY**, born 26 Aug 1909; married Bee COKER, 12 Jun 1967; married Merlin KING, Sep 1931; died 5 May 1999.
285	ii.	**Joe Raymond BUSSEY**, born 31 Oct 1911; married Hazel HORN, Sep 1931; married Alta MOORE, 2 Mar 1953; died 12 Aug 1987, Salina, CA.
286	iii.	**Floyd Francis BUSSEY**, born 10 May 1913; married Evaughna THOMPSON, 9 May 1937; died Coweta, Wagoner Co., OK.
287	iv.	**Georgell BUSSEY**, born 9 Mar 1916, Winfield, Marion Co., AL; married Gladys Lou GAYLER, 3 Sep 1938.
288	v.	**Mary Ruth BUSSEY**, born 17 Dec 1918; married Paul NORTHCUTT, 1936.
289	vi.	**Willie Everette BUSSEY**, born 28 Oct 1920; died 3 May 1959, Henryetta, McIntosh Co., OK.
	vii.	**Lavora BUSSEY** was born on 16 Feb 1923. She died in Dec 1927 at the age of 4.
290	viii.	**Bobby BUSSEY**, born 15 Mar 1926, Hitchita, McIntosh Co., OK; married Christina WORTHAM, 27 Mar 1948, Henryetta, McIntosh Co., OK.
291	ix.	**Ernest Eugene BUSSEY**, born 10 Dec 1928; married Dorothy LINDSAY, 7 Aug 1948.
292	x.	**Jimmy Ray BUSSEY**, born 15 Oct 1933, Hitchita, McIntosh Co., OK; married Betty KOBLECHECK,

1982; married June Rose MORRIS, 1 Feb 1951, Okmulgee, OK.
293 xi. **Gladys Sue BUSSEY**, born 25 Dec 1936, Hitchita, McIntosh Co., OK; married Danny Ray POWELL, 18 Dec 1953, Henryetta, McIntosh Co., OK.

173. **Oscar BUSSEY** (Benjamin Harm-11, Martha (Malinda) Moseley-10, George-9, Margaret Vann-8, Edward Ned-7, Mary Lewis Barnes-6, April-Tkikami Hop Turkey-5, Big Turkey Hop-4, Hokolesqua Opechan-3, Cleopatra the Shawano Powhatan-2, Wahunsonacock-1) was born on 24 Oct 1887. He died on 29 Jul 1966 at the age of 78.

Mabel Elzora BURKS was born (date unknown).

174. **Mary Ellen BUSSEY** (Benjamin Harm-11, Martha (Malinda) Moseley-10, George-9, Margaret Vann-8, Edward Ned-7, Mary Lewis Barnes-6, April-Tkikami Hop Turkey-5, Big Turkey Hop-4, Hokolesqua Opechan-3, Cleopatra the Shawano Powhatan-2, Wahunsonacock-1) was born on 20 Jun 1889. She died in 1951 at the age of 62.

Frank A. ROSE Jr., son of Frank Alexander ROSE and Ann Elizabeth "Lulu" POSTON, held the title of Jr..

Frank A. ROSE and Mary Ellen BUSSEY had the following children:

 i. **Frank Howard ROSE** was born (date unknown).
 ii. **Robert ROSE** was born (date unknown).
 iii. **Unk ROSE** was born (date unknown).

175. **Alma Eudora BUSSEY** (Benjamin Harm-11, Martha (Malinda) Moseley-10, George-9, Margaret Vann-8, Edward Ned-7, Mary Lewis Barnes-6, April-Tkikami Hop Turkey-5, Big Turkey Hop-4, Hokolesqua Opechan-3, Cleopatra the Shawano Powhatan-2, Wahunsonacock-1) was born on 27 Jun 1892. She died on 7 Dec 1975 at the age of 83.

Alma Eudora BUSSEY and William Lee BOWLING were married on 15 Dec 1912. **William Lee BOWLING**, son of Martin Coston BOWLING and Unk BRIDGES, was born in 1875. He died in 1943 at the age of 68.

William Lee BOWLING and Alma Eudora BUSSEY had the following children:

294 i. **Willie Virginia BOWLING**, born 29 Nov 1924.
 ii. **Infant BOWLING** was born on 15 Oct 1913. He/she died on 15 Oct 1913 at the age of 0.
295 iii. **Verita Mae BOWLING**, born 5 Jun 1916; married Arvel Parks HOSCH; died 6 Jul 2009, Winfield, Marion Co., AL.
296 iv. **Everette DeWayne BOWLING**, born 4 Jul 1922.

176. **Emma Ollie BUSSEY** (Edmund Moody-11, Martha (Malinda) Moseley-10, George-9, Margaret Vann-8, Edward Ned-7, Mary Lewis Barnes-6, April-Tkikami Hop Turkey-5, Big Turkey Hop-4, Hokolesqua Opechan-3, Cleopatra the Shawano Powhatan-2, Wahunsonacock-1) was born on 5 Dec 1880. She died on 19 Dec 1972 at the age of 92.

John T. WASHINGTON, son of William WASHINGTON and Margaret E. ALLMAN, was born in 1877. He died in 1957

Descendants of Chief Wahunsonacock Powhatan

26 January 2012

at the age of 80.

John T. WASHINGTON and Emma Ollie BUSSEY had the following children:

	i.	**Lester WASHINGTON** was born in Dec 1896.
297	ii.	**Edward Moody WASHINGTON**, born 11 Nov 1898; married Lorene DUTTON.
298	iii.	**Tressie Olene WASHINGTON**, born 4 May 1902; married Thomas HARRISON.
299	iv.	**Earl WASHINGTON**, born 18 Mar 1904; married Fleta STEWART.
	v.	**Roy WASHINGTON** was born (date unknown).
300	vi.	**Helen WASHINGTON**, born 13 Apr 1912, Dora, Walker Co., AL; married James Leslie SANFORD; died 10 Aug 2001, Dora, Walker Co., AL.
301	vii.	**Tee Ester WASHINGTON**, married Arthur William BLACKBURN.

177. **Lon A. BUSSEY** (Edmund Moody-11, Martha (Malinda) Moseley-10, George-9, Margaret Vann-8, Edward Ned-7, Mary Lewis Barnes-6, April-Tkikami Hop Turkey-5, Big Turkey Hop-4, Hokolesqua Opechan-3, Cleopatra the Shawano Powhatan-2, Wahunsonacock-1) was born on 11 May 1883.

Lon A. BUSSEY and Annie L. were married. **Annie L.** was born in 1883 in AL.

Lon A. BUSSEY and Annie L. had the following children:

302	i.	**Nettie C. BUSSEY**, born 1904, AL; married GLOVER.
	ii.	**Clyde Thomas? BUSSEY** was born in 1910 in AL.
	iii.	**Mary Ena BUSSEY** was born in 1918 in AL.

178. **Luanna BUSSEY** (Edmund Moody-11, Martha (Malinda) Moseley-10, George-9, Margaret Vann-8, Edward Ned-7, Mary Lewis Barnes-6, April-Tkikami Hop Turkey-5, Big Turkey Hop-4, Hokolesqua Opechan-3, Cleopatra the Shawano Powhatan-2, Wahunsonacock-1) was born on 6 Jun 1886. She died on 12 Aug 1912 at the age of 26. She was buried on 14 Aug 1912 in Crews Cemetery, Beaverton, Lamar Co., AL.

Luanna BUSSEY and Lonnie Alonzo GUYTON were married on 9 Jun 1904 in Lamar Co, AL. **Lonnie Alonzo GUYTON**, son of Aaron P. GUYTON and Sarah Kathryn (Sally) HARRIS, was born on 24 Apr 1880. He died on 20 May 1943 at the age of 63. He was buried on 22 May 1943 in Crews Cemetery, Beaverton, Lamar Co., AL.

Lonnie Alonzo GUYTON and Luanna BUSSEY had the following children:

	i.	**Tommy T. GUYTON** was born (date unknown).
	ii.	**Dewey GUYTON** was born (date unknown).
	iii.	**Willie Atmus GUYTON** was born on 25 Apr 1908 in Lamar Co, AL.
303	iv.	**Ernest Paul GUYTON**, born 25 Jan 1912, Lamar Co, AL; married Daisy Cardell HARRIS; married Katie LOVELACE; died 11 Sep 1971, Lamar Co, AL.

179. **Rufus Thomas BUSSEY** (Edmund Moody-11, Martha (Malinda) Moseley-10, George-9, Margaret Vann-8, Edward Ned-7, Mary Lewis Barnes-6, April-Tkikami Hop Turkey-5, Big Turkey Hop-4, Hokolesqua Opechan-3, Cleopatra the Shawano Powhatan-2, Wahunsonacock-1) was born on 3 Mar 1886 in Arkadelphia, Cullman Co., AL. He died on 23 Oct 1947 at the age of 61 in Prestonburg, KY.

Descendants of Chief Wahunsonacock Powhatan

26 January 2012

Rufus Thomas BUSSEY and Luried Navada CLARK were married on 23 Dec 1908 in Dora, Walker Co., AL. **Luried Navada CLARK**, daughter of Marion CLARK and Daisy JEFFERSON, was born on 3 May 1893 in Dora, Walker Co., AL. She died on 25 Sep 1954 at the age of 61 in Prestonburg, KY.

Rufus Thomas BUSSEY and Luried Navada CLARK had the following children:

- 304   i.   **Otis Howard BUSSEY**, born 4 Jun 1911, Dora, Walker Co., AL; married Ora Lorien SANFORD, 3 Jan 1931, Dora, AL; died 24 Jul 1975, Prestonburg, KY.
- 305   ii.   **Dawson Ellard BUSSEY**, born 4 Jun 1913, Dora, Walker Co., AL; married Nova Jean HICKS, Oct 1936, KY; died 26 Feb 1972, Prestonburg, KY.
- 306   iii.   **Mildred Ethel BUSSEY**, born 12 Jun 1915; married Bruce CONLEY, 31 Oct 1936, Paintsville, KY; died 27 Nov 1971, Marion, OH.
- 307   iv.   **Marion Edward "Fat" BUSSEY**, born 7 Jan 1917, Dora, AL; died 2 May 1964, Union City, NJ.
- 308   v.   **Rufus Terry BUSSEY**, born 20 Apr 1920; married Lorene LAWSON.
- 309   vi.   **Gwendolyn BUSSEY**, born 29 Sep 1921; married Jacque Leonard WYNN, 15 Mar 1947, Brooklin Hts., OH.
- 310   vii.   **Emmy Sue BUSSEY**, born 15 Jul 1925, Dora, Walker Co., AL; married Charles J. GIGANTI, 10 Jun 1946, Cleveland, OH.
- 311   viii.   **Tommie Lee BUSSEY**, born 2 Jun 1925, Dora, Walker Co., AL; died 30 Aug 1980, Pikeville, KY.
- 312   ix.   **Naoma "Naomi" BUSSEY**, born 23 Feb 1927, Dora, Walker Co., AL; married William Hollie CONLEY, 27 Jan 1945, Leatha, KY.

180. **Milton Travis BUSSEY** (Edmund Moody-11, Martha (Malinda) Moseley-10, George-9, Margaret Vann-8, Edward Ned-7, Mary Lewis Barnes-6, April-Tkikami Hop Turkey-5, Big Turkey Hop-4, Hokolesqua Opechan-3, Cleopatra the Shawano Powhatan-2, Wahunsonacock-1) was born on 12 Feb 1889. He died on 6 May 1945 at the age of 56. He was buried on 8 May 1945 in East Dora Cemetery, Dora, Walker Co., AL.

Lucy EITSON was born on 19 May 1899. She died on 4 Mar 1955 at the age of 55. She was buried on 6 Mar 1955 in East Dora Cemetery, Dora, Walker Co., AL.

Milton Travis BUSSEY and Lucy EITSON had the following children:

- 313   i.   **Virginia BUSSEY**, born 1919, AL; married GRISSOM.
- 314   ii.   **Dora Oliver BUSSEY**, married GOSSETT.
- 315   iii.   **Wonnell (Nell) BUSSEY**, born 4 Feb 1933; died 20 Jul 1984.

181. **Elizabeth "Lizzie Beth" BUSSEY** (Edmund Moody-11, Martha (Malinda) Moseley-10, George-9, Margaret Vann-8, Edward Ned-7, Mary Lewis Barnes-6, April-Tkikami Hop Turkey-5, Big Turkey Hop-4, Hokolesqua Opechan-3, Cleopatra the Shawano Powhatan-2, Wahunsonacock-1) was born on 5 Apr 1892 in Arkadelphia, Cullman Co., AL. She died on 21 Apr 1974 at the age of 82 in Graysville, Jefferson Co., AL. She was buried on 23 Apr 1974 in East Dora Cemetery, Dora, Walker Co., AL.

Elizabeth "Lizzie Beth" BUSSEY and James Martin WEEKS were married on 16 Jan 1908. **James Martin WEEKS**, son of James Perry WEEKS and Josephine Louise PAGE, was born on 23 Jun 1883 in Crews, Lamar Co., AL. He died on 21 Mar 1961 at the age of 77 in Graysville, Jefferson Co., AL. He was buried on 23 Mar 1961 in East Dora Cemetery, Dora, Walker Co., AL.

Descendants of Chief Wahunsonacock Powhatan

26 January 2012

James Martin WEEKS and Elizabeth "Lizzie Beth" BUSSEY had the following children:

316	i.	**Cullen Dexter WEEKS**, born 30 Apr 1909, Lamar Co, AL; married Velma A. WELCH, abt 1936, Smithville, MS; died 3 Aug 1944, St. Lo, France.
317	ii.	**Era Earl WEEKS**, born 22 May 1910, Detroit, Lamar Co, AL; married Lillie Myrtle HEATHERLY, 29 Jun 1930, Cullman County, AL; died 24 Jun 1983, Gardendale, Jefferson Co., AL.
318	iii.	**Venice Myrtle WEEKS**, born 3 Apr 1912, Lamar Co, AL; died 21 May 1990, Birmingham, Jefferson Co., AL.
	iv.	**Willard Earnest WEEKS** was born on 9 Oct 1913 in Lamar Co, AL. He died on 5 Mar 1916 at the age of 2 in Lamar Co, AL. He was buried on 7 Mar 1916 in Carter Cemetery, Detroit, Lamar Co., AL.
319	v.	**Marvin Benson WEEKS**, born 28 Jan 1914, Lamar Co, AL; died Sep 1982.
320	vi.	**Verda Louise WEEKS**, born 21 Mar 1917, Lamar Co, AL; married Arthur Lee "Pete" HAMILTON, 1936; died 26 May 1944, Birmingham, Jefferson Co., AL.

182. **Minnie Malinda BUSSEY** (Edmund Moody-11, Martha (Malinda) Moseley-10, George-9, Margaret Vann-8, Edward Ned-7, Mary Lewis Barnes-6, April-Tkikami Hop Turkey-5, Big Turkey Hop-4, Hokolesqua Opechan-3, Cleopatra the Shawano Powhatan-2, Wahunsonacock-1) was born on 12 Feb 1895.

Thomas Earl LOWERY was born (date unknown).

Thomas Earl LOWERY and Minnie Malinda BUSSEY had the following children:

321	i.	**John William "Billy" LOWERY**, married Ethel MATHEWS.
322	ii.	**Mattie Bee LOWERY**, born 27 Jan 1917; married R.J. BOSHELLE.
323	iii.	**Margaret Ruth LOWERY**, born 1923; married Lehman LOLLAR.
	iv.	**Joe Stanley LOWERY** was born (date unknown).
324	v.	**Mary Louise LOWERY**, born 27 Feb 1924; married Adrian O'Neal MCKINNEY.
	vi.	**Lois Christine LOWERY** was born in 1926.
325	vii.	**Thomas Harold LOWERY**, born 9 Jan 1928; married Doris PARKER.
326	viii.	**Clarence Howard LOWERY**, born 19 Jul 1931; married Rochelle TUCKER.

183. **Willie Benjamin "Will" BUSSEY** (Edmund Moody-11, Martha (Malinda) Moseley-10, George-9, Margaret Vann-8, Edward Ned-7, Mary Lewis Barnes-6, April-Tkikami Hop Turkey-5, Big Turkey Hop-4, Hokolesqua Opechan-3, Cleopatra the Shawano Powhatan-2, Wahunsonacock-1) was born on 12 Feb 1895. He was buried in East Dora Cemetery, Dora, Walker Co., AL.

Willie Benjamin "Will" BUSSEY and Ruby WARD were married. **Ruby WARD** was born on 1 Aug 1902. She died on 4 Jul 1980 at the age of 77. She was buried on 6 Jul 1980 in East Dora Cemetery, Dora, Walker Co., AL.

Pearl was born on 22 Jun 1894. She died on 17 Feb 1943 at the age of 48. She was buried on 19 Feb 1943 in East Dora Cemetery, Dora, Walker Co., AL.

Willie Benjamin "Will" BUSSEY and Pearl had the following child:

i. **William C. BUSSEY** was born in 1917 in AL.

Descendants of Chief Wahunsonacock Powhatan

184. **Mattie Marie "Sweetie" BUSSEY** (Edmund Moody-11, Martha (Malinda) Moseley-10, George-9, Margaret Vann-8, Edward Ned-7, Mary Lewis Barnes-6, April-Tkikami Hop Turkey-5, Big Turkey Hop-4, Hokolesqua Opechan-3, Cleopatra the Shawano Powhatan-2, Wahunsonacock-1) was born in May 1898. She died on 9 Dec 1971 at the age of 73.

Mattie Marie "Sweetie" BUSSEY and Charlie E. HOLLIS were married. **Charlie E. HOLLIS**, son of John R. HOLLIS and Minnie E., was born in Feb 1892 in AL.

Charlie E. HOLLIS and Mattie Marie "Sweetie" BUSSEY had the following child:

    327   i. **Aileen HOLLIS**, married Jesse B. MCCRARY.

185. **Edward "Ed" BUSSEY** (Edmund Moody-11, Martha (Malinda) Moseley-10, George-9, Margaret Vann-8, Edward Ned-7, Mary Lewis Barnes-6, April-Tkikami Hop Turkey-5, Big Turkey Hop-4, Hokolesqua Opechan-3, Cleopatra the Shawano Powhatan-2, Wahunsonacock-1) was born on 18 Jan 1905. He died on 4 Jun 1967 at the age of 62. He was buried on 6 Jun 1967 at Morgan Cemetery, Old Sumiton Road in Sumiton, Walker Co., AL.

Flora Mae SELLERS was born (date unknown).

Edward "Ed" BUSSEY and Flora Mae SELLERS had the following child:

    328   i. **James Edward BUSSEY**, born 31 Aug 1931; died 11 Feb 2008.

Edward "Ed" BUSSEY and Marion GRIFFITH were married. **Marion GRIFFITH** was born on 27 Jul 1928. She died in Mar 1974 at the age of 45.

Edward "Ed" BUSSEY and Marion GRIFFITH had the following children:

        i. **Edward Junior BUSSEY** was born on 12 Sep 1954.
       ii. **Willard Van BUSSEY** was born on 11 Apr 1958.

186. **Richmond Hobson Pearson BUSSEY** (Edmund Moody-11, Martha (Malinda) Moseley-10, George-9, Margaret Vann-8, Edward Ned-7, Mary Lewis Barnes-6, April-Tkikami Hop Turkey-5, Big Turkey Hop-4, Hokolesqua Opechan-3, Cleopatra the Shawano Powhatan-2, Wahunsonacock-1) was born in 1905. He died in 1948 at the age of 43. He was buried in 1948 in East Dora Cemetery, Dora, Walker Co., AL.

Pauline SANDERS was born (date unknown).

Richmond Hobson Pearson BUSSEY and Pauline SANDERS had the following child:

        i. **Eugene BUSSEY** was born (date unknown).

Descendants of Chief Wahunsonacock Powhatan

26 January 2012

187. Charlie BUSSEY (Edmund Moody-11, Martha (Malinda) Moseley-10, George-9, Margaret Vann-8, Edward Ned-7, Mary Lewis Barnes-6, April-Tkikami Hop Turkey-5, Big Turkey Hop-4, Hokolesqua Opechan-3, Cleopatra the Shawano Powhatan-2, Wahunsonacock-1) was born in 1912. He died in 1968 at the age of 56. He was buried in 1968.

Katy HILL was born (date unknown).

Charlie BUSSEY and Katy HILL had the following children:

      i. **Charles BUSSEY** was born (date unknown).
      ii. **Kaye BUSSEY** was born (date unknown).
      iii. **Lynn BUSSEY** was born (date unknown).

188. Ruby Lee BUSSEY (Edmund Moody-11, Martha (Malinda) Moseley-10, George-9, Margaret Vann-8, Edward Ned-7, Mary Lewis Barnes-6, April-Tkikami Hop Turkey-5, Big Turkey Hop-4, Hokolesqua Opechan-3, Cleopatra the Shawano Powhatan-2, Wahunsonacock-1) was born on 11 Jan 1915. She died on 19 Aug 2008 at the age of 93 in Empire, Walker Co., AL. She was buried on 21 Aug 2008 in Morgan Cemetery, Sumiton, Walker Co., AL.

Ruby Lee BUSSEY and Thomas Clarence PARR were married on 9 Jun 1936. **Thomas Clarence PARR** was born on 10 Jan 1908.

Thomas Clarence PARR and Ruby Lee BUSSEY had the following children:

329	i.	**Iva Jean PARR**, born 4 Apr 1947, AL; married KEY; died 3 Sep 1977, AL.
	ii.	**Lawrence Ray PARR** was born on 3 Jul 1947.
330	iii.	**James Thomas PARR**, married Joyce .
331	iv.	**William Wilford PARR**, born 1938; married Elizabeth Ann .

189. Euell BUSSEY (Edmund Moody-11, Martha (Malinda) Moseley-10, George-9, Margaret Vann-8, Edward Ned-7, Mary Lewis Barnes-6, April-Tkikami Hop Turkey-5, Big Turkey Hop-4, Hokolesqua Opechan-3, Cleopatra the Shawano Powhatan-2, Wahunsonacock-1) was born in 1917.

Ruth ROBINSON was born (date unknown).

Euell BUSSEY and Ruth ROBINSON had the following children:

332	i.	**Sue BUSSEY**.
	ii.	**Billie BUSSEY** was born (date unknown).
	iii.	**Gary BUSSEY** was born (date unknown).
	iv.	**Ronnie BUSSEY** was born (date unknown).

Wavey RIDDER was born (date unknown).

190. Frank BUSSEY (Edmund Moody-11, Martha (Malinda) Moseley-10, George-9, Margaret Vann-8, Edward Ned-7,

Descendants of Chief Wahunsonacock Powhatan

26 January 2012

Mary Lewis Barnes-6, April-Tkikami Hop Turkey-5, Big Turkey Hop-4, Hokolesqua Opechan-3, Cleopatra the Shawano Powhatan-2, Wahunsonacock-1) was born in 1919. He died in Feb 1999 at the age of 80 in Walker Co., AL.

Frank BUSSEY and Lillian Tolbert ROBINSON were married on 18 Nov 1942. **Lillian Tolbert ROBINSON** was born (date unknown).

Frank BUSSEY and Lillian Tolbert ROBINSON had the following children:

    333   i.   **Marshall BUSSEY**.
    334   ii. **Sheila Faye BUSSEY**.
               iii. **Mitchell Lee BUSSEY** was born (date unknown).

191. **Johnny BUSSEY** (Edmund Moody-11, Martha (Malinda) Moseley-10, George-9, Margaret Vann-8, Edward Ned-7, Mary Lewis Barnes-6, April-Tkikami Hop Turkey-5, Big Turkey Hop-4, Hokolesqua Opechan-3, Cleopatra the Shawano Powhatan-2, Wahunsonacock-1) was born on 22 Jul 1922 in Walker Co., AL. He died on 18 Nov 2008 at the age of 86 in Dora, Walker Co., AL. He was buried on 21 Nov 2008 in New Horizon Memorial Gardens, Dora, Walker Co., AL.

Johnny BUSSEY and Edith BOX were married on 2 Jan 1941 in Dora, Walker Co., AL. **Edith BOX** was born (date unknown).

Johnny BUSSEY and Edith BOX had the following children:

    335   i.   **Carolyn BUSSEY**, born 31 Aug 1942.
    336   ii. **Jimmy Carroll BUSSEY**, born 5 Apr 1944.
    337   iii. **Roy Charles BUSSEY**, born 12 Nov 1946.
    338   iv. **Sandra "Sandy) BUSSEY**, born 6 Apr 1949; died 22 Nov 1996.
    339   v. **Charlotte Loretta BUSSEY**, born 20 Jun 1952.
    340   vi. **Gwendolyn Joan BUSSEY**, born 18 Dec 1954.
    341   vii. **Roxann BUSSEY**, born 17 Feb 1957.

192. **Gertrude BUSSEY** (Edmund Moody-11, Martha (Malinda) Moseley-10, George-9, Margaret Vann-8, Edward Ned-7, Mary Lewis Barnes-6, April-Tkikami Hop Turkey-5, Big Turkey Hop-4, Hokolesqua Opechan-3, Cleopatra the Shawano Powhatan-2, Wahunsonacock-1) was born in Dec 1926 in Lamar Co, AL.

Gertrude BUSSEY and Mabrie STYLES were married on 22 Feb 1946. **Mabrie STYLES** was born (date unknown).

193. **Ludie ABBOTT** (Adra "Addie" BUSSEY-11, Martha (Malinda) Moseley-10, George-9, Margaret Vann-8, Edward Ned-7, Mary Lewis Barnes-6, April-Tkikami Hop Turkey-5, Big Turkey Hop-4, Hokolesqua Opechan-3, Cleopatra the Shawano Powhatan-2, Wahunsonacock-1) was born (date unknown).

Tidie CREW was born (date unknown).

Tidie CREW and Ludie ABBOTT had the following child:

Descendants of Chief Wahunsonacock Powhatan

    342   i. **Gilbert CREW**.

194. **Lillian (Lillie) Chester BUSSEY** (William M. (Will)-11, Martha (Malinda) Moseley-10, George-9, Margaret Vann-8, Edward Ned-7, Mary Lewis Barnes-6, April-Tkikami Hop Turkey-5, Big Turkey Hop-4, Hokolesqua Opechan-3, Cleopatra the Shawano Powhatan-2, Wahunsonacock-1) was born in 1894. She died in 1986 at the age of 92.

Lillian (Lillie) Chester BUSSEY and William Newton NASH were married in 1910 in Coleman, TX. **William Newton NASH** was born (date unknown).

195. **Myrtle Katherine BUSSEY** (William M. (Will)-11, Martha (Malinda) Moseley-10, George-9, Margaret Vann-8, Edward Ned-7, Mary Lewis Barnes-6, April-Tkikami Hop Turkey-5, Big Turkey Hop-4, Hokolesqua Opechan-3, Cleopatra the Shawano Powhatan-2, Wahunsonacock-1) was born in 1897. She died in 1981 at the age of 84.

Myrtle Katherine BUSSEY and HENDERSON were married. **HENDERSON** was born (date unknown).

Myrtle Katherine BUSSEY and James Elbert BUSE were married. **James Elbert BUSE** was born (date unknown).

196. **Addie BUSSEY** (William M. (Will)-11, Martha (Malinda) Moseley-10, George-9, Margaret Vann-8, Edward Ned-7, Mary Lewis Barnes-6, April-Tkikami Hop Turkey-5, Big Turkey Hop-4, Hokolesqua Opechan-3, Cleopatra the Shawano Powhatan-2, Wahunsonacock-1) was born in 1903. She died in 1980 at the age of 77.

Addie BUSSEY and Fred NUNCIO were married. **Fred NUNCIO** was born in 1897. He died in 1963 at the age of 66.

197. **Lizzie Irene MOSLEY** (Hiram Mace-11, William Lafayette-10, George-9, Margaret Vann-8, Edward Ned-7, Mary Lewis Barnes-6, April-Tkikami Hop Turkey-5, Big Turkey Hop-4, Hokolesqua Opechan-3, Cleopatra the Shawano Powhatan-2, Wahunsonacock-1) was born on 24 Nov 1892 in AL. She died on 3 May 1983 at the age of 90 in Addison, Winston Co., AL. She was buried on 5 May 1983 in Arkadelphia Cemetery, Arkadelphia, Cullman Co., AL.

Lizzie Irene MOSLEY and Tommie Pierce OGLETREE were married. **Tommie Pierce OGLETREE** was born on 26 Mar 1890. He died on 18 Feb 1965 at the age of 74. He was buried on 20 Feb 1965 in Arkadelphia Cemetery, Arkadelphia, Cullman Co., AL.

198. **Alice Mae MOSLEY** (Hiram Mace-11, William Lafayette-10, George-9, Margaret Vann-8, Edward Ned-7, Mary Lewis Barnes-6, April-Tkikami Hop Turkey-5, Big Turkey Hop-4, Hokolesqua Opechan-3, Cleopatra the Shawano

Descendants of Chief Wahunsonacock Powhatan

26 January 2012

Powhatan-2, Wahunsonacock-1) was born on 31 Oct 1893 in Jefferson Co., AL. She died on 3 Aug 1955 at the age of 61 in Birmingham, Jefferson Co., AL. She was buried on 5 Aug 1955 in Peasant Mount Cemetery, Blount Co., AL.

Alice Mae MOSLEY and Lonnie WINNETT were married. **Lonnie WINNETT** was born (date unknown).

Alice Mae MOSLEY and Arthur Jackson BRADY Sr. were married on 6 Sep 1917 in Hamilton Co., TN. **Arthur Jackson BRADY Sr.** was born on 4 Apr 1871. He died on 8 Oct 1954 at the age of 83 in Tuscaloosa, Tuscaloosa Co., AL. He held the title of Sr..

199. **Travis Forrest MOSLEY Sr.** (Hiram Mace-11, William Lafayette-10, George-9, Margaret Vann-8, Edward Ned-7, Mary Lewis Barnes-6, April-Tkikami Hop Turkey-5, Big Turkey Hop-4, Hokolesqua Opechan-3, Cleopatra the Shawano Powhatan-2, Wahunsonacock-1) was born on 9 Apr 1895 in AL. He died on 15 Nov 1979 at the age of 84 in Morris, Jefferson Co., AL. He was buried on 17 Nov 1979 in Liberty Baptist Church Cemetery, Morris, Jefferson Co., AL. Travis held the title of Sr..

Travis Forrest MOSLEY Sr. and Gertrude Lenora REED were married on 20 Jul 1913. **Gertrude Lenora REED** was born on 10 Feb 1898 in AL. She died on 6 Nov 1985 at the age of 87 in AL. She was buried on 8 Nov 1985 in Liberty Baptist Church Cemetery, Morris, Jefferson Co., AL.

Travis Forrest MOSLEY and Gertrude Lenora REED had the following children:

	i.	**Earl Frank MOSLEY** was born on 13 Jun 1914 in Jefferson Co., AL. He died on 20 Oct 1993 at the age of 79 in Morris, Jefferson Co., AL.
	ii.	**Edward Neely MOSLEY** was born on 7 Sep 1915 in Jefferson Co., AL. He died on 4 Feb 1991 at the age of 75 in MS.
	iii.	**Evelyn Eleanor MOSLEY** was born on 31 Dec 1917 in Jefferson Co., AL. She died on 1 Nov 1991 at the age of 73 in Morris, Jefferson Co., AL.
	iv.	**Florence MOSLEY** was born in Dec 1919 in Jefferson Co., AL.
343	v.	**Travis Forrest MOSLEY Jr.**, born 21 Jan 1920, AL; married Earlene KNIGHT; married Jackie Edins LOCKHART; died 4 Mar 1993, San Antonio, Bexar Co., TX.
	vi.	**Jennie Inez MOSLEY** was born on 1 Jul 1922 in Morris, Jefferson Co., AL. She died on 10 Jul 2003 at the age of 81 in Charlotte, Mecklenburg, NC.

200. **Annie MOSLEY** (Hiram Mace-11, William Lafayette-10, George-9, Margaret Vann-8, Edward Ned-7, Mary Lewis Barnes-6, April-Tkikami Hop Turkey-5, Big Turkey Hop-4, Hokolesqua Opechan-3, Cleopatra the Shawano Powhatan-2, Wahunsonacock-1) was born on 27 Aug 1896 in AL. She died on 8 Mar 1965 at the age of 68 in AL. She was buried on 10 Mar 1965 in Liberty Baptist Church Cemetery, Morris, Jefferson Co., AL.

Annie MOSLEY and Ranzy DOSS were married. **Ranzy DOSS** was born on 9 Feb 1891 in AL. He died on 15 Apr 1967 at the age of 76 in Warrior, Jefferson Co., AL. He was buried on 17 Apr 1967 in Liberty Baptist Church Cemetery, Morris, Jefferson Co., AL.

Descendants of Chief Wahunsonacock Powhatan

201. Bessie MOSLEY (Hiram Mace-11, William Lafayette-10, George-9, Margaret Vann-8, Edward Ned-7, Mary Lewis Barnes-6, April-Tkikami Hop Turkey-5, Big Turkey Hop-4, Hokolesqua Opechan-3, Cleopatra the Shawano Powhatan-2, Wahunsonacock-1) was born on 10 Jul 1900 in Kimberly, Jefferson Co., AL. She died on 13 Oct 1980 at the age of 80 in Birmingham, Jefferson Co., AL. She was buried on 15 Oct 1980 in Valhalla Cemetery, Birmingham, Jefferson Co., AL.

Bessie MOSLEY and William McKinley BYRD were married on 3 Feb 1923. **William McKinley BYRD** was born (date unknown).

Bessie MOSLEY and Hobart Garet BYRD were married on 4 Jun 1962. **Hobart Garet BYRD** was born (date unknown).

202. Matilda MOSLEY (Hiram Mace-11, William Lafayette-10, George-9, Margaret Vann-8, Edward Ned-7, Mary Lewis Barnes-6, April-Tkikami Hop Turkey-5, Big Turkey Hop-4, Hokolesqua Opechan-3, Cleopatra the Shawano Powhatan-2, Wahunsonacock-1) was born on 21 Sep 1901 in Kimberly, Jefferson Co., AL. She died on 19 Apr 1964 at the age of 62 in AL.

Matilda MOSLEY and Dennis HUGHES were married on 12 Dec 1923. **Dennis HUGHES** was born on 28 Jan 1901. He died on 13 Jul 1990 at the age of 89 in Gardendale, Jefferson Co., AL. He was buried on 15 Jul 1990 in New Bethel Baptist Church Cemetery, Gardendale, Jefferson Co., AL.

203. Robert Herman MOSLEY (Hiram Mace-11, William Lafayette-10, George-9, Margaret Vann-8, Edward Ned-7, Mary Lewis Barnes-6, April-Tkikami Hop Turkey-5, Big Turkey Hop-4, Hokolesqua Opechan-3, Cleopatra the Shawano Powhatan-2, Wahunsonacock-1) was born on 29 Apr 1904 in Kimberly, Jefferson Co., AL. He died on 2 Dec 1981 at the age of 77 in Morris, Jefferson Co., AL. He was buried on 4 Dec 1981 at Liberty Baptist Church Cemetery in Morris, Jefferson Co., AL.

Robert Herman MOSLEY and Mary Amy Bell CHRESTMAN were married on 23 Jan 1926. **Mary Amy Bell CHRESTMAN**, daughter of Willie CHRESTMAN and Clara COLLINS, was born about 1907 in Tallahatchie Co., MS. She died on 4 Jan 1991 at the age of 84 in Morris, Jefferson Co., AL.

Robert Herman MOSLEY and Mary Amy Bell CHRESTMAN had the following children:

	i.	**Clyde Herman MOSLEY** was born on 29 Dec 1926 in Jefferson Co., AL.
	ii.	**Bobby Edward MOSLEY** was born on 11 Nov 1928 in Jefferson Co., AL.
344	iii.	**Sarah Pauline MOSLEY**, born Jefferson Co., AL; married Thomas STAFFORD.
345	iv.	**John Wesley MOSLEY**, born Jefferson Co., AL; married Kathleen HAYES.
346	v.	**Frank Hiram MOSLEY**, born 22 Nov 1935, Jefferson Co., AL.
	vi.	**Eugene Nolan MOSLEY** was born in Jefferson Co., AL.
347	vii.	**Dan Wilson MOSLEY**, born Jefferson Co., AL; married Sharon NEELY.
348	viii.	**Douglas McArthur MOSLEY**, born 31 May 1943, Jefferson Co., AL; married Juanita MELTON; died 21 Dec 1964.
	ix.	**Leon Wayne MOSLEY** was born on 13 Mar 1946.
	x.	**Joe MOSLEY** was born (date unknown).

204. **S.E. MOSLEY** (Hiram Mace-11, William Lafayette-10, George-9, Margaret Vann-8, Edward Ned-7, Mary Lewis Barnes-6, April-Tkikami Hop Turkey-5, Big Turkey Hop-4, Hokolesqua Opechan-3, Cleopatra the Shawano Powhatan-2, Wahunsonacock-1) was born on 21 Apr 1908 in Kimberly, Jefferson Co., AL. She died on 9 Aug 1971 at the age of 63 in AL. She was buried on 11 Aug 1971 in Liberty Minter Cemetery, Morris, Jefferson Co., AL.

S.E. MOSLEY and James Ernest SELF were married. **James Ernest SELF** was born (date unknown).

James Ernest SELF and S.E. MOSLEY had the following child:

    349   i. **Nora Louise SELF**, born 4 Jan 1929, Morris, Jefferson Co., AL; married William Cuthbert WOOD.

S.E. MOSLEY and George Melvin CRANE were married. **George Melvin CRANE** was born on 3 Oct 1893. He died on 8 Feb 1964 at the age of 70 in AL.

205. **Stella EATON** (Adrin Bethiah Mosley-11, William Lafayette-10, George-9, Margaret Vann-8, Edward Ned-7, Mary Lewis Barnes-6, April-Tkikami Hop Turkey-5, Big Turkey Hop-4, Hokolesqua Opechan-3, Cleopatra the Shawano Powhatan-2, Wahunsonacock-1) was born on 26 Sep 1888 in Morris, Jefferson Co., AL.

Stella EATON and John REEVES were married. **John REEVES** was born (date unknown).

Stella EATON and Henry OWENS were married. **Henry OWENS** was born (date unknown).

206. **Will EATON** (Adrin Bethiah Mosley-11, William Lafayette-10, George-9, Margaret Vann-8, Edward Ned-7, Mary Lewis Barnes-6, April-Tkikami Hop Turkey-5, Big Turkey Hop-4, Hokolesqua Opechan-3, Cleopatra the Shawano Powhatan-2, Wahunsonacock-1) was born on 21 Mar 1891 in Jefferson Co., AL.

Will EATON and Minnie were married. **Minnie** was born (date unknown).

207. **Grover EATON** (Adrin Bethiah Mosley-11, William Lafayette-10, George-9, Margaret Vann-8, Edward Ned-7, Mary Lewis Barnes-6, April-Tkikami Hop Turkey-5, Big Turkey Hop-4, Hokolesqua Opechan-3, Cleopatra the Shawano Powhatan-2, Wahunsonacock-1) was born on 26 Feb 1893 in Jefferson Co., AL.

Grover EATON and BYARS were married. **BYARS** was born (date unknown).

Descendants of Chief Wahunsonacock Powhatan

26 January 2012

208. **Mary Lou EATON** (Adrin Bethiah Mosley-11, William Lafayette-10, George-9, Margaret Vann-8, Edward Ned-7, Mary Lewis Barnes-6, April-Tkikami Hop Turkey-5, Big Turkey Hop-4, Hokolesqua Opechan-3, Cleopatra the Shawano Powhatan-2, Wahunsonacock-1) was born on 20 Apr 1894 in Jefferson Co., AL. She died on 8 Nov 1979 at the age of 85 in Gardendale, Jefferson Co., AL.

Mary Lou EATON and Dan REEVES were married. **Dan REEVES** was born (date unknown).

209. **Eula EATON** (Adrin Bethiah Mosley-11, William Lafayette-10, George-9, Margaret Vann-8, Edward Ned-7, Mary Lewis Barnes-6, April-Tkikami Hop Turkey-5, Big Turkey Hop-4, Hokolesqua Opechan-3, Cleopatra the Shawano Powhatan-2, Wahunsonacock-1) was born on 31 Dec 1895 in Jefferson Co., AL.

Eula EATON and BRONFIELD were married. **BRONFIELD** was born (date unknown).

210. **George EATON** (Adrin Bethiah Mosley-11, William Lafayette-10, George-9, Margaret Vann-8, Edward Ned-7, Mary Lewis Barnes-6, April-Tkikami Hop Turkey-5, Big Turkey Hop-4, Hokolesqua Opechan-3, Cleopatra the Shawano Powhatan-2, Wahunsonacock-1) was born on 23 Mar 1903 in Jefferson Co., AL.

George EATON and Bertie TUCKER were married. **Bertie TUCKER** was born (date unknown).

211. **Jeffery Terence MOSLEY** (James Augusta-11, William Lafayette-10, George-9, Margaret Vann-8, Edward Ned-7, Mary Lewis Barnes-6, April-Tkikami Hop Turkey-5, Big Turkey Hop-4, Hokolesqua Opechan-3, Cleopatra the Shawano Powhatan-2, Wahunsonacock-1) was born (date unknown).

Jeffery Terence MOSLEY had the following child:

      i. **Karen S. MOSLEY** was born (date unknown).

212. **Grover Cecil MOSLEY** (James Augusta-11, William Lafayette-10, George-9, Margaret Vann-8, Edward Ned-7, Mary Lewis Barnes-6, April-Tkikami Hop Turkey-5, Big Turkey Hop-4, Hokolesqua Opechan-3, Cleopatra the Shawano Powhatan-2, Wahunsonacock-1) was born (date unknown).

Grover Cecil MOSLEY and Frances were married. **Frances** was born (date unknown).

Descendants of Chief Wahunsonacock Powhatan

26 January 2012

213. **Etta MOSLEY** (James Augusta-11, William Lafayette-10, George-9, Margaret Vann-8, Edward Ned-7, Mary Lewis Barnes-6, April-Tkikami Hop Turkey-5, Big Turkey Hop-4, Hokolesqua Opechan-3, Cleopatra the Shawano Powhatan-2, Wahunsonacock-1) was born (date unknown).

Etta MOSLEY and Norman THEEL were married. **Norman THEEL** was born (date unknown).

214. **Eleanora MOSLEY** (James Augusta-11, William Lafayette-10, George-9, Margaret Vann-8, Edward Ned-7, Mary Lewis Barnes-6, April-Tkikami Hop Turkey-5, Big Turkey Hop-4, Hokolesqua Opechan-3, Cleopatra the Shawano Powhatan-2, Wahunsonacock-1) was born (date unknown).

Eleanora MOSLEY and MCNEICE were married. **MCNEICE** was born (date unknown).

215. **Bethia MOSLEY** (James Augusta-11, William Lafayette-10, George-9, Margaret Vann-8, Edward Ned-7, Mary Lewis Barnes-6, April-Tkikami Hop Turkey-5, Big Turkey Hop-4, Hokolesqua Opechan-3, Cleopatra the Shawano Powhatan-2, Wahunsonacock-1) was born (date unknown).

Bethia MOSLEY and WINSTANLEY were married. **WINSTANLEY** was born (date unknown).

216. **Colleen MOSLEY** (William Lee-11, William Lafayette-10, George-9, Margaret Vann-8, Edward Ned-7, Mary Lewis Barnes-6, April-Tkikami Hop Turkey-5, Big Turkey Hop-4, Hokolesqua Opechan-3, Cleopatra the Shawano Powhatan-2, Wahunsonacock-1) was born on 18 Mar 1924 in Jefferson Co., AL.

Colleen MOSLEY and Arthur Leonard DANIEL were married. **Arthur Leonard DANIEL** was born on 25 Mar 1923 in Jefferson Co., AL.

217. **Daphne MOSLEY** (William Lee-11, William Lafayette-10, George-9, Margaret Vann-8, Edward Ned-7, Mary Lewis Barnes-6, April-Tkikami Hop Turkey-5, Big Turkey Hop-4, Hokolesqua Opechan-3, Cleopatra the Shawano Powhatan-2, Wahunsonacock-1) was born on 1 Feb 1926.

Daphne MOSLEY and Vernon WATSON were married. **Vernon WATSON** was born (date unknown).

218. **Royce George MOSLEY** (William Lee-11, William Lafayette-10, George-9, Margaret Vann-8, Edward Ned-7, Mary Lewis Barnes-6, April-Tkikami Hop Turkey-5, Big Turkey Hop-4, Hokolesqua Opechan-3, Cleopatra the Shawano Powhatan-2, Wahunsonacock-1) was born on 14 Nov 1927 in Morris, Jefferson Co., AL. He died on 16 Sep 1987 at the age of 59 in Warrior, Jefferson Co., AL. He was buried on 18 Sep 1987 in Morris Cemetery, Morris, Jefferson Co., AL.

Descendants of Chief Wahunsonacock Powhatan

26 January 2012

Royce George MOSLEY and Martha Nan GOODWIN were married on 30 Jul 1950 in Morris, Jefferson Co., AL. **Martha Nan GOODWIN** was born on 4 Oct 1931 in Warrior, Jefferson Co., AL. She was buried in Morris Cemetery, Morris, Jefferson Co., AL.

Royce George MOSLEY and Martha Nan GOODWIN had the following children:

350	i.	**Pamela Sue MOSLEY**, born 25 Mar 1954; married Charles CORSENTINO.
	ii.	**Thomas Lee MOSLEY** was born on 31 Dec 1956 in Arrington, England.
	iii.	**Michael Royce MOSLEY** was born on 17 Feb 1958 in Arrington, England.
	iv.	**Charles Ray MOSLEY** was born on 23 Apr 1961 in Kansas City, MO.
	v.	**Nancy Lee MOSLEY** was born on 19 Apr 1963 in Kansas City, MO.
351	vi.	**Keith Alan MOSLEY**, born 8 Mar 1965, Wahiawa, Hawaii; married Wanda Glenn CRANE.

219. **J.D. MOSLEY** (William Lee-11, William Lafayette-10, George-9, Margaret Vann-8, Edward Ned-7, Mary Lewis Barnes-6, April-Tkikami Hop Turkey-5, Big Turkey Hop-4, Hokolesqua Opechan-3, Cleopatra the Shawano Powhatan-2, Wahunsonacock-1) was born on 25 Sep 1929 in Village Springs, Jefferson Co., AL.

J.D. MOSLEY and Jackie MCCOMBS were married. **Jackie MCCOMBS**, daughter of Robert MCCOMBS and Juanita COX, was born on 23 Jun 1932 in Morris, Jefferson Co., AL.

J.D. MOSLEY and Jackie MCCOMBS had the following children:

	i.	**Sherwin Anita MOSLEY** was born on 17 Dec 1951.
	ii.	**Barry Michael MOSLEY** was born on 15 Dec 1953.
352	iii.	**Mark Duane MOSLEY**, born 30 Aug 1956; married Dorothy Renee RICE.

220. **Gerald Olaf MOSLEY** (William Lee-11, William Lafayette-10, George-9, Margaret Vann-8, Edward Ned-7, Mary Lewis Barnes-6, April-Tkikami Hop Turkey-5, Big Turkey Hop-4, Hokolesqua Opechan-3, Cleopatra the Shawano Powhatan-2, Wahunsonacock-1) was born on 16 Feb 1931 in Morris, Jefferson Co., AL. He died on 7 Jan 2000 at the age of 68 in Morris, Jefferson Co., AL. He was buried on 9 Jan 2000 in Morris Cemetery, Morris, Jefferson Co., AL.

Gerald Olaf MOSLEY and Billie MCCOMBS were married. **Billie MCCOMBS**, daughter of Robert MCCOMBS and Juanita COX, was born (date unknown).

Gerald Olaf MOSLEY and Billie MCCOMBS had the following children:

	i.	**Jerri Leigh MOSLEY** was born (date unknown).
353	ii.	**Barbara MOSLEY**, married Bobby TRUELOVE.
354	iii.	**Billy MOSLEY**, married Carol Ann .
	iv.	**Gregory MOSLEY** was born (date unknown).
355	v.	**Daniel MOSLEY**, married Kathy .

221. **Thelma Mae MOSLEY** (William Lee-11, William Lafayette-10, George-9, Margaret Vann-8, Edward Ned-7, Mary Lewis Barnes-6, April-Tkikami Hop Turkey-5, Big Turkey Hop-4, Hokolesqua Opechan-3, Cleopatra the Shawano Powhatan-2, Wahunsonacock-1) was born on 2 May 1904 in Winston Co., AL. She died on 25 Aug 1975 at the age of 71 in

Descendants of Chief Wahunsonacock Powhatan

Bessemer, Jefferson Co., AL.

Thelma Mae MOSLEY and George JOHNSON were married on 17 Feb 1923 in Guntersville, Marshall Co., AL. **George JOHNSON**, son of Isaac JOHNSON and Mellie WELLS, was born on 27 Oct 1905 in Jefferson Co., AL. He died on 1 Dec 1975 at the age of 70 in Bessemer, Jefferson Co., AL.

222. **Clarence Lee MOSLEY** (William Lee-11, William Lafayette-10, George-9, Margaret Vann-8, Edward Ned-7, Mary Lewis Barnes-6, April-Tkikami Hop Turkey-5, Big Turkey Hop-4, Hokolesqua Opechan-3, Cleopatra the Shawano Powhatan-2, Wahunsonacock-1) was born on 17 Jan 1906 in AL. He died on 26 Mar 1989 at the age of 83 in Jefferson Co., AL.

Clarence Lee MOSLEY and Helen GUTHERIE were married. **Helen GUTHERIE** was born (date unknown).

Clarence Lee MOSLEY and Helen GUTHERIE had the following children:

    356   i. **Karen MOSLEY**, married Eric Allan JONES.
    357   ii. **Jill Stone MOSLEY**, married PAWSON.
    358   iii. **Ashley Nell MOSLEY**, married MARTIN.

223. **Fannie Sue MOSLEY** (William Lee-11, William Lafayette-10, George-9, Margaret Vann-8, Edward Ned-7, Mary Lewis Barnes-6, April-Tkikami Hop Turkey-5, Big Turkey Hop-4, Hokolesqua Opechan-3, Cleopatra the Shawano Powhatan-2, Wahunsonacock-1) was born on 19 Jan 1908 in AL. She died on 22 Dec 1999 at the age of 91 in West Blockton, Bibb Co., AL.

Fannie Sue MOSLEY and David PICKETT were married in 1926. **David PICKETT** was born on 22 Oct 1907. He died on 15 Sep 1990 at the age of 82.

224. **Myrtle Lucile MOSLEY** (William Lee-11, William Lafayette-10, George-9, Margaret Vann-8, Edward Ned-7, Mary Lewis Barnes-6, April-Tkikami Hop Turkey-5, Big Turkey Hop-4, Hokolesqua Opechan-3, Cleopatra the Shawano Powhatan-2, Wahunsonacock-1) was born on 1 Nov 1909 in AL. She died on 7 Nov 1997 at the age of 88 in Pinson, Jefferson Co., AL.

Myrtle Lucile MOSLEY and Wiley Mason MCCOMBS were married. **Wiley Mason MCCOMBS**, son of Elisha MCCOMBS and Lucy MERRILL, was born on 18 Aug 1907. He died on 29 Aug 2002 at the age of 95 in Pinson, Jefferson Co., AL.

Wiley Mason MCCOMBS and Myrtle Lucile MOSLEY had the following children:

    i. **Linda MCCOMBS** was born (date unknown).
    ii. **Wiley Michael MCCOMBS** was born (date unknown).

Descendants of Chief Wahunsonacock Powhatan

26 January 2012

225. **Ruby Estelle MOSLEY** (Robert Elisha-11, William Lafayette-10, George-9, Margaret Vann-8, Edward Ned-7, Mary Lewis Barnes-6, April-Tkikami Hop Turkey-5, Big Turkey Hop-4, Hokolesqua Opechan-3, Cleopatra the Shawano Powhatan-2, Wahunsonacock-1) was born on 12 Sep 1906 in Jefferson Co., AL. She died on 25 Sep 1966 at the age of 60 in Kimberly, Jefferson Co., AL.

Ruby Estelle MOSLEY and Ollie Lee MCCURRY were married. **Ollie Lee MCCURRY** was born on 5 Dec 1905. He died on 20 Aug 1980 at the age of 74 in Kimberly, Jefferson Co., AL.

226. **Minnie Pearl MOSLEY** (Robert Elisha-11, William Lafayette-10, George-9, Margaret Vann-8, Edward Ned-7, Mary Lewis Barnes-6, April-Tkikami Hop Turkey-5, Big Turkey Hop-4, Hokolesqua Opechan-3, Cleopatra the Shawano Powhatan-2, Wahunsonacock-1) was born on 11 Jan 1914 in Jefferson Co., AL.

Minnie Pearl MOSLEY and Clayton BURTRAM were married. **Clayton BURTRAM** was born (date unknown).

227. **Trudy Sylvia WHISENANT** (Myrtle Addie Mosley-11, William Lafayette-10, George-9, Margaret Vann-8, Edward Ned-7, Mary Lewis Barnes-6, April-Tkikami Hop Turkey-5, Big Turkey Hop-4, Hokolesqua Opechan-3, Cleopatra the Shawano Powhatan-2, Wahunsonacock-1) was born on 3 Oct 1906 in Jefferson Co., AL. She died on 1 Jun 1990 at the age of 83 in Gardendale, Jefferson Co., AL. She was buried on 3 Jun 1990 in Moncrief Cemetery, Gardendale, Jefferson Co., AL.

Trudy Sylvia WHISENANT and JACKS were married. **JACKS** was born (date unknown).

JACKS and Trudy Sylvia WHISENANT had the following children:

- 359   i. **Helen JACKS**, married PARKER.
- ii. **Douglas E. JACKS** was born (date unknown).

228. **Clyde Earl WHISENANT** (Myrtle Addie Mosley-11, William Lafayette-10, George-9, Margaret Vann-8, Edward Ned-7, Mary Lewis Barnes-6, April-Tkikami Hop Turkey-5, Big Turkey Hop-4, Hokolesqua Opechan-3, Cleopatra the Shawano Powhatan-2, Wahunsonacock-1) was born on 21 Dec 1907 in Jefferson Co., AL. He died on 25 Jun 1979 at the age of 71 in Gardendale, Jefferson Co., AL. He was buried on 27 Jun 1979 in Old Walker's Chapel Cemetery, Fultondale, Jefferson Co., AL.

Clyde Earl WHISENANT and Lilly Mae were married. **Lilly Mae** was born (date unknown).

Clyde Earl WHISENANT and Lilly Mae had the following children:

- i. **Clyde Earl WHISENANT Jr.** was born (date unknown).
- ii. **William WHISENANT** was born (date unknown).

229. **Olive Inez WHISENANT** (Myrtle Addie Mosley-11, William Lafayette-10, George-9, Margaret Vann-8, Edward Ned-7, Mary Lewis Barnes-6, April-Tkikami Hop Turkey-5, Big Turkey Hop-4, Hokolesqua Opechan-3, Cleopatra the Shawano

Descendants of Chief Wahunsonacock Powhatan

Powhatan-2, Wahunsonacock-1) was born on 15 Jan 1910 in Jefferson Co., AL. She died on 28 Nov 1995 at the age of 85 in Warrior, Jefferson Co., AL.

Olive Inez WHISENANT and BLAIKIE were married. **BLAIKIE** was born (date unknown).

230. **Nightie Mae WHISENANT** (Myrtle Addie Mosley-11, William Lafayette-10, George-9, Margaret Vann-8, Edward Ned-7, Mary Lewis Barnes-6, April-Tkikami Hop Turkey-5, Big Turkey Hop-4, Hokolesqua Opechan-3, Cleopatra the Shawano Powhatan-2, Wahunsonacock-1) was born in Jefferson Co., AL.

Nightie Mae WHISENANT and CASSIDY were married. **CASSIDY** was born (date unknown).

231. **Mary Louise WHISENANT** (Myrtle Addie Mosley-11, William Lafayette-10, George-9, Margaret Vann-8, Edward Ned-7, Mary Lewis Barnes-6, April-Tkikami Hop Turkey-5, Big Turkey Hop-4, Hokolesqua Opechan-3, Cleopatra the Shawano Powhatan-2, Wahunsonacock-1) was born in Kimberly, Jefferson Co., AL.

Mary Louise WHISENANT and RASCO were married. **RASCO** was born (date unknown).

232. **Robert Pytchlynn POLAND** (William Pytchlynn-11, William Henry-10, Hannah Moseley-9, Margaret Vann-8, Edward Ned-7, Mary Lewis Barnes-6, April-Tkikami Hop Turkey-5, Big Turkey Hop-4, Hokolesqua Opechan-3, Cleopatra the Shawano Powhatan-2, Wahunsonacock-1) was born in Sep 1879.

Emer Mildred GRIGSBY was born (date unknown).

Robert Pytchlynn POLAND and Emer Mildred GRIGSBY had the following child:

    360   i. **Daniel Grigsby POLAND**, born 30 Jun 1901.

233. **Lucy POLAND** (William Pytchlynn-11, William Henry-10, Hannah Moseley-9, Margaret Vann-8, Edward Ned-7, Mary Lewis Barnes-6, April-Tkikami Hop Turkey-5, Big Turkey Hop-4, Hokolesqua Opechan-3, Cleopatra the Shawano Powhatan-2, Wahunsonacock-1) was born (date unknown).

COOK was born (date unknown).

COOK and Lucy POLAND had the following children:

    361   i. **William COOK**.
            ii. **Jack A. COOK** was born (date unknown).
           iii. **Charles COOK** was born (date unknown).

Descendants of Chief Wahunsonacock Powhatan

234. **Donnis BUSSEY** (Margaret "Maggie" Boyd-11, Margaret E. Moseley-10, Mason-9, Margaret Vann-8, Edward Ned-7, Mary Lewis Barnes-6, April-Tkikami Hop Turkey-5, Big Turkey Hop-4, Hokolesqua Opechan-3, Cleopatra the Shawano Powhatan-2, Wahunsonacock-1) was born about 1885 in Upshur Co., TX.

Donnis BUSSEY and J.P. FORD were married on 22 Dec 1911 in Gregg Co., TX. **J.P. FORD** was born (date unknown).

Donnis BUSSEY and HORTON were married. **HORTON** was born (date unknown).

235. **Elbert J. GEE** (Clary BUSSEY-11, Hezekiah-10, Mahulda Hulda Moseley-9, Margaret Vann-8, Edward Ned-7, Mary Lewis Barnes-6, April-Tkikami Hop Turkey-5, Big Turkey Hop-4, Hokolesqua Opechan-3, Cleopatra the Shawano Powhatan-2, Wahunsonacock-1) was born in Feb 1877 in Upshur Co., TX.

Elbert J. GEE and Fannie were married in 1897. **Fannie** was born in Dec 1881 in TX.

Elbert J. GEE and Fannie had the following children:

- 362   i. **Lucile GEE**, born Jul 1899, Upshur Co., TX; married LARU.
- ii. **Frances GEE** was born about 1905 in TX.
- iii. **Robert GEE** was born about 1910 in TX.

Elbert J. GEE and Josephine N. were married in 1928. **Josephine N.** was born about 1904.

236. **Dr. J. Everette BUSSEY** (Edward "Eddie" H.-11, Hezekiah-10, Mahulda Hulda Moseley-9, Margaret Vann-8, Edward Ned-7, Mary Lewis Barnes-6, April-Tkikami Hop Turkey-5, Big Turkey Hop-4, Hokolesqua Opechan-3, Cleopatra the Shawano Powhatan-2, Wahunsonacock-1) was born in 1898 in TX.

Dr. J. Everette BUSSEY and Vivian were married. **Vivian** was born in 1899 in TX.

237. **Drue Milton MOORE** (Sarah "Sally" Mahulda Bowles-11, Sarah Ann BUSSEY-10, Mahulda Hulda Moseley-9, Margaret Vann-8, Edward Ned-7, Mary Lewis Barnes-6, April-Tkikami Hop Turkey-5, Big Turkey Hop-4, Hokolesqua Opechan-3, Cleopatra the Shawano Powhatan-2, Wahunsonacock-1) was born on 21 Dec 1881 in Harrison Co., TX.

Drue Milton MOORE and Dallvore "Dolly" Frances HARRIS were married in 1904 in Harrison Co., TX. **Dallvore "Dolly" Frances HARRIS** was born in 1886 in TX.

Drue Milton MOORE and Dallvore "Dolly" Frances HARRIS had the following children:

Descendants of Chief Wahunsonacock Powhatan

	i.	**Henry Chester MOORE** was born (date unknown).
363	ii.	**Emery L. MOORE**, born 1905, Harrison Co., TX; married Carman Balbee SLASHRE.
364	iii.	**Milton Earl MOORE**, born 1908, Harrison Co., TX; married Kathrine STEVENS.
365	iv.	**Estelle MOORE**, born 1 Sep 1910, Harrison Co., TX; married Albert Abb CRAWFORD; died 15 Oct 1966.
366	v.	**Winnie Easter MOORE**, born 1911, Harrison Co., TX; married Clyde H. KILPATRICK.
367	vi.	**John Wilson Bill MOORE**, born 1914, Harrison Co., TX; married Mildred WOLF.
368	vii.	**Edith Mozelle MOORE**, born 1921, Harrison Co., TX; married J.R. Bob MCKENLEY Jr..

238. **Annie Louvenia Lou MOORE** (Sarah "Sally" Mahulda Bowles-11, Sarah Ann BUSSEY-10, Mahulda Hulda Moseley-9, Margaret Vann-8, Edward Ned-7, Mary Lewis Barnes-6, April-Tkikami Hop Turkey-5, Big Turkey Hop-4, Hokolesqua Opechan-3, Cleopatra the Shawano Powhatan-2, Wahunsonacock-1) was born in May 1883 in Harrison Co., TX.

Annie Louvenia Lou MOORE and Jesse Monroe MOORE were married in 1900 in Harrison Co., TX. **Jesse Monroe MOORE** was born in 1871 in AR.

Jesse Monroe MOORE and Annie Louvenia Lou MOORE had the following children:

369	i.	**Harold Gusse MOORE**, born 1901, Harrison Co., TX; married Ira Annie HUFFMAN.
370	ii.	**Albert Roy MOORE**, born 1902, Harrison Co., TX; married Clara Alice HALL.
371	iii.	**Clarence William MOORE**, born 1904, Harrison Co., TX; married Clara MILLER.
372	iv.	**Murrah Lee MOORE**, born 1908, Harrison Co., TX; married Bernice HENIGAN.
373	v.	**Jesse Milton MOORE**, married Mary Eleven EVERITT.
374	vi.	**Sible MOORE**, married WOODSON.
	vii.	**Marton MOORE** was born (date unknown).

239. **Gus Lewis MOORE** (Sarah "Sally" Mahulda Bowles-11, Sarah Ann BUSSEY-10, Mahulda Hulda Moseley-9, Margaret Vann-8, Edward Ned-7, Mary Lewis Barnes-6, April-Tkikami Hop Turkey-5, Big Turkey Hop-4, Hokolesqua Opechan-3, Cleopatra the Shawano Powhatan-2, Wahunsonacock-1) was born in Dec 1884 in Harrison Co., TX.

Gus Lewis MOORE and Lorena S. "Lola" SMITH were married in 1909 in Harrison Co., TX. **Lorena S. "Lola" SMITH** was born on 16 Jun 1890 in Harrison Co., TX.

Gus Lewis MOORE and Lorena S. "Lola" SMITH had the following children:

375	i.	**Aralree Elna Bussey MOORE**, born 1910, Harrison Co., TX; married Oliver JOHNSON; married M. RICHARDS.
	ii.	**Hubert Lewis MOORE** was born on 11 Apr 1912 in Harrison Co., TX.
376	iii.	**Philip Morton MOORE**, born 1915, Harrison Co., TX; married Mary M. LINXWITER.
	iv.	**Floyd Enice MOORE** was born on 21 Apr 1919 in Harrison Co., TX.
	v.	**Eunice Mae MOORE** was born on 18 Jan 1921.

240. **Johnnie MOORE** (Sarah "Sally" Mahulda Bowles-11, Sarah Ann BUSSEY-10, Mahulda Hulda Moseley-9, Margaret Vann-8, Edward Ned-7, Mary Lewis Barnes-6, April-Tkikami Hop Turkey-5, Big Turkey Hop-4, Hokolesqua Opechan-3, Cleopatra the Shawano Powhatan-2, Wahunsonacock-1) was born in Aug 1889 in Harrison Co., TX.

Descendants of Chief Wahunsonacock Powhatan

26 January 2012

Johnnie MOORE and Ross PITTS were married. **Ross PITTS** was born (date unknown).

Ross PITTS and Johnnie MOORE had the following child:

    i. **Leland PITTS** was born (date unknown).

241. **Lillie Mande MOORE** (Sarah "Sally" Mahulda Bowles-11, Sarah Ann BUSSEY-10, Mahulda Hulda Moseley-9, Margaret Vann-8, Edward Ned-7, Mary Lewis Barnes-6, April-Tkikami Hop Turkey-5, Big Turkey Hop-4, Hokolesqua Opechan-3, Cleopatra the Shawano Powhatan-2, Wahunsonacock-1) was born on 9 Apr 1893 in Harrison Co., TX.

Lillie Mande MOORE and Leon Hill DICKARD were married. **Leon Hill DICKARD**, son of Frank Emmanuel DICKARD and Susan Roland COLEMAN, was born (date unknown).

Leon Hill DICKARD and Lillie Mande MOORE had the following children:

377	i.	**Leon Hill DICKARD Jr.**, married Doris BOWLES.
378	ii.	**Ruth Waudell DICKARD**, married Delvin Fat HILL.
379	iii.	**Claudia DICKARD**, married Hiram Bewitt HICKEY.

242. **Guy Ellis MOORE** (Sarah "Sally" Mahulda Bowles-11, Sarah Ann BUSSEY-10, Mahulda Hulda Moseley-9, Margaret Vann-8, Edward Ned-7, Mary Lewis Barnes-6, April-Tkikami Hop Turkey-5, Big Turkey Hop-4, Hokolesqua Opechan-3, Cleopatra the Shawano Powhatan-2, Wahunsonacock-1) was born in Dec 1894 in Hallsville, Harrison Co., TX.

Guy Ellis MOORE and Clara Lucile ONEY were married. **Clara Lucile ONEY** was born (date unknown).

Guy Ellis MOORE and Clara Lucile ONEY had the following child:

    i. **Vernon Odell MOORE** was born on 28 Mar 1918.

Guy Ellis MOORE and UNK were married. **UNK** was born (date unknown).

Guy Ellis MOORE and UNK had the following child:

    i. **Orvele MOORE** was born (date unknown).

243. **Grace BOWLES** (Edward Augustus "Gus"-11, Sarah Ann BUSSEY-10, Mahulda Hulda Moseley-9, Margaret Vann-8, Edward Ned-7, Mary Lewis Barnes-6, April-Tkikami Hop Turkey-5, Big Turkey Hop-4, Hokolesqua Opechan-3, Cleopatra the Shawano Powhatan-2, Wahunsonacock-1) was born on 25 Apr 1895. She died on 22 Jul 1976 at the age of 81.

Grace BOWLES and Marton SMITH were married. **Marton SMITH** was born (date unknown).

Marton SMITH and Grace BOWLES had the following child:

i. **Edward SMITH** was born (date unknown).

244. **Perry H. BOWLES** (Edward Augustus "Gus"-11, Sarah Ann BUSSEY-10, Mahulda Hulda Moseley-9, Margaret Vann-8, Edward Ned-7, Mary Lewis Barnes-6, April-Tkikami Hop Turkey-5, Big Turkey Hop-4, Hokolesqua Opechan-3, Cleopatra the Shawano Powhatan-2, Wahunsonacock-1) was born in 1903 in Harrison Co., TX.

Perry H. BOWLES and Alma were married in 1923 in Harrison Co., TX. **Alma** was born in 1903 in GA.

245. **Albert MCFARLAND** (Mary Mollie Antoniette Killingsworth-11, Mary Lou Tassie BUSSEY-10, Mahulda Hulda Moseley-9, Margaret Vann-8, Edward Ned-7, Mary Lewis Barnes-6, April-Tkikami Hop Turkey-5, Big Turkey Hop-4, Hokolesqua Opechan-3, Cleopatra the Shawano Powhatan-2, Wahunsonacock-1) was born (date unknown).

Albert MCFARLAND and Dorothy PATTERSON were married. **Dorothy PATTERSON** was born (date unknown).

Albert MCFARLAND and Dorothy PATTERSON had the following children:

i. **Harold MCFARLAND** was born (date unknown).
ii. **Edith MCFARLAND** was born (date unknown).
iii. **William "Billy" MCFARLAND** was born (date unknown).
iv. **Ruth MCFARLAND** was born (date unknown).

246. **Myrtis Edith BRADLEY** (Frances Maud BUSSEY-11, William J.-10, Mahulda Hulda Moseley-9, Margaret Vann-8, Edward Ned-7, Mary Lewis Barnes-6, April-Tkikami Hop Turkey-5, Big Turkey Hop-4, Hokolesqua Opechan-3, Cleopatra the Shawano Powhatan-2, Wahunsonacock-1) was born (date unknown).

Myrtis Edith BRADLEY and COLLARD were married. **COLLARD** was born (date unknown).

247. **Maud BRADLEY** (Frances Maud BUSSEY-11, William J.-10, Mahulda Hulda Moseley-9, Margaret Vann-8, Edward Ned-7, Mary Lewis Barnes-6, April-Tkikami Hop Turkey-5, Big Turkey Hop-4, Hokolesqua Opechan-3, Cleopatra the Shawano Powhatan-2, Wahunsonacock-1) was born (date unknown).

Maud BRADLEY and ARTHUR were married. **ARTHUR** was born (date unknown).

248. **Lois Mae VANN** (James Albert-11, James Mason-10, Mason M.-9, Mason M.-8, Edward Ned-7, Mary Lewis Barnes-6, April-Tkikami Hop Turkey-5, Big Turkey Hop-4, Hokolesqua Opechan-3, Cleopatra the Shawano Powhatan-2, Wahunsonacock-1) was born on 3 Mar 1920. She died on 12 Mar 1985 at the age of 65.

Descendants of Chief Wahunsonacock Powhatan

Lois Mae VANN and James Franklin MORGAN were married. **James Franklin MORGAN** was born (date unknown).

249. **Grace Loyce MCCASLIN** (Letty Annety Riley-11, Mary Lavisa Cothern-10, Lavica Jane Vann-9, Mason M.-8, Edward Ned-7, Mary Lewis Barnes-6, April-Tkikami Hop Turkey-5, Big Turkey Hop-4, Hokolesqua Opechan-3, Cleopatra the Shawano Powhatan-2, Wahunsonacock-1) was born on 24 Nov 1916 in Hartshorne, Pittsburg Co., OK. She died on 4 Mar 1989 at the age of 72 in Tulsa, Tulsa Co., OK.

Grace Loyce MCCASLIN and Leslie Eugene SAVAGE were married on 6 Jul 1948 in Greenwood, Sebastian Co., AR. **Leslie Eugene SAVAGE** was born on 5 Feb 1922.

250. **Arthur Leonard RILEY** (Andrew Leonard-11, Mary Lavisa Cothern-10, Lavica Jane Vann-9, Mason M.-8, Edward Ned-7, Mary Lewis Barnes-6, April-Tkikami Hop Turkey-5, Big Turkey Hop-4, Hokolesqua Opechan-3, Cleopatra the Shawano Powhatan-2, Wahunsonacock-1) was born on 25 Nov 1918 in OK.

Arthur Leonard RILEY and Winnie BRITTON were married on 7 Feb 1941 in OK. **Winnie BRITTON** was born (date unknown).

251. **William Leon RILEY** (Andrew Leonard-11, Mary Lavisa Cothern-10, Lavica Jane Vann-9, Mason M.-8, Edward Ned-7, Mary Lewis Barnes-6, April-Tkikami Hop Turkey-5, Big Turkey Hop-4, Hokolesqua Opechan-3, Cleopatra the Shawano Powhatan-2, Wahunsonacock-1) was born on 31 Jan 1921 in OK.

William Leon RILEY and Mavis WOLFORD were married on 16 Nov 1940 in OK. **Mavis WOLFORD** was born (date unknown).

252. **Mary Louise RILEY** (Andrew Leonard-11, Mary Lavisa Cothern-10, Lavica Jane Vann-9, Mason M.-8, Edward Ned-7, Mary Lewis Barnes-6, April-Tkikami Hop Turkey-5, Big Turkey Hop-4, Hokolesqua Opechan-3, Cleopatra the Shawano Powhatan-2, Wahunsonacock-1) was born on 10 Jan 1923 in OK.

Mary Louise RILEY and Howard STOTTS were married on 6 Sep 1942 in OK. **Howard STOTTS** was born (date unknown).

253. **Andrew Lawrence RILEY** (Andrew Leonard-11, Mary Lavisa Cothern-10, Lavica Jane Vann-9, Mason M.-8, Edward Ned-7, Mary Lewis Barnes-6, April-Tkikami Hop Turkey-5, Big Turkey Hop-4, Hokolesqua Opechan-3, Cleopatra the Shawano Powhatan-2, Wahunsonacock-1) was born on 29 Jul 1925 in OK. He died on 23 Aug 1947 at the age of 22 in OK.

Andrew Lawrence RILEY and Sue LOVELACE were married in OK. **Sue LOVELACE** was born (date unknown).

254. **Annie Mae LYONS** (Farrie Cothern-11, Walter-10, Lavica Jane Vann-9, Mason M.-8, Edward Ned-7, Mary Lewis Barnes-6, April-Tkikami Hop Turkey-5, Big Turkey Hop-4, Hokolesqua Opechan-3, Cleopatra the Shawano Powhatan-2, Wahunsonacock-1) was born (date unknown).

Annie Mae LYONS and BURNETT were married. **BURNETT** was born (date unknown).

Annie Mae LYONS and Gill GILBREATH were married. **Gill GILBREATH** was born (date unknown).

Descendants of Chief Wahunsonacock Powhatan

Thirteenth Generation

255. **Ella Mae ROGERS** (Sallie Armstrong-12, Monroe Griffin-11, Sarah Ann Poland-10, Nancy Naomi Moseley-9, Margaret Vann-8, Edward Ned-7, Mary Lewis Barnes-6, April-Tkikami Hop Turkey-5, Big Turkey Hop-4, Hokolesqua Opechan-3, Cleopatra the Shawano Powhatan-2, Wahunsonacock-1) was born in Aug 1900 in Jonesville, Harrison Co., TX. She died in 1989 at the age of 89.

Ella Mae ROGERS and Alda W. HINCHMAN M.D. were married. **Alda W. HINCHMAN M.D.** was born in 1896. He died in Jan 1976 at the age of 80.

Alda W. HINCHMAN and Ella Mae ROGERS had the following child:

380	i.	**Warren HINCHMAN**, born 16 Feb 1921, TX; married Lillian KNIGHT; died 3 Sep 2006.

256. **Nelle WATKINS** (Leslie Virginia Latta-12, Lenora Lee Poland-11, John Stratton-10, Nancy Naomi Moseley-9, Margaret Vann-8, Edward Ned-7, Mary Lewis Barnes-6, April-Tkikami Hop Turkey-5, Big Turkey Hop-4, Hokolesqua Opechan-3, Cleopatra the Shawano Powhatan-2, Wahunsonacock-1) was born (date unknown).

Hampton Oscar MARLEY was born (date unknown).

257. **Flay Latta WATKINS** (Leslie Virginia Latta-12, Lenora Lee Poland-11, John Stratton-10, Nancy Naomi Moseley-9, Margaret Vann-8, Edward Ned-7, Mary Lewis Barnes-6, April-Tkikami Hop Turkey-5, Big Turkey Hop-4, Hokolesqua Opechan-3, Cleopatra the Shawano Powhatan-2, Wahunsonacock-1) was born on 6 May 1892 in Dyersburg, TN. She died on 27 Dec 1911 at the age of 19 in Dyersburg, TN.

Robert Jones BEASLEY Sr. was born on 15 Apr 1884 in Beeville, TX. He died on 26 Dec 1945 at the age of 61 in Beeville, TX. He held the title of Sr..

Robert Jones BEASLEY and Flay Latta WATKINS had the following children:

	i.	**Robert Jones BEASLEY Jr.** was born on 26 Jan 1912 in Beeville, TX. He held the title of Jr..
381	ii.	**Dorothy Latta BEASLEY**, born 19 May 1914, Beeville, TX; married James Meece RUHMANN, 14 Aug 1946.

258. **Louella SMITH** (Thomas Poland-12, Mary A. Poland-11, Thomas-10, Nancy Naomi Moseley-9, Margaret Vann-8, Edward Ned-7, Mary Lewis Barnes-6, April-Tkikami Hop Turkey-5, Big Turkey Hop-4, Hokolesqua Opechan-3, Cleopatra the Shawano Powhatan-2, Wahunsonacock-1) was born (date unknown).

RICHARDSON was born (date unknown).

Descendants of Chief Wahunsonacock Powhatan

26 January 2012

259. **Oscar Newton "Junior" MOSLEY** (William Alexander (Oscar)-12, William Alexander Newton-11, George Benjamin Alexander-10, George-9, Margaret Vann-8, Edward Ned-7, Mary Lewis Barnes-6, April-Tkikami Hop Turkey-5, Big Turkey Hop-4, Hokolesqua Opechan-3, Cleopatra the Shawano Powhatan-2, Wahunsonacock-1) was born in 1916 in Florala, Covington Co., AL. He died in 1995 at the age of 79 in Pensacola, Escambia Co., FL.

Oscar Newton "Junior" MOSLEY and Ruby Lee WARREN were married. **Ruby Lee WARREN** was born in 1919 in Florala, Covington Co., AL. She died in 1997 at the age of 78 in Pensacola, Escambia Co., FL.

Oscar Newton "Junior" MOSLEY and Ruby Lee WARREN had the following child:

382   i. **Linda MOSLEY**, born Escambia Co., FL; married Robert CHAVIS.

260. **Sudie "Sue" MOSLEY** (William Alexander (Oscar)-12, William Alexander Newton-11, George Benjamin Alexander-10, George-9, Margaret Vann-8, Edward Ned-7, Mary Lewis Barnes-6, April-Tkikami Hop Turkey-5, Big Turkey Hop-4, Hokolesqua Opechan-3, Cleopatra the Shawano Powhatan-2, Wahunsonacock-1) was born in 1918 in Covington Co., AL. She died in 1968 at the age of 50 in Florala, Covington Co., AL.

Sudie "Sue" MOSLEY and Dale TWITCHELL were married. **Dale TWITCHELL** was born (date unknown).

Dale TWITCHELL and Sudie "Sue" MOSLEY had the following children:

- i. **Dale Carlton TWITCHELL** was born (date unknown).
- ii. **Michael Lee TWITCHELL** was born (date unknown).
- iii. **Roger Bruce TWITCHELL** was born (date unknown).
- iv. **Pamela Ellen TWITCHELL** was born (date unknown).
- v. **Vickie Sue TWITCHELL** was born (date unknown).

261. **Ferrolyn MOSLEY** (William Alexander (Oscar)-12, William Alexander Newton-11, George Benjamin Alexander-10, George-9, Margaret Vann-8, Edward Ned-7, Mary Lewis Barnes-6, April-Tkikami Hop Turkey-5, Big Turkey Hop-4, Hokolesqua Opechan-3, Cleopatra the Shawano Powhatan-2, Wahunsonacock-1) was born on 1 Aug 1921 in Lockhart, Covington Co., AL.

Ferrolyn MOSLEY and Walter Lafayette STINSON Jr. were married in Florala, Covington Co., AL. **Walter Lafayette STINSON Jr.**, son of Walter STINSON and Myrtie TAYLOR, was born on 6 Feb 1920 in River Falls, Covington Co., AL. He died on 12 Dec 1995 at the age of 75 in Florala, Covington Co., AL. He held the title of Jr..

Walter Lafayette STINSON and Ferrolyn MOSLEY had the following children:

383   i. **Gregory Weylan STINSON**, born 13 Oct 1940, Florala, Covington Co., AL; married Susan YEAMAN; married Sarah Winnette BASS, 30 Jun 1979, Thomasville, Thomas Co., GA.
384   ii. **Sue Angela STINSON**, born 8 Aug 1942, Covington Co., AL; married Robert LAWSON, abt 1964; married Charles GOOLSBY, abt 1989.
        iii. **Rebecca Louise STINSON** was born (date unknown).
385   iv. **Rae Evelyn STINSON**, born 1 Dec 1945, Florala, Covington Co., AL; married Whit GOOLSBY.

262. Martha Louise MOSLEY (William Alexander (Oscar)-12, William Alexander Newton-11, George Benjamin Alexander-10, George-9, Margaret Vann-8, Edward Ned-7, Mary Lewis Barnes-6, April-Tkikami Hop Turkey-5, Big Turkey Hop-4, Hokolesqua Opechan-3, Cleopatra the Shawano Powhatan-2, Wahunsonacock-1) was born on 7 Apr 1924 in Lockhart, Covington Co., AL. She died on 23 Jan 2001 at the age of 76 in Florala, Covington Co., AL.

Martha Louise MOSLEY and John M. RAY were married. **John M. RAY** was born on 6 Sep 1921 in AL. He died on 5 Jun 1979 at the age of 57 in Florala, Covington Co., AL.

John M. RAY and Martha Louise MOSLEY had the following children:

          i. **Bill RAY** was born in Florala, Covington Co., AL.
         ii. **Carole RAY** was born in Covington Co., AL.
386   iii. **Cathy RAY**, born Florala, Covington Co., AL; married Mark STANLEY.
        iv. **Johnny RAY** was born in Covington Co., AL.

263. John Edythe "Edie" MOSLEY (William Alexander (Oscar)-12, William Alexander Newton-11, George Benjamin Alexander-10, George-9, Margaret Vann-8, Edward Ned-7, Mary Lewis Barnes-6, April-Tkikami Hop Turkey-5, Big Turkey Hop-4, Hokolesqua Opechan-3, Cleopatra the Shawano Powhatan-2, Wahunsonacock-1) was born in Florala, Covington Co., AL.

John Edythe "Edie" MOSLEY and Roak TITTLE were married. **Roak TITTLE** died in Jonesboro, Clayton Co., GA.

Roak TITTLE and John Edythe "Edie" MOSLEY had the following children:

      i. **Timothy TITTLE** was born (date unknown).
     ii. **Donna TITTLE** was born (date unknown).
    iii. **Joann TITTLE** was born (date unknown).
    iv. **Barbara TITTLE** was born (date unknown).

264. Betty CRAUSWELL (Spencer Avis "Skinny"-12, Virginia Moseley-11, George Benjamin Alexander-10, George-9, Margaret Vann-8, Edward Ned-7, Mary Lewis Barnes-6, April-Tkikami Hop Turkey-5, Big Turkey Hop-4, Hokolesqua Opechan-3, Cleopatra the Shawano Powhatan-2, Wahunsonacock-1) was born (date unknown).

Bill CLARK was born (date unknown).

265. Betty J. FREEMAN (Trixie Ethelyn Crauswell-12, Virginia Moseley-11, George Benjamin Alexander-10, George-9, Margaret Vann-8, Edward Ned-7, Mary Lewis Barnes-6, April-Tkikami Hop Turkey-5, Big Turkey Hop-4, Hokolesqua Opechan-3, Cleopatra the Shawano Powhatan-2, Wahunsonacock-1) was born (date unknown).

Betty J. FREEMAN and Frank SELLERS were married. **Frank SELLERS** was born (date unknown).

Descendants of Chief Wahunsonacock Powhatan

266. L.C. RUSSELL (Trixie Ethelyn Crauswell-12, Virginia Moseley-11, George Benjamin Alexander-10, George-9, Margaret Vann-8, Edward Ned-7, Mary Lewis Barnes-6, April-Tkikami Hop Turkey-5, Big Turkey Hop-4, Hokolesqua Opechan-3, Cleopatra the Shawano Powhatan-2, Wahunsonacock-1) was born (date unknown).

L.C. RUSSELL and Elizabeth were married. **Elizabeth** was born (date unknown).

267. Thomas S. RUSSELL (Trixie Ethelyn Crauswell-12, Virginia Moseley-11, George Benjamin Alexander-10, George-9, Margaret Vann-8, Edward Ned-7, Mary Lewis Barnes-6, April-Tkikami Hop Turkey-5, Big Turkey Hop-4, Hokolesqua Opechan-3, Cleopatra the Shawano Powhatan-2, Wahunsonacock-1) was born (date unknown).

Thomas S. RUSSELL and Pat were married. **Pat** was born (date unknown).

268. Gladys Lula BUSSEY (Charles Drennen-12, Benjamin Harm-11, Martha (Malinda) Moseley-10, George-9, Margaret Vann-8, Edward Ned-7, Mary Lewis Barnes-6, April-Tkikami Hop Turkey-5, Big Turkey Hop-4, Hokolesqua Opechan-3, Cleopatra the Shawano Powhatan-2, Wahunsonacock-1) was born on 6 Mar 1899 in Lamar Co, AL. She died on 7 Dec 1980 at the age of 81.

Gladys Lula BUSSEY and James Allen SMITH were married about 1918. **James Allen SMITH**, son of Joel Henry SMITH and Mary Frances MOON, was born on 1 Aug 1890 in Lamar Co, AL. He died on 13 Sep 1972 at the age of 82.

James Allen SMITH and Gladys Lula BUSSEY had the following children:

387	i.	**Lillian SMITH**, born 1920.
	ii.	**Henry Arlington SMITH** was born (date unknown).
388	iii.	**Mary Belle SMITH**.
389	iv.	**Dorothy Lee SMITH**, born 25 Nov 1928, Winfield, Marion Co., AL; married Jess Willard JOHNSON, 6 Apr 1946, Marion Co., AL.
	v.	**Charles Edwin SMITH** was born (date unknown).
390	vi.	**Wynonia SMITH**, born 1931.
391	vii.	**Peggy SMITH**, born 1933.

Dewey PRESCOTT was born (date unknown).

269. Velma Leona BUSSEY (Charles Drennen-12, Benjamin Harm-11, Martha (Malinda) Moseley-10, George-9, Margaret Vann-8, Edward Ned-7, Mary Lewis Barnes-6, April-Tkikami Hop Turkey-5, Big Turkey Hop-4, Hokolesqua Opechan-3, Cleopatra the Shawano Powhatan-2, Wahunsonacock-1) was born on 18 Jan 1901. She died on 19 Dec 1988 at the age of 87.

Glenn SHEARER was born (date unknown).

Glenn SHEARER and Velma Leona BUSSEY had the following children:

Descendants of Chief Wahunsonacock Powhatan

      i. **Patricia Ann SHEARER** was born (date unknown).
     ii. **Joyce Glenda SHEARER** was born (date unknown).
    iii. **Norman SHEARER** was born (date unknown).
    iv. **William Verlan SHEARER** was born (date unknown).
     v. **Edmund SHEARER** was born (date unknown).
    vi. **Hazel Valerie SHEARER** was born (date unknown).
   vii. **Dora Frances SHEARER** was born (date unknown).
  viii. **Robert Lee SHEARER** was born (date unknown).
    ix. **Pauline Mildred SHEARER** was born (date unknown).
     x. **Lola Faye SHEARER** was born (date unknown).

Frank LAFFOOD was born (date unknown).

270. **Felix Hobson BUSSEY** (Charles Drennen-12, Benjamin Harm-11, Martha (Malinda) Moseley-10, George-9, Margaret Vann-8, Edward Ned-7, Mary Lewis Barnes-6, April-Tkikami Hop Turkey-5, Big Turkey Hop-4, Hokolesqua Opechan-3, Cleopatra the Shawano Powhatan-2, Wahunsonacock-1) was born on 4 Sep 1903. He died in 1979 at the age of 76.

Georgia KELLOGG was born (date unknown).

Felix Hobson BUSSEY and Georgia KELLOGG had the following children:

392	i.	**Earlene BUSSEY**.
	ii.	**Myrtle Belle BUSSEY** was born (date unknown).
	iii.	**Wanda Lee BUSSEY** was born (date unknown).
	iv.	**Winifred BUSSEY** was born (date unknown).
393	v.	**Hazel BUSSEY**.
394	vi.	**Levicy BUSSEY**.

Arlene LONG was born (date unknown).

271. **Delora BUSSEY** (Charles Drennen-12, Benjamin Harm-11, Martha (Malinda) Moseley-10, George-9, Margaret Vann-8, Edward Ned-7, Mary Lewis Barnes-6, April-Tkikami Hop Turkey-5, Big Turkey Hop-4, Hokolesqua Opechan-3, Cleopatra the Shawano Powhatan-2, Wahunsonacock-1) was born on 26 Jun 1906. She died in 1960 at the age of 54.

Clarence WELCH was born (date unknown).

Clarence WELCH and Delora BUSSEY had the following children:

395	i.	**Illa Mae WELCH**, married Stanley Theodore STOYANOSKI, 20 Oct 1956.
396	ii.	**Dorothy WELCH**.

Descendants of Chief Wahunsonacock Powhatan

26 January 2012

272. **Flora BUSSEY** (Charles Drennen-12, Benjamin Harm-11, Martha (Malinda) Moseley-10, George-9, Margaret Vann-8, Edward Ned-7, Mary Lewis Barnes-6, April-Tkikami Hop Turkey-5, Big Turkey Hop-4, Hokolesqua Opechan-3, Cleopatra the Shawano Powhatan-2, Wahunsonacock-1) was born on 7 Feb 1909. She died on 13 Nov 1999 at the age of 90.

Lawrence HIBDON was born (date unknown).

Lawrence HIBDON and Flora BUSSEY had the following children:

    397   i. **Joanne HIBDON**.
    398   ii. **Louise HIBDON**.

273. **Charles Marshall BUSSEY** (Charles Drennen-12, Benjamin Harm-11, Martha (Malinda) Moseley-10, George-9, Margaret Vann-8, Edward Ned-7, Mary Lewis Barnes-6, April-Tkikami Hop Turkey-5, Big Turkey Hop-4, Hokolesqua Opechan-3, Cleopatra the Shawano Powhatan-2, Wahunsonacock-1) was born on 10 Apr 1912 in Winfield, Marion Co., AL.

Charles Marshall BUSSEY and Louise JEFFERIES were married in 1937 in Watsonville, CA. They were divorced in 1945. **Louise JEFFERIES** was born (date unknown).

Charles Marshall BUSSEY and Louise JEFFERIES had the following children:

           i. **Barbara Jean BUSSEY** was born on 11 May 1938 in Bakersville, Kern Co., CA.
    399   ii. **Charles Freddie BUSSEY**, born 4 Sep 1939, Boley, OK; married Mildred Joy COLEMAN, 7 Sep 1961, Gregory, TX.
    400   iii. **Delora Joan BUSSEY**, born 7 Dec 1943.

Charles Marshall BUSSEY and Esther M. BYINGTON were married on 26 Jul 1946. **Esther M. BYINGTON** was born on 15 Jan 1926 in Haworth, OK.

274. **Oral Lee BUSSEY** (Walter-12, Benjamin Harm-11, Martha (Malinda) Moseley-10, George-9, Margaret Vann-8, Edward Ned-7, Mary Lewis Barnes-6, April-Tkikami Hop Turkey-5, Big Turkey Hop-4, Hokolesqua Opechan-3, Cleopatra the Shawano Powhatan-2, Wahunsonacock-1) was born in Jul 1902.

Thaddeus WALKER was born (date unknown).

Thaddeus WALKER and Oral Lee BUSSEY had the following children:

        i. **Thad WALKER** was born (date unknown).
        ii. **Bill WALKER** was born (date unknown).
        iii. **Eugene WALKER** was born (date unknown).
        iv. **Robert WALKER** was born (date unknown).

275. **Blanche Mae BUSSEY** (Walter-12, Benjamin Harm-11, Martha (Malinda) Moseley-10, George-9, Margaret Vann-8,

Descendants of Chief Wahunsonacock Powhatan

Edward Ned-7, Mary Lewis Barnes-6, April-Tkikami Hop Turkey-5, Big Turkey Hop-4, Hokolesqua Opechan-3, Cleopatra the Shawano Powhatan-2, Wahunsonacock-1) was born in 1910.

Floyd LAWRENCE died on 4 Jul 1986.

Floyd LAWRENCE and Blanche Mae BUSSEY had the following children:

              i. **Bob LAWRENCE** was born (date unknown).
401   ii. **William LAWRENCE**.

276. **Catherine BUSSEY** (Walter-12, Benjamin Harm-11, Martha (Malinda) Moseley-10, George-9, Margaret Vann-8, Edward Ned-7, Mary Lewis Barnes-6, April-Tkikami Hop Turkey-5, Big Turkey Hop-4, Hokolesqua Opechan-3, Cleopatra the Shawano Powhatan-2, Wahunsonacock-1) was born in 1915.

Luther THOMPSON was born (date unknown).

Luther THOMPSON and Catherine BUSSEY had the following children:

              i. **Ann THOMPSON** was born (date unknown).
             ii. **Gerald THOMPSON** was born (date unknown).
            iii. **Mary THOMPSON** was born (date unknown).

277. **Hazel BUSSEY** (Walter-12, Benjamin Harm-11, Martha (Malinda) Moseley-10, George-9, Margaret Vann-8, Edward Ned-7, Mary Lewis Barnes-6, April-Tkikami Hop Turkey-5, Big Turkey Hop-4, Hokolesqua Opechan-3, Cleopatra the Shawano Powhatan-2, Wahunsonacock-1) was born in 1917.

James ALFORD was born (date unknown).

James ALFORD and Hazel BUSSEY had the following children:

              i. **Judy ALFORD** was born (date unknown).
             ii. **Rachel ALFORD** was born (date unknown).
            iii. **Susan ALFORD** was born (date unknown).
            iv. **Melissa ALFORD** was born (date unknown).
             v. **James ALFORD** was born (date unknown).

278. **Daisy BUSSEY** (Walter-12, Benjamin Harm-11, Martha (Malinda) Moseley-10, George-9, Margaret Vann-8, Edward Ned-7, Mary Lewis Barnes-6, April-Tkikami Hop Turkey-5, Big Turkey Hop-4, Hokolesqua Opechan-3, Cleopatra the Shawano Powhatan-2, Wahunsonacock-1) was born in 1917.

Tommy CORKIN was born (date unknown).

Descendants of Chief Wahunsonacock Powhatan

26 January 2012

279. **Walter Edwin BUSSEY** (Walter-12, Benjamin Harm-11, Martha (Malinda) Moseley-10, George-9, Margaret Vann-8, Edward Ned-7, Mary Lewis Barnes-6, April-Tkikami Hop Turkey-5, Big Turkey Hop-4, Hokolesqua Opechan-3, Cleopatra the Shawano Powhatan-2, Wahunsonacock-1) was born in 1924.

Linda PARR was born (date unknown).

Walter Edwin BUSSEY and Linda PARR had the following children:

      i. **Lynne BUSSEY** was born (date unknown).
     ii. **Steve BUSSEY** was born (date unknown).

280. **Bennie Lucas BUSSEY** (Walter-12, Benjamin Harm-11, Martha (Malinda) Moseley-10, George-9, Margaret Vann-8, Edward Ned-7, Mary Lewis Barnes-6, April-Tkikami Hop Turkey-5, Big Turkey Hop-4, Hokolesqua Opechan-3, Cleopatra the Shawano Powhatan-2, Wahunsonacock-1) was born (date unknown).

Leona FRANKS was born (date unknown).

Annie HOWTON was born (date unknown).

Bennie Lucas BUSSEY and Annie HOWTON had the following children:

      i. **Joe BUSSEY** was born (date unknown).
     ii. **Frankie BUSSEY** was born (date unknown).
    iii. **Beatrice BUSSEY** was born (date unknown).
    iv. **Mary Sue BUSSEY** was born (date unknown).
     v. **Bennie Lou BUSSEY** was born (date unknown).
    vi. **Sara BUSSEY** was born (date unknown).
   vii. **James BUSSEY** was born (date unknown).
  viii. **Betty BUSSEY** was born (date unknown).
    ix. **Barbara BUSSEY** was born (date unknown).

281. **Mattie Marie BUSSEY** (James "Jimmy" David-12, Benjamin Harm-11, Martha (Malinda) Moseley-10, George-9, Margaret Vann-8, Edward Ned-7, Mary Lewis Barnes-6, April-Tkikami Hop Turkey-5, Big Turkey Hop-4, Hokolesqua Opechan-3, Cleopatra the Shawano Powhatan-2, Wahunsonacock-1) was born on 6 Sep 1906 in Carbon Hill, Walker Co., AL.

Mattie Marie BUSSEY and Frank Julius FALGOUT were married on 19 Aug 1929. **Frank Julius FALGOUT** died on 11 Jul 1998 in Greenville, Washington Co., MS.

Frank Julius FALGOUT and Mattie Marie BUSSEY had the following child:

  402   i. **Winfred Marie FALGOUT**, born 23 Jun 1932.

Descendants of Chief Wahunsonacock Powhatan

26 January 2012

282. **Mable Ellen BUSSEY** (James "Jimmy" David-12, Benjamin Harm-11, Martha (Malinda) Moseley-10, George-9, Margaret Vann-8, Edward Ned-7, Mary Lewis Barnes-6, April-Tkikami Hop Turkey-5, Big Turkey Hop-4, Hokolesqua Opechan-3, Cleopatra the Shawano Powhatan-2, Wahunsonacock-1) was born on 31 Jan 1911 in Winfield, Marion Co., AL.

James Mikel ROWCLIFF died on 28 Nov 1971 in Greenville, Washington Co., MS.

James Mikel ROWCLIFF and Mable Ellen BUSSEY had the following child:

403   i. **James Mikel, Jr. ROWCLIFF**, born 23 Jun 1946.

Lewis HARTSHORN was born (date unknown).

283. **Ruby Elizabeth BUSSEY** (James "Jimmy" David-12, Benjamin Harm-11, Martha (Malinda) Moseley-10, George-9, Margaret Vann-8, Edward Ned-7, Mary Lewis Barnes-6, April-Tkikami Hop Turkey-5, Big Turkey Hop-4, Hokolesqua Opechan-3, Cleopatra the Shawano Powhatan-2, Wahunsonacock-1) was born on 3 Oct 1912 in Winfield, Marion Co., AL.

Ruby Elizabeth BUSSEY and Merico Cesare "Mike Chester" MANDOLINI were married on 18 Dec 1929. **Merico Cesare "Mike Chester" MANDOLINI** was born on 17 Jun 1908 in Glen Allen, Washington Co., MS. He died on 26 Aug 2000 at the age of 92 in Green Forest, Carroll Co., AR.

Merico Cesare "Mike Chester" MANDOLINI and Ruby Elizabeth BUSSEY had the following children:

404   i. **Ann Elizabeth MANDOLINI**, born 1 Jan 1934, Washington City, Washington Co., MS; married Alton Boman COALTER, 10 Apr 1955, Greenville, Washington Co., MS.
405   ii. **Carl Chester MANDOLINI**, born 20 Feb 1936.

284. **Christina BUSSEY** (George Washington-12, Benjamin Harm-11, Martha (Malinda) Moseley-10, George-9, Margaret Vann-8, Edward Ned-7, Mary Lewis Barnes-6, April-Tkikami Hop Turkey-5, Big Turkey Hop-4, Hokolesqua Opechan-3, Cleopatra the Shawano Powhatan-2, Wahunsonacock-1) was born on 26 Aug 1909. She died on 5 May 1999 at the age of 89.

Christina BUSSEY and Bee COKER were married on 12 Jun 1967. **Bee COKER** was born (date unknown).

Christina BUSSEY and Merlin KING were married in Sep 1931. **Merlin KING** was born on 31 Oct 1911. He died on 17 May 1961 at the age of 49.

Merlin KING and Christina BUSSEY had the following children:

     i. **Pauline KING** was born (date unknown).
     ii. **Buford KING** was born (date unknown).
     iii. **Mildred KING** was born (date unknown).
     iv. **Helen KING** was born (date unknown).

285. **Joe Raymond BUSSEY** (George Washington-12, Benjamin Harm-11, Martha (Malinda) Moseley-10, George-9, Margaret Vann-8, Edward Ned-7, Mary Lewis Barnes-6, April-Tkikami Hop Turkey-5, Big Turkey Hop-4, Hokolesqua Opechan-3, Cleopatra the Shawano Powhatan-2, Wahunsonacock-1) was born on 31 Oct 1911. He died on 12 Aug 1987 at the age of 75 in Salina, CA.

Joe Raymond BUSSEY and Hazel HORN were married in Sep 1931. **Hazel HORN** was born (date unknown).

Joe Raymond BUSSEY and Hazel HORN had the following children:

    i. **JoAnn BUSSEY** was born (date unknown).
    ii. **Leon BUSSEY** was born (date unknown).
    iii. **Marilyn BUSSEY** was born (date unknown).
    iv. **Maudine BUSSEY** was born (date unknown).

Joe Raymond BUSSEY and Alta MOORE were married on 2 Mar 1953. **Alta MOORE** was born (date unknown).

286. **Floyd Francis BUSSEY** (George Washington-12, Benjamin Harm-11, Martha (Malinda) Moseley-10, George-9, Margaret Vann-8, Edward Ned-7, Mary Lewis Barnes-6, April-Tkikami Hop Turkey-5, Big Turkey Hop-4, Hokolesqua Opechan-3, Cleopatra the Shawano Powhatan-2, Wahunsonacock-1) was born on 10 May 1913. He died in Coweta, Wagoner Co., OK.

Floyd Francis BUSSEY and Evaughna THOMPSON were married on 9 May 1937. **Evaughna THOMPSON** was born (date unknown).

Floyd Francis BUSSEY and Evaughna THOMPSON had the following children:

    i. **Carl BUSSEY** was born (date unknown).
    ii. **Floyd BUSSEY** was born (date unknown).
    iii. **Judy BUSSEY** was born (date unknown).

287. **Georgell BUSSEY** (George Washington-12, Benjamin Harm-11, Martha (Malinda) Moseley-10, George-9, Margaret Vann-8, Edward Ned-7, Mary Lewis Barnes-6, April-Tkikami Hop Turkey-5, Big Turkey Hop-4, Hokolesqua Opechan-3, Cleopatra the Shawano Powhatan-2, Wahunsonacock-1) was born on 9 Mar 1916 in Winfield, Marion Co., AL.

Georgell BUSSEY and Gladys Lou GAYLER were married on 3 Sep 1938. **Gladys Lou GAYLER** was born on 17 Dec 1918.

Georgell BUSSEY and Gladys Lou GAYLER had the following child:

    i. **Donna Gaylene BUSSEY** was born (date unknown).

288. **Mary Ruth BUSSEY** (George Washington-12, Benjamin Harm-11, Martha (Malinda) Moseley-10, George-9,

Descendants of Chief Wahunsonacock Powhatan

Margaret Vann-8, Edward Ned-7, Mary Lewis Barnes-6, April-Tkikami Hop Turkey-5, Big Turkey Hop-4, Hokolesqua Opechan-3, Cleopatra the Shawano Powhatan-2, Wahunsonacock-1) was born on 17 Dec 1918.

Mary Ruth BUSSEY and Paul NORTHCUTT were married in 1936. **Paul NORTHCUTT** was born (date unknown).

Paul NORTHCUTT and Mary Ruth BUSSEY had the following children:

- i. **Louie Dean NORTHCUTT** was born (date unknown).
- 406   ii. **Ladona NORTHCUTT**.
- iii. **Juanita NORTHCUTT** was born (date unknown).
- iv. **Maurine NORTHCUTT** was born (date unknown).

289. **Willie Everette BUSSEY** (George Washington-12, Benjamin Harm-11, Martha (Malinda) Moseley-10, George-9, Margaret Vann-8, Edward Ned-7, Mary Lewis Barnes-6, April-Tkikami Hop Turkey-5, Big Turkey Hop-4, Hokolesqua Opechan-3, Cleopatra the Shawano Powhatan-2, Wahunsonacock-1) was born on 28 Oct 1920. He died on 3 May 1959 at the age of 38 in Henryetta, McIntosh Co., OK.

Louella SCHALSKI, daughter of Thomas SCHALSKI and Bertha SIVILS, was born (date unknown).

Willie Everette BUSSEY and Louella SCHALSKI had the following children:

- i. **Billy Wayne BUSSEY** was born (date unknown).
- ii. **Don Thomas BUSSEY** was born (date unknown).

Ruth SMOCK was born (date unknown).

Willie Everette BUSSEY and Ruth SMOCK had the following children:

- i. **Gayle BUSSEY** was born (date unknown).
- ii. **Brenda Jean BUSSEY** was born (date unknown).

Judy UNK was born (date unknown).

290. **Bobby BUSSEY** (George Washington-12, Benjamin Harm-11, Martha (Malinda) Moseley-10, George-9, Margaret Vann-8, Edward Ned-7, Mary Lewis Barnes-6, April-Tkikami Hop Turkey-5, Big Turkey Hop-4, Hokolesqua Opechan-3, Cleopatra the Shawano Powhatan-2, Wahunsonacock-1) was born on 15 Mar 1926 in Hitchita, McIntosh Co., OK.

Bobby BUSSEY and Christina WORTHAM were married on 27 Mar 1948 in Henryetta, McIntosh Co., OK. **Christina WORTHAM**, daughter of Benjamin WORTHAM and Lula Mae POLLARD, was born (date unknown).

Bobby BUSSEY and Christina WORTHAM had the following children:

- i. **Sharon Faye BUSSEY** was born (date unknown).
- ii. **Ronald David BUSSEY** was born (date unknown).

Descendants of Chief Wahunsonacock Powhatan

26 January 2012

291. **Ernest Eugene BUSSEY** (George Washington-12, Benjamin Harm-11, Martha (Malinda) Moseley-10, George-9, Margaret Vann-8, Edward Ned-7, Mary Lewis Barnes-6, April-Tkikami Hop Turkey-5, Big Turkey Hop-4, Hokolesqua Opechan-3, Cleopatra the Shawano Powhatan-2, Wahunsonacock-1) was born on 10 Dec 1928.

Ernest Eugene BUSSEY and Dorothy LINDSAY were married on 7 Aug 1948. **Dorothy LINDSAY** was born on 3 Oct 1932 in Henryetta, McIntosh Co., OK.

Ernest Eugene BUSSEY and Dorothy LINDSAY had the following children:

    i. **Joe BUSSEY** was born (date unknown).
    ii. **Mary L. BUSSEY** was born (date unknown).

292. **Jimmy Ray BUSSEY** (George Washington-12, Benjamin Harm-11, Martha (Malinda) Moseley-10, George-9, Margaret Vann-8, Edward Ned-7, Mary Lewis Barnes-6, April-Tkikami Hop Turkey-5, Big Turkey Hop-4, Hokolesqua Opechan-3, Cleopatra the Shawano Powhatan-2, Wahunsonacock-1) was born on 15 Oct 1933 in Hitchita, McIntosh Co., OK.

Jimmy Ray BUSSEY and Betty KOBLECHECK were married in 1982. **Betty KOBLECHECK** was born (date unknown).

Jimmy Ray BUSSEY and June Rose MORRIS were married on 1 Feb 1951 in Okmulgee, OK. **June Rose MORRIS** was born on 15 Sep 1934 in Hanna, OK.

Jimmy Ray BUSSEY and June Rose MORRIS had the following children:

407	i.	**Deborah Jean BUSSEY**, born 31 Dec 1951, Henryetta, McIntosh Co., OK; married Norman J. CUMMINGS, 15 May 1969, Henryetta, McIntosh Co., OK; married Jerry Thomas CAPLE, 21 Oct 1977.
408	ii.	**Jimmy Eugene BUSSEY**, born 20 Feb 1956, Henryetta, McIntosh Co., OK; married Barbara STUART, 25 Sep, Henryetta, McIntosh Co., OK.

293. **Gladys Sue BUSSEY** (George Washington-12, Benjamin Harm-11, Martha (Malinda) Moseley-10, George-9, Margaret Vann-8, Edward Ned-7, Mary Lewis Barnes-6, April-Tkikami Hop Turkey-5, Big Turkey Hop-4, Hokolesqua Opechan-3, Cleopatra the Shawano Powhatan-2, Wahunsonacock-1) was born on 25 Dec 1936 in Hitchita, McIntosh Co., OK.

Gladys Sue BUSSEY and Danny Ray POWELL were married on 18 Dec 1953 in Henryetta, McIntosh Co., OK. **Danny Ray POWELL**, son of John Wesley POWELL and Susie MIZELL, was born on 30 Jun 1929 in Gennylind, AR.

Danny Ray POWELL and Gladys Sue BUSSEY had the following children:

409	i.	**Kenneth Ray POWELL**, born 5 Oct 1954, Henryetta, Okmulgee Co., OK; married Kay DETURK, Henryetta, Okmulgee Co., OK.
	ii.	**Danny Everette POWELL** was born (date unknown).

Descendants of Chief Wahunsonacock Powhatan

    iii. **Mike Eugene POWELL** was born (date unknown).
    iv. **Stacey Don POWELL** was born (date unknown).

294. **Willie Virginia BOWLING** (Alma Eudora BUSSEY-12, Benjamin Harm-11, Martha (Malinda) Moseley-10, George-9, Margaret Vann-8, Edward Ned-7, Mary Lewis Barnes-6, April-Tkikami Hop Turkey-5, Big Turkey Hop-4, Hokolesqua Opechan-3, Cleopatra the Shawano Powhatan-2, Wahunsonacock-1) was born on 29 Nov 1924.

Hurbert PORTER was born on 28 Oct 1922. He died on 13 Jul 1980 at the age of 57.

Hurbert PORTER and Willie Virginia BOWLING had the following child:

   410   i. **Judy PORTER**.

295. **Verita Mae BOWLING** (Alma Eudora BUSSEY-12, Benjamin Harm-11, Martha (Malinda) Moseley-10, George-9, Margaret Vann-8, Edward Ned-7, Mary Lewis Barnes-6, April-Tkikami Hop Turkey-5, Big Turkey Hop-4, Hokolesqua Opechan-3, Cleopatra the Shawano Powhatan-2, Wahunsonacock-1) was born on 5 Jun 1916. She died on 6 Jul 2009 at the age of 93 in Winfield, Marion Co., AL. She was buried on 8 Jul 2009.

Verita Mae BOWLING and Arvel Parks HOSCH were married. **Arvel Parks HOSCH** was born on 14 Dec 1911. He was buried in Nov 1998 in Goodwater Cemetery, Winfield, Marion Co., AL. He died on 26 Nov 1998 at the age of 86.

296. **Everette DeWayne BOWLING** (Alma Eudora BUSSEY-12, Benjamin Harm-11, Martha (Malinda) Moseley-10, George-9, Margaret Vann-8, Edward Ned-7, Mary Lewis Barnes-6, April-Tkikami Hop Turkey-5, Big Turkey Hop-4, Hokolesqua Opechan-3, Cleopatra the Shawano Powhatan-2, Wahunsonacock-1) was born on 4 Jul 1922.

Florence MAYS was born (date unknown).

Everette DeWayne BOWLING and Florence MAYS had the following children:

    i. **Gary BOWLING** was born on 1 Jan 1943.
    ii. **Roger BOWLING** was born on 5 Nov 1944.
    iii. **Ricky BOWLING** was born in 1948.

297. **Edward Moody WASHINGTON** (Emma Ollie BUSSEY-12, Edmund Moody-11, Martha (Malinda) Moseley-10, George-9, Margaret Vann-8, Edward Ned-7, Mary Lewis Barnes-6, April-Tkikami Hop Turkey-5, Big Turkey Hop-4, Hokolesqua Opechan-3, Cleopatra the Shawano Powhatan-2, Wahunsonacock-1) was born on 11 Nov 1898.

Edward Moody WASHINGTON and Lorene DUTTON were married. **Lorene DUTTON** was born (date unknown).

Edward Moody WASHINGTON and Lorene DUTTON had the following children:

    i. **Agnes WASHINGTON** was born (date unknown).

Descendants of Chief Wahunsonacock Powhatan

26 January 2012

      ii. **Thomas Anders WASHINGTON** was born (date unknown).

298. **Tressie Olene WASHINGTON** (Emma Ollie BUSSEY-12, Edmund Moody-11, Martha (Malinda) Moseley-10, George-9, Margaret Vann-8, Edward Ned-7, Mary Lewis Barnes-6, April-Tkikami Hop Turkey-5, Big Turkey Hop-4, Hokolesqua Opechan-3, Cleopatra the Shawano Powhatan-2, Wahunsonacock-1) was born on 4 May 1902.

Tressie Olene WASHINGTON and Thomas HARRISON were married. **Thomas HARRISON** was born (date unknown).

Thomas HARRISON and Tressie Olene WASHINGTON had the following children:

      i. **John T. HARRISON** was born (date unknown).
      ii. **Audoline HARRISON** was born (date unknown).
      iii. **Robert Earl HARRISON** was born (date unknown).

299. **Earl WASHINGTON** (Emma Ollie BUSSEY-12, Edmund Moody-11, Martha (Malinda) Moseley-10, George-9, Margaret Vann-8, Edward Ned-7, Mary Lewis Barnes-6, April-Tkikami Hop Turkey-5, Big Turkey Hop-4, Hokolesqua Opechan-3, Cleopatra the Shawano Powhatan-2, Wahunsonacock-1) was born on 18 Mar 1904.

Earl WASHINGTON and Fleta STEWART were married. **Fleta STEWART** was born (date unknown).

Earl WASHINGTON and Fleta STEWART had the following children:

      i. **John Edward WASHINGTON** was born (date unknown).
      ii. **Peggy Sue WASHINGTON** was born (date unknown).
      iii. **Earline WASHINGTON** was born (date unknown).

300. **Helen WASHINGTON** (Emma Ollie BUSSEY-12, Edmund Moody-11, Martha (Malinda) Moseley-10, George-9, Margaret Vann-8, Edward Ned-7, Mary Lewis Barnes-6, April-Tkikami Hop Turkey-5, Big Turkey Hop-4, Hokolesqua Opechan-3, Cleopatra the Shawano Powhatan-2, Wahunsonacock-1) was born on 13 Apr 1912 in Dora, Walker Co., AL. She died on 10 Aug 2001 at the age of 89 in Dora, Walker Co., AL. She was buried on 12 Aug 2001 in East Dora Cemetery, Dora, Walker Co., AL.

Helen WASHINGTON and James Leslie SANFORD were married. **James Leslie SANFORD**, son of William SANFORD and Lillie HAYNES, was born on 2 Oct 1903. He died on 14 Jun 1973 at the age of 69.

James Leslie SANFORD and Helen WASHINGTON had the following children:

  411   i. **Imogene SANFORD**, born 13 Dec 1928; married Fred SIDES; died Oct 1996, Dora, Walker Co., AL.
  412   ii. **Nina SANFORD**, born 1931; married Dennis SAWYER.

301. **Tee Ester WASHINGTON** (Emma Ollie BUSSEY-12, Edmund Moody-11, Martha (Malinda) Moseley-10, George-9, Margaret Vann-8, Edward Ned-7, Mary Lewis Barnes-6, April-Tkikami Hop Turkey-5, Big Turkey Hop-4, Hokolesqua Opechan-3, Cleopatra the Shawano Powhatan-2, Wahunsonacock-1) was born (date unknown).

Descendants of Chief Wahunsonacock Powhatan

26 January 2012

Tee Ester WASHINGTON and Arthur William BLACKBURN were married. **Arthur William BLACKBURN** was born (date unknown).

Arthur William BLACKBURN and Tee Ester WASHINGTON had the following children:

413	i.	**Frances BLACKBURN**, married Ollie William MCCRARY.
	ii.	**Mary Elizabeth BLACKBURN** was born (date unknown).
	iii.	**Arthur William BLACKBURN Jr.** was born (date unknown).

302. **Nettie C. BUSSEY** (Lon A.-12, Edmund Moody-11, Martha (Malinda) Moseley-10, George-9, Margaret Vann-8, Edward Ned-7, Mary Lewis Barnes-6, April-Tkikami Hop Turkey-5, Big Turkey Hop-4, Hokolesqua Opechan-3, Cleopatra the Shawano Powhatan-2, Wahunsonacock-1) was born in 1904 in AL.

Nettie C. BUSSEY and GLOVER were married. **GLOVER** was born (date unknown).

303. **Ernest Paul GUYTON** (Luanna BUSSEY-12, Edmund Moody-11, Martha (Malinda) Moseley-10, George-9, Margaret Vann-8, Edward Ned-7, Mary Lewis Barnes-6, April-Tkikami Hop Turkey-5, Big Turkey Hop-4, Hokolesqua Opechan-3, Cleopatra the Shawano Powhatan-2, Wahunsonacock-1) was born on 25 Jan 1912 in Lamar Co, AL. He died on 11 Sep 1971 at the age of 59 in Lamar Co, AL.

Ernest Paul GUYTON and Daisy Cardell HARRIS were married. **Daisy Cardell HARRIS**, daughter of Ozie Dixie HARRIS and Ozema PORMER, was born in 1916. She died on 19 Nov 1952 at the age of 36 in Lamar Co, AL.

Ernest Paul GUYTON and Daisy Cardell HARRIS had the following children:

	i.	**Willie C. GUYTON** was born in 1940 in Lamar Co, AL. He died on 21 Jul 2005 at the age of 65 in Clearwater, FL.
414	ii.	**Roger Dale GUYTON**, born 4 Aug 1948; married Rose Marie MARTIN.
415	iii.	**Helen Faye GUYTON**, born Lamar Co, AL; married Oscar Harry PARKER; died 2002, Gainsville, FL.
416	iv.	**Grady Benton GUYTON**, married Lana KELLEY.
417	v.	**Carolyn Sue GUYTON**, married Farrell LOVVORN.
418	vi.	**Patricia Anne GUYTON**, married Wayne URBAN.

Ernest Paul GUYTON and Katie LOVELACE were married. **Katie LOVELACE** was born (date unknown).

Ernest Paul GUYTON and Katie LOVELACE had the following child:

	i.	**Raymond Paul GUYTON** was born (date unknown).

304. **Otis Howard BUSSEY** (Rufus Thomas-12, Edmund Moody-11, Martha (Malinda) Moseley-10, George-9, Margaret Vann-8, Edward Ned-7, Mary Lewis Barnes-6, April-Tkikami Hop Turkey-5, Big Turkey Hop-4, Hokolesqua Opechan-3, Cleopatra the Shawano Powhatan-2, Wahunsonacock-1) was born on 4 Jun 1911 in Dora, Walker Co., AL. He died on 24 Jul

Descendants of Chief Wahunsonacock Powhatan

26 January 2012

1975 at the age of 64 in Prestonburg, KY.

Otis Howard BUSSEY and Ora Lorien SANFORD were married on 3 Jan 1931 in Dora, AL. **Ora Lorien SANFORD**, daughter of William Oliver SANFORD and Lillie Perry Lou Ada HAYNES, was born on 13 May 1911.

Otis Howard BUSSEY and Ora Lorien SANFORD had the following children:

419	i.	**Daisy Wonnell BUSSEY**, born 6 May 1932, Allock, KY; married Garland D. GODSEY, 7 Apr 1952.
420	ii.	**William Thomas BUSSEY**, born 31 May 1934, Wayland, Floyd Co., KY; married Uldeen CLINE, 7 Nov 1952, Scott Air Force Base, Bellville, IL; married Maria Alberta SOLIS, 25 Sep 1974, El Paso, TX.

305. **Dawson Ellard BUSSEY** (Rufus Thomas-12, Edmund Moody-11, Martha (Malinda) Moseley-10, George-9, Margaret Vann-8, Edward Ned-7, Mary Lewis Barnes-6, April-Tkikami Hop Turkey-5, Big Turkey Hop-4, Hokolesqua Opechan-3, Cleopatra the Shawano Powhatan-2, Wahunsonacock-1) was born on 4 Jun 1913 in Dora, Walker Co., AL. He died on 26 Feb 1972 at the age of 58 in Prestonburg, KY.

Dawson Ellard BUSSEY and Nova Jean HICKS were married in Oct 1936 in KY. **Nova Jean HICKS**, daughter of John HICKS and Liz GUNNEL, was born on 14 Oct 1919 in Mousie, Knott Co., KY. She died on 29 Dec 1985 at the age of 66 in Tutor Key, KY.

Dawson Ellard BUSSEY and Nova Jean HICKS had the following children:

421	i.	**Peggy Jean BUSSEY**, born 6 May 1937, Wayland, Floyd Co., KY; married William Ray COLLINS, 11 Apr 1953, David, KY; married Harold AUGUSTINE, 8 Jun 1963, Delaware, OH; married Elmer RHULE, 21 Dec 1973, Frenchburg, KY; died 6 Jul 2009, Morehead, KY.
422	ii.	**Toby Ann BUSSEY**, born 30 Mar 1939, Wayland, Floyd Co., KY; married Bruce Lewis HOWARD, 19 Nov 1960, Prestonburg, KY.
423	iii.	**Judith Sharon BUSSEY**, born 31 Jul 1943, Paintsville, KY; married Thomas Benton SMITH, 29 Jan 1962, Williamson, WV.
424	iv.	**Rodney Clark BUSSEY**, born 2 Apr 1941, Wayland, Floyd Co., KY; married Helen Elizabeth ADAMS, 25 Jan 1964, Berea College, KY.
425	v.	**Karen Rae BUSSEY**, born 8 Oct 1945; married Thomas John O'ROURKE, 3 Feb 1968, Cynthiana, KY.
426	vi.	**John Rufus BUSSEY**, born 5 Apr 1949, Prestonburg, KY; married Diana Hope LYKINS, 16 Aug 1968, Cannel City, KY; married Edadean BOYD, 18 May 1990, Prestonburg, KY.

306. **Mildred Ethel BUSSEY** (Rufus Thomas-12, Edmund Moody-11, Martha (Malinda) Moseley-10, George-9, Margaret Vann-8, Edward Ned-7, Mary Lewis Barnes-6, April-Tkikami Hop Turkey-5, Big Turkey Hop-4, Hokolesqua Opechan-3, Cleopatra the Shawano Powhatan-2, Wahunsonacock-1) was born on 12 Jun 1915. She died on 27 Nov 1971 at the age of 56 in Marion, OH.

Mildred Ethel BUSSEY and Bruce CONLEY were married on 31 Oct 1936 in Paintsville, KY. **Bruce CONLEY**, son of William CONLEY and Martha CANTRILL, was born on 17 Apr 1907 in Salyersville, KY. He died in Mar 1987 at the age of 79 in Marion, OH.

Bruce CONLEY and Mildred Ethel BUSSEY had the following children:

427	i.	**Ivan Duell CONLEY**, born 1937, Wayland, Floyd Co., KY; married Kathryn PARSONS, Marion, OH.
428	ii.	**Jeffrey Lynn CONLEY**, born 15 Jun 1943, Cleveland, OH; married Margaret HITT, 1967, Marion, OH.

Descendants of Chief Wahunsonacock Powhatan

    429   iii. **Henry Thomas CONLEY**, born 21 Mar 1946, Cleveland, OH; married Freeda Darlene THOMPSON, 30 Aug 1975, Marion, OH.

    430   iv. **Timothy Bruce CONLEY**, born 20 Jan 1952, Cleveland, OH; married Marla JEWEL, 18 Jan 1975, Marion, OH.

307. **Marion Edward "Fat" BUSSEY** (Rufus Thomas-12, Edmund Moody-11, Martha (Malinda) Moseley-10, George-9, Margaret Vann-8, Edward Ned-7, Mary Lewis Barnes-6, April-Tkikami Hop Turkey-5, Big Turkey Hop-4, Hokolesqua Opechan-3, Cleopatra the Shawano Powhatan-2, Wahunsonacock-1) was born on 7 Jan 1917 in Dora, AL. He died on 2 May 1964 at the age of 47 in Union City, NJ.

Helen COLLINS was born (date unknown).

Marion Edward "Fat" BUSSEY and Helen COLLINS had the following children:

    431   i. **Carolyn Sue BUSSEY**, born Marion, OH; married BUTLER.
    432   ii. **Sheila Ann BUSSEY**, born Marion, OH; married GARRISON.
            iii. **Larry BUSSEY** was born (date unknown).

308. **Rufus Terry BUSSEY** (Rufus Thomas-12, Edmund Moody-11, Martha (Malinda) Moseley-10, George-9, Margaret Vann-8, Edward Ned-7, Mary Lewis Barnes-6, April-Tkikami Hop Turkey-5, Big Turkey Hop-4, Hokolesqua Opechan-3, Cleopatra the Shawano Powhatan-2, Wahunsonacock-1) was born on 20 Apr 1920.

Rufus Terry BUSSEY and Lorene LAWSON were married. **Lorene LAWSON** was born on 2 Feb 1924 in Wayland, Floyd Co., KY.

309. **Gwendolyn BUSSEY** (Rufus Thomas-12, Edmund Moody-11, Martha (Malinda) Moseley-10, George-9, Margaret Vann-8, Edward Ned-7, Mary Lewis Barnes-6, April-Tkikami Hop Turkey-5, Big Turkey Hop-4, Hokolesqua Opechan-3, Cleopatra the Shawano Powhatan-2, Wahunsonacock-1) was born on 29 Sep 1921.

Gwendolyn BUSSEY and Jacque Leonard WYNN were married on 15 Mar 1947 in Brooklin Hts., OH. **Jacque Leonard WYNN** was born on 14 Dec 1924 in Cleveland, OH. He died on 19 Oct 1996 at the age of 71 in Cleveland, OH. He was buried on 21 Oct 1996 in Acacia Memorial Park Cemetery.

Jacque Leonard WYNN and Gwendolyn BUSSEY had the following children:

    433   i. **Cynthia Beth WYNN**, born 9 Oct 1948; married Kenneth Lewis JAFFE, 21 Nov 1970, Cleveland, OH.
    434   ii. **Nancy WYNN**, born 16 Jul 1951, Cleveland, OH; married Glenn KOYL, 10 Aug 1973.
    435   iii. **Jacqueline WYNN**, born 15 Jan 1958; married Robert Eric KENNEDY, 20 Dec 1986.
    436   iv. **Susan WYNN**, born 10 Aug 1963; married Scott ALLBEE, 8 Aug 1987.

310. **Emmy Sue BUSSEY** (Rufus Thomas-12, Edmund Moody-11, Martha (Malinda) Moseley-10, George-9, Margaret Vann-8, Edward Ned-7, Mary Lewis Barnes-6, April-Tkikami Hop Turkey-5, Big Turkey Hop-4, Hokolesqua Opechan-3,

Descendants of Chief Wahunsonacock Powhatan

Cleopatra the Shawano Powhatan-2, Wahunsonacock-1) was born on 15 Jul 1925 in Dora, Walker Co., AL.

Emmy Sue BUSSEY and Charles J. GIGANTI were married on 10 Jun 1946 in Cleveland, OH. **Charles J. GIGANTI** was born on 23 Apr 1922 in Cleveland, OH. He died on 20 Aug 1987 at the age of 65 in Cleveland, OH.

Charles J. GIGANTI and Emmy Sue BUSSEY had the following children:

437	i.	**Frank Charles GIGANTI**, born 20 Apr 1950; married Kelly JOYCE, 14 Nov 1981.
438	ii.	**Catherine Ann GIGANTI**, born 1 Jun 1947, Cleveland, OH.

311. **Tommie Lee BUSSEY** (Rufus Thomas-12, Edmund Moody-11, Martha (Malinda) Moseley-10, George-9, Margaret Vann-8, Edward Ned-7, Mary Lewis Barnes-6, April-Tkikami Hop Turkey-5, Big Turkey Hop-4, Hokolesqua Opechan-3, Cleopatra the Shawano Powhatan-2, Wahunsonacock-1) was born on 2 Jun 1925 in Dora, Walker Co., AL. She died on 30 Aug 1980 at the age of 55 in Pikeville, KY.

Maurice E. HALL was born on 31 May 1923 in KY. He died on 29 Jun 1979 at the age of 56 in Pikeville, Pike Co., KY.

Maurice E. HALL and Tommie Lee BUSSEY had the following children:

439	i.	**Patricia HALL**, born 14 Jun 1945; married Arthur Winford CRAIG, 19 Aug 1967.
440	ii.	**Frances Michelle HALL**, born 6 Jul 1950, Pikeville, Pike Co., KY; married James David ENGLAND, 8 Aug 1970, Pike Co., KY.

312. **Naoma "Naomi" BUSSEY** (Rufus Thomas-12, Edmund Moody-11, Martha (Malinda) Moseley-10, George-9, Margaret Vann-8, Edward Ned-7, Mary Lewis Barnes-6, April-Tkikami Hop Turkey-5, Big Turkey Hop-4, Hokolesqua Opechan-3, Cleopatra the Shawano Powhatan-2, Wahunsonacock-1) was born on 23 Feb 1927 in Dora, Walker Co., AL.

Naoma "Naomi" BUSSEY and William Hollie CONLEY were married on 27 Jan 1945 in Leatha, KY. **William Hollie CONLEY**, son of John CONLEY and Hattie HUNLEY, was born on 26 Jun 1925 in Leatha, KY. He died on 2 Nov 1993 at the age of 68 in Burnside, KY.

William Hollie CONLEY and Naoma "Naomi" BUSSEY had the following children:

441	i.	**William Hollie "Bill", Jr. CONLEY**, born 19 Jun 1946, Leatha, KY; married Joyce Lynn MCNEARNY, Maple Hts., Cleveland, OH; married Mary Frances JORDAN, 28 May 1988, Moonachie, NJ.
	ii.	**Navada Ann CONLEY** was born on 7 Dec 1947 in Cleveland, OH.
442	iii.	**Timothy Lee CONLEY**, born 7 Feb 1956, Medina, OH; married Kathlee RAGER, 9 Nov 1974, Cleveland, OH.
443	iv.	**Gregory Christopher CONLEY**, born 20 Jul 1953, Cleveland, OH; married Elizabeth Anne , 29 Dec 1978, Lakewood, OH.

313. **Virginia BUSSEY** (Milton Travis-12, Edmund Moody-11, Martha (Malinda) Moseley-10, George-9, Margaret Vann-8, Edward Ned-7, Mary Lewis Barnes-6, April-Tkikami Hop Turkey-5, Big Turkey Hop-4, Hokolesqua Opechan-3, Cleopatra the Shawano Powhatan-2, Wahunsonacock-1) was born in 1919 in AL.

Descendants of Chief Wahunsonacock Powhatan

Virginia BUSSEY and GRISSOM were married. **GRISSOM** was born (date unknown).

314. **Dora Oliver BUSSEY** (Milton Travis-12, Edmund Moody-11, Martha (Malinda) Moseley-10, George-9, Margaret Vann-8, Edward Ned-7, Mary Lewis Barnes-6, April-Tkikami Hop Turkey-5, Big Turkey Hop-4, Hokolesqua Opechan-3, Cleopatra the Shawano Powhatan-2, Wahunsonacock-1) was born (date unknown).

Dora Oliver BUSSEY and GOSSETT were married. **GOSSETT** was born (date unknown).

315. **Wonnell (Nell) BUSSEY** (Milton Travis-12, Edmund Moody-11, Martha (Malinda) Moseley-10, George-9, Margaret Vann-8, Edward Ned-7, Mary Lewis Barnes-6, April-Tkikami Hop Turkey-5, Big Turkey Hop-4, Hokolesqua Opechan-3, Cleopatra the Shawano Powhatan-2, Wahunsonacock-1) was born on 4 Feb 1933. She died on 20 Jul 1984 at the age of 51. She was buried on 22 Jul 1984 in East Dora Cemetery, Dora, Walker Co., AL.

MILLIGAN was born (date unknown).

316. **Cullen Dexter WEEKS** (Elizabeth "Lizzie Beth" BUSSEY-12, Edmund Moody-11, Martha (Malinda) Moseley-10, George-9, Margaret Vann-8, Edward Ned-7, Mary Lewis Barnes-6, April-Tkikami Hop Turkey-5, Big Turkey Hop-4, Hokolesqua Opechan-3, Cleopatra the Shawano Powhatan-2, Wahunsonacock-1) was born on 30 Apr 1909 in Lamar Co, AL. He died on 3 Aug 1944 at the age of 35 in St. Lo, France. He was buried on 4 Aug 1944 in U.S. Military Cemetery, St. Laurent-Sur Mer #1, France. Cullen was buried about 15 Dec 1948 in East Dora Cemetery, Dora, Walker Co., AL.

Cullen Dexter WEEKS and Velma A. WELCH were married about 1936 in Smithville, MS. **Velma A. WELCH**, daughter of Carl L. WELCH and Dora Catherine BOWLING, was born in 1915 in MS. She died on 12 Aug 1956 at the age of 41 in Birmingham, Jefferson Co., AL.

317. **Era Earl WEEKS** (Elizabeth "Lizzie Beth" BUSSEY-12, Edmund Moody-11, Martha (Malinda) Moseley-10, George-9, Margaret Vann-8, Edward Ned-7, Mary Lewis Barnes-6, April-Tkikami Hop Turkey-5, Big Turkey Hop-4, Hokolesqua Opechan-3, Cleopatra the Shawano Powhatan-2, Wahunsonacock-1) was born on 22 May 1910 in Detroit, Lamar Co, AL. He died on 24 Jun 1983 at the age of 73 in Gardendale, Jefferson Co., AL. He was buried on 26 Jun 1983 in Jefferson Memorial Gardens, Trussville, Jefferson Co., AL.

Era Earl WEEKS and Lillie Myrtle HEATHERLY were married on 29 Jun 1930 in Cullman County, AL. **Lillie Myrtle HEATHERLY**, daughter of John Wesley HEATHERLY and Sarah Jane FREEMAN, was born on 24 Nov 1911 in Cullman County, AL. She died on 4 Dec 1982 at the age of 71 in Birmingham, Jefferson Co., AL. She was buried on 6 Dec 1982 in Jefferson Memorial Gardens, Trussville, Jefferson Co., AL.

Era Earl WEEKS and Lillie Myrtle HEATHERLY had the following children:

Descendants of Chief Wahunsonacock Powhatan

    444   i.   **J.D. WEEKS**, born 12 Apr 1937, Cullman County, AL; married Jane Lynn PEARSON, 6 Jul 1956.

    445   ii.   **Bobbie Jo WEEKS**, born 10 Aug 1938, Birmingham, Jefferson Co., AL; married Bob DAVIS, 4 Sep 1959; died 6 Nov 2011, Douglasville, Douglas Co., GA.

318. **Venice Myrtle WEEKS** (Elizabeth "Lizzie Beth" BUSSEY-12, Edmund Moody-11, Martha (Malinda) Moseley-10, George-9, Margaret Vann-8, Edward Ned-7, Mary Lewis Barnes-6, April-Tkikami Hop Turkey-5, Big Turkey Hop-4, Hokolesqua Opechan-3, Cleopatra the Shawano Powhatan-2, Wahunsonacock-1) was born on 3 Apr 1912 in Lamar Co, AL. She died on 21 May 1990 at the age of 78 at BMC Princeton in Birmingham, Jefferson Co., AL. She was buried on 23 May 1990 at Crestview Memorial Gardends in Adamsville, Jefferson Co., AL.

Troy William PALMER died on 7 Aug in Graysville, Jefferson Co., AL.

Troy William PALMER and Venice Myrtle WEEKS had the following children:

    446   i.   **Mary Sue PALMER**.

                 ii.   **Gene PALMER** was born (date unknown).

    447   iii. **James Walter PALMER**, born 1928; married JoAnn RODEN; died 26 Feb 1995.

319. **Marvin Benson WEEKS** (Elizabeth "Lizzie Beth" BUSSEY-12, Edmund Moody-11, Martha (Malinda) Moseley-10, George-9, Margaret Vann-8, Edward Ned-7, Mary Lewis Barnes-6, April-Tkikami Hop Turkey-5, Big Turkey Hop-4, Hokolesqua Opechan-3, Cleopatra the Shawano Powhatan-2, Wahunsonacock-1) was born on 28 Jan 1914 in Lamar Co, AL. He died in Sep 1982 at the age of 68.

Tommie Lucille HAMBLEY was born in 1922. She died on 15 May 1995 at the age of 73. She was buried on 17 May 1995 at Highland Memorial Gardens in Bessemer, AL.

Marvin Benson WEEKS and Tommie Lucille HAMBLEY had the following children:

    448   i.   **Wayne Martin WEEKS**, married Ann SMITH.

    449   ii.   **Jerry Earl WEEKS**.

    450   iii. **Wanda Gay WEEKS**.

320. **Verda Louise WEEKS** (Elizabeth "Lizzie Beth" BUSSEY-12, Edmund Moody-11, Martha (Malinda) Moseley-10, George-9, Margaret Vann-8, Edward Ned-7, Mary Lewis Barnes-6, April-Tkikami Hop Turkey-5, Big Turkey Hop-4, Hokolesqua Opechan-3, Cleopatra the Shawano Powhatan-2, Wahunsonacock-1) was born on 21 Mar 1917 in Lamar Co, AL. She died on 26 May 1944 at the age of 27 in Birmingham, Jefferson Co., AL. She was buried on 28 May 1944 in East Dora Cemetery, Dora, Walker Co., AL.

Verda Louise WEEKS and Arthur Lee "Pete" HAMILTON were married in 1936. **Arthur Lee "Pete" HAMILTON**, son of George Huston HAMILTON and Laura , was born on 10 Jul 1914. He died on 5 Jul 1971 at the age of 56.

Arthur Lee "Pete" HAMILTON and Verda Louise WEEKS had the following children:

    451   i.   **Betty Lou HAMILTON**, born 11 Jun 1937; died 10 Jun 1970.

    452   ii.   **Ronnie Lee HAMILTON**, born 26 Apr 1941; married Wanda Faye HANNAH, 1959; died 2 Jul 2010, GA.

321. **John William "Billy" LOWERY** (Minnie Malinda BUSSEY-12, Edmund Moody-11, Martha (Malinda) Moseley-10, George-9, Margaret Vann-8, Edward Ned-7, Mary Lewis Barnes-6, April-Tkikami Hop Turkey-5, Big Turkey Hop-4, Hokolesqua Opechan-3, Cleopatra the Shawano Powhatan-2, Wahunsonacock-1) was born (date unknown).

John William "Billy" LOWERY and Ethel MATHEWS were married. **Ethel MATHEWS** was born (date unknown).

322. **Mattie Bee LOWERY** (Minnie Malinda BUSSEY-12, Edmund Moody-11, Martha (Malinda) Moseley-10, George-9, Margaret Vann-8, Edward Ned-7, Mary Lewis Barnes-6, April-Tkikami Hop Turkey-5, Big Turkey Hop-4, Hokolesqua Opechan-3, Cleopatra the Shawano Powhatan-2, Wahunsonacock-1) was born on 27 Jan 1917.

Mattie Bee LOWERY and R.J. BOSHELLE were married. **R.J. BOSHELLE** was born (date unknown).

R.J. BOSHELLE and Mattie Bee LOWERY had the following children:

      i. **Ronnie BOSHELLE** was born (date unknown).
      ii. **Brenda BOSHELLE** was born (date unknown).

323. **Margaret Ruth LOWERY** (Minnie Malinda BUSSEY-12, Edmund Moody-11, Martha (Malinda) Moseley-10, George-9, Margaret Vann-8, Edward Ned-7, Mary Lewis Barnes-6, April-Tkikami Hop Turkey-5, Big Turkey Hop-4, Hokolesqua Opechan-3, Cleopatra the Shawano Powhatan-2, Wahunsonacock-1) was born in 1923.

Margaret Ruth LOWERY and Lehman LOLLAR were married. **Lehman LOLLAR** was born (date unknown).

Lehman LOLLAR and Margaret Ruth LOWERY had the following children:

      i. **Melinda LOLLAR** was born (date unknown).
      ii. **Michael LOLLAR** was born (date unknown).

324. **Mary Louise LOWERY** (Minnie Malinda BUSSEY-12, Edmund Moody-11, Martha (Malinda) Moseley-10, George-9, Margaret Vann-8, Edward Ned-7, Mary Lewis Barnes-6, April-Tkikami Hop Turkey-5, Big Turkey Hop-4, Hokolesqua Opechan-3, Cleopatra the Shawano Powhatan-2, Wahunsonacock-1) was born on 27 Feb 1924.

Mary Louise LOWERY and Adrian O'Neal MCKINNEY were married. **Adrian O'Neal MCKINNEY** was born on 11 Jan 1922.

Adrian O'Neal MCKINNEY and Mary Louise LOWERY had the following children:

   453   i. **Sandra MCKINNEY**, born 29 May 1944; married STORM.
          ii. **Peggy MCKINNEY** was born on 18 Dec 1951.
          iii. **Teresa MCKINNEY** was born on 6 Apr 1962.

Descendants of Chief Wahunsonacock Powhatan

26 January 2012

325. **Thomas Harold LOWERY** (Minnie Malinda BUSSEY-12, Edmund Moody-11, Martha (Malinda) Moseley-10, George-9, Margaret Vann-8, Edward Ned-7, Mary Lewis Barnes-6, April-Tkikami Hop Turkey-5, Big Turkey Hop-4, Hokolesqua Opechan-3, Cleopatra the Shawano Powhatan-2, Wahunsonacock-1) was born on 9 Jan 1928.

Thomas Harold LOWERY and Doris PARKER were married. **Doris PARKER** was born (date unknown).

Thomas Harold LOWERY and Doris PARKER had the following children:

      i. **Rose Marie LOWERY** was born (date unknown).
      ii. **Thomas Howard LOWERY Jr.** held the title of Jr..
      iii. **Billy Ralph LOWERY** was born (date unknown).
      iv. **Jenny LOWERY** was born (date unknown).

326. **Clarence Howard LOWERY** (Minnie Malinda BUSSEY-12, Edmund Moody-11, Martha (Malinda) Moseley-10, George-9, Margaret Vann-8, Edward Ned-7, Mary Lewis Barnes-6, April-Tkikami Hop Turkey-5, Big Turkey Hop-4, Hokolesqua Opechan-3, Cleopatra the Shawano Powhatan-2, Wahunsonacock-1) was born on 19 Jul 1931.

Clarence Howard LOWERY and Rochelle TUCKER were married. **Rochelle TUCKER** was born (date unknown).

Clarence Howard LOWERY and Rochelle TUCKER had the following children:

      i. **Kelly LOWERY** was born (date unknown).
      ii. **Howard Keith LOWERY** was born (date unknown).
      iii. **Cory LOWERY** was born (date unknown).

327. **Aileen HOLLIS** (Mattie Marie "Sweetie" BUSSEY-12, Edmund Moody-11, Martha (Malinda) Moseley-10, George-9, Margaret Vann-8, Edward Ned-7, Mary Lewis Barnes-6, April-Tkikami Hop Turkey-5, Big Turkey Hop-4, Hokolesqua Opechan-3, Cleopatra the Shawano Powhatan-2, Wahunsonacock-1) was born (date unknown).

Aileen HOLLIS and Jesse B. MCCRARY were married. **Jesse B. MCCRARY** was born (date unknown).

Jesse B. MCCRARY and Aileen HOLLIS had the following children:

      i. **Billy Douglas MCCRARY** was born on 25 Mar 1939.
      ii. **Rodney Wayne MCCRARY** was born on 24 Feb 1944. He died on 20 Feb 1991 at the age of 46.
454   iii. **Debbie MCCRARY**, born 1955; married Bill HILL.

328. **James Edward BUSSEY** (Edward "Ed"-12, Edmund Moody-11, Martha (Malinda) Moseley-10, George-9, Margaret Vann-8, Edward Ned-7, Mary Lewis Barnes-6, April-Tkikami Hop Turkey-5, Big Turkey Hop-4, Hokolesqua Opechan-3, Cleopatra the Shawano Powhatan-2, Wahunsonacock-1) was born on 31 Aug 1931. He died on 11 Feb 2008 at the age of 76.

Nell AARON was born (date unknown).

Descendants of Chief Wahunsonacock Powhatan

James Edward BUSSEY and Nell AARON had the following children:

    i. **Jerry Wayne BUSSEY** was born (date unknown).
    ii. **Carolyn Ann BUSSEY** was born (date unknown).
    iii. **James Arnold BUSSEY** was born (date unknown).

329. **Iva Jean PARR** (Ruby Lee BUSSEY-12, Edmund Moody-11, Martha (Malinda) Moseley-10, George-9, Margaret Vann-8, Edward Ned-7, Mary Lewis Barnes-6, April-Tkikami Hop Turkey-5, Big Turkey Hop-4, Hokolesqua Opechan-3, Cleopatra the Shawano Powhatan-2, Wahunsonacock-1) was born on 4 Apr 1947 in AL. She died on 3 Sep 1977 at the age of 30 in AL. She was buried on 5 Sep 1977 in Morgan Chapel Cemetery, Walker Co., AL.

Iva Jean PARR and KEY were married. **KEY** was born (date unknown).

330. **James Thomas PARR** (Ruby Lee BUSSEY-12, Edmund Moody-11, Martha (Malinda) Moseley-10, George-9, Margaret Vann-8, Edward Ned-7, Mary Lewis Barnes-6, April-Tkikami Hop Turkey-5, Big Turkey Hop-4, Hokolesqua Opechan-3, Cleopatra the Shawano Powhatan-2, Wahunsonacock-1) was born (date unknown).

James Thomas PARR and Joyce were married. **Joyce** was born (date unknown).

331. **William Wilford PARR** (Ruby Lee BUSSEY-12, Edmund Moody-11, Martha (Malinda) Moseley-10, George-9, Margaret Vann-8, Edward Ned-7, Mary Lewis Barnes-6, April-Tkikami Hop Turkey-5, Big Turkey Hop-4, Hokolesqua Opechan-3, Cleopatra the Shawano Powhatan-2, Wahunsonacock-1) was born in 1938.

William Wilford PARR and Elizabeth Ann were married. **Elizabeth Ann** was born (date unknown).

William Wilford PARR and Elizabeth Ann had the following child:

    i. **James PARR** was born (date unknown).

332. **Sue BUSSEY** (Euell-12, Edmund Moody-11, Martha (Malinda) Moseley-10, George-9, Margaret Vann-8, Edward Ned-7, Mary Lewis Barnes-6, April-Tkikami Hop Turkey-5, Big Turkey Hop-4, Hokolesqua Opechan-3, Cleopatra the Shawano Powhatan-2, Wahunsonacock-1) was born (date unknown).

George RIDDER was born (date unknown).

333. **Marshall BUSSEY** (Frank-12, Edmund Moody-11, Martha (Malinda) Moseley-10, George-9, Margaret Vann-8,

Descendants of Chief Wahunsonacock Powhatan

26 January 2012

Edward Ned-7, Mary Lewis Barnes-6, April-Tkikami Hop Turkey-5, Big Turkey Hop-4, Hokolesqua Opechan-3, Cleopatra the Shawano Powhatan-2, Wahunsonacock-1) was born (date unknown).

Eloise LIGHT was born (date unknown).

Marshall BUSSEY and Eloise LIGHT had the following children:

    i. **Kerry Marshall BUSSEY** was born in Sep 1973.
    ii. **Joey Lemer BUSSEY** was born (date unknown).
    iii. **Kimberly Kay BUSSEY** was born (date unknown).

334. **Sheila Faye BUSSEY** (Frank-12, Edmund Moody-11, Martha (Malinda) Moseley-10, George-9, Margaret Vann-8, Edward Ned-7, Mary Lewis Barnes-6, April-Tkikami Hop Turkey-5, Big Turkey Hop-4, Hokolesqua Opechan-3, Cleopatra the Shawano Powhatan-2, Wahunsonacock-1) was born (date unknown).

Joe HOFFMAN was born (date unknown).

335. **Carolyn BUSSEY** (Johnny-12, Edmund Moody-11, Martha (Malinda) Moseley-10, George-9, Margaret Vann-8, Edward Ned-7, Mary Lewis Barnes-6, April-Tkikami Hop Turkey-5, Big Turkey Hop-4, Hokolesqua Opechan-3, Cleopatra the Shawano Powhatan-2, Wahunsonacock-1) was born on 31 Aug 1942.

Kenneth SMITH died in 1979.

Kenneth SMITH and Carolyn BUSSEY had the following children:

    i. **Steve SMITH** was born on 14 Jul 1960.
455   ii. **Kimberly SMITH**, born 10 Nov 1963.

Michael KEY was born (date unknown).

336. **Jimmy Carroll BUSSEY** (Johnny-12, Edmund Moody-11, Martha (Malinda) Moseley-10, George-9, Margaret Vann-8, Edward Ned-7, Mary Lewis Barnes-6, April-Tkikami Hop Turkey-5, Big Turkey Hop-4, Hokolesqua Opechan-3, Cleopatra the Shawano Powhatan-2, Wahunsonacock-1) was born on 5 Apr 1944.

Linda STEAGER was born (date unknown).

Jimmy Carroll BUSSEY and Linda STEAGER had the following children:

    i. **Johnny BUSSEY** was born (date unknown).
    ii. **Jimmy BUSSEY Jr.** held the title of Jr..
    iii. **Tommy BUSSEY** was born (date unknown).

Descendants of Chief Wahunsonacock Powhatan

337. **Roy Charles BUSSEY** (Johnny-12, Edmund Moody-11, Martha (Malinda) Moseley-10, George-9, Margaret Vann-8, Edward Ned-7, Mary Lewis Barnes-6, April-Tkikami Hop Turkey-5, Big Turkey Hop-4, Hokolesqua Opechan-3, Cleopatra the Shawano Powhatan-2, Wahunsonacock-1) was born on 12 Nov 1946.

Connie ALEXANDER was born (date unknown).

Roy Charles BUSSEY and Connie ALEXANDER had the following children:

      i. **Scott BUSSEY** was born (date unknown).
     ii. **Jason BUSSEY** was born (date unknown).
    iii. **Brandi BUSSEY** was born (date unknown).

338. **Sandra "Sandy) BUSSEY** (Johnny-12, Edmund Moody-11, Martha (Malinda) Moseley-10, George-9, Margaret Vann-8, Edward Ned-7, Mary Lewis Barnes-6, April-Tkikami Hop Turkey-5, Big Turkey Hop-4, Hokolesqua Opechan-3, Cleopatra the Shawano Powhatan-2, Wahunsonacock-1) was born on 6 Apr 1949. She died on 22 Nov 1996 at the age of 47.

David CAPPS was born (date unknown).

David CAPPS and Sandra "Sandy) BUSSEY had the following children:

      i. **Mike CAPPS** was born (date unknown).
     ii. **Scott CAPPS** was born (date unknown).
    iii. **Tracy CAPPS** was born (date unknown).

339. **Charlotte Loretta BUSSEY** (Johnny-12, Edmund Moody-11, Martha (Malinda) Moseley-10, George-9, Margaret Vann-8, Edward Ned-7, Mary Lewis Barnes-6, April-Tkikami Hop Turkey-5, Big Turkey Hop-4, Hokolesqua Opechan-3, Cleopatra the Shawano Powhatan-2, Wahunsonacock-1) was born on 20 Jun 1952.

Michael CAMPBELL was born (date unknown).

Michael CAMPBELL and Charlotte Loretta BUSSEY had the following child:

      i. **Stacy CAMPBELL** was born (date unknown).

340. **Gwendolyn Joan BUSSEY** (Johnny-12, Edmund Moody-11, Martha (Malinda) Moseley-10, George-9, Margaret Vann-8, Edward Ned-7, Mary Lewis Barnes-6, April-Tkikami Hop Turkey-5, Big Turkey Hop-4, Hokolesqua Opechan-3, Cleopatra the Shawano Powhatan-2, Wahunsonacock-1) was born on 18 Dec 1954.

Vernon Ray "Bo" ANDERSON was born (date unknown).

Vernon Ray "Bo" ANDERSON and Gwendolyn Joan BUSSEY had the following children:

Descendants of Chief Wahunsonacock Powhatan

26 January 2012

      i. **Christie ANDERSON** was born (date unknown).
     ii. **Christopher ANDERSON** was born (date unknown).

341. **Roxann BUSSEY** (Johnny-12, Edmund Moody-11, Martha (Malinda) Moseley-10, George-9, Margaret Vann-8, Edward Ned-7, Mary Lewis Barnes-6, April-Tkikami Hop Turkey-5, Big Turkey Hop-4, Hokolesqua Opechan-3, Cleopatra the Shawano Powhatan-2, Wahunsonacock-1) was born on 17 Feb 1957.

Bruce HILL was born (date unknown).

Bruce HILL and Roxann BUSSEY had the following child:

      i. **Jennifer HILL** was born (date unknown).

342. **Gilbert CREW** (Ludie ABBOTT-12, Adra "Addie" BUSSEY-11, Martha (Malinda) Moseley-10, George-9, Margaret Vann-8, Edward Ned-7, Mary Lewis Barnes-6, April-Tkikami Hop Turkey-5, Big Turkey Hop-4, Hokolesqua Opechan-3, Cleopatra the Shawano Powhatan-2, Wahunsonacock-1) was born (date unknown).

Lucille was born (date unknown).

343. **Travis Forrest MOSLEY Jr.** (Travis Forrest-12, Hiram Mace-11, William Lafayette-10, George-9, Margaret Vann-8, Edward Ned-7, Mary Lewis Barnes-6, April-Tkikami Hop Turkey-5, Big Turkey Hop-4, Hokolesqua Opechan-3, Cleopatra the Shawano Powhatan-2, Wahunsonacock-1) was born on 21 Jan 1920 in AL. He died on 4 Mar 1993 at the age of 73 in San Antonio, Bexar Co., TX. He held the title of Jr..

Travis Forrest MOSLEY Jr. and Earlene KNIGHT were married. **Earlene KNIGHT** was born (date unknown).

Travis Forrest MOSLEY Jr. and Jackie Edins LOCKHART were married. **Jackie Edins LOCKHART** was born on 16 Jul 1926. She died on 17 Jan 1999 at the age of 72.

344. **Sarah Pauline MOSLEY** (Robert Herman-12, Hiram Mace-11, William Lafayette-10, George-9, Margaret Vann-8, Edward Ned-7, Mary Lewis Barnes-6, April-Tkikami Hop Turkey-5, Big Turkey Hop-4, Hokolesqua Opechan-3, Cleopatra the Shawano Powhatan-2, Wahunsonacock-1) was born in Jefferson Co., AL.

Sarah Pauline MOSLEY and Thomas STAFFORD were married. **Thomas STAFFORD** was born (date unknown).

Descendants of Chief Wahunsonacock Powhatan

26 January 2012

345. **John Wesley MOSLEY** (Robert Herman-12, Hiram Mace-11, William Lafayette-10, George-9, Margaret Vann-8, Edward Ned-7, Mary Lewis Barnes-6, April-Tkikami Hop Turkey-5, Big Turkey Hop-4, Hokolesqua Opechan-3, Cleopatra the Shawano Powhatan-2, Wahunsonacock-1) was born in Jefferson Co., AL.

John Wesley MOSLEY and Kathleen HAYES were married. **Kathleen HAYES** was born (date unknown).

346. **Frank Hiram MOSLEY** (Robert Herman-12, Hiram Mace-11, William Lafayette-10, George-9, Margaret Vann-8, Edward Ned-7, Mary Lewis Barnes-6, April-Tkikami Hop Turkey-5, Big Turkey Hop-4, Hokolesqua Opechan-3, Cleopatra the Shawano Powhatan-2, Wahunsonacock-1) was born on 22 Nov 1935 in Jefferson Co., AL.

Frank Hiram MOSLEY had the following children:

       i. **Michael Frank MOSLEY** was born (date unknown).
      ii. **Susan Leigh MOSLEY** was born (date unknown).
456 iii. **Sandra MOSLEY**, born 2 Jan 1962; married George Lewis HAWKINS, 22 Oct 2004; married Phillip Anthony ROPER, 1963, Jefferson Co., AL.
     iv. **Patricia Diane MOSLEY** was born (date unknown).

347. **Dan Wilson MOSLEY** (Robert Herman-12, Hiram Mace-11, William Lafayette-10, George-9, Margaret Vann-8, Edward Ned-7, Mary Lewis Barnes-6, April-Tkikami Hop Turkey-5, Big Turkey Hop-4, Hokolesqua Opechan-3, Cleopatra the Shawano Powhatan-2, Wahunsonacock-1) was born in Jefferson Co., AL.

Dan Wilson MOSLEY and Sharon NEELY were married. **Sharon NEELY** was born (date unknown).

348. **Douglas McArthur MOSLEY** (Robert Herman-12, Hiram Mace-11, William Lafayette-10, George-9, Margaret Vann-8, Edward Ned-7, Mary Lewis Barnes-6, April-Tkikami Hop Turkey-5, Big Turkey Hop-4, Hokolesqua Opechan-3, Cleopatra the Shawano Powhatan-2, Wahunsonacock-1) was born on 31 May 1943 in Jefferson Co., AL. He died on 21 Dec 1964 at the age of 21.

Douglas McArthur MOSLEY and Juanita MELTON were married. **Juanita MELTON** was born (date unknown).

349. **Nora Louise SELF** (S.E. Mosley-12, Hiram Mace-11, William Lafayette-10, George-9, Margaret Vann-8, Edward Ned-7, Mary Lewis Barnes-6, April-Tkikami Hop Turkey-5, Big Turkey Hop-4, Hokolesqua Opechan-3, Cleopatra the Shawano Powhatan-2, Wahunsonacock-1) was born on 4 Jan 1929 in Morris, Jefferson Co., AL.

Nora Louise SELF and William Cuthbert WOOD were married. **William Cuthbert WOOD** was born (date unknown).

William Cuthbert WOOD and Nora Louise SELF had the following child:

    i. **Tammie Lynne WOOD** was born on 25 Jun 1959 in Birmingham, Jefferson Co., AL.

350. **Pamela Sue MOSLEY** (Royce George-12, William Lee-11, William Lafayette-10, George-9, Margaret Vann-8, Edward Ned-7, Mary Lewis Barnes-6, April-Tkikami Hop Turkey-5, Big Turkey Hop-4, Hokolesqua Opechan-3, Cleopatra the Shawano Powhatan-2, Wahunsonacock-1) was born on 25 Mar 1954.

Pamela Sue MOSLEY and Charles CORSENTINO were married. **Charles CORSENTINO** was born on 12 Jun 1942 in Fairfield, Jefferson Co., AL.

351. **Keith Alan MOSLEY** (Royce George-12, William Lee-11, William Lafayette-10, George-9, Margaret Vann-8, Edward Ned-7, Mary Lewis Barnes-6, April-Tkikami Hop Turkey-5, Big Turkey Hop-4, Hokolesqua Opechan-3, Cleopatra the Shawano Powhatan-2, Wahunsonacock-1) was born on 8 Mar 1965 in Wahiawa, Hawaii.

Keith Alan MOSLEY and Wanda Glenn CRANE were married. **Wanda Glenn CRANE** was born on 25 Nov 1964 in Warrior, Jefferson Co., AL.

Keith Alan MOSLEY and Wanda Glenn CRANE had the following child:

    i. **Elizabeth Crane MOSLEY** was born on 25 Apr 1991.

352. **Mark Duane MOSLEY** (J.D.-12, William Lee-11, William Lafayette-10, George-9, Margaret Vann-8, Edward Ned-7, Mary Lewis Barnes-6, April-Tkikami Hop Turkey-5, Big Turkey Hop-4, Hokolesqua Opechan-3, Cleopatra the Shawano Powhatan-2, Wahunsonacock-1) was born on 30 Aug 1956.

Mark Duane MOSLEY and Dorothy Renee RICE were married. **Dorothy Renee RICE** was born (date unknown).

353. **Barbara MOSLEY** (Gerald Olaf-12, William Lee-11, William Lafayette-10, George-9, Margaret Vann-8, Edward Ned-7, Mary Lewis Barnes-6, April-Tkikami Hop Turkey-5, Big Turkey Hop-4, Hokolesqua Opechan-3, Cleopatra the Shawano Powhatan-2, Wahunsonacock-1) was born (date unknown).

Barbara MOSLEY and Bobby TRUELOVE were married. **Bobby TRUELOVE** was born (date unknown).

354. **Billy MOSLEY** (Gerald Olaf-12, William Lee-11, William Lafayette-10, George-9, Margaret Vann-8, Edward Ned-7, Mary Lewis Barnes-6, April-Tkikami Hop Turkey-5, Big Turkey Hop-4, Hokolesqua Opechan-3, Cleopatra the Shawano

Powhatan-2, Wahunsonacock-1) was born (date unknown).

Billy MOSLEY and Carol Ann were married. **Carol Ann** was born (date unknown).

355. **Daniel MOSLEY** (Gerald Olaf-12, William Lee-11, William Lafayette-10, George-9, Margaret Vann-8, Edward Ned-7, Mary Lewis Barnes-6, April-Tkikami Hop Turkey-5, Big Turkey Hop-4, Hokolesqua Opechan-3, Cleopatra the Shawano Powhatan-2, Wahunsonacock-1) was born (date unknown).

Daniel MOSLEY and Kathy were married. **Kathy** was born (date unknown).

356. **Karen MOSLEY** (Clarence Lee-12, William Lee-11, William Lafayette-10, George-9, Margaret Vann-8, Edward Ned-7, Mary Lewis Barnes-6, April-Tkikami Hop Turkey-5, Big Turkey Hop-4, Hokolesqua Opechan-3, Cleopatra the Shawano Powhatan-2, Wahunsonacock-1) was born (date unknown).

Karen MOSLEY and Eric Allan JONES were married. **Eric Allan JONES** was born (date unknown).

357. **Jill Stone MOSLEY** (Clarence Lee-12, William Lee-11, William Lafayette-10, George-9, Margaret Vann-8, Edward Ned-7, Mary Lewis Barnes-6, April-Tkikami Hop Turkey-5, Big Turkey Hop-4, Hokolesqua Opechan-3, Cleopatra the Shawano Powhatan-2, Wahunsonacock-1) was born (date unknown).

Jill Stone MOSLEY and PAWSON were married. **PAWSON** was born (date unknown).

358. **Ashley Nell MOSLEY** (Clarence Lee-12, William Lee-11, William Lafayette-10, George-9, Margaret Vann-8, Edward Ned-7, Mary Lewis Barnes-6, April-Tkikami Hop Turkey-5, Big Turkey Hop-4, Hokolesqua Opechan-3, Cleopatra the Shawano Powhatan-2, Wahunsonacock-1) was born (date unknown).

Ashley Nell MOSLEY and MARTIN were married. **MARTIN** was born (date unknown).

359. **Helen JACKS** (Trudy Sylvia Whisenant-12, Myrtle Addie Mosley-11, William Lafayette-10, George-9, Margaret Vann-8, Edward Ned-7, Mary Lewis Barnes-6, April-Tkikami Hop Turkey-5, Big Turkey Hop-4, Hokolesqua Opechan-3, Cleopatra the Shawano Powhatan-2, Wahunsonacock-1) was born (date unknown).

Helen JACKS and PARKER were married. **PARKER** was born (date unknown).

360. **Daniel Grigsby POLAND** (Robert Pytchlynn-12, William Pytchlynn-11, William Henry-10, Hannah Moseley-9, Margaret Vann-8, Edward Ned-7, Mary Lewis Barnes-6, April-Tkikami Hop Turkey-5, Big Turkey Hop-4, Hokolesqua Opechan-3, Cleopatra the Shawano Powhatan-2, Wahunsonacock-1) was born on 30 Jun 1901.

Adalyn J. YOUNG was born on 11 Nov 1903.

361. **William COOK** (Lucy Poland-12, William Pytchlynn-11, William Henry-10, Hannah Moseley-9, Margaret Vann-8, Edward Ned-7, Mary Lewis Barnes-6, April-Tkikami Hop Turkey-5, Big Turkey Hop-4, Hokolesqua Opechan-3, Cleopatra the Shawano Powhatan-2, Wahunsonacock-1) was born (date unknown).

Mary Lil DICKENS was born (date unknown).

362. **Lucile GEE** (Elbert J.-12, Clary BUSSEY-11, Hezekiah-10, Mahulda Hulda Moseley-9, Margaret Vann-8, Edward Ned-7, Mary Lewis Barnes-6, April-Tkikami Hop Turkey-5, Big Turkey Hop-4, Hokolesqua Opechan-3, Cleopatra the Shawano Powhatan-2, Wahunsonacock-1) was born in Jul 1899 in Upshur Co., TX.

Lucile GEE and LARU were married. **LARU** was born (date unknown).

LARU and Lucile GEE had the following child:

    i. **Elizabeth J. LARU** was born about 1917 in TX.

363. **Emery L. MOORE** (Drue Milton-12, Sarah "Sally" Mahulda Bowles-11, Sarah Ann BUSSEY-10, Mahulda Hulda Moseley-9, Margaret Vann-8, Edward Ned-7, Mary Lewis Barnes-6, April-Tkikami Hop Turkey-5, Big Turkey Hop-4, Hokolesqua Opechan-3, Cleopatra the Shawano Powhatan-2, Wahunsonacock-1) was born in 1905 in Harrison Co., TX.

Emery L. MOORE and Carman Balbee SLASHRE were married. **Carman Balbee SLASHRE** was born (date unknown).

364. **Milton Earl MOORE** (Drue Milton-12, Sarah "Sally" Mahulda Bowles-11, Sarah Ann BUSSEY-10, Mahulda Hulda Moseley-9, Margaret Vann-8, Edward Ned-7, Mary Lewis Barnes-6, April-Tkikami Hop Turkey-5, Big Turkey Hop-4, Hokolesqua Opechan-3, Cleopatra the Shawano Powhatan-2, Wahunsonacock-1) was born in 1908 in Harrison Co., TX.

Milton Earl MOORE and Kathrine STEVENS were married. **Kathrine STEVENS** was born (date unknown).

Milton Earl MOORE and Kathrine STEVENS had the following children:

    i. **Bobbie MOORE** was born (date unknown).

ii. **Robben MOORE** was born (date unknown).
  iii. **Kesley Earil MOORE** was born (date unknown).

365. **Estelle MOORE** (Drue Milton-12, Sarah "Sally" Mahulda Bowles-11, Sarah Ann BUSSEY-10, Mahulda Hulda Moseley-9, Margaret Vann-8, Edward Ned-7, Mary Lewis Barnes-6, April-Tkikami Hop Turkey-5, Big Turkey Hop-4, Hokolesqua Opechan-3, Cleopatra the Shawano Powhatan-2, Wahunsonacock-1) was born on 1 Sep 1910 in Harrison Co., TX. She died on 15 Oct 1966 at the age of 56.

Estelle MOORE and Albert Abb CRAWFORD were married. **Albert Abb CRAWFORD** was born (date unknown).

Albert Abb CRAWFORD and Estelle MOORE had the following children:

  i. **John CRAWFORD** was born (date unknown).
  ii. **Bobby CRAWFORD** was born (date unknown).
  iii. **Carland CRAWFORD** was born (date unknown).
  iv. **Arnold Wayne CRAWFORD** was born (date unknown).

366. **Winnie Easter MOORE** (Drue Milton-12, Sarah "Sally" Mahulda Bowles-11, Sarah Ann BUSSEY-10, Mahulda Hulda Moseley-9, Margaret Vann-8, Edward Ned-7, Mary Lewis Barnes-6, April-Tkikami Hop Turkey-5, Big Turkey Hop-4, Hokolesqua Opechan-3, Cleopatra the Shawano Powhatan-2, Wahunsonacock-1) was born in 1911 in Harrison Co., TX.

Winnie Easter MOORE and Clyde H. KILPATRICK were married. **Clyde H. KILPATRICK** was born (date unknown).

Clyde H. KILPATRICK and Winnie Easter MOORE had the following children:

  i. **Doris Marie KILPATRICK** was born (date unknown).
  ii. **David KILPATRICK** was born (date unknown).
  iii. **Betty Ruth KILPATRICK** was born (date unknown).

367. **John Wilson Bill MOORE** (Drue Milton-12, Sarah "Sally" Mahulda Bowles-11, Sarah Ann BUSSEY-10, Mahulda Hulda Moseley-9, Margaret Vann-8, Edward Ned-7, Mary Lewis Barnes-6, April-Tkikami Hop Turkey-5, Big Turkey Hop-4, Hokolesqua Opechan-3, Cleopatra the Shawano Powhatan-2, Wahunsonacock-1) was born in 1914 in Harrison Co., TX.

John Wilson Bill MOORE and Mildred WOLF were married. **Mildred WOLF** was born (date unknown).

John Wilson Bill MOORE and Mildred WOLF had the following children:

  i. **Janet Dall MOORE** was born (date unknown).
  ii. **Mary MOORE** was born (date unknown).
  iii. **Nance MOORE** was born (date unknown).

368. **Edith Mozelle MOORE** (Drue Milton-12, Sarah "Sally" Mahulda Bowles-11, Sarah Ann BUSSEY-10, Mahulda Hulda Moseley-9, Margaret Vann-8, Edward Ned-7, Mary Lewis Barnes-6, April-Tkikami Hop Turkey-5, Big Turkey Hop-4,

Hokolesqua Opechan-3, Cleopatra the Shawano Powhatan-2, Wahunsonacock-1) was born in 1921 in Harrison Co., TX.

Edith Mozelle MOORE and J.R. Bob MCKENLEY Jr. were married. **J.R. Bob MCKENLEY Jr.** held the title of Jr..

J.R. Bob MCKENLEY and Edith Mozelle MOORE had the following children:

    i. **Rob MCKENLEY** was born (date unknown).
    ii. **Lande MCKENLEY** was born (date unknown).
    iii. **Steve MCKENLEY** was born (date unknown).

369. **Harold Gusse MOORE** (Annie Louvenia Lou Moore-12, Sarah "Sally" Mahulda Bowles-11, Sarah Ann BUSSEY-10, Mahulda Hulda Moseley-9, Margaret Vann-8, Edward Ned-7, Mary Lewis Barnes-6, April-Tkikami Hop Turkey-5, Big Turkey Hop-4, Hokolesqua Opechan-3, Cleopatra the Shawano Powhatan-2, Wahunsonacock-1) was born in 1901 in Harrison Co., TX.

Harold Gusse MOORE and Ira Annie HUFFMAN were married. **Ira Annie HUFFMAN** was born (date unknown).

Harold Gusse MOORE and Ira Annie HUFFMAN had the following children:

    i. **Jesse Marion MOORE** was born (date unknown).
    ii. **Nelwyn Marie MOORE** was born (date unknown).
    iii. **John Wilbur MOORE** was born (date unknown).
    iv. **Mildred MOORE** was born (date unknown).

370. **Albert Roy MOORE** (Annie Louvenia Lou Moore-12, Sarah "Sally" Mahulda Bowles-11, Sarah Ann BUSSEY-10, Mahulda Hulda Moseley-9, Margaret Vann-8, Edward Ned-7, Mary Lewis Barnes-6, April-Tkikami Hop Turkey-5, Big Turkey Hop-4, Hokolesqua Opechan-3, Cleopatra the Shawano Powhatan-2, Wahunsonacock-1) was born in 1902 in Harrison Co., TX.

Albert Roy MOORE and Clara Alice HALL were married. **Clara Alice HALL** was born (date unknown).

Albert Roy MOORE and Clara Alice HALL had the following children:

    i. **Roy Albert MOORE** was born (date unknown).
    ii. **Annie Jewel MOORE** was born (date unknown).
    iii. **Sible Gale MOORE** was born (date unknown).
    iv. **Alfred Lamar "Al" MOORE** was born (date unknown).

371. **Clarence William MOORE** (Annie Louvenia Lou Moore-12, Sarah "Sally" Mahulda Bowles-11, Sarah Ann BUSSEY-10, Mahulda Hulda Moseley-9, Margaret Vann-8, Edward Ned-7, Mary Lewis Barnes-6, April-Tkikami Hop Turkey-5, Big Turkey Hop-4, Hokolesqua Opechan-3, Cleopatra the Shawano Powhatan-2, Wahunsonacock-1) was born in 1904 in Harrison Co., TX.

Clarence William MOORE and Clara MILLER were married. **Clara MILLER** was born (date unknown).

Descendants of Chief Wahunsonacock Powhatan

26 January 2012

Clarence William MOORE and Clara MILLER had the following children:

    i. **June MOORE** was born (date unknown).
    ii. **Jerry MOORE** was born (date unknown).
    iii. **Ronald C. MOORE** was born (date unknown).
    iv. **Donald E. MOORE** was born (date unknown).
    v. **Clarence William "Billy" MOORE** was born (date unknown).

372. **Murrah Lee MOORE** (Annie Louvenia Lou Moore-12, Sarah "Sally" Mahulda Bowles-11, Sarah Ann BUSSEY-10, Mahulda Hulda Moseley-9, Margaret Vann-8, Edward Ned-7, Mary Lewis Barnes-6, April-Tkikami Hop Turkey-5, Big Turkey Hop-4, Hokolesqua Opechan-3, Cleopatra the Shawano Powhatan-2, Wahunsonacock-1) was born in 1908 in Harrison Co., TX.

Murrah Lee MOORE and Bernice HENIGAN were married. **Bernice HENIGAN** was born (date unknown).

Murrah Lee MOORE and Bernice HENIGAN had the following children:

    i. **Samuel David MOORE** was born (date unknown).
    ii. **Mary Louise MOORE** was born (date unknown).
    iii. **Murrah Lee Moe MOORE** was born (date unknown).
    iv. **Charles Vernon MOORE** was born (date unknown).

373. **Jesse Milton MOORE** (Annie Louvenia Lou Moore-12, Sarah "Sally" Mahulda Bowles-11, Sarah Ann BUSSEY-10, Mahulda Hulda Moseley-9, Margaret Vann-8, Edward Ned-7, Mary Lewis Barnes-6, April-Tkikami Hop Turkey-5, Big Turkey Hop-4, Hokolesqua Opechan-3, Cleopatra the Shawano Powhatan-2, Wahunsonacock-1) was born (date unknown).

Jesse Milton MOORE and Mary Eleven EVERITT were married. **Mary Eleven EVERITT** was born (date unknown).

Jesse Milton MOORE and Mary Eleven EVERITT had the following children:

    i. **Mary Eleven MOORE** was born (date unknown).
    ii. **Bobby Glynda MOORE** was born (date unknown).
    iii. **Thomas K. MOORE** was born (date unknown).
    iv. **Jesse Daine MOORE** was born (date unknown).

374. **Sible MOORE** (Annie Louvenia Lou Moore-12, Sarah "Sally" Mahulda Bowles-11, Sarah Ann BUSSEY-10, Mahulda Hulda Moseley-9, Margaret Vann-8, Edward Ned-7, Mary Lewis Barnes-6, April-Tkikami Hop Turkey-5, Big Turkey Hop-4, Hokolesqua Opechan-3, Cleopatra the Shawano Powhatan-2, Wahunsonacock-1) was born (date unknown).

Sible MOORE and WOODSON were married. **WOODSON** was born (date unknown).

WOODSON and Sible MOORE had the following child:

    i. **Richard Sible WOODSON** was born (date unknown).

Harvey BOLLINS was born (date unknown).

375. **Aralree Elna Bussey MOORE** (Gus Lewis-12, Sarah "Sally" Mahulda Bowles-11, Sarah Ann BUSSEY-10, Mahulda Hulda Moseley-9, Margaret Vann-8, Edward Ned-7, Mary Lewis Barnes-6, April-Tkikami Hop Turkey-5, Big Turkey Hop-4, Hokolesqua Opechan-3, Cleopatra the Shawano Powhatan-2, Wahunsonacock-1) was born in 1910 in Harrison Co., TX.

Aralree Elna Bussey MOORE and Oliver JOHNSON were married. **Oliver JOHNSON** was born (date unknown).

Aralree Elna Bussey MOORE and M. RICHARDS were married. **M. RICHARDS** was born (date unknown).

376. **Philip Morton MOORE** (Gus Lewis-12, Sarah "Sally" Mahulda Bowles-11, Sarah Ann BUSSEY-10, Mahulda Hulda Moseley-9, Margaret Vann-8, Edward Ned-7, Mary Lewis Barnes-6, April-Tkikami Hop Turkey-5, Big Turkey Hop-4, Hokolesqua Opechan-3, Cleopatra the Shawano Powhatan-2, Wahunsonacock-1) was born in 1915 in Harrison Co., TX.

Philip Morton MOORE and Mary M. LINXWITER were married. **Mary M. LINXWITER** was born (date unknown).

Philip Morton MOORE and Mary M. LINXWITER had the following children:

    i. **Linda M. MOORE** was born (date unknown).
    ii. **Philip Dennis MOORE** was born (date unknown).
    iii. **Susan Marie MOORE** was born (date unknown).

377. **Leon Hill DICKARD Jr.** (Lillie Mande Moore-12, Sarah "Sally" Mahulda Bowles-11, Sarah Ann BUSSEY-10, Mahulda Hulda Moseley-9, Margaret Vann-8, Edward Ned-7, Mary Lewis Barnes-6, April-Tkikami Hop Turkey-5, Big Turkey Hop-4, Hokolesqua Opechan-3, Cleopatra the Shawano Powhatan-2, Wahunsonacock-1) held the title of Jr..

Leon Hill DICKARD Jr. and Doris BOWLES were married. **Doris BOWLES** was born (date unknown).

Leon Hill DICKARD and Doris BOWLES had the following children:

    i. **Robert Dale DICKARD** was born (date unknown).
    ii. **Leon Hall DICKARD** was born (date unknown).

378. **Ruth Waudell DICKARD** (Lillie Mande Moore-12, Sarah "Sally" Mahulda Bowles-11, Sarah Ann BUSSEY-10, Mahulda Hulda Moseley-9, Margaret Vann-8, Edward Ned-7, Mary Lewis Barnes-6, April-Tkikami Hop Turkey-5, Big Turkey Hop-4, Hokolesqua Opechan-3, Cleopatra the Shawano Powhatan-2, Wahunsonacock-1) was born (date unknown).

Ruth Waudell DICKARD and Delvin Fat HILL were married. **Delvin Fat HILL** was born (date unknown).

Delvin Fat HILL and Ruth Waudell DICKARD had the following children:

    i. **Elsie Ruth HILL** was born (date unknown).
    ii. **Billie HILL** was born (date unknown).

379. **Claudia DICKARD** (Lillie Mande Moore-12, Sarah "Sally" Mahulda Bowles-11, Sarah Ann BUSSEY-10, Mahulda Hulda Moseley-9, Margaret Vann-8, Edward Ned-7, Mary Lewis Barnes-6, April-Tkikami Hop Turkey-5, Big Turkey Hop-4, Hokolesqua Opechan-3, Cleopatra the Shawano Powhatan-2, Wahunsonacock-1) was born (date unknown).

Claudia DICKARD and Hiram Bewitt HICKEY were married. **Hiram Bewitt HICKEY** was born (date unknown).

Hiram Bewitt HICKEY and Claudia DICKARD had the following children:

    i. **Hiram Dewitt HICKEY** was born (date unknown).
    ii. **Alfred Hill HICKEY** was born (date unknown).

Descendants of Chief Wahunsonacock Powhatan

Fourteenth Generation

380. **Warren HINCHMAN** (Ella Mae Rogers-13, Sallie Armstrong-12, Monroe Griffin-11, Sarah Ann Poland-10, Nancy Naomi Moseley-9, Margaret Vann-8, Edward Ned-7, Mary Lewis Barnes-6, April-Tkikami Hop Turkey-5, Big Turkey Hop-4, Hokolesqua Opechan-3, Cleopatra the Shawano Powhatan-2, Wahunsonacock-1) was born on 16 Feb 1921 in TX. He died on 3 Sep 2006 at the age of 85.

Warren HINCHMAN and Lillian KNIGHT were married. **Lillian KNIGHT** was born on 6 Oct 1922.

Warren HINCHMAN and Lillian KNIGHT had the following child:

    457   i. **Sally Darlene HINCHMAN**, born 4 Sep 1942, Brady, TX; married Jerry Duaine MCANULTY.

381. **Dorothy Latta BEASLEY** (Flay Latta Watkins-13, Leslie Virginia Latta-12, Lenora Lee Poland-11, John Stratton-10, Nancy Naomi Moseley-9, Margaret Vann-8, Edward Ned-7, Mary Lewis Barnes-6, April-Tkikami Hop Turkey-5, Big Turkey Hop-4, Hokolesqua Opechan-3, Cleopatra the Shawano Powhatan-2, Wahunsonacock-1) was born on 19 May 1914 in Beeville, TX.

Dorothy Latta BEASLEY and James Meece RUHMANN were married on 14 Aug 1946. **James Meece RUHMANN** was born on 17 Feb 1912 in Kenedy, Karnes Co., TX.

James Meece RUHMANN and Dorothy Latta BEASLEY had the following children:

    458   i. **Latta Lillian RUHMANN**, born 26 Oct 1947, Beeville, TX; married Donley Randall STEPHENSON, Austin, Travis Co., TX.
           ii. **Nance Ann RUHMANN** was born on 26 Oct 1948 in Beeville, TX.

382. **Linda MOSLEY** (Oscar Newton "Junior"-13, William Alexander (Oscar)-12, William Alexander Newton-11, George Benjamin Alexander-10, George-9, Margaret Vann-8, Edward Ned-7, Mary Lewis Barnes-6, April-Tkikami Hop Turkey-5, Big Turkey Hop-4, Hokolesqua Opechan-3, Cleopatra the Shawano Powhatan-2, Wahunsonacock-1) was born in Escambia Co., FL.

Linda MOSLEY and Robert CHAVIS were married. **Robert CHAVIS** was born about 1940. He died about 1980 at the age of 40 in Pensacola, Escambia Co., FL.

383. **Gregory Weylan STINSON** (Ferrolyn MOSLEY-13, William Alexander (Oscar)-12, William Alexander Newton-11, George Benjamin Alexander-10, George-9, Margaret Vann-8, Edward Ned-7, Mary Lewis Barnes-6, April-Tkikami Hop Turkey-5, Big Turkey Hop-4, Hokolesqua Opechan-3, Cleopatra the Shawano Powhatan-2, Wahunsonacock-1) was born on 13 Oct 1940 in Florala, Covington Co., AL.

Gregory Weylan STINSON and Susan YEAMAN were married. **Susan YEAMAN** was born in Florala, Covington Co., AL.

Gregory Weylan STINSON and Susan YEAMAN had the following child:

    i. **Jama Chernault STINSON** was born on 9 Sep 1963 in Florala, Covington Co., AL.

Gregory Weylan STINSON and Sarah Winnette BASS were married on 30 Jun 1979 in Thomasville, Thomas Co., GA. **Sarah Winnette BASS** was born on 20 Jul 1944 in Thomasville, Thomas Co., GA.

384. **Sue Angela STINSON** (Ferrolyn MOSLEY-13, William Alexander (Oscar)-12, William Alexander Newton-11, George Benjamin Alexander-10, George-9, Margaret Vann-8, Edward Ned-7, Mary Lewis Barnes-6, April-Tkikami Hop Turkey-5, Big Turkey Hop-4, Hokolesqua Opechan-3, Cleopatra the Shawano Powhatan-2, Wahunsonacock-1) was born on 8 Aug 1942 in Covington Co., AL.

Sue Angela STINSON and Robert LAWSON were married about 1964. **Robert LAWSON** was born on 24 May 1926 in Florala, Covington Co., AL. He died on 11 Mar 1993 at the age of 66 in Jefferson Co., AL.

Robert LAWSON and Sue Angela STINSON had the following children:

    i. **Michael LAWSON** was born in Florala, Covington Co., AL.
459 ii. **Robert LAWSON**, born Covington Co., AL; married Jan .

Sue Angela STINSON and Charles GOOLSBY were married about 1989. **Charles GOOLSBY** was born about 1938 in Florala, Covington Co., AL.

385. **Rae Evelyn STINSON** (Ferrolyn MOSLEY-13, William Alexander (Oscar)-12, William Alexander Newton-11, George Benjamin Alexander-10, George-9, Margaret Vann-8, Edward Ned-7, Mary Lewis Barnes-6, April-Tkikami Hop Turkey-5, Big Turkey Hop-4, Hokolesqua Opechan-3, Cleopatra the Shawano Powhatan-2, Wahunsonacock-1) was born on 1 Dec 1945 in Florala, Covington Co., AL.

Rae Evelyn STINSON and Whit GOOLSBY were married. **Whit GOOLSBY** was born in AL.

Whit GOOLSBY and Rae Evelyn STINSON had the following child:

460 i. **Craig GOOLSBY**, born abt 1963, Florala, Covington Co., AL; married Sonjia SCOTT.

386. **Cathy RAY** (Martha Louise MOSLEY-13, William Alexander (Oscar)-12, William Alexander Newton-11, George Benjamin Alexander-10, George-9, Margaret Vann-8, Edward Ned-7, Mary Lewis Barnes-6, April-Tkikami Hop Turkey-5, Big Turkey Hop-4, Hokolesqua Opechan-3, Cleopatra the Shawano Powhatan-2, Wahunsonacock-1) was born in Florala, Covington Co., AL.

Cathy RAY and Mark STANLEY were married. **Mark STANLEY** was born in VA.

387. **Lillian SMITH** (Gladys Lula BUSSEY-13, Charles Drennen-12, Benjamin Harm-11, Martha (Malinda) Moseley-10, George-9, Margaret Vann-8, Edward Ned-7, Mary Lewis Barnes-6, April-Tkikami Hop Turkey-5, Big Turkey Hop-4, Hokolesqua Opechan-3, Cleopatra the Shawano Powhatan-2, Wahunsonacock-1) was born in 1920.

Eugene RIFFIE was born (date unknown).

388. **Mary Belle SMITH** (Gladys Lula BUSSEY-13, Charles Drennen-12, Benjamin Harm-11, Martha (Malinda) Moseley-10, George-9, Margaret Vann-8, Edward Ned-7, Mary Lewis Barnes-6, April-Tkikami Hop Turkey-5, Big Turkey Hop-4, Hokolesqua Opechan-3, Cleopatra the Shawano Powhatan-2, Wahunsonacock-1) was born (date unknown).

Unk MAYS was born (date unknown).

389. **Dorothy Lee SMITH** (Gladys Lula BUSSEY-13, Charles Drennen-12, Benjamin Harm-11, Martha (Malinda) Moseley-10, George-9, Margaret Vann-8, Edward Ned-7, Mary Lewis Barnes-6, April-Tkikami Hop Turkey-5, Big Turkey Hop-4, Hokolesqua Opechan-3, Cleopatra the Shawano Powhatan-2, Wahunsonacock-1) was born on 25 Nov 1928 in Winfield, Marion Co., AL.

Dorothy Lee SMITH and Jess Willard JOHNSON were married on 6 Apr 1946 in Marion Co., AL. **Jess Willard JOHNSON**, son of Freeman JOHNSON and Byrd WILSON, was born on 7 May 1916 in Walker Co., AL. He died on 25 Sep 1976 at the age of 60 in Kokomo IN. He was buried on 27 Sep 1976 in Memorial Park Cemetery, Kokomo, IN.

Jess Willard JOHNSON and Dorothy Lee SMITH had the following children:

	i.	**James W. JOHNSON** was born on 27 Jan 1947 in AL. He died on 8 Aug 1999 at the age of 52 in Indianapolis, IN. He was buried on 11 Aug 1999 in Beech Grove Cemetery.
461	ii.	**Vivia June JOHNSON**, born 18 Jun 1948, AL; married Lonnie DURBIN, 27 Mar 1971, Spring Hill, TN.
462	iii.	**Larry Jim JOHNSON**, born 15 Aug 1950, Kokomo IN; married Darlene Ann DAVIS, 15 Jul 1972, Kokomo IN.
463	iv.	**Jesse H. JOHNSON**, born 4 Dec 1954, Kokomo IN; married Sue Dorothy ROSSOW, 10 Jul 1993, St. Louis, MO.
	v.	**Janice L. JOHNSON** was born on 25 Nov 1957 in Kokomo IN.
	vi.	**Phillip Michael JOHNSON** was born on 6 Jun 1962 in Kokomo IN.

390. **Wynonia SMITH** (Gladys Lula BUSSEY-13, Charles Drennen-12, Benjamin Harm-11, Martha (Malinda) Moseley-10, George-9, Margaret Vann-8, Edward Ned-7, Mary Lewis Barnes-6, April-Tkikami Hop Turkey-5, Big Turkey Hop-4, Hokolesqua Opechan-3, Cleopatra the Shawano Powhatan-2, Wahunsonacock-1) was born in 1931.

William LAWRENCE, son of Floyd LAWRENCE and Blanche Mae BUSSEY, was born (date unknown).

391. **Peggy SMITH** (Gladys Lula BUSSEY-13, Charles Drennen-12, Benjamin Harm-11, Martha (Malinda) Moseley-10, George-9, Margaret Vann-8, Edward Ned-7, Mary Lewis Barnes-6, April-Tkikami Hop Turkey-5, Big Turkey Hop-4, Hokolesqua Opechan-3, Cleopatra the Shawano Powhatan-2, Wahunsonacock-1) was born in 1933.

Leslie P. "Pete" COX was born (date unknown).

Leslie P. "Pete" COX and Peggy SMITH had the following child:

      i. **Marina COX** was born (date unknown).

392. **Earlene BUSSEY** (Felix Hobson-13, Charles Drennen-12, Benjamin Harm-11, Martha (Malinda) Moseley-10, George-9, Margaret Vann-8, Edward Ned-7, Mary Lewis Barnes-6, April-Tkikami Hop Turkey-5, Big Turkey Hop-4, Hokolesqua Opechan-3, Cleopatra the Shawano Powhatan-2, Wahunsonacock-1) was born (date unknown).

Unk RICH was born (date unknown).

393. **Hazel BUSSEY** (Felix Hobson-13, Charles Drennen-12, Benjamin Harm-11, Martha (Malinda) Moseley-10, George-9, Margaret Vann-8, Edward Ned-7, Mary Lewis Barnes-6, April-Tkikami Hop Turkey-5, Big Turkey Hop-4, Hokolesqua Opechan-3, Cleopatra the Shawano Powhatan-2, Wahunsonacock-1) was born (date unknown).

Unk BROWN was born (date unknown).

394. **Levicy BUSSEY** (Felix Hobson-13, Charles Drennen-12, Benjamin Harm-11, Martha (Malinda) Moseley-10, George-9, Margaret Vann-8, Edward Ned-7, Mary Lewis Barnes-6, April-Tkikami Hop Turkey-5, Big Turkey Hop-4, Hokolesqua Opechan-3, Cleopatra the Shawano Powhatan-2, Wahunsonacock-1) was born (date unknown).

Unk MURPHY was born (date unknown).

395. **Illa Mae WELCH** (Delora BUSSEY-13, Charles Drennen-12, Benjamin Harm-11, Martha (Malinda) Moseley-10, George-9, Margaret Vann-8, Edward Ned-7, Mary Lewis Barnes-6, April-Tkikami Hop Turkey-5, Big Turkey Hop-4, Hokolesqua Opechan-3, Cleopatra the Shawano Powhatan-2, Wahunsonacock-1) was born (date unknown).

Illa Mae WELCH and Stanley Theodore STOYANOSKI were married on 20 Oct 1956. **Stanley Theodore STOYANOSKI** was born on 17 Nov 1919 in Jessup, Lackawanna Co., PA. He died on 17 Jun 1985 at the age of 65 in Muskogee, Muskogee Co., OK. He was buried on 21 Jun 1985 in Ft. Gibson National Cemetery, Ft. Gibson, Muskogee Co., OK.

Descendants of Chief Wahunsonacock Powhatan

26 January 2012

Stanley Theodore STOYANOSKI and Illa Mae WELCH had the following children:

    i. **Anna STOYANOSKI** was born (date unknown).
    ii. **Vincent STOYANOSKI** was born (date unknown).

396. **Dorothy WELCH** (Delora BUSSEY-13, Charles Drennen-12, Benjamin Harm-11, Martha (Malinda) Moseley-10, George-9, Margaret Vann-8, Edward Ned-7, Mary Lewis Barnes-6, April-Tkikami Hop Turkey-5, Big Turkey Hop-4, Hokolesqua Opechan-3, Cleopatra the Shawano Powhatan-2, Wahunsonacock-1) was born (date unknown).

John CADMANN was born (date unknown).

397. **Joanne HIBDON** (Flora BUSSEY-13, Charles Drennen-12, Benjamin Harm-11, Martha (Malinda) Moseley-10, George-9, Margaret Vann-8, Edward Ned-7, Mary Lewis Barnes-6, April-Tkikami Hop Turkey-5, Big Turkey Hop-4, Hokolesqua Opechan-3, Cleopatra the Shawano Powhatan-2, Wahunsonacock-1) was born (date unknown).

Unk WIEBERDINK was born (date unknown).

398. **Louise HIBDON** (Flora BUSSEY-13, Charles Drennen-12, Benjamin Harm-11, Martha (Malinda) Moseley-10, George-9, Margaret Vann-8, Edward Ned-7, Mary Lewis Barnes-6, April-Tkikami Hop Turkey-5, Big Turkey Hop-4, Hokolesqua Opechan-3, Cleopatra the Shawano Powhatan-2, Wahunsonacock-1) was born (date unknown).

Unk MOUNCE was born (date unknown).

399. **Charles Freddie BUSSEY** (Charles Marshall-13, Charles Drennen-12, Benjamin Harm-11, Martha (Malinda) Moseley-10, George-9, Margaret Vann-8, Edward Ned-7, Mary Lewis Barnes-6, April-Tkikami Hop Turkey-5, Big Turkey Hop-4, Hokolesqua Opechan-3, Cleopatra the Shawano Powhatan-2, Wahunsonacock-1) was born on 4 Sep 1939 in Boley, OK.

Charles Freddie BUSSEY and Mildred Joy COLEMAN were married on 7 Sep 1961 in Gregory, TX. **Mildred Joy COLEMAN** was born (date unknown).

400. **Delora Joan BUSSEY** (Charles Marshall-13, Charles Drennen-12, Benjamin Harm-11, Martha (Malinda) Moseley-10, George-9, Margaret Vann-8, Edward Ned-7, Mary Lewis Barnes-6, April-Tkikami Hop Turkey-5, Big Turkey Hop-4, Hokolesqua Opechan-3, Cleopatra the Shawano Powhatan-2, Wahunsonacock-1) was born on 7 Dec 1943.

Eddie DEATON was born (date unknown).

Descendants of Chief Wahunsonacock Powhatan

26 January 2012

401. **William LAWRENCE** (Blanche Mae BUSSEY-13, Walter-12, Benjamin Harm-11, Martha (Malinda) Moseley-10, George-9, Margaret Vann-8, Edward Ned-7, Mary Lewis Barnes-6, April-Tkikami Hop Turkey-5, Big Turkey Hop-4, Hokolesqua Opechan-3, Cleopatra the Shawano Powhatan-2, Wahunsonacock-1) was born (date unknown).

Wynonia SMITH, daughter of James Allen SMITH and Gladys Lula BUSSEY, was born in 1931.

402. **Winfred Marie FALGOUT** (Mattie Marie BUSSEY-13, James "Jimmy" David-12, Benjamin Harm-11, Martha (Malinda) Moseley-10, George-9, Margaret Vann-8, Edward Ned-7, Mary Lewis Barnes-6, April-Tkikami Hop Turkey-5, Big Turkey Hop-4, Hokolesqua Opechan-3, Cleopatra the Shawano Powhatan-2, Wahunsonacock-1) was born on 23 Jun 1932.

Doyle Daphney JONES was born on 28 Apr 1931.

Doyle Daphney JONES and Winfred Marie FALGOUT had the following children:

- 464   i. **Susan Marie JONES**, married George Allen WILKINSON, 15 Aug 1965; married J. Thomas BRAKEFIELD, Dec 1975.
- 465   ii. **Phillip Wayne JONES**.

403. **James Mikel, Jr. ROWCLIFF** (Mable Ellen BUSSEY-13, James "Jimmy" David-12, Benjamin Harm-11, Martha (Malinda) Moseley-10, George-9, Margaret Vann-8, Edward Ned-7, Mary Lewis Barnes-6, April-Tkikami Hop Turkey-5, Big Turkey Hop-4, Hokolesqua Opechan-3, Cleopatra the Shawano Powhatan-2, Wahunsonacock-1) was born on 23 Jun 1946.

Dorothy AVANT was born (date unknown).

James Mikel, Jr. ROWCLIFF and Dorothy AVANT had the following child:

- i. **James Mikel, III ROWCLIFF** was born on 3 Mar 1967.

404. **Ann Elizabeth MANDOLINI** (Ruby Elizabeth BUSSEY-13, James "Jimmy" David-12, Benjamin Harm-11, Martha (Malinda) Moseley-10, George-9, Margaret Vann-8, Edward Ned-7, Mary Lewis Barnes-6, April-Tkikami Hop Turkey-5, Big Turkey Hop-4, Hokolesqua Opechan-3, Cleopatra the Shawano Powhatan-2, Wahunsonacock-1) was born on 1 Jan 1934 in Washington City, Washington Co., MS.

Ann Elizabeth MANDOLINI and Alton Boman COALTER were married on 10 Apr 1955 in Greenville, Washington Co., MS. **Alton Boman COALTER** was born on 17 Sep 1931 in Belzoni, Humphreys Co., MS. He died on 17 May 1998 at the age of 66 in Green Forest, Carroll Co., AR.

Alton Boman COALTER and Ann Elizabeth MANDOLINI had the following children:

Descendants of Chief Wahunsonacock Powhatan

26 January 2012

 466   i. **Beverly Carolann COALTER**, born 14 Feb 1956, Greenville, Washington Co., MS; married Calvin Wayne NEFF, 1 May 1981, Huntsville, AR.
 467   ii. **Alton Bayne, Jr. COALTER**, born 5 Dec 1957, Greenville, Washington Co., MS; married Pamela Joyce KELLY, 15 May 1976, Fayetteville, AR.
    iii. **Terry Michael COALTER** was born on 25 Mar 1960 in Greenville, Washington Co., MS.
    iv. **David Andrew COALTER** was born on 12 Nov 1968 in Greenville, Washington Co., MS.
    v. **Elizabeth Jo COALTER** was born on 28 Dec 1970 in Berryville, Carroll Co., AR.

405. **Carl Chester MANDOLINI** (Ruby Elizabeth BUSSEY-13, James "Jimmy" David-12, Benjamin Harm-11, Martha (Malinda) Moseley-10, George-9, Margaret Vann-8, Edward Ned-7, Mary Lewis Barnes-6, April-Tkikami Hop Turkey-5, Big Turkey Hop-4, Hokolesqua Opechan-3, Cleopatra the Shawano Powhatan-2, Wahunsonacock-1) was born on 20 Feb 1936.

Maxine FRIDDLE was born (date unknown).

Carl Chester MANDOLINI and Maxine FRIDDLE had the following child:

   i. **Carla MANDOLINI** was born on 17 Oct 1961. She died on 4 Nov 1971 at the age of 10.

406. **Ladona NORTHCUTT** (Mary Ruth BUSSEY-13, George Washington-12, Benjamin Harm-11, Martha (Malinda) Moseley-10, George-9, Margaret Vann-8, Edward Ned-7, Mary Lewis Barnes-6, April-Tkikami Hop Turkey-5, Big Turkey Hop-4, Hokolesqua Opechan-3, Cleopatra the Shawano Powhatan-2, Wahunsonacock-1) was born (date unknown).

Gene AUTRY was born (date unknown).

Gene AUTRY and Ladona NORTHCUTT had the following children:

   i. **Sherry Lynn AUTRY** was born (date unknown).
   ii. **Brenda Jean AUTRY** was born (date unknown).
   iii. **Shawna Lee AUTRY** was born (date unknown).

407. **Deborah Jean BUSSEY** (Jimmy Ray-13, George Washington-12, Benjamin Harm-11, Martha (Malinda) Moseley-10, George-9, Margaret Vann-8, Edward Ned-7, Mary Lewis Barnes-6, April-Tkikami Hop Turkey-5, Big Turkey Hop-4, Hokolesqua Opechan-3, Cleopatra the Shawano Powhatan-2, Wahunsonacock-1) was born on 31 Dec 1951 in Henryetta, McIntosh Co., OK.

Deborah Jean BUSSEY and Norman J. CUMMINGS were married on 15 May 1969 in Henryetta, McIntosh Co., OK. **Norman J. CUMMINGS** was born on 15 May 1947.

Deborah Jean BUSSEY and Jerry Thomas CAPLE were married on 21 Oct 1977. **Jerry Thomas CAPLE** was born on 5 Jul 1954 in New Albany, Union Co., MS.

Descendants of Chief Wahunsonacock Powhatan

408. **Jimmy Eugene BUSSEY** (Jimmy Ray-13, George Washington-12, Benjamin Harm-11, Martha (Malinda) Moseley-10, George-9, Margaret Vann-8, Edward Ned-7, Mary Lewis Barnes-6, April-Tkikami Hop Turkey-5, Big Turkey Hop-4, Hokolesqua Opechan-3, Cleopatra the Shawano Powhatan-2, Wahunsonacock-1) was born on 20 Feb 1956 in Henryetta, McIntosh Co., OK.

Jimmy Eugene BUSSEY and Barbara STUART were married on 25 Sep in Henryetta, McIntosh Co., OK. **Barbara STUART**, daughter of Robert STUART and Dorothy UNK, was born in Henryetta, McIntosh Co., OK.

Jimmy Eugene BUSSEY and Barbara STUART had the following children:

    i. **Kandle Melissa BUSSEY** was born on 28 Mar 1977.
    ii. **Zackery James Bryan BUSSEY** was born on 3 Dec 1983.

409. **Kenneth Ray POWELL** (Gladys Sue BUSSEY-13, George Washington-12, Benjamin Harm-11, Martha (Malinda) Moseley-10, George-9, Margaret Vann-8, Edward Ned-7, Mary Lewis Barnes-6, April-Tkikami Hop Turkey-5, Big Turkey Hop-4, Hokolesqua Opechan-3, Cleopatra the Shawano Powhatan-2, Wahunsonacock-1) was born on 5 Oct 1954 in Henryetta, Okmulgee Co., OK.

Kenneth Ray POWELL and Kay DETURK were married in Henryetta, Okmulgee Co., OK. **Kay DETURK**, daughter of Bill DETURK, was born on 15 Oct 1957.

410. **Judy PORTER** (Willie Virginia Bowling-13, Alma Eudora BUSSEY-12, Benjamin Harm-11, Martha (Malinda) Moseley-10, George-9, Margaret Vann-8, Edward Ned-7, Mary Lewis Barnes-6, April-Tkikami Hop Turkey-5, Big Turkey Hop-4, Hokolesqua Opechan-3, Cleopatra the Shawano Powhatan-2, Wahunsonacock-1) was born (date unknown).

Unk SMITH was born (date unknown).

411. **Imogene SANFORD** (Helen WASHINGTON-13, Emma Ollie BUSSEY-12, Edmund Moody-11, Martha (Malinda) Moseley-10, George-9, Margaret Vann-8, Edward Ned-7, Mary Lewis Barnes-6, April-Tkikami Hop Turkey-5, Big Turkey Hop-4, Hokolesqua Opechan-3, Cleopatra the Shawano Powhatan-2, Wahunsonacock-1) was born on 13 Dec 1928. She died in Oct 1996 at the age of 67 in Dora, Walker Co., AL.

Imogene SANFORD and Fred SIDES were married. **Fred SIDES** was born (date unknown).

412. **Nina SANFORD** (Helen WASHINGTON-13, Emma Ollie BUSSEY-12, Edmund Moody-11, Martha (Malinda) Moseley-10, George-9, Margaret Vann-8, Edward Ned-7, Mary Lewis Barnes-6, April-Tkikami Hop Turkey-5, Big Turkey

Descendants of Chief Wahunsonacock Powhatan

Hop-4, Hokolesqua Opechan-3, Cleopatra the Shawano Powhatan-2, Wahunsonacock-1) was born in 1931.

Nina SANFORD and Dennis SAWYER were married. **Dennis SAWYER** was born (date unknown).

413. **Frances BLACKBURN** (Tee Ester WASHINGTON-13, Emma Ollie BUSSEY-12, Edmund Moody-11, Martha (Malinda) Moseley-10, George-9, Margaret Vann-8, Edward Ned-7, Mary Lewis Barnes-6, April-Tkikami Hop Turkey-5, Big Turkey Hop-4, Hokolesqua Opechan-3, Cleopatra the Shawano Powhatan-2, Wahunsonacock-1) was born (date unknown).

Frances BLACKBURN and Ollie William MCCRARY were married. **Ollie William MCCRARY** was born (date unknown).

Ollie William MCCRARY and Frances BLACKBURN had the following child:

    468   i.   **Charles William MCCRARY**, married Virginia DICKINSON.

414. **Roger Dale GUYTON** (Ernest Paul-13, Luanna BUSSEY-12, Edmund Moody-11, Martha (Malinda) Moseley-10, George-9, Margaret Vann-8, Edward Ned-7, Mary Lewis Barnes-6, April-Tkikami Hop Turkey-5, Big Turkey Hop-4, Hokolesqua Opechan-3, Cleopatra the Shawano Powhatan-2, Wahunsonacock-1) was born on 4 Aug 1948.

Roger Dale GUYTON and Rose Marie MARTIN were married. **Rose Marie MARTIN**, daughter of Jim Joe MARTIN and Frances DUNN, was born on 19 Jul 1954.

Roger Dale GUYTON and Rose Marie MARTIN had the following children:

    469   i.   **Roger Dale GUYTON II**, born 7 Nov 1974; married Jennifer Sue AUTRY.
    470   ii.   **Erin Nicole GUYTON**, born 16 Feb 1981, Florence, Lauderdale Co., AL; married Edward Steven LARKIN, 1 Jun 2002.

415. **Helen Faye GUYTON** (Ernest Paul-13, Luanna BUSSEY-12, Edmund Moody-11, Martha (Malinda) Moseley-10, George-9, Margaret Vann-8, Edward Ned-7, Mary Lewis Barnes-6, April-Tkikami Hop Turkey-5, Big Turkey Hop-4, Hokolesqua Opechan-3, Cleopatra the Shawano Powhatan-2, Wahunsonacock-1) died in 2002 in Gainsville, FL. She was born in Lamar Co, AL.

Helen Faye GUYTON and Oscar Harry PARKER were married. **Oscar Harry PARKER** was born (date unknown).

416. **Grady Benton GUYTON** (Ernest Paul-13, Luanna BUSSEY-12, Edmund Moody-11, Martha (Malinda) Moseley-10, George-9, Margaret Vann-8, Edward Ned-7, Mary Lewis Barnes-6, April-Tkikami Hop Turkey-5, Big Turkey Hop-4, Hokolesqua Opechan-3, Cleopatra the Shawano Powhatan-2, Wahunsonacock-1) was born (date unknown).

Grady Benton GUYTON and Lana KELLEY were married. **Lana KELLEY** was born (date unknown).

Descendants of Chief Wahunsonacock Powhatan

26 January 2012

Grady Benton GUYTON and Lana KELLEY had the following children:

      i. **Marie Cardell GUYTON** was born (date unknown).
     ii. **Kelley Jo GUYTON** was born (date unknown).
    iii. **Todd GUYTON** was born (date unknown).

417. **Carolyn Sue GUYTON** (Ernest Paul-13, Luanna BUSSEY-12, Edmund Moody-11, Martha (Malinda) Moseley-10, George-9, Margaret Vann-8, Edward Ned-7, Mary Lewis Barnes-6, April-Tkikami Hop Turkey-5, Big Turkey Hop-4, Hokolesqua Opechan-3, Cleopatra the Shawano Powhatan-2, Wahunsonacock-1) was born (date unknown).

Carolyn Sue GUYTON and Farrell LOVVORN were married. **Farrell LOVVORN** was born (date unknown).

Farrell LOVVORN and Carolyn Sue GUYTON had the following children:

      i. **Scott LOVVORN** was born (date unknown).
     ii. **Shannon LOVVORN** was born (date unknown).
    iii. **Sean LOVVORN** was born on 20 Feb 1980.

418. **Patricia Anne GUYTON** (Ernest Paul-13, Luanna BUSSEY-12, Edmund Moody-11, Martha (Malinda) Moseley-10, George-9, Margaret Vann-8, Edward Ned-7, Mary Lewis Barnes-6, April-Tkikami Hop Turkey-5, Big Turkey Hop-4, Hokolesqua Opechan-3, Cleopatra the Shawano Powhatan-2, Wahunsonacock-1) was born (date unknown).

Patricia Anne GUYTON and Wayne URBAN were married. **Wayne URBAN** was born (date unknown).

419. **Daisy Wonnell BUSSEY** (Otis Howard-13, Rufus Thomas-12, Edmund Moody-11, Martha (Malinda) Moseley-10, George-9, Margaret Vann-8, Edward Ned-7, Mary Lewis Barnes-6, April-Tkikami Hop Turkey-5, Big Turkey Hop-4, Hokolesqua Opechan-3, Cleopatra the Shawano Powhatan-2, Wahunsonacock-1) was born on 6 May 1932 in Allock, KY.

Daisy Wonnell BUSSEY and Garland D. GODSEY were married on 7 Apr 1952. **Garland D. GODSEY**, son of Eura GODSEY and Arminta COMBS, was born in 1932 in Harland Co., KY.

Garland D. GODSEY and Daisy Wonnell BUSSEY had the following children:

471   i. **Cheryl Lynn GODSEY**, born 16 Nov 1954, Prestonburg, KY; married Darrell Keith LESLIE, 13 Jan 1973, Prestonburg, KY.
        ii. **Linda Lorene GODSEY** was born on 25 Mar 1956 in Fairbanks, AK.
472   iii. **Nancy GODSEY**, born 15 Feb 1961, Louisville, Jefferson Co., KY; married Lawrence Bradley BAKER, 13 Jul 1985, Prestonburg, KY.

420. **William Thomas BUSSEY** (Otis Howard-13, Rufus Thomas-12, Edmund Moody-11, Martha (Malinda) Moseley-10, George-9, Margaret Vann-8, Edward Ned-7, Mary Lewis Barnes-6, April-Tkikami Hop Turkey-5, Big Turkey Hop-4,

Hokolesqua Opechan-3, Cleopatra the Shawano Powhatan-2, Wahunsonacock-1) was born on 31 May 1934 in Wayland, Floyd Co., KY.

William Thomas BUSSEY and Uldeen CLINE were married on 7 Nov 1952 in Scott Air Force Base, Bellville, IL. **Uldeen CLINE**, daughter of James CLINE and Lackie WILLIAMS, was born on 2 Feb 1935 in Auxier, KY. She died about 1973 at the age of 38 in Ft. Lauderdale, FL.

William Thomas BUSSEY and Uldeen CLINE had the following children:

- 473   i. **William Thomas, Jr. BUSSEY**, born 10 Aug 1954, Anchorage, AK; married Dana DECKER, Ft. Lauderdale, FL.
- 474   ii. **James Howard BUSSEY**, born 21 Aug 1957, Ft. Knox, KY; married Connie Francis EAGEN, 21 Aug 1978, Keleen, TX; married Sharon Elizabeth FLEMING, 15 Jun 1996, Boynton Beach, Palm Beach Co., FL.

William Thomas BUSSEY and Maria Alberta SOLIS were married on 25 Sep 1974 in El Paso, TX. **Maria Alberta SOLIS**, daughter of Pete SOLIS and Maria LOPEZ, was born (date unknown).

William Thomas BUSSEY and Maria Alberta SOLIS had the following child:

- i. **Bianca Malina BUSSEY** was born on 4 Jun 1976.

421. Peggy Jean BUSSEY (Dawson Ellard-13, Rufus Thomas-12, Edmund Moody-11, Martha (Malinda) Moseley-10, George-9, Margaret Vann-8, Edward Ned-7, Mary Lewis Barnes-6, April-Tkikami Hop Turkey-5, Big Turkey Hop-4, Hokolesqua Opechan-3, Cleopatra the Shawano Powhatan-2, Wahunsonacock-1) was born on 6 May 1937 in Wayland, Floyd Co., KY. She died on 6 Jul 2009 at the age of 72 in Morehead, KY.

Peggy Jean BUSSEY and William Ray COLLINS were married on 11 Apr 1953 in David, KY. **William Ray COLLINS** was born on 4 Sep 1934 in Prestonburg, KY.

William Ray COLLINS and Peggy Jean BUSSEY had the following children:

- 475   i. **Jerra Rae COLLINS**, born 3 May 1953; married David Morton CAMPBELL, 12 Jun 1971, Clintwood, VA.
- 476   ii. **Margaret Elizabeth COLLINS**, born 22 Jul 1955; married Ballard HYDEN, 5 Mar 1977.

Peggy Jean BUSSEY and Harold AUGUSTINE were married on 8 Jun 1963 in Delaware, OH. **Harold AUGUSTINE** was born on 29 Apr 1939 in Delaware, OH.

Peggy Jean BUSSEY and Elmer RHULE were married on 21 Dec 1973 in Frenchburg, KY. **Elmer RHULE** was born on 17 Sep 1924 in Clay City, KY. He died in 1993 at the age of 69.

Descendants of Chief Wahunsonacock Powhatan

26 January 2012

422. **Toby Ann BUSSEY** (Dawson Ellard-13, Rufus Thomas-12, Edmund Moody-11, Martha (Malinda) Moseley-10, George-9, Margaret Vann-8, Edward Ned-7, Mary Lewis Barnes-6, April-Tkikami Hop Turkey-5, Big Turkey Hop-4, Hokolesqua Opechan-3, Cleopatra the Shawano Powhatan-2, Wahunsonacock-1) was born on 30 Mar 1939 in Wayland, Floyd Co., KY.

Toby Ann BUSSEY and Bruce Lewis HOWARD were married on 19 Nov 1960 in Prestonburg, KY. **Bruce Lewis HOWARD** was born on 17 Nov 1938 in Tutor Key, KY.

Bruce Lewis HOWARD and Toby Ann BUSSEY had the following children:

477	i.	**Elizabeth Rae HOWARD**, born 22 Dec 1961, Paintsville, KY; married Jeffrey Oran PECK, 9 Dec 1978, Clintwood, VA.
478	ii.	**Melissa Ann HOWARD**, born 29 Dec 1966, West Liberty, KY; married Evertt Dwight BLAIR, 8 Jun 1985, Paintsville, KY; married Gary Darrell BLAIR, 2 May 1992, Middlefork, KY.
	iii.	**Robert Bruce HOWARD** was born on 18 Oct 1975 in Prestonburg, KY.

423. **Judith Sharon BUSSEY** (Dawson Ellard-13, Rufus Thomas-12, Edmund Moody-11, Martha (Malinda) Moseley-10, George-9, Margaret Vann-8, Edward Ned-7, Mary Lewis Barnes-6, April-Tkikami Hop Turkey-5, Big Turkey Hop-4, Hokolesqua Opechan-3, Cleopatra the Shawano Powhatan-2, Wahunsonacock-1) was born on 31 Jul 1943 in Paintsville, KY.

Judith Sharon BUSSEY and Thomas Benton SMITH were married on 29 Jan 1962 in Williamson, WV. **Thomas Benton SMITH** was born on 3 Mar 1942 in Pike Co., KY. He died in Aug 1999 at the age of 57.

Thomas Benton SMITH and Judith Sharon BUSSEY had the following children:

479	i.	**Sandra Gayle SMITH**, born 3 May 1963, Williamson, WV.
480	ii.	**Thomas Benton, Jr. SMITH**, born 22 Sep 1964, Williamson, WV; married Sherry Lou JONES, 22 Aug 1991, Lexington, KY.

424. **Rodney Clark BUSSEY** (Dawson Ellard-13, Rufus Thomas-12, Edmund Moody-11, Martha (Malinda) Moseley-10, George-9, Margaret Vann-8, Edward Ned-7, Mary Lewis Barnes-6, April-Tkikami Hop Turkey-5, Big Turkey Hop-4, Hokolesqua Opechan-3, Cleopatra the Shawano Powhatan-2, Wahunsonacock-1) was born on 2 Apr 1941 in Wayland, Floyd Co., KY.

Rodney Clark BUSSEY and Helen Elizabeth ADAMS were married on 25 Jan 1964 in Berea College, KY. **Helen Elizabeth ADAMS**, daughter of Steven ADAMS and Mildred RATCLIFFE, was born on 3 Mar 1944 in Wytheville, VA.

Rodney Clark BUSSEY and Helen Elizabeth ADAMS had the following children:

481	i.	**Kelly Anne BUSSEY**, born 20 Feb 1965, Huntington, NY; married Keene JONES, 4 May 1985, Berea, KY; married Howard Clay EVANS, 18 Jul 1987, Gatlinburg, TN.
482	ii.	**Kimberly Adams BUSSEY**, born 9 Nov 1967, Lexington, KY; married Patrick Benjamin GAY, 7 May 1994, Berea, KY.

425. **Karen Rae BUSSEY** (Dawson Ellard-13, Rufus Thomas-12, Edmund Moody-11, Martha (Malinda) Moseley-10, George-9, Margaret Vann-8, Edward Ned-7, Mary Lewis Barnes-6, April-Tkikami Hop Turkey-5, Big Turkey Hop-4,

Descendants of Chief Wahunsonacock Powhatan

Hokolesqua Opechan-3, Cleopatra the Shawano Powhatan-2, Wahunsonacock-1) was born on 8 Oct 1945.

Karen Rae BUSSEY and Thomas John O'ROURKE were married on 3 Feb 1968 in Cynthiana, KY. **Thomas John O'ROURKE** was born on 2 Jan 1945 in Latrobe, PA.

Thomas John O'ROURKE and Karen Rae BUSSEY had the following children:

483	i.	**Kelly Jane O'ROURKE**, born 25 Aug 1970, Decatur, GA.
484	ii.	**Amy Katherine O'ROURKE**, born 10 Mar 1973, Decatur, GA; married Adam Kelly EDWARD, 16 Jun 1995, Lawrenvile, GA.
	iii.	**Daniel Thomas O'ROURKE** was born on 4 Jan 1976 in Decatur, GA.

426. **John Rufus BUSSEY** (Dawson Ellard-13, Rufus Thomas-12, Edmund Moody-11, Martha (Malinda) Moseley-10, George-9, Margaret Vann-8, Edward Ned-7, Mary Lewis Barnes-6, April-Tkikami Hop Turkey-5, Big Turkey Hop-4, Hokolesqua Opechan-3, Cleopatra the Shawano Powhatan-2, Wahunsonacock-1) was born on 5 Apr 1949 in Prestonburg, KY.

John Rufus BUSSEY and Diana Hope LYKINS were married on 16 Aug 1968 in Cannel City, KY. **Diana Hope LYKINS** was born on 11 Aug 1952 in Cannel City, KY.

John Rufus BUSSEY and Diana Hope LYKINS had the following children:

485	i.	**Johnny Bruce BUSSEY**, born 25 Nov 1970, Williamson, WV; married Amy UNK, 4 Jan 1997, Salyersville, KY.
	ii.	**Jason Clark BUSSEY** was born on 3 Aug 1975 in Prestonburg, KY.

John Rufus BUSSEY and Edadean BOYD were married on 18 May 1990 in Prestonburg, KY. **Edadean BOYD**, daughter of Montis BOYD and Destraphine FUGATE, was born on 30 Mar 1961 in Prestonburg, KY.

John Rufus BUSSEY and Edadean BOYD had the following child:

  i. **Bethany Claire BUSSEY** was born on 10 Mar 1986 in Lexington, KY.

427. **Ivan Duell CONLEY** (Mildred Ethel BUSSEY-13, Rufus Thomas-12, Edmund Moody-11, Martha (Malinda) Moseley-10, George-9, Margaret Vann-8, Edward Ned-7, Mary Lewis Barnes-6, April-Tkikami Hop Turkey-5, Big Turkey Hop-4, Hokolesqua Opechan-3, Cleopatra the Shawano Powhatan-2, Wahunsonacock-1) was born in 1937 in Wayland, Floyd Co., KY.

Ivan Duell CONLEY and Kathryn PARSONS were married in Marion, OH. **Kathryn PARSONS** was born (date unknown).

Ivan Duell CONLEY and Kathryn PARSONS had the following children:

  i. **Rhonda Yvette CONLEY** was born (date unknown).
  ii. **Ivan Duell, Jr. CONLEY** was born on 10 Dec 1958.

Descendants of Chief Wahunsonacock Powhatan

26 January 2012

428. **Jeffrey Lynn CONLEY** (Mildred Ethel BUSSEY-13, Rufus Thomas-12, Edmund Moody-11, Martha (Malinda) Moseley-10, George-9, Margaret Vann-8, Edward Ned-7, Mary Lewis Barnes-6, April-Tkikami Hop Turkey-5, Big Turkey Hop-4, Hokolesqua Opechan-3, Cleopatra the Shawano Powhatan-2, Wahunsonacock-1) was born on 15 Jun 1943 in Cleveland, OH.

Jeffrey Lynn CONLEY and Margaret HITT were married in 1967 in Marion, OH. **Margaret HITT** was born (date unknown).

Jeffrey Lynn CONLEY and Margaret HITT had the following children:

      i. **Heidi Go CONLEY** was born on 1 Nov 1974.
     ii. **Holly Sue CONLEY** was born on 15 Jun 1975.

429. **Henry Thomas CONLEY** (Mildred Ethel BUSSEY-13, Rufus Thomas-12, Edmund Moody-11, Martha (Malinda) Moseley-10, George-9, Margaret Vann-8, Edward Ned-7, Mary Lewis Barnes-6, April-Tkikami Hop Turkey-5, Big Turkey Hop-4, Hokolesqua Opechan-3, Cleopatra the Shawano Powhatan-2, Wahunsonacock-1) was born on 21 Mar 1946 in Cleveland, OH.

Henry Thomas CONLEY and Freeda Darlene THOMPSON were married on 30 Aug 1975 in Marion, OH. **Freeda Darlene THOMPSON** was born on 3 Jul 1941.

430. **Timothy Bruce CONLEY** (Mildred Ethel BUSSEY-13, Rufus Thomas-12, Edmund Moody-11, Martha (Malinda) Moseley-10, George-9, Margaret Vann-8, Edward Ned-7, Mary Lewis Barnes-6, April-Tkikami Hop Turkey-5, Big Turkey Hop-4, Hokolesqua Opechan-3, Cleopatra the Shawano Powhatan-2, Wahunsonacock-1) was born on 20 Jan 1952 in Cleveland, OH.

Timothy Bruce CONLEY and Marla JEWEL were married on 18 Jan 1975 in Marion, OH. **Marla JEWEL**, daughter of Erwin JEWEL and Ida BRUNSON, was born on 10 Mar 1953 in Marion, OH.

Timothy Bruce CONLEY and Marla JEWEL had the following children:

      i. **Kiersten CONLEY** was born on 22 Nov 1979 in Canton, OH.
     ii. **Kerra Brienne CONLEY** was born on 7 May 1986 in Canton, OH.
    iii. **Timothy Devin CONLEY** was born on 18 Aug 1982 in Canton, OH.

431. **Carolyn Sue BUSSEY** (Marion Edward "Fat"-13, Rufus Thomas-12, Edmund Moody-11, Martha (Malinda) Moseley-10, George-9, Margaret Vann-8, Edward Ned-7, Mary Lewis Barnes-6, April-Tkikami Hop Turkey-5, Big Turkey Hop-4, Hokolesqua Opechan-3, Cleopatra the Shawano Powhatan-2, Wahunsonacock-1) was born in Marion, OH.

Carolyn Sue BUSSEY and BUTLER were married. **BUTLER** was born (date unknown).

Descendants of Chief Wahunsonacock Powhatan

432. Sheila Ann BUSSEY (Marion Edward "Fat"-13, Rufus Thomas-12, Edmund Moody-11, Martha (Malinda) Moseley-10, George-9, Margaret Vann-8, Edward Ned-7, Mary Lewis Barnes-6, April-Tkikami Hop Turkey-5, Big Turkey Hop-4, Hokolesqua Opechan-3, Cleopatra the Shawano Powhatan-2, Wahunsonacock-1) was born in Marion, OH.

Sheila Ann BUSSEY and GARRISON were married. **GARRISON** was born (date unknown).

433. Cynthia Beth WYNN (Gwendolyn BUSSEY-13, Rufus Thomas-12, Edmund Moody-11, Martha (Malinda) Moseley-10, George-9, Margaret Vann-8, Edward Ned-7, Mary Lewis Barnes-6, April-Tkikami Hop Turkey-5, Big Turkey Hop-4, Hokolesqua Opechan-3, Cleopatra the Shawano Powhatan-2, Wahunsonacock-1) was born on 9 Oct 1948.

Cynthia Beth WYNN and Kenneth Lewis JAFFE were married on 21 Nov 1970 in Cleveland, OH. **Kenneth Lewis JAFFE** was born on 14 Oct 1948.

Kenneth Lewis JAFFE and Cynthia Beth WYNN had the following children:

      i. **Kevin Eric JAFFE** was born on 12 Oct 1973.
     ii. **Jennifer Lea JAFFE** was born on 20 Jan 1977.

434. Nancy WYNN (Gwendolyn BUSSEY-13, Rufus Thomas-12, Edmund Moody-11, Martha (Malinda) Moseley-10, George-9, Margaret Vann-8, Edward Ned-7, Mary Lewis Barnes-6, April-Tkikami Hop Turkey-5, Big Turkey Hop-4, Hokolesqua Opechan-3, Cleopatra the Shawano Powhatan-2, Wahunsonacock-1) was born on 16 Jul 1951 in Cleveland, OH.

Nancy WYNN and Glenn KOYL were married on 10 Aug 1973. **Glenn KOYL** was born (date unknown).

Glenn KOYL and Nancy WYNN had the following children:

      i. **Glenn Wynn KOYL** was born on 10 Aug 1973.
     ii. **Ben Wynn KOYL** was born on 16 Aug 1980.
    iii. **Sam Wynn KOYL** was born on 1 Mar 1985.

435. Jacqueline WYNN (Gwendolyn BUSSEY-13, Rufus Thomas-12, Edmund Moody-11, Martha (Malinda) Moseley-10, George-9, Margaret Vann-8, Edward Ned-7, Mary Lewis Barnes-6, April-Tkikami Hop Turkey-5, Big Turkey Hop-4, Hokolesqua Opechan-3, Cleopatra the Shawano Powhatan-2, Wahunsonacock-1) was born on 15 Jan 1958.

Jacqueline WYNN and Robert Eric KENNEDY were married on 20 Dec 1986. **Robert Eric KENNEDY** was born on 5 Aug 1955 in Cleveland, OH.

Robert Eric KENNEDY and Jacqueline WYNN had the following children:

      i. **Robert Jacque KENNEDY** was born on 26 Dec 1991.
     ii. **Alexandra Charles KENNEDY** was born on 27 May 1990.
    iii. **Madison Wynn KENNEDY** was born on 1 Sep 1995 in Cleveland, OH.

436. **Susan WYNN** (Gwendolyn BUSSEY-13, Rufus Thomas-12, Edmund Moody-11, Martha (Malinda) Moseley-10, George-9, Margaret Vann-8, Edward Ned-7, Mary Lewis Barnes-6, April-Tkikami Hop Turkey-5, Big Turkey Hop-4, Hokolesqua Opechan-3, Cleopatra the Shawano Powhatan-2, Wahunsonacock-1) was born on 10 Aug 1963.

Susan WYNN and Scott ALLBEE were married on 8 Aug 1987. **Scott ALLBEE** was born on 5 Aug 1955 in Cleveland, OH.

Scott ALLBEE and Susan WYNN had the following child:

    i. **Coltyn Wynn ALLBEE** was born on 18 Jan 1994.

437. **Frank Charles GIGANTI** (Emmy Sue BUSSEY-13, Rufus Thomas-12, Edmund Moody-11, Martha (Malinda) Moseley-10, George-9, Margaret Vann-8, Edward Ned-7, Mary Lewis Barnes-6, April-Tkikami Hop Turkey-5, Big Turkey Hop-4, Hokolesqua Opechan-3, Cleopatra the Shawano Powhatan-2, Wahunsonacock-1) was born on 20 Apr 1950.

Frank Charles GIGANTI and Kelly JOYCE were married on 14 Nov 1981. **Kelly JOYCE** was born on 10 Sep 1960.

Frank Charles GIGANTI and Kelly JOYCE had the following children:

    i. **Kate GIGANTI** was born on 4 Nov 1982.
    ii. **Charles Francesco GIGANTI** was born on 1 Apr 1986.
    iii. **Joseph GIGANTI** was born in Apr 1988. He died in Feb 1989 at the age of 0.

438. **Catherine Ann GIGANTI** (Emmy Sue BUSSEY-13, Rufus Thomas-12, Edmund Moody-11, Martha (Malinda) Moseley-10, George-9, Margaret Vann-8, Edward Ned-7, Mary Lewis Barnes-6, April-Tkikami Hop Turkey-5, Big Turkey Hop-4, Hokolesqua Opechan-3, Cleopatra the Shawano Powhatan-2, Wahunsonacock-1) was born on 1 Jun 1947 in Cleveland, OH.

Robert GILLESPIE was born on 13 Mar 1947 in Cleveland, OH.

Robert GILLESPIE and Catherine Ann GIGANTI had the following children:

    i. **Amy Elizabeth GILLESPIE** was born on 5 Oct 1976 in Toledo, OH.
    ii. **Nancy Maureen GILLESPIE** was born on 6 Nov 1977 in Toledo, OH.

439. **Patricia HALL** (Tommie Lee BUSSEY-13, Rufus Thomas-12, Edmund Moody-11, Martha (Malinda) Moseley-10, George-9, Margaret Vann-8, Edward Ned-7, Mary Lewis Barnes-6, April-Tkikami Hop Turkey-5, Big Turkey Hop-4, Hokolesqua Opechan-3, Cleopatra the Shawano Powhatan-2, Wahunsonacock-1) was born on 14 Jun 1945.

Patricia HALL and Arthur Winford CRAIG were married on 19 Aug 1967. **Arthur Winford CRAIG** was born on 5 Sep 1944.

Arthur Winford CRAIG and Patricia HALL had the following child:

Descendants of Chief Wahunsonacock Powhatan

26 January 2012

      i. **Hallie Michelle CRAIG** was born on 10 Jun 1980.

440. **Frances Michelle HALL** (Tommie Lee BUSSEY-13, Rufus Thomas-12, Edmund Moody-11, Martha (Malinda) Moseley-10, George-9, Margaret Vann-8, Edward Ned-7, Mary Lewis Barnes-6, April-Tkikami Hop Turkey-5, Big Turkey Hop-4, Hokolesqua Opechan-3, Cleopatra the Shawano Powhatan-2, Wahunsonacock-1) was born on 6 Jul 1950 in Pikeville, Pike Co., KY.

Frances Michelle HALL and James David ENGLAND were married on 8 Aug 1970 in Pike Co., KY. **James David ENGLAND** was born on 2 Mar 1948 in Pikeville, KY.

James David ENGLAND and Frances Michelle HALL had the following children:

    486   i. **Cynthia Lynn ENGLAND**, born 23 May 1972; married John David "JD" HUGHES, 30 Dec 1995, Pikeville, Pike Co., KY.
          ii. **Amanda Lee ENGLAND** was born on 22 Apr 1976.

441. **William Hollie "Bill", Jr. CONLEY** (Naoma "Naomi" BUSSEY-13, Rufus Thomas-12, Edmund Moody-11, Martha (Malinda) Moseley-10, George-9, Margaret Vann-8, Edward Ned-7, Mary Lewis Barnes-6, April-Tkikami Hop Turkey-5, Big Turkey Hop-4, Hokolesqua Opechan-3, Cleopatra the Shawano Powhatan-2, Wahunsonacock-1) was born on 19 Jun 1946 in Leatha, KY.

Pamela Sue MANSFIELD was born on 12 May 1973 in Ashland, KY.

William Hollie "Bill", Jr. CONLEY and Pamela Sue MANSFIELD had the following child:

      i. **Lovinda Adiar CONLEY** was born on 12 May 1973.

William Hollie "Bill", Jr. CONLEY and Joyce Lynn MCNEARNY were married in Maple Hts., Cleveland, OH. **Joyce Lynn MCNEARNY** was born (date unknown).

William Hollie "Bill", Jr. CONLEY and Mary Frances JORDAN were married on 28 May 1988 in Moonachie, NJ. **Mary Frances JORDAN**, daughter of Raymand JORDAN and Constance PUGLIA, was born (date unknown).

William Hollie "Bill", Jr. CONLEY and Mary Frances JORDAN had the following children:

      i. **Louvinda Adiar CONLEY** was born on 12 May 1973.
      ii. **William Brian CONLEY** was born on 18 Feb 1975.
      iii. **Michael Patrick CONLEY** was born on 27 Aug 1977.
      iv. **James Evans CONLEY** was born on 1 Aug 1978 in Hackensack, NY.
      v. **Mark David CONLEY** was born on 5 Dec 1981 in Cleveland, OH.

442. **Timothy Lee CONLEY** (Naoma "Naomi" BUSSEY-13, Rufus Thomas-12, Edmund Moody-11, Martha (Malinda)

Descendants of Chief Wahunsonacock Powhatan
26 January 2012

Moseley-10, George-9, Margaret Vann-8, Edward Ned-7, Mary Lewis Barnes-6, April-Tkikami Hop Turkey-5, Big Turkey Hop-4, Hokolesqua Opechan-3, Cleopatra the Shawano Powhatan-2, Wahunsonacock-1) was born on 7 Feb 1956 in Medina, OH.

Timothy Lee CONLEY and Kathlee RAGER were married on 9 Nov 1974 in Cleveland, OH. **Kathlee RAGER** was born on 23 Oct 1956.

Timothy Lee CONLEY and Kathlee RAGER had the following children:

    i. **Timothy Paul CONLEY** was born on 14 May 1985 in Springfield, MO.
    ii. **Ethan Andrew CONLEY** was born on 3 Sep 1988 in Springfield, MO.

443. **Gregory Christopher CONLEY** (Naoma "Naomi" BUSSEY-13, Rufus Thomas-12, Edmund Moody-11, Martha (Malinda) Moseley-10, George-9, Margaret Vann-8, Edward Ned-7, Mary Lewis Barnes-6, April-Tkikami Hop Turkey-5, Big Turkey Hop-4, Hokolesqua Opechan-3, Cleopatra the Shawano Powhatan-2, Wahunsonacock-1) was born on 20 Jul 1953 in Cleveland, OH.

Gregory Christopher CONLEY and Elizabeth Anne were married on 29 Dec 1978 in Lakewood, OH. **Elizabeth Anne** was born on 12 Feb 1953.

Gregory Christopher CONLEY and Elizabeth Anne had the following children:

    i. **Christopher Gregory CONLEY** was born on 17 Jun 1981 in Cleveland, OH.
    ii. **Jonathan William CONLEY** was born on 19 Sep 1982 in Cleveland, OH.
    iii. **Patrick Edward CONLEY** was born on 30 Jul 1985 in Cleveland, OH.
    iv. **Michael Adam CONLEY** was born on 2 May 1990 in Cleveland, OH.

444. **J.D. WEEKS** (Era Earl-13, Elizabeth "Lizzie Beth" BUSSEY-12, Edmund Moody-11, Martha (Malinda) Moseley-10, George-9, Margaret Vann-8, Edward Ned-7, Mary Lewis Barnes-6, April-Tkikami Hop Turkey-5, Big Turkey Hop-4, Hokolesqua Opechan-3, Cleopatra the Shawano Powhatan-2, Wahunsonacock-1) was born on 12 Apr 1937 in Cullman County, AL.

J.D. WEEKS and Jane Lynn PEARSON were married on 6 Jul 1956. They were divorced on 13 Aug 1974. **Jane Lynn PEARSON**, daughter of Delmar Lynn PEARSON and Dorothy Louise MIDDLETON, was born on 8 Nov 1938 in Meridian, Lauderdale Co., MS.

J.D. WEEKS and Jane Lynn PEARSON had the following children:

487	i.	**Stephen Douglas WEEKS**, born 6 Jan 1959, Birmingham, Jefferson Co., AL; married Slavomira MELIORISOVA, 6 Apr 1991, Tranava, Czechoslovakia.
488	ii.	**Jennifer Lynn WEEKS**, born 17 Mar 1961, Birmingham, Jefferson Co., AL; married Danny Joe BRITTIAN, 15 Dec 1979, Gardendale, Jefferson Co., AL.
489	iii.	**Catherine Marie WEEKS**, born 28 Mar 1963, Birmingham, Jefferson Co., AL; married Christopher Alan SHELNUTT, 14 Oct 1988, Gardendale, Jefferson Co., AL.

445. **Bobbie Jo WEEKS** (Era Earl-13, Elizabeth "Lizzie Beth" BUSSEY-12, Edmund Moody-11, Martha (Malinda)

Descendants of Chief Wahunsonacock Powhatan

Moseley-10, George-9, Margaret Vann-8, Edward Ned-7, Mary Lewis Barnes-6, April-Tkikami Hop Turkey-5, Big Turkey Hop-4, Hokolesqua Opechan-3, Cleopatra the Shawano Powhatan-2, Wahunsonacock-1) was born on 10 Aug 1938 in Birmingham, Jefferson Co., AL. She died on 6 Nov 2011 at the age of 73 at Garden Terrace Nursing Home in Douglasville, Douglas Co., GA.

Bobbie Jo WEEKS and Bob DAVIS were married on 4 Sep 1959. **Bob DAVIS** was born on 11 Apr 1938.

Bob DAVIS and Bobbie Jo WEEKS had the following children:

- 490   i. **Donna Rene DAVIS**, born 9 Feb 1961; married Joseph Gordon LONG; married Frank Newton FINCHER.
- 491   ii. **Michael Ray DAVIS**, born 30 Sep 1963; married Lori .

446. **Mary Sue PALMER** (Venice Myrtle WEEKS-13, Elizabeth "Lizzie Beth" BUSSEY-12, Edmund Moody-11, Martha (Malinda) Moseley-10, George-9, Margaret Vann-8, Edward Ned-7, Mary Lewis Barnes-6, April-Tkikami Hop Turkey-5, Big Turkey Hop-4, Hokolesqua Opechan-3, Cleopatra the Shawano Powhatan-2, Wahunsonacock-1) was born (date unknown).

Robert HANNAH was born (date unknown).

Robert HANNAH and Mary Sue PALMER had the following children:

- 492   i. **Michael Lester HANNAH**, married Vickie HOLDEN; married Brenda .
- 493   ii. **Jeffery Lawrence HANNAH**, married Debra .
- 494   iii. **Robert Bradley HANNAH**, married Joyce SHAW.

447. **James Walter PALMER** (Venice Myrtle WEEKS-13, Elizabeth "Lizzie Beth" BUSSEY-12, Edmund Moody-11, Martha (Malinda) Moseley-10, George-9, Margaret Vann-8, Edward Ned-7, Mary Lewis Barnes-6, April-Tkikami Hop Turkey-5, Big Turkey Hop-4, Hokolesqua Opechan-3, Cleopatra the Shawano Powhatan-2, Wahunsonacock-1) was born in 1928. He died on 26 Feb 1995 at the age of 67. He was buried on 28 Feb 1995 in Cordova, Alabama.

James Walter PALMER and JoAnn RODEN were married. **JoAnn RODEN** was born (date unknown).

James Walter PALMER and JoAnn RODEN had the following children:

- 495   i. **Jon Randle "Randy" PALMER**.
- 496   ii. **William Andrew (Bill) PALMER**, married Donna WATTS.
- 497   iii. **Mark Dexter PALMER**, married Anna BLACK.
- 498   iv. **Paul Greg PALMER**, married Michelle ENGLAND.

448. **Wayne Martin WEEKS** (Marvin Benson-13, Elizabeth "Lizzie Beth" BUSSEY-12, Edmund Moody-11, Martha (Malinda) Moseley-10, George-9, Margaret Vann-8, Edward Ned-7, Mary Lewis Barnes-6, April-Tkikami Hop Turkey-5, Big Turkey Hop-4, Hokolesqua Opechan-3, Cleopatra the Shawano Powhatan-2, Wahunsonacock-1) was born (date unknown).

Descendants of Chief Wahunsonacock Powhatan

26 January 2012

Wayne Martin WEEKS and Ann SMITH were married. **Ann SMITH** was born (date unknown).

Wayne Martin WEEKS and Ann SMITH had the following children:

499	i.	**Donald Wayne WEEKS**, married Patricia Jo ; married Pierina GALLO.
500	ii.	**Cynthia Diane WEEKS**, married Michael MARTIN.
501	iii.	**Lisa Anne WEEKS**, married David LE.

449. **Jerry Earl WEEKS** (Marvin Benson-13, Elizabeth "Lizzie Beth" BUSSEY-12, Edmund Moody-11, Martha (Malinda) Moseley-10, George-9, Margaret Vann-8, Edward Ned-7, Mary Lewis Barnes-6, April-Tkikami Hop Turkey-5, Big Turkey Hop-4, Hokolesqua Opechan-3, Cleopatra the Shawano Powhatan-2, Wahunsonacock-1) was born (date unknown).

Elizabeth WADSWORTH was born (date unknown).

Jerry Earl WEEKS and Elizabeth WADSWORTH had the following children:

502	i.	**David Earl WEEKS**, born 4 Sep 1968; died 8 Dec 2001, FL.
503	ii.	**Allison WEEKS**, married Dale YIELDING.

450. **Wanda Gay WEEKS** (Marvin Benson-13, Elizabeth "Lizzie Beth" BUSSEY-12, Edmund Moody-11, Martha (Malinda) Moseley-10, George-9, Margaret Vann-8, Edward Ned-7, Mary Lewis Barnes-6, April-Tkikami Hop Turkey-5, Big Turkey Hop-4, Hokolesqua Opechan-3, Cleopatra the Shawano Powhatan-2, Wahunsonacock-1) was born (date unknown).

Harold "Buddy" HUBBARD was born (date unknown).

Harold "Buddy" HUBBARD and Wanda Gay WEEKS had the following child:

i. **Christopher Benson WEEKS** was born (date unknown).

451. **Betty Lou HAMILTON** (Verda Louise WEEKS-13, Elizabeth "Lizzie Beth" BUSSEY-12, Edmund Moody-11, Martha (Malinda) Moseley-10, George-9, Margaret Vann-8, Edward Ned-7, Mary Lewis Barnes-6, April-Tkikami Hop Turkey-5, Big Turkey Hop-4, Hokolesqua Opechan-3, Cleopatra the Shawano Powhatan-2, Wahunsonacock-1) was born on 11 Jun 1937. She was buried in Jun 1970 in East Dora Cemetery, Dora, Walker Co., AL. She died on 10 Jun 1970 at the age of 32.

Kenneth BEAM, son of Chatman Loys BEAM and Lillie Mae BUSHARD, was born on 17 Sep 1934. He died in 2005 at the age of 71 in Jefferson Co., AL.

Kenneth BEAM and Betty Lou HAMILTON had the following children:

504	i.	**Donna Jo BEAM**, born 2 Nov 1955.
505	ii.	**Kathy Louise BEAM**, born 18 Apr 1957.
506	iii.	**Elizabeth Kay BEAM**, born 26 Mar 1958.
507	iv.	**Martin Eric BEAM**, born 28 Apr 1960.

Descendants of Chief Wahunsonacock Powhatan

James Vernon CORK was born on 8 Aug 1924. He died on 13 Mar 1993 at the age of 68.

James Vernon CORK and Betty Lou HAMILTON had the following children:

            i. **Rose Diane CORK** was born on 9 Jan 1964.
508   ii. **James Earl (Jim) CORK**, born 9 Jan 1965; married Theresa MCCAUGHREN.

452. **Ronnie Lee HAMILTON** (Verda Louise WEEKS-13, Elizabeth "Lizzie Beth" BUSSEY-12, Edmund Moody-11, Martha (Malinda) Moseley-10, George-9, Margaret Vann-8, Edward Ned-7, Mary Lewis Barnes-6, April-Tkikami Hop Turkey-5, Big Turkey Hop-4, Hokolesqua Opechan-3, Cleopatra the Shawano Powhatan-2, Wahunsonacock-1) was born on 26 Apr 1941. He died on 2 Jul 2010 at the age of 69 in GA. He was buried on 6 Jul 2010 in Jefferson, GA.

Ronnie Lee HAMILTON and Wanda Faye HANNAH were married in 1959. **Wanda Faye HANNAH** was born on 24 Nov 1940.

Ronnie Lee HAMILTON and Wanda Faye HANNAH had the following children:

509   i. **Russell Allen HAMILTON**, born 16 Nov 1961.
510   ii. **Ronnie Todd HAMILTON**, born 18 Sep 1967.

453. **Sandra MCKINNEY** (Mary Louise LOWERY-13, Minnie Malinda BUSSEY-12, Edmund Moody-11, Martha (Malinda) Moseley-10, George-9, Margaret Vann-8, Edward Ned-7, Mary Lewis Barnes-6, April-Tkikami Hop Turkey-5, Big Turkey Hop-4, Hokolesqua Opechan-3, Cleopatra the Shawano Powhatan-2, Wahunsonacock-1) was born on 29 May 1944.

Sandra MCKINNEY and STORM were married. **STORM** was born (date unknown).

STORM and Sandra MCKINNEY had the following child:

            i. **Joseph Erik STORM** was born in 1962.

454. **Debbie MCCRARY** (Aileen Hollis-13, Mattie Marie "Sweetie" BUSSEY-12, Edmund Moody-11, Martha (Malinda) Moseley-10, George-9, Margaret Vann-8, Edward Ned-7, Mary Lewis Barnes-6, April-Tkikami Hop Turkey-5, Big Turkey Hop-4, Hokolesqua Opechan-3, Cleopatra the Shawano Powhatan-2, Wahunsonacock-1) was born in 1955.

Debbie MCCRARY and Bill HILL were married. **Bill HILL** was born in 1949.

Bill HILL and Debbie MCCRARY had the following children:

511   i. **Lindsay Hyche HILL**, born 25 Mar 1976; married Clyde L. BARLOW.
512   ii. **Mary Hyche HILL**, born 10 Mar 1979; married Conner ; died 11 Mar 2007.

455. **Kimberly SMITH** (Carolyn BUSSEY-13, Johnny-12, Edmund Moody-11, Martha (Malinda) Moseley-10, George-9, Margaret Vann-8, Edward Ned-7, Mary Lewis Barnes-6, April-Tkikami Hop Turkey-5, Big Turkey Hop-4, Hokolesqua Opechan-3, Cleopatra the Shawano Powhatan-2, Wahunsonacock-1) was born on 10 Nov 1963.

Dennis MCDONALD was born (date unknown).

456. **Sandra MOSLEY** (Frank Hiram-13, Robert Herman-12, Hiram Mace-11, William Lafayette-10, George-9, Margaret Vann-8, Edward Ned-7, Mary Lewis Barnes-6, April-Tkikami Hop Turkey-5, Big Turkey Hop-4, Hokolesqua Opechan-3, Cleopatra the Shawano Powhatan-2, Wahunsonacock-1) was born on 2 Jan 1962.

Sandra MOSLEY and George Lewis HAWKINS were married on 22 Oct 2004. **George Lewis HAWKINS** was born on 15 Sep 1950 in The Dalles, OR.

Sandra MOSLEY and Phillip Anthony ROPER were married in 1963 in Jefferson Co., AL. **Phillip Anthony ROPER** was born (date unknown).

Phillip Anthony ROPER and Sandra MOSLEY had the following child:

    513   i. **Teresa Michelle ROPER**, born 7 Mar 1983.

Descendants of Chief Wahunsonacock Powhatan

Fifteenth Generation

457. **Sally Darlene HINCHMAN** (Warren-14, Ella Mae Rogers-13, Sallie Armstrong-12, Monroe Griffin-11, Sarah Ann Poland-10, Nancy Naomi Moseley-9, Margaret Vann-8, Edward Ned-7, Mary Lewis Barnes-6, April-Tkikami Hop Turkey-5, Big Turkey Hop-4, Hokolesqua Opechan-3, Cleopatra the Shawano Powhatan-2, Wahunsonacock-1) was born on 4 Sep 1942 in Brady, TX.

Sally Darlene HINCHMAN and Jerry Duaine MCANULTY were married. **Jerry Duaine MCANULTY** was born on 5 Jan 1940 in TX.

Jerry Duaine MCANULTY and Sally Darlene HINCHMAN had the following child:

    i. **Lisa Darlene MCANULTY** was born (date unknown).

458. **Latta Lillian RUHMANN** (Dorothy Latta Beasley-14, Flay Latta Watkins-13, Leslie Virginia Latta-12, Lenora Lee Poland-11, John Stratton-10, Nancy Naomi Moseley-9, Margaret Vann-8, Edward Ned-7, Mary Lewis Barnes-6, April-Tkikami Hop Turkey-5, Big Turkey Hop-4, Hokolesqua Opechan-3, Cleopatra the Shawano Powhatan-2, Wahunsonacock-1) was born on 26 Oct 1947 in Beeville, TX.

Latta Lillian RUHMANN and Donley Randall STEPHENSON were married in Austin, Travis Co., TX. **Donley Randall STEPHENSON** was born on 1 Feb 1944.

459. **Robert LAWSON** (Sue Angela Stinson-14, Ferrolyn MOSLEY-13, William Alexander (Oscar)-12, William Alexander Newton-11, George Benjamin Alexander-10, George-9, Margaret Vann-8, Edward Ned-7, Mary Lewis Barnes-6, April-Tkikami Hop Turkey-5, Big Turkey Hop-4, Hokolesqua Opechan-3, Cleopatra the Shawano Powhatan-2, Wahunsonacock-1) was born in Covington Co., AL.

Robert LAWSON and Jan were married. **Jan** was born (date unknown).

460. **Craig GOOLSBY** (Rae Evelyn Stinson-14, Ferrolyn MOSLEY-13, William Alexander (Oscar)-12, William Alexander Newton-11, George Benjamin Alexander-10, George-9, Margaret Vann-8, Edward Ned-7, Mary Lewis Barnes-6, April-Tkikami Hop Turkey-5, Big Turkey Hop-4, Hokolesqua Opechan-3, Cleopatra the Shawano Powhatan-2, Wahunsonacock-1) was born about 1963 in Florala, Covington Co., AL.

Craig GOOLSBY and Sonjia SCOTT were married. **Sonjia SCOTT** was born about 1965 in FL.

461. **Vivia June JOHNSON** (Dorothy Lee Smith-14, Gladys Lula BUSSEY-13, Charles Drennen-12, Benjamin Harm-11, Martha (Malinda) Moseley-10, George-9, Margaret Vann-8, Edward Ned-7, Mary Lewis Barnes-6, April-Tkikami Hop

Descendants of Chief Wahunsonacock Powhatan   26 January 2012

Turkey-5, Big Turkey Hop-4, Hokolesqua Opechan-3, Cleopatra the Shawano Powhatan-2, Wahunsonacock-1) was born on 18 Jun 1948 in AL.

Vivia June JOHNSON and Lonnie DURBIN were married on 27 Mar 1971 in Spring Hill, TN. **Lonnie DURBIN** was born on 16 Apr 1940 in Center, IN.

Lonnie DURBIN and Vivia June JOHNSON had the following children:

    i. **Mitchell DURBIN** was born on 18 Feb 1968 in Kokomo IN.
    ii. **Tim DURBIN** was born on 31 Jul 1969 in Kokomo IN.
    iii. **Curtis DURBIN** was born on 9 Nov 1971 in Kokomo IN.
    iv. **Daniel DURBIN** was born on 9 Feb 1974 in Kokomo IN.

462. **Larry Jim JOHNSON** (Dorothy Lee Smith-14, Gladys Lula BUSSEY-13, Charles Drennen-12, Benjamin Harm-11, Martha (Malinda) Moseley-10, George-9, Margaret Vann-8, Edward Ned-7, Mary Lewis Barnes-6, April-Tkikami Hop Turkey-5, Big Turkey Hop-4, Hokolesqua Opechan-3, Cleopatra the Shawano Powhatan-2, Wahunsonacock-1) was born on 15 Aug 1950 in Kokomo IN.

Larry Jim JOHNSON and Darlene Ann DAVIS were married on 15 Jul 1972 in Kokomo IN. **Darlene Ann DAVIS** was born on 9 Dec 1953 in Chelsea, MA.

Larry Jim JOHNSON and Darlene Ann DAVIS had the following children:

  514   i. **Melanie A. JOHNSON**, born 10 Mar 1975, Fort Knox, KY; married Chad E. SPRAKER, 21 Nov 1998, Frankfort, IN.
    ii. **Crystal L. JOHNSON** was born on 13 Jun 1980 in Fort Hood, TX.
    iii. **Aaron M. JOHNSON** was born on 10 Sep 1990 in Kokomo IN.

463. **Jesse H. JOHNSON** (Dorothy Lee Smith-14, Gladys Lula BUSSEY-13, Charles Drennen-12, Benjamin Harm-11, Martha (Malinda) Moseley-10, George-9, Margaret Vann-8, Edward Ned-7, Mary Lewis Barnes-6, April-Tkikami Hop Turkey-5, Big Turkey Hop-4, Hokolesqua Opechan-3, Cleopatra the Shawano Powhatan-2, Wahunsonacock-1) was born on 4 Dec 1954 in Kokomo IN.

Jesse H. JOHNSON and Sue Dorothy ROSSOW were married on 10 Jul 1993 in St. Louis, MO. **Sue Dorothy ROSSOW** was born on 4 Dec 1955.

464. **Susan Marie JONES** (Winfred Marie Falgout-14, Mattie Marie BUSSEY-13, James "Jimmy" David-12, Benjamin Harm-11, Martha (Malinda) Moseley-10, George-9, Margaret Vann-8, Edward Ned-7, Mary Lewis Barnes-6, April-Tkikami Hop Turkey-5, Big Turkey Hop-4, Hokolesqua Opechan-3, Cleopatra the Shawano Powhatan-2, Wahunsonacock-1) was born (date unknown).

Susan Marie JONES and George Allen WILKINSON were married on 15 Aug 1965. **George Allen WILKINSON** was born (date unknown).

Descendants of Chief Wahunsonacock Powhatan

26 January 2012

George Allen WILKINSON and Susan Marie JONES had the following child:

    515   i. **Jana Marie WILKINSON**, born 13 May 1968.

Susan Marie JONES and J. Thomas BRAKEFIELD were married in Dec 1975. **J. Thomas BRAKEFIELD** died in May 1993.

465. **Phillip Wayne JONES** (Winfred Marie Falgout-14, Mattie Marie BUSSEY-13, James "Jimmy" David-12, Benjamin Harm-11, Martha (Malinda) Moseley-10, George-9, Margaret Vann-8, Edward Ned-7, Mary Lewis Barnes-6, April-Tkikami Hop Turkey-5, Big Turkey Hop-4, Hokolesqua Opechan-3, Cleopatra the Shawano Powhatan-2, Wahunsonacock-1) was born (date unknown).

Pat THOMAS was born (date unknown).

466. **Beverly Carolann COALTER** (Ann Elizabeth Mandolini-14, Ruby Elizabeth BUSSEY-13, James "Jimmy" David-12, Benjamin Harm-11, Martha (Malinda) Moseley-10, George-9, Margaret Vann-8, Edward Ned-7, Mary Lewis Barnes-6, April-Tkikami Hop Turkey-5, Big Turkey Hop-4, Hokolesqua Opechan-3, Cleopatra the Shawano Powhatan-2, Wahunsonacock-1) was born on 14 Feb 1956 in Greenville, Washington Co., MS.

Beverly Carolann COALTER and Calvin Wayne NEFF were married on 1 May 1981 in Huntsville, AR. **Calvin Wayne NEFF** was born on 23 Oct 1957.

Calvin Wayne NEFF and Beverly Carolann COALTER had the following children:

        i. **Issac Eugene NEFF** was born on 31 Aug 1984 in Eureka Springs, Carroll Co., AR.
       ii. **Charity Elizabeth NEFF** was born on 11 Sep 1987.

467. **Alton Bayne, Jr. COALTER** (Ann Elizabeth Mandolini-14, Ruby Elizabeth BUSSEY-13, James "Jimmy" David-12, Benjamin Harm-11, Martha (Malinda) Moseley-10, George-9, Margaret Vann-8, Edward Ned-7, Mary Lewis Barnes-6, April-Tkikami Hop Turkey-5, Big Turkey Hop-4, Hokolesqua Opechan-3, Cleopatra the Shawano Powhatan-2, Wahunsonacock-1) was born on 5 Dec 1957 in Greenville, Washington Co., MS.

Alton Bayne, Jr. COALTER and Pamela Joyce KELLY were married on 15 May 1976 in Fayetteville, AR. **Pamela Joyce KELLY** was born on 9 Aug 1956 in Minneapolis, MN.

Alton Bayne, Jr. COALTER and Pamela Joyce KELLY had the following child:

    516   i. **Emily Jennette COALTER**, born 17 Jan 1979, Clarendon, Monroe Co., AR; married Peter Nathan WILLIAMSON, 26 Jul 1997, Auburn, Sangamon Co., IL.

Descendants of Chief Wahunsonacock Powhatan

468. **Charles William MCCRARY** (Frances Blackburn-14, Tee Ester WASHINGTON-13, Emma Ollie BUSSEY-12, Edmund Moody-11, Martha (Malinda) Moseley-10, George-9, Margaret Vann-8, Edward Ned-7, Mary Lewis Barnes-6, April-Tkikami Hop Turkey-5, Big Turkey Hop-4, Hokolesqua Opechan-3, Cleopatra the Shawano Powhatan-2, Wahunsonacock-1) was born (date unknown).

Charles William MCCRARY and Virginia DICKINSON were married. **Virginia DICKINSON** was born (date unknown).

Charles William MCCRARY and Virginia DICKINSON had the following child:

　　i. **Charles Dennis MCCRARY** was born on 26 Oct 1956 in Jefferson Co., AL.

469. **Roger Dale GUYTON II** (Roger Dale-14, Ernest Paul-13, Luanna BUSSEY-12, Edmund Moody-11, Martha (Malinda) Moseley-10, George-9, Margaret Vann-8, Edward Ned-7, Mary Lewis Barnes-6, April-Tkikami Hop Turkey-5, Big Turkey Hop-4, Hokolesqua Opechan-3, Cleopatra the Shawano Powhatan-2, Wahunsonacock-1) was born on 7 Nov 1974. He held the title of II.

Roger Dale GUYTON II and Jennifer Sue AUTRY were married. **Jennifer Sue AUTRY** was born (date unknown).

470. **Erin Nicole GUYTON** (Roger Dale-14, Ernest Paul-13, Luanna BUSSEY-12, Edmund Moody-11, Martha (Malinda) Moseley-10, George-9, Margaret Vann-8, Edward Ned-7, Mary Lewis Barnes-6, April-Tkikami Hop Turkey-5, Big Turkey Hop-4, Hokolesqua Opechan-3, Cleopatra the Shawano Powhatan-2, Wahunsonacock-1) was born on 16 Feb 1981 in Florence, Lauderdale Co., AL.

Erin Nicole GUYTON and Edward Steven LARKIN were married on 1 Jun 2002. **Edward Steven LARKIN**, son of Edward LARKIN and Debbie CURRY, was born on 18 Sep 1971 in Philadelphia, PA.

Edward Steven LARKIN and Erin Nicole GUYTON had the following child:

　　i. **Child LARKIN** was born (date unknown).

471. **Cheryl Lynn GODSEY** (Daisy Wonnell BUSSEY-14, Otis Howard-13, Rufus Thomas-12, Edmund Moody-11, Martha (Malinda) Moseley-10, George-9, Margaret Vann-8, Edward Ned-7, Mary Lewis Barnes-6, April-Tkikami Hop Turkey-5, Big Turkey Hop-4, Hokolesqua Opechan-3, Cleopatra the Shawano Powhatan-2, Wahunsonacock-1) was born on 16 Nov 1954 in Prestonburg, KY.

Cheryl Lynn GODSEY and Darrell Keith LESLIE were married on 13 Jan 1973 in Prestonburg, KY. **Darrell Keith LESLIE**, son of Frank LESLIE and Hester WOODS, was born on 24 Oct 1954.

Darrell Keith LESLIE and Cheryl Lynn GODSEY had the following children:

　　i. **Jonathan Keith LESLIE** was born on 20 Jul 1973 in Lexington, KY.
　　ii. **Darrell Blake LESLIE** was born on 28 Aug 1977 in Lexington, KY.

Descendants of Chief Wahunsonacock Powhatan

26 January 2012

472. **Nancy GODSEY** (Daisy Wonnell BUSSEY-14, Otis Howard-13, Rufus Thomas-12, Edmund Moody-11, Martha (Malinda) Moseley-10, George-9, Margaret Vann-8, Edward Ned-7, Mary Lewis Barnes-6, April-Tkikami Hop Turkey-5, Big Turkey Hop-4, Hokolesqua Opechan-3, Cleopatra the Shawano Powhatan-2, Wahunsonacock-1) was born on 15 Feb 1961 in Louisville, Jefferson Co., KY.

Nancy GODSEY and Lawrence Bradley BAKER were married on 13 Jul 1985 in Prestonburg, KY. **Lawrence Bradley BAKER**, son of William BAKER and Barbara HILL, was born on 14 Jul 1962 in Davis Co., KY.

Lawrence Bradley BAKER and Nancy GODSEY had the following child:

    i. **Worth BAKER** was born on 22 Aug 1993.

473. **William Thomas, Jr. BUSSEY** (William Thomas-14, Otis Howard-13, Rufus Thomas-12, Edmund Moody-11, Martha (Malinda) Moseley-10, George-9, Margaret Vann-8, Edward Ned-7, Mary Lewis Barnes-6, April-Tkikami Hop Turkey-5, Big Turkey Hop-4, Hokolesqua Opechan-3, Cleopatra the Shawano Powhatan-2, Wahunsonacock-1) was born on 10 Aug 1954 in Anchorage, AK.

William Thomas, Jr. BUSSEY and Dana DECKER were married in Ft. Lauderdale, FL. **Dana DECKER** was born (date unknown).

474. **James Howard BUSSEY** (William Thomas-14, Otis Howard-13, Rufus Thomas-12, Edmund Moody-11, Martha (Malinda) Moseley-10, George-9, Margaret Vann-8, Edward Ned-7, Mary Lewis Barnes-6, April-Tkikami Hop Turkey-5, Big Turkey Hop-4, Hokolesqua Opechan-3, Cleopatra the Shawano Powhatan-2, Wahunsonacock-1) was born on 21 Aug 1957 in Ft. Knox, KY.

Sandra UNK was born (date unknown).

James Howard BUSSEY and Connie Francis EAGEN were married on 21 Aug 1978 in Keleen, TX. **Connie Francis EAGEN** was born (date unknown).

James Howard BUSSEY and Connie Francis EAGEN had the following children:

    i. **Elizabeth Francis BUSSEY** was born on 24 Sep 1980.
   ii. **Jennifer BUSSEY** was born on 12 Sep 1981.

James Howard BUSSEY and Sharon Elizabeth FLEMING were married on 15 Jun 1996 in Boynton Beach, Palm Beach Co., FL. **Sharon Elizabeth FLEMING**, daughter of Francis FLEMING and Judy SWEET, was born on 30 Jul 1969 in Boynton Beach, Palm Beach Co., FL.

Descendants of Chief Wahunsonacock Powhatan

26 January 2012

475. **Jerra Rae COLLINS** (Peggy Jean BUSSEY-14, Dawson Ellard-13, Rufus Thomas-12, Edmund Moody-11, Martha (Malinda) Moseley-10, George-9, Margaret Vann-8, Edward Ned-7, Mary Lewis Barnes-6, April-Tkikami Hop Turkey-5, Big Turkey Hop-4, Hokolesqua Opechan-3, Cleopatra the Shawano Powhatan-2, Wahunsonacock-1) was born on 3 May 1953.

Jerra Rae COLLINS and David Morton CAMPBELL were married on 12 Jun 1971 in Clintwood, VA. **David Morton CAMPBELL**, son of Asa CAMPBELL and Hazel UNK, was born on 14 Nov 1944 in Wolfe Co., KY.

David Morton CAMPBELL and Jerra Rae COLLINS had the following children:

      i. **David CAMPBELL** was born on 10 Dec 1973 in Campton, KY.
     ii. **Lori Rae CAMPBELL** was born on 19 Nov 1975.

476. **Margaret Elizabeth COLLINS** (Peggy Jean BUSSEY-14, Dawson Ellard-13, Rufus Thomas-12, Edmund Moody-11, Martha (Malinda) Moseley-10, George-9, Margaret Vann-8, Edward Ned-7, Mary Lewis Barnes-6, April-Tkikami Hop Turkey-5, Big Turkey Hop-4, Hokolesqua Opechan-3, Cleopatra the Shawano Powhatan-2, Wahunsonacock-1) was born on 22 Jul 1955.

Margaret Elizabeth COLLINS and Ballard HYDEN were married on 5 Mar 1977. **Ballard HYDEN** was born (date unknown).

Ballard HYDEN and Margaret Elizabeth COLLINS had the following child:

517   i. **Nova Rebecca HYDEN**, born 11 Feb 1978.

477. **Elizabeth Rae HOWARD** (Toby Ann BUSSEY-14, Dawson Ellard-13, Rufus Thomas-12, Edmund Moody-11, Martha (Malinda) Moseley-10, George-9, Margaret Vann-8, Edward Ned-7, Mary Lewis Barnes-6, April-Tkikami Hop Turkey-5, Big Turkey Hop-4, Hokolesqua Opechan-3, Cleopatra the Shawano Powhatan-2, Wahunsonacock-1) was born on 22 Dec 1961 in Paintsville, KY.

Elizabeth Rae HOWARD and Jeffrey Oran PECK were married on 9 Dec 1978 in Clintwood, VA. **Jeffrey Oran PECK** was born on 24 Jul 1958.

Jeffrey Oran PECK and Elizabeth Rae HOWARD had the following children:

      i. **Joshua Howard PECK** was born on 21 Oct 1980 in West Liberty, KY.
     ii. **Jesse Ray PECK** was born on 14 Aug 1982 in Martin, KY.
    iii. **Jodi Kathryn PECK** was born on 11 Nov 1987 in Prestonburg, KY.

478. **Melissa Ann HOWARD** (Toby Ann BUSSEY-14, Dawson Ellard-13, Rufus Thomas-12, Edmund Moody-11, Martha (Malinda) Moseley-10, George-9, Margaret Vann-8, Edward Ned-7, Mary Lewis Barnes-6, April-Tkikami Hop Turkey-5, Big Turkey Hop-4, Hokolesqua Opechan-3, Cleopatra the Shawano Powhatan-2, Wahunsonacock-1) was born on 29 Dec 1966 in West Liberty, KY.

Descendants of Chief Wahunsonacock Powhatan

Michael Dean PRESTON was born (date unknown).

Michael Dean PRESTON and Melissa Ann HOWARD had the following child:

    i. **Maggie Ann HOWARD** was born on 17 Jan 1983 in Ashland, KY.

Gary Dean JONES was born (date unknown).

Gary Dean JONES and Melissa Ann HOWARD had the following child:

    i. **Micaela Dominique BLAIR** was born on 24 Aug 1991 in Prestonburg, KY.

Melissa Ann HOWARD and Evertt Dwight BLAIR were married on 8 Jun 1985 in Paintsville, KY. **Evertt Dwight BLAIR** was born on 30 Oct 1967.

Evertt Dwight BLAIR and Melissa Ann HOWARD had the following child:

    i. **Jon-Erik Dwight BLAIR** was born on 23 Sep 1988 in Ashland, KY.

Melissa Ann HOWARD and Gary Darrell BLAIR were married on 2 May 1992 in Middlefork, KY. **Gary Darrell BLAIR** was born (date unknown).

Gary Darrell BLAIR and Melissa Ann HOWARD had the following child:

    i. **Cari Amber BLAIR** was born on 8 May 1995 in Prestonburg, KY.

479. **Sandra Gayle SMITH** (Judith Sharon BUSSEY-14, Dawson Ellard-13, Rufus Thomas-12, Edmund Moody-11, Martha (Malinda) Moseley-10, George-9, Margaret Vann-8, Edward Ned-7, Mary Lewis Barnes-6, April-Tkikami Hop Turkey-5, Big Turkey Hop-4, Hokolesqua Opechan-3, Cleopatra the Shawano Powhatan-2, Wahunsonacock-1) was born on 3 May 1963 in Williamson, WV.

Mark Lincoln MASSIE was born on 6 Dec 1960 in Phoenix, AZ. He died on 7 Mar 1991 at the age of 30.

Mark Lincoln MASSIE and Sandra Gayle SMITH had the following child:

    i. **Savannah Marie MASSIE** was born on 23 Mar 1991 in Lexington, KY.

480. **Thomas Benton, Jr. SMITH** (Judith Sharon BUSSEY-14, Dawson Ellard-13, Rufus Thomas-12, Edmund Moody-11, Martha (Malinda) Moseley-10, George-9, Margaret Vann-8, Edward Ned-7, Mary Lewis Barnes-6, April-Tkikami Hop Turkey-5, Big Turkey Hop-4, Hokolesqua Opechan-3, Cleopatra the Shawano Powhatan-2, Wahunsonacock-1) was born on 22 Sep 1964 in Williamson, WV.

Thomas Benton, Jr. SMITH and Sherry Lou JONES were married on 22 Aug 1991 in Lexington, KY. **Sherry Lou JONES** was born on 20 Jul 1960.

Thomas Benton, Jr. SMITH and Sherry Lou JONES had the following child:

    i. **Dawson Oliver Reed SMITH** was born on 21 Oct 1994 in Lexington, KY.

481. **Kelly Anne BUSSEY** (Rodney Clark-14, Dawson Ellard-13, Rufus Thomas-12, Edmund Moody-11, Martha (Malinda) Moseley-10, George-9, Margaret Vann-8, Edward Ned-7, Mary Lewis Barnes-6, April-Tkikami Hop Turkey-5, Big Turkey Hop-4, Hokolesqua Opechan-3, Cleopatra the Shawano Powhatan-2, Wahunsonacock-1) was born on 20 Feb 1965 in Huntington, NY.

Kelly Anne BUSSEY and Keene JONES were married on 4 May 1985 in Berea, KY. **Keene JONES** was born on 27 Mar 1964 in Richmond, KY.

Kelly Anne BUSSEY and Howard Clay EVANS were married on 18 Jul 1987 in Gatlinburg, TN. **Howard Clay EVANS** was born on 29 Jan 1957.

Howard Clay EVANS and Kelly Anne BUSSEY had the following children:

    i. **Austin Clay EVANS** was born on 7 Dec 1990 in Lexington, KY.
    ii. **Andrew Blake EVANS** was born on 17 May 1995 in Lexington, KY.

482. **Kimberly Adams BUSSEY** (Rodney Clark-14, Dawson Ellard-13, Rufus Thomas-12, Edmund Moody-11, Martha (Malinda) Moseley-10, George-9, Margaret Vann-8, Edward Ned-7, Mary Lewis Barnes-6, April-Tkikami Hop Turkey-5, Big Turkey Hop-4, Hokolesqua Opechan-3, Cleopatra the Shawano Powhatan-2, Wahunsonacock-1) was born on 9 Nov 1967 in Lexington, KY.

Kimberly Adams BUSSEY and Patrick Benjamin GAY were married on 7 May 1994 in Berea, KY. **Patrick Benjamin GAY** was born on 7 Jan 1967 in Berea, KY.

Patrick Benjamin GAY and Kimberly Adams BUSSEY had the following children:

    i. **Benjamin Patrick Bussey GAY** was born on 22 Dec 1994 in Lexington, KY.
    ii. **Braeden Harding GAY** was born on 12 Nov 1999.

483. **Kelly Jane O'ROURKE** (Karen Rae BUSSEY-14, Dawson Ellard-13, Rufus Thomas-12, Edmund Moody-11, Martha (Malinda) Moseley-10, George-9, Margaret Vann-8, Edward Ned-7, Mary Lewis Barnes-6, April-Tkikami Hop Turkey-5, Big Turkey Hop-4, Hokolesqua Opechan-3, Cleopatra the Shawano Powhatan-2, Wahunsonacock-1) was born on 25 Aug 1970 in Decatur, GA.

David HARMS was born (date unknown).

Descendants of Chief Wahunsonacock Powhatan

26 January 2012

David HARMS and Kelly Jane O'ROURKE had the following child:

    i. **Mackenzie Rose HARMS** was born in Oct 1999.

484. **Amy Katherine O'ROURKE** (Karen Rae BUSSEY-14, Dawson Ellard-13, Rufus Thomas-12, Edmund Moody-11, Martha (Malinda) Moseley-10, George-9, Margaret Vann-8, Edward Ned-7, Mary Lewis Barnes-6, April-Tkikami Hop Turkey-5, Big Turkey Hop-4, Hokolesqua Opechan-3, Cleopatra the Shawano Powhatan-2, Wahunsonacock-1) was born on 10 Mar 1973 in Decatur, GA.

Amy Katherine O'ROURKE and Adam Kelly EDWARD were married on 16 Jun 1995 in Lawrenvile, GA. **Adam Kelly EDWARD** was born on 10 Jan 1970.

485. **Johnny Bruce BUSSEY** (John Rufus-14, Dawson Ellard-13, Rufus Thomas-12, Edmund Moody-11, Martha (Malinda) Moseley-10, George-9, Margaret Vann-8, Edward Ned-7, Mary Lewis Barnes-6, April-Tkikami Hop Turkey-5, Big Turkey Hop-4, Hokolesqua Opechan-3, Cleopatra the Shawano Powhatan-2, Wahunsonacock-1) was born on 25 Nov 1970 in Williamson, WV.

Johnny Bruce BUSSEY and Amy UNK were married on 4 Jan 1997 in Salyersville, KY. **Amy UNK** was born in Salyersville, KY.

Johnny Bruce BUSSEY and Amy UNK had the following child:

    i. **Taylor Elizabeth Hope BUSSEY** was born on 11 May 2000.

486. **Cynthia Lynn ENGLAND** (Frances Michelle Hall-14, Tommie Lee BUSSEY-13, Rufus Thomas-12, Edmund Moody-11, Martha (Malinda) Moseley-10, George-9, Margaret Vann-8, Edward Ned-7, Mary Lewis Barnes-6, April-Tkikami Hop Turkey-5, Big Turkey Hop-4, Hokolesqua Opechan-3, Cleopatra the Shawano Powhatan-2, Wahunsonacock-1) was born on 23 May 1972.

Cynthia Lynn ENGLAND and John David "JD" HUGHES were married on 30 Dec 1995 in Pikeville, Pike Co., KY. **John David "JD" HUGHES** was born on 15 Apr 1971 in Pikeville, KY.

John David "JD" HUGHES and Cynthia Lynn ENGLAND had the following child:

    i. **Emily HUGHES** was born on 13 Oct 1998 in Lexington, KY.

487. **Stephen Douglas WEEKS** (J.D.-14, Era Earl-13, Elizabeth "Lizzie Beth" BUSSEY-12, Edmund Moody-11, Martha (Malinda) Moseley-10, George-9, Margaret Vann-8, Edward Ned-7, Mary Lewis Barnes-6, April-Tkikami Hop Turkey-5, Big Turkey Hop-4, Hokolesqua Opechan-3, Cleopatra the Shawano Powhatan-2, Wahunsonacock-1) was born on 6 Jan 1959 in Birmingham, Jefferson Co., AL. He was baptized in Birmingham, Jefferson Co., AL.

Stephen Douglas WEEKS and Slavomira MELIORISOVA were married on 6 Apr 1991 in Tranava, Czechoslovakia.

Descendants of Chief Wahunsonacock Powhatan

Slavomira MELIORISOVA, daughter of Stefan MELIORIS and Alzbeta VALASOVA, was born on 20 Aug 1964 in Levoca, Slovakia.

Stephen Douglas WEEKS and Slavomira MELIORISOVA had the following children:

  i. **Stephen Middleton WEEKS** was born on 30 Sep 1992 in Decatur, Morgan Co., AL. He died on 10 Jan 1994 at the age of 1 in Houston, TX. He was buried on 14 Jan 1994 in Birmingham, Jefferson Co., AL. Stephen was baptized in Birmingham, Jefferson Co., AL.
  ii. **Edmund Douglas WEEKS** was born on 31 Jan 1994 in Houston, TX. He was baptized on 22 May 1994 in Houston, TX.
  iii. **Hugh Middleton WEEKS** was born on 2 Aug 1995 in Houston, TX.
  iv. **Richard Pearson WEEKS** was born on 14 Jul 2006 in Moscow, Russia.

488. **Jennifer Lynn WEEKS** (J.D.-14, Era Earl-13, Elizabeth "Lizzie Beth" BUSSEY-12, Edmund Moody-11, Martha (Malinda) Moseley-10, George-9, Margaret Vann-8, Edward Ned-7, Mary Lewis Barnes-6, April-Tkikami Hop Turkey-5, Big Turkey Hop-4, Hokolesqua Opechan-3, Cleopatra the Shawano Powhatan-2, Wahunsonacock-1) was born on 17 Mar 1961 in Birmingham, Jefferson Co., AL.

Jennifer Lynn WEEKS and Danny Joe BRITTIAN were married on 15 Dec 1979 in Gardendale, Jefferson Co., AL. **Danny Joe BRITTIAN**, son of James Colley BRITTIAN and Carolyn Jeanette HOLLIS, was born on 24 Aug 1960 in AL.

Danny Joe BRITTIAN and Jennifer Lynn WEEKS had the following children:

  i. **Jarred Michael BRITTIAN** was born on 24 Jan 1988 in Birmingham, Jefferson Co., AL.
  ii. **James Ryan BRITTIAN** was born on 11 Dec 1991 in Birmingham, Jefferson Co., AL.

489. **Catherine Marie WEEKS** (J.D.-14, Era Earl-13, Elizabeth "Lizzie Beth" BUSSEY-12, Edmund Moody-11, Martha (Malinda) Moseley-10, George-9, Margaret Vann-8, Edward Ned-7, Mary Lewis Barnes-6, April-Tkikami Hop Turkey-5, Big Turkey Hop-4, Hokolesqua Opechan-3, Cleopatra the Shawano Powhatan-2, Wahunsonacock-1) was born on 28 Mar 1963 in Birmingham, Jefferson Co., AL.

Catherine Marie WEEKS and Christopher Alan SHELNUTT were married on 14 Oct 1988 in Gardendale, Jefferson Co., AL. **Christopher Alan SHELNUTT**, son of Thomas Floyd SHELNUTT and Willie Faye THOMAS, was born on 25 Jan 1964 in South Highland Hospital, Birmingham, AL.

Christopher Alan SHELNUTT and Catherine Marie WEEKS had the following children:

  i. **Christopher Michael SHELNUTT** was born on 6 Oct 1989 in Birmingham, Jefferson Co., AL.
  ii. **Joseph Matthew SHELNUTT** was born on 1 Nov 1991 in Birmingham, Jefferson Co., AL.
  iii. **Elizabeth Jane SHELNUTT** was born on 10 Oct 1996 in Birmingham, Jefferson Co., AL.
  iv. **Jonathan Thomas SHELNUTT** was born on 26 Jun 1998 in Birmingham, Jefferson Co., AL.

490. **Donna Rene DAVIS** (Bobbie Jo WEEKS-14, Era Earl-13, Elizabeth "Lizzie Beth" BUSSEY-12, Edmund Moody-11, Martha (Malinda) Moseley-10, George-9, Margaret Vann-8, Edward Ned-7, Mary Lewis Barnes-6, April-Tkikami Hop Turkey-5, Big Turkey Hop-4, Hokolesqua Opechan-3, Cleopatra the Shawano Powhatan-2, Wahunsonacock-1) was born on 9 Feb 1961.

Descendants of Chief Wahunsonacock Powhatan

26 January 2012

Donna Rene DAVIS and Joseph Gordon LONG were married. **Joseph Gordon LONG** was born (date unknown).

Joseph Gordon LONG and Donna Rene DAVIS had the following child:

    i. **Chad Mikel LONG** was born on 20 Feb 1988 in Douglasville, Douglas Co., GA.

Donna Rene DAVIS and Frank Newton FINCHER were married. **Frank Newton FINCHER** was born on 21 Aug 1962.

Frank Newton FINCHER and Donna Rene DAVIS had the following child:

    i. **Corey Isaac FINCHER** was born on 23 Apr 1992 in Douglasville, Douglas Co., GA.

491. **Michael Ray DAVIS** (Bobbie Jo WEEKS-14, Era Earl-13, Elizabeth "Lizzie Beth" BUSSEY-12, Edmund Moody-11, Martha (Malinda) Moseley-10, George-9, Margaret Vann-8, Edward Ned-7, Mary Lewis Barnes-6, April-Tkikami Hop Turkey-5, Big Turkey Hop-4, Hokolesqua Opechan-3, Cleopatra the Shawano Powhatan-2, Wahunsonacock-1) was born on 30 Sep 1963.

Michael Ray DAVIS and Lori were married. **Lori** was born in 1969.

Michael Ray DAVIS and Lori had the following children:

    i. **Emily DAVIS** was born in 1992.
    ii. **Madison DAVIS** was born in 2002.

492. **Michael Lester HANNAH** (Mary Sue PALMER-14, Venice Myrtle WEEKS-13, Elizabeth "Lizzie Beth" BUSSEY-12, Edmund Moody-11, Martha (Malinda) Moseley-10, George-9, Margaret Vann-8, Edward Ned-7, Mary Lewis Barnes-6, April-Tkikami Hop Turkey-5, Big Turkey Hop-4, Hokolesqua Opechan-3, Cleopatra the Shawano Powhatan-2, Wahunsonacock-1) was born (date unknown).

Michael Lester HANNAH and Vickie HOLDEN were married. **Vickie HOLDEN** was born (date unknown).

Michael Lester HANNAH and Vickie HOLDEN had the following child:

    i. **Jennifer HANNAH** was born (date unknown).

Michael Lester HANNAH and Brenda were married. **Brenda** was born (date unknown).

493. **Jeffery Lawrence HANNAH** (Mary Sue PALMER-14, Venice Myrtle WEEKS-13, Elizabeth "Lizzie Beth" BUSSEY-12, Edmund Moody-11, Martha (Malinda) Moseley-10, George-9, Margaret Vann-8, Edward Ned-7, Mary Lewis Barnes-6, April-Tkikami Hop Turkey-5, Big Turkey Hop-4, Hokolesqua Opechan-3, Cleopatra the Shawano Powhatan-2,

Descendants of Chief Wahunsonacock Powhatan

26 January 2012

Wahunsonacock-1) was born (date unknown).

Jeffery Lawrence HANNAH and Debra were married. **Debra** was born (date unknown).

Jeffery Lawrence HANNAH and Debra had the following child:

    i. **Matthew HANNAH** was born (date unknown).

494. **Robert Bradley HANNAH** (Mary Sue PALMER-14, Venice Myrtle WEEKS-13, Elizabeth "Lizzie Beth" BUSSEY-12, Edmund Moody-11, Martha (Malinda) Moseley-10, George-9, Margaret Vann-8, Edward Ned-7, Mary Lewis Barnes-6, April-Tkikami Hop Turkey-5, Big Turkey Hop-4, Hokolesqua Opechan-3, Cleopatra the Shawano Powhatan-2, Wahunsonacock-1) was born (date unknown).

Robert Bradley HANNAH and Joyce SHAW were married. **Joyce SHAW** was born (date unknown).

Robert Bradley HANNAH and Joyce SHAW had the following children:

    i. **Angela Faye HANNAH** was born (date unknown).
    ii. **Jessica Marie HANNAH** was born (date unknown).
    iii. **Stacey Leigh HANNAH** was born (date unknown).

495. **Jon Randle "Randy" PALMER** (James Walter-14, Venice Myrtle WEEKS-13, Elizabeth "Lizzie Beth" BUSSEY-12, Edmund Moody-11, Martha (Malinda) Moseley-10, George-9, Margaret Vann-8, Edward Ned-7, Mary Lewis Barnes-6, April-Tkikami Hop Turkey-5, Big Turkey Hop-4, Hokolesqua Opechan-3, Cleopatra the Shawano Powhatan-2, Wahunsonacock-1) was born (date unknown).

Karen CORDELL was born (date unknown).

Jon Randle "Randy" PALMER and Karen CORDELL had the following child:

    i. **Brady PALMER** was born (date unknown).

496. **William Andrew (Bill) PALMER** (James Walter-14, Venice Myrtle WEEKS-13, Elizabeth "Lizzie Beth" BUSSEY-12, Edmund Moody-11, Martha (Malinda) Moseley-10, George-9, Margaret Vann-8, Edward Ned-7, Mary Lewis Barnes-6, April-Tkikami Hop Turkey-5, Big Turkey Hop-4, Hokolesqua Opechan-3, Cleopatra the Shawano Powhatan-2, Wahunsonacock-1) was born (date unknown).

William Andrew (Bill) PALMER and Donna WATTS were married. **Donna WATTS** was born (date unknown).

William Andrew (Bill) PALMER and Donna WATTS had the following child:

    i. **Lauren Elizabeth PALMER** was born (date unknown).

Descendants of Chief Wahunsonacock Powhatan

497. Mark Dexter PALMER (James Walter-14, Venice Myrtle WEEKS-13, Elizabeth "Lizzie Beth" BUSSEY-12, Edmund Moody-11, Martha (Malinda) Moseley-10, George-9, Margaret Vann-8, Edward Ned-7, Mary Lewis Barnes-6, April-Tkikami Hop Turkey-5, Big Turkey Hop-4, Hokolesqua Opechan-3, Cleopatra the Shawano Powhatan-2, Wahunsonacock-1) was born (date unknown).

Mark Dexter PALMER and Anna BLACK were married. **Anna BLACK** was born (date unknown).

Mark Dexter PALMER and Anna BLACK had the following child:

    i. **Anna Lee PALMER** was born (date unknown).

498. Paul Greg PALMER (James Walter-14, Venice Myrtle WEEKS-13, Elizabeth "Lizzie Beth" BUSSEY-12, Edmund Moody-11, Martha (Malinda) Moseley-10, George-9, Margaret Vann-8, Edward Ned-7, Mary Lewis Barnes-6, April-Tkikami Hop Turkey-5, Big Turkey Hop-4, Hokolesqua Opechan-3, Cleopatra the Shawano Powhatan-2, Wahunsonacock-1) was born (date unknown).

Paul Greg PALMER and Michelle ENGLAND were married. **Michelle ENGLAND** was born (date unknown).

499. Donald Wayne WEEKS (Wayne Martin-14, Marvin Benson-13, Elizabeth "Lizzie Beth" BUSSEY-12, Edmund Moody-11, Martha (Malinda) Moseley-10, George-9, Margaret Vann-8, Edward Ned-7, Mary Lewis Barnes-6, April-Tkikami Hop Turkey-5, Big Turkey Hop-4, Hokolesqua Opechan-3, Cleopatra the Shawano Powhatan-2, Wahunsonacock-1) was born (date unknown).

Donald Wayne WEEKS and Patricia Jo were married. **Patricia Jo** was born (date unknown).

Donald Wayne WEEKS and Pierina GALLO were married. **Pierina GALLO** was born (date unknown).

500. Cynthia Diane WEEKS (Wayne Martin-14, Marvin Benson-13, Elizabeth "Lizzie Beth" BUSSEY-12, Edmund Moody-11, Martha (Malinda) Moseley-10, George-9, Margaret Vann-8, Edward Ned-7, Mary Lewis Barnes-6, April-Tkikami Hop Turkey-5, Big Turkey Hop-4, Hokolesqua Opechan-3, Cleopatra the Shawano Powhatan-2, Wahunsonacock-1) was born (date unknown).

Cynthia Diane WEEKS and Michael MARTIN were married. **Michael MARTIN** was born (date unknown).

Michael MARTIN and Cynthia Diane WEEKS had the following children:

    i. **Robbie MARTIN** was born (date unknown).
    ii. **Joshua MARTIN** was born (date unknown).

Descendants of Chief Wahunsonacock Powhatan

26 January 2012

501. **Lisa Anne WEEKS** (Wayne Martin-14, Marvin Benson-13, Elizabeth "Lizzie Beth" BUSSEY-12, Edmund Moody-11, Martha (Malinda) Moseley-10, George-9, Margaret Vann-8, Edward Ned-7, Mary Lewis Barnes-6, April-Tkikami Hop Turkey-5, Big Turkey Hop-4, Hokolesqua Opechan-3, Cleopatra the Shawano Powhatan-2, Wahunsonacock-1) was born (date unknown).

Lisa Anne WEEKS and David LE were married. **David LE** was born (date unknown).

David LE and Lisa Anne WEEKS had the following child:

    i. **Noah LE** was born (date unknown).

502. **David Earl WEEKS** (Jerry Earl-14, Marvin Benson-13, Elizabeth "Lizzie Beth" BUSSEY-12, Edmund Moody-11, Martha (Malinda) Moseley-10, George-9, Margaret Vann-8, Edward Ned-7, Mary Lewis Barnes-6, April-Tkikami Hop Turkey-5, Big Turkey Hop-4, Hokolesqua Opechan-3, Cleopatra the Shawano Powhatan-2, Wahunsonacock-1) was born on 4 Sep 1968. He died on 8 Dec 2001 at the age of 33 in FL. He was buried on 12 Dec 2001 in New Horizon Cemetery, Sumiton, Walker Co., AL.

Lori was born (date unknown).

David Earl WEEKS and Lori had the following child:

    i. **Jason WEEKS** was born (date unknown).

503. **Allison WEEKS** (Jerry Earl-14, Marvin Benson-13, Elizabeth "Lizzie Beth" BUSSEY-12, Edmund Moody-11, Martha (Malinda) Moseley-10, George-9, Margaret Vann-8, Edward Ned-7, Mary Lewis Barnes-6, April-Tkikami Hop Turkey-5, Big Turkey Hop-4, Hokolesqua Opechan-3, Cleopatra the Shawano Powhatan-2, Wahunsonacock-1) was born (date unknown).

Allison WEEKS and Dale YIELDING were married. **Dale YIELDING** was born (date unknown).

Dale YIELDING and Allison WEEKS had the following children:

    i. **Rachael YIELDING** was born (date unknown).
    ii. **Jared YIELDING** was born (date unknown).

504. **Donna Jo BEAM** (Betty Lou HAMILTON-14, Verda Louise WEEKS-13, Elizabeth "Lizzie Beth" BUSSEY-12, Edmund Moody-11, Martha (Malinda) Moseley-10, George-9, Margaret Vann-8, Edward Ned-7, Mary Lewis Barnes-6, April-Tkikami Hop Turkey-5, Big Turkey Hop-4, Hokolesqua Opechan-3, Cleopatra the Shawano Powhatan-2, Wahunsonacock-1) was born on 2 Nov 1955.

Cecil Leon CLICK was born on 16 Aug 1942.

Cecil Leon CLICK and Donna Jo BEAM had the following child:

518 i. **Teri Jeanette CLICK**, born 3 May 1980; married Matthew Scott RICHARDSON.

505. **Kathy Louise BEAM** (Betty Lou HAMILTON-14, Verda Louise WEEKS-13, Elizabeth "Lizzie Beth" BUSSEY-12, Edmund Moody-11, Martha (Malinda) Moseley-10, George-9, Margaret Vann-8, Edward Ned-7, Mary Lewis Barnes-6, April-Tkikami Hop Turkey-5, Big Turkey Hop-4, Hokolesqua Opechan-3, Cleopatra the Shawano Powhatan-2, Wahunsonacock-1) was born on 18 Apr 1957.

Roger Dale ELLISON was born on 30 Aug 1953.

Roger Dale ELLISON and Kathy Louise BEAM had the following child:

519 i. **Betty Marie ELLISON**, born 21 Aug 1974; married Carson Joseph TORGENSON.

James David Allen BROWN was born on 28 Nov 1959.

James David Allen BROWN and Kathy Louise BEAM had the following children:

  i. **James David Allen, Jr. BROWN** was born on 15 Nov 1986.
  ii. **Kaylon Matthew BROWN** was born on 14 Aug 1988.

506. **Elizabeth Kay BEAM** (Betty Lou HAMILTON-14, Verda Louise WEEKS-13, Elizabeth "Lizzie Beth" BUSSEY-12, Edmund Moody-11, Martha (Malinda) Moseley-10, George-9, Margaret Vann-8, Edward Ned-7, Mary Lewis Barnes-6, April-Tkikami Hop Turkey-5, Big Turkey Hop-4, Hokolesqua Opechan-3, Cleopatra the Shawano Powhatan-2, Wahunsonacock-1) was born on 26 Mar 1958.

Charles Samuel MOORE Jr. was born on 11 Mar 1960. He held the title of Jr..

Charles Samuel MOORE and Elizabeth Kay BEAM had the following children:

520 i. **Cristy Diane MOORE**, born 15 Feb 1978; married Shannon MIMS; married Philip Wayne WHITE Jr..
521 ii. **James Derrick MOORE**, born 17 Mar 1980; married Tia .

507. **Martin Eric BEAM** (Betty Lou HAMILTON-14, Verda Louise WEEKS-13, Elizabeth "Lizzie Beth" BUSSEY-12, Edmund Moody-11, Martha (Malinda) Moseley-10, George-9, Margaret Vann-8, Edward Ned-7, Mary Lewis Barnes-6, April-Tkikami Hop Turkey-5, Big Turkey Hop-4, Hokolesqua Opechan-3, Cleopatra the Shawano Powhatan-2, Wahunsonacock-1) was born on 28 Apr 1960.

Janet Lynn BAILEY was born on 27 Apr 1964.

Descendants of Chief Wahunsonacock Powhatan

508. **James Earl (Jim) CORK** (Betty Lou HAMILTON-14, Verda Louise WEEKS-13, Elizabeth "Lizzie Beth" BUSSEY-12, Edmund Moody-11, Martha (Malinda) Moseley-10, George-9, Margaret Vann-8, Edward Ned-7, Mary Lewis Barnes-6, April-Tkikami Hop Turkey-5, Big Turkey Hop-4, Hokolesqua Opechan-3, Cleopatra the Shawano Powhatan-2, Wahunsonacock-1) was born on 9 Jan 1965.

James Earl (Jim) CORK and Theresa MCCAUGHREN were married. **Theresa MCCAUGHREN** was born (date unknown).

Rhonda NORTON was born on 14 Nov 1963.

509. **Russell Allen HAMILTON** (Ronnie Lee-14, Verda Louise WEEKS-13, Elizabeth "Lizzie Beth" BUSSEY-12, Edmund Moody-11, Martha (Malinda) Moseley-10, George-9, Margaret Vann-8, Edward Ned-7, Mary Lewis Barnes-6, April-Tkikami Hop Turkey-5, Big Turkey Hop-4, Hokolesqua Opechan-3, Cleopatra the Shawano Powhatan-2, Wahunsonacock-1) was born on 16 Nov 1961.

Teri DUNCAN was born on 11 May 1957.

510. **Ronnie Todd HAMILTON** (Ronnie Lee-14, Verda Louise WEEKS-13, Elizabeth "Lizzie Beth" BUSSEY-12, Edmund Moody-11, Martha (Malinda) Moseley-10, George-9, Margaret Vann-8, Edward Ned-7, Mary Lewis Barnes-6, April-Tkikami Hop Turkey-5, Big Turkey Hop-4, Hokolesqua Opechan-3, Cleopatra the Shawano Powhatan-2, Wahunsonacock-1) was born on 18 Sep 1967.

Stephanie SHARP was born on 4 Feb 1966.

Ronnie Todd HAMILTON and Stephanie SHARP had the following children:

   i. **Lindsay Hannah HAMILTON** was born (date unknown).
   ii. **Will HAMILTON** was born (date unknown).

511. **Lindsay Hyche HILL** (Debbie McCrary-14, Aileen Hollis-13, Mattie Marie "Sweetie" BUSSEY-12, Edmund Moody-11, Martha (Malinda) Moseley-10, George-9, Margaret Vann-8, Edward Ned-7, Mary Lewis Barnes-6, April-Tkikami Hop Turkey-5, Big Turkey Hop-4, Hokolesqua Opechan-3, Cleopatra the Shawano Powhatan-2, Wahunsonacock-1) was born on 25 Mar 1976.

Lindsay Hyche HILL and Clyde L. BARLOW were married. **Clyde L. BARLOW** was born in 1978.

Clyde L. BARLOW and Lindsay Hyche HILL had the following children:

   i. **Bodie Jay BARLOW** was born on 12 Jul 2006.
   ii. **Kenzie Mae BARLOW** was born on 6 Dec 2007.

512. **Mary Hyche HILL** (Debbie McCrary-14, Aileen Hollis-13, Mattie Marie "Sweetie" BUSSEY-12, Edmund Moody-11, Martha (Malinda) Moseley-10, George-9, Margaret Vann-8, Edward Ned-7, Mary Lewis Barnes-6, April-Tkikami Hop Turkey-5, Big Turkey Hop-4, Hokolesqua Opechan-3, Cleopatra the Shawano Powhatan-2, Wahunsonacock-1) was born on 10 Mar 1979. She died on 11 Mar 2007 at the age of 28.

Mary Hyche HILL and Conner were married. **Conner** was born (date unknown).

Conner and Mary Hyche HILL had the following child:

    i. **Mims Howard CONNER IV** was born on 26 Aug 2005.

513. **Teresa Michelle ROPER** (Sandra Mosley-14, Frank Hiram-13, Robert Herman-12, Hiram Mace-11, William Lafayette-10, George-9, Margaret Vann-8, Edward Ned-7, Mary Lewis Barnes-6, April-Tkikami Hop Turkey-5, Big Turkey Hop-4, Hokolesqua Opechan-3, Cleopatra the Shawano Powhatan-2, Wahunsonacock-1) was born on 7 Mar 1983.

Teresa Michelle ROPER had the following child:

    i. **Grayson HAWKINS** was born (date unknown).

Descendants of Chief Wahunsonacock Powhatan

Sixteenth Generation

514. **Melanie A. JOHNSON** (Larry Jim-15, Dorothy Lee Smith-14, Gladys Lula BUSSEY-13, Charles Drennen-12, Benjamin Harm-11, Martha (Malinda) Moseley-10, George-9, Margaret Vann-8, Edward Ned-7, Mary Lewis Barnes-6, April-Tkikami Hop Turkey-5, Big Turkey Hop-4, Hokolesqua Opechan-3, Cleopatra the Shawano Powhatan-2, Wahunsonacock-1) was born on 10 Mar 1975 in Fort Knox, KY.

Melanie A. JOHNSON and Chad E. SPRAKER were married on 21 Nov 1998 in Frankfort, IN. **Chad E. SPRAKER** was born on 28 May 1978 in Culter, IN.

Chad E. SPRAKER and Melanie A. JOHNSON had the following child:

      i. **Lauren M. SPRAKER** was born on 3 Aug 1999.

515. **Jana Marie WILKINSON** (Susan Marie Jones-15, Winfred Marie Falgout-14, Mattie Marie BUSSEY-13, James "Jimmy" David-12, Benjamin Harm-11, Martha (Malinda) Moseley-10, George-9, Margaret Vann-8, Edward Ned-7, Mary Lewis Barnes-6, April-Tkikami Hop Turkey-5, Big Turkey Hop-4, Hokolesqua Opechan-3, Cleopatra the Shawano Powhatan-2, Wahunsonacock-1) was born on 13 May 1968.

John Pierce MCCANDLISH was born (date unknown).

John Pierce MCCANDLISH and Jana Marie WILKINSON had the following child:

      i. **Alexandra Marie MCCANDLISH** was born (date unknown).

516. **Emily Jennette COALTER** (Alton Bayne, Jr.-15, Ann Elizabeth Mandolini-14, Ruby Elizabeth BUSSEY-13, James "Jimmy" David-12, Benjamin Harm-11, Martha (Malinda) Moseley-10, George-9, Margaret Vann-8, Edward Ned-7, Mary Lewis Barnes-6, April-Tkikami Hop Turkey-5, Big Turkey Hop-4, Hokolesqua Opechan-3, Cleopatra the Shawano Powhatan-2, Wahunsonacock-1) was born on 17 Jan 1979 in Clarendon, Monroe Co., AR.

Emily Jennette COALTER and Peter Nathan WILLIAMSON were married on 26 Jul 1997 in Auburn, Sangamon Co., IL. **Peter Nathan WILLIAMSON** was born on 22 Jan 1978 in Oak Park, IL.

517. **Nova Rebecca HYDEN** (Margaret Elizabeth Collins-15, Peggy Jean BUSSEY-14, Dawson Ellard-13, Rufus Thomas-12, Edmund Moody-11, Martha (Malinda) Moseley-10, George-9, Margaret Vann-8, Edward Ned-7, Mary Lewis Barnes-6, April-Tkikami Hop Turkey-5, Big Turkey Hop-4, Hokolesqua Opechan-3, Cleopatra the Shawano Powhatan-2, Wahunsonacock-1) was born on 11 Feb 1978.

Nova Rebecca HYDEN had the following child:

i. **Nova Peggy HYDEN** was born in Jul 1996.

518. **Teri Jeanette CLICK** (Donna Jo Beam-15, Betty Lou HAMILTON-14, Verda Louise WEEKS-13, Elizabeth "Lizzie Beth" BUSSEY-12, Edmund Moody-11, Martha (Malinda) Moseley-10, George-9, Margaret Vann-8, Edward Ned-7, Mary Lewis Barnes-6, April-Tkikami Hop Turkey-5, Big Turkey Hop-4, Hokolesqua Opechan-3, Cleopatra the Shawano Powhatan-2, Wahunsonacock-1) was born on 3 May 1980.

Teri Jeanette CLICK and Matthew Scott RICHARDSON were married. **Matthew Scott RICHARDSON** was born (date unknown).

Matthew Scott RICHARDSON and Teri Jeanette CLICK had the following children:

i. **Alexandria Raine RICHARDSON** was born (date unknown).
ii. **Matthew Cash RICHARDSON** was born (date unknown).

519. **Betty Marie ELLISON** (Kathy Louise Beam-15, Betty Lou HAMILTON-14, Verda Louise WEEKS-13, Elizabeth "Lizzie Beth" BUSSEY-12, Edmund Moody-11, Martha (Malinda) Moseley-10, George-9, Margaret Vann-8, Edward Ned-7, Mary Lewis Barnes-6, April-Tkikami Hop Turkey-5, Big Turkey Hop-4, Hokolesqua Opechan-3, Cleopatra the Shawano Powhatan-2, Wahunsonacock-1) was born on 21 Aug 1974.

Betty Marie ELLISON and Carson Joseph TORGENSON were married. **Carson Joseph TORGENSON** was born (date unknown).

520. **Cristy Diane MOORE** (Elizabeth Kay Beam-15, Betty Lou HAMILTON-14, Verda Louise WEEKS-13, Elizabeth "Lizzie Beth" BUSSEY-12, Edmund Moody-11, Martha (Malinda) Moseley-10, George-9, Margaret Vann-8, Edward Ned-7, Mary Lewis Barnes-6, April-Tkikami Hop Turkey-5, Big Turkey Hop-4, Hokolesqua Opechan-3, Cleopatra the Shawano Powhatan-2, Wahunsonacock-1) was born on 15 Feb 1978.

Cristy Diane MOORE and Shannon MIMS were married. **Shannon MIMS** was born (date unknown).

Shannon MIMS and Cristy Diane MOORE had the following child:

i. **Kayla Lynn MIMS** was born (date unknown).

Cristy Diane MOORE and Philip Wayne WHITE Jr. were married. **Philip Wayne WHITE Jr.** held the title of Jr..

Philip Wayne WHITE and Cristy Diane MOORE had the following child:

i. **Emily Elizabeth WHITE** was born (date unknown).

521. **James Derrick MOORE** (Elizabeth Kay Beam-15, Betty Lou HAMILTON-14, Verda Louise WEEKS-13, Elizabeth "Lizzie Beth" BUSSEY-12, Edmund Moody-11, Martha (Malinda) Moseley-10, George-9, Margaret Vann-8, Edward Ned-7, Mary Lewis Barnes-6, April-Tkikami Hop Turkey-5, Big Turkey Hop-4, Hokolesqua Opechan-3, Cleopatra the Shawano Powhatan-2, Wahunsonacock-1) was born on 17 Mar 1980.

James Derrick MOORE and Tia were married. **Tia** was born (date unknown).

James Derrick MOORE and Tia had the following child:

    i. **Jasmine Alexis MOORE** was born (date unknown).

Preparer:
JD Weeks
1636 Magnolia Street
Gardendale, AL 35071
jd@jdweeks.com

Kinship List - Chief Wahunsonacock Powhatan

26 January 2012

Relative	Relationship
, Alma	Spouse of ninth great grandson
, Anna E.	Spouse of seventh great grandson
, Annie L.	Spouse of ninth great grandson
, Brenda	Spouse of twelfth great grandson
, Carol Ann	Spouse of tenth great grandson
, Chalakatha Woman	Spouse of great grandson
, Cinquoateck Woman	Spouse of brother
, Conner	Spouse of twelfth great granddaughter
, Debra	Spouse of twelfth great grandson
, Elizabeth	Spouse of tenth great grandson
, Elizabeth	Spouse of seventh great grandson
, Elizabeth Ann	Spouse of tenth great grandson
, Elizabeth Anne	Spouse of eleventh great grandson
, Fannie	Spouse of ninth great grandson
, Frances	Spouse of ninth great grandson
, Jan	Spouse of twelfth great grandson
, Josephine N.	Spouse of ninth great grandson
, Joyce	Spouse of tenth great grandson
, Kathy	Spouse of tenth great grandson
, Lilly Mae	Spouse of ninth great grandson
, Lori	Spouse of twelfth great grandson
, Lori	Spouse of twelfth great grandson
, Lucille	Spouse of tenth great grandson
, Lucinda	Spouse of seventh great grandson
, Mattaponi Woman	Spouse of brother
, Minnie	Spouse of ninth great grandson
, Nitka	Spouse of seventh great grandson
, Nonoma	Spouse of grandson
, Pamukey Woman	Spouse of first cousin
, Pamukey Woman	Spouse of first cousin
, Pat	Spouse of tenth great grandson
, Patricia Jo	Spouse of twelfth great grandson
, Pearl	Spouse of ninth great grandson
, Peggy	Spouse of fourth great grandson
, Powhatan Woman	Spouse of brother
, Powhatan Woman	Spouse of brother
, Sarah Ann	Spouse of seventh great grandson
, Scent Flower	Grandmother
, Shawano Chief	Spouse of mother
, Tia	Spouse of thirteenth great grandson
, Vivian	Spouse of ninth great grandson
, Werewocomoco Woman	Spouse of brother
AARON, Nell	Spouse of tenth great grandson
ABBOTT	Spouse of eighth great granddaughter
ABBOTT, George	Spouse of eighth great granddaughter
ABBOTT, Ludie	Ninth great granddaughter
ADAMS, Helen Elizabeth	Spouse of eleventh great grandson
AGRRETT, Emma Lucy	Spouse of eighth great grandson
ALEXANDER	Spouse of seventh great granddaughter
ALEXANDER, Connie	Spouse of tenth great grandson
ALEXANDER, Mary Jane	Spouse of seventh great grandson
ALFORD, James	Spouse of tenth great granddaughter
ALFORD, James	Eleventh great grandson
ALFORD, Judy	Eleventh great granddaughter

Kinship List - Chief Wahunsonacock Powhatan

26 January 2012

Relative	Relationship
ALFORD, Melissa	Eleventh great granddaughter
ALFORD, Rachel	Eleventh great granddaughter
ALFORD, Susan	Eleventh great granddaughter
ALLBEE, Coltyn Wynn	Twelfth great grandchild
ALLBEE, Scott	Spouse of eleventh great granddaughter
AMOPOTUSKEE, Bear Clan Shawano	Spouse
ANDERSON, Christie	Eleventh great granddaughter
ANDERSON, Christopher	Eleventh great grandson
ANDERSON, Vernon Ray "Bo"	Spouse of tenth great granddaughter
APPIMMONOISKE, Tauxenent	Spouse
APPOMOSISCUT, Pamukey	Spouse
ARMSTRONG, John Kittle	Spouse of seventh great granddaughter
ARMSTRONG, Monroe Griffin	Spouse of ninth great granddaughter
ARMSTRONG, Monroe Griffin	Spouse of ninth great granddaughter
ARMSTRONG, Sallie	Ninth great granddaughter
ARTHUR	Spouse of ninth great granddaughter
ARTOUGHNOISKE	Spouse
ASHETOISKE	Spouse
ATTOSSOCOMISKE, Sockobeck	Spouse
AUGUSTINE, Harold	Spouse of eleventh great granddaughter
AUTRY, Brenda Jean	Twelfth great granddaughter
AUTRY, Gene	Spouse of eleventh great granddaughter
AUTRY, Jennifer Sue	Spouse of twelfth great grandson
AUTRY, Shawna Lee	Twelfth great granddaughter
AUTRY, Sherry Lynn	Twelfth great granddaughter
AVANT, Dorothy	Spouse of eleventh great grandson
BAILEY, Janet Lynn	Spouse of twelfth great grandson
BAIRD, Ola	Spouse of ninth great grandson
BAKER, Lawrence Bradley	Spouse of twelfth great granddaughter
BAKER, Worth	Thirteenth great grandson
BARLOW, Bodie Jay	Thirteenth great grandson
BARLOW, Clyde L.	Spouse of twelfth great granddaughter
BARLOW, Kenzie Mae	Thirteenth great granddaughter
BARNES, Charity	Third great granddaughter
BARNES, Mary Lewis	Third great granddaughter
BARNES, Richard	Spouse of second great granddaughter
BARTON, Hannah Suttizie (Tizie)	Spouse of eighth great grandson
BASDEN, Ann	Spouse of eighth great grandson
BASS, Sarah Winnette	Spouse of eleventh great grandson
BEACH, John Wesley Jr.	Spouse of eighth great granddaughter
BEAM, Donna Jo	Twelfth great granddaughter
BEAM, Elizabeth Kay	Twelfth great granddaughter
BEAM, Kathy Louise	Twelfth great granddaughter
BEAM, Kenneth	Spouse of eleventh great granddaughter
BEAM, Martin Eric	Twelfth great grandson
BEAMER, John	Spouse of second great granddaughter
BEASLEY, Dorothy Latta	Eleventh great granddaughter
BEASLEY, Robert Jones Sr.	Spouse of tenth great granddaughter
BEASLEY, Robert Jones Jr.	Eleventh great grandson
BELEW, John	Spouse of sixth great granddaughter
BEVILS, Mildred Rosa	Spouse of eighth great grandson
BLACK, Anna	Spouse of twelfth great grandson
BLACKBURN, Arthur William	Spouse of tenth great granddaughter
BLACKBURN, Arthur William Jr.	Eleventh great grandson

Kinship List - Chief Wahunsonacock Powhatan

26 January 2012

Relative	Relationship
BLACKBURN, Frances	Eleventh great granddaughter
BLACKBURN, Mary Elizabeth	Eleventh great granddaughter
BLACKWOOD, Mary	Spouse of fifth great grandson
BLAIKIE	Spouse of ninth great granddaughter
BLAIR, Cari Amber	Thirteenth great granddaughter
BLAIR, Evertt Dwight	Spouse of twelfth great granddaughter
BLAIR, Gary Darrell	Spouse of twelfth great granddaughter
BLAIR, Jon-Erik Dwight	Thirteenth great grandson
BLAIR, Micaela Dominique	Thirteenth great grandchild
BLANTON, Addie M.	Spouse of eighth great grandson
BOLLING, Robert	Spouse of great granddaughter
BOLLINS, Harvey	Spouse of tenth great granddaughter
BONHAM, J.H. I/L?	Ninth great grandson
BONHAM, James W.	Spouse of eighth great granddaughter
BOSHELLE, Brenda	Eleventh great granddaughter
BOSHELLE, R.J.	Spouse of tenth great granddaughter
BOSHELLE, Ronnie	Eleventh great grandson
BOWLES, Anna	Eighth great granddaughter
BOWLES, Annie E.	Ninth great granddaughter
BOWLES, Doris	Spouse of tenth great grandson
BOWLES, Edward Augustus "Gus"	Eighth great grandson
BOWLES, Edward R. "Eddie"	Ninth great grandson
BOWLES, Ethel	Ninth great granddaughter
BOWLES, Ethel M.	Ninth great granddaughter
BOWLES, Eva M.	Ninth great granddaughter
BOWLES, Ghigoneli	Third great grandchild
BOWLES, Grace	Ninth great granddaughter
BOWLES, Gussie Olive	Ninth great granddaughter
BOWLES, H. Augustus	Spouse of seventh great granddaughter
BOWLES, Ina Ruth	Ninth great granddaughter
BOWLES, John	Spouse of second great granddaughter
BOWLES, John Thomas	Eighth great grandson
BOWLES, Mary Christine	Ninth great granddaughter
BOWLES, Maticia J. "Mattie"	Eighth great granddaughter
BOWLES, Maybelle	Ninth great granddaughter
BOWLES, Pearl	Ninth great granddaughter
BOWLES, Perry H.	Ninth great grandson
BOWLES, Richard Bassett	Ninth great grandson
BOWLES, Samuel	Eighth great grandson
BOWLES, Sarah "Sally" Mahulda	Eighth great granddaughter
BOWLES, William	Eighth great grandson
BOWLES, Willie A.	Ninth great grandson
BOWLING, Everette DeWayne	Tenth great grandson
BOWLING, Gary	Eleventh great grandson
BOWLING, Infant	Tenth great grandchild
BOWLING, Ricky	Eleventh great grandson
BOWLING, Roger	Eleventh great grandson
BOWLING, Verita Mae	Tenth great granddaughter
BOWLING, William Lee	Spouse of ninth great granddaughter
BOWLING, Willie Virginia	Tenth great granddaughter
BOX, Edith	Spouse of ninth great grandson
BOYD, Alabama Texana	Eighth great granddaughter
BOYD, Anna T.	Eighth great granddaughter
BOYD, Bessie	Eighth great granddaughter

Kinship List - Chief Wahunsonacock Powhatan

26 January 2012

Relative	Relationship
BOYD, Edadean	Spouse of eleventh great grandson
BOYD, Emma	Eighth great granddaughter
BOYD, Hezekiah	Spouse of seventh great granddaughter
BOYD, Hezekiah Jr.	Eighth great grandson
BOYD, Infant	Eighth great grandchild
BOYD, J. Walter	Spouse of seventh great granddaughter
BOYD, James Watson	Eighth great grandson
BOYD, Letitia Jane	Eighth great granddaughter
BOYD, Levina Pamelia	Eighth great granddaughter
BOYD, Mae (May)	Eighth great granddaughter
BOYD, Margaret "Maggie"	Spouse of eighth great grandson
BOYD, Martha	Eighth great granddaughter
BOYD, Mary Virginia	Eighth great granddaughter
BOYD, Thomas	Spouse of sixth great granddaughter
BOYD, Walter Jr.	Eighth great grandson
BOYETTE, Grady	Tenth great grandson
BOYETTE, John Thomas	Spouse of ninth great granddaughter
BOYETTE, Troy	Tenth great grandson
BOYETTE, Unk	Tenth great granddaughter
BRADLEY, Dennis Houghton	Ninth great grandson
BRADLEY, Horace Grady	Ninth great grandson
BRADLEY, James Thurman	Ninth great grandson
BRADLEY, James William	Spouse of eighth great granddaughter
BRADLEY, Maud	Ninth great granddaughter
BRADLEY, Myrtis Edith	Ninth great granddaughter
BRADY, Arthur Jackson Sr.	Spouse of ninth great granddaughter
BRAKEFIELD, J. Thomas	Spouse of twelfth great granddaughter
BRANCH, Henry	Spouse of eighth great granddaughter
BRITTIAN, Danny Joe	Spouse of twelfth great granddaughter
BRITTIAN, James Ryan	Thirteenth great grandson
BRITTIAN, Jarred Michael	Thirteenth great grandson
BRITTON, Winnie	Spouse of ninth great grandson
BRONFIELD	Spouse of ninth great granddaughter
BROWN, James	Spouse of fourth great granddaughter
BROWN, James David Allen, Jr.	Thirteenth great grandson
BROWN, James David Allen	Spouse of twelfth great granddaughter
BROWN, Kaylon Matthew	Thirteenth great grandson
BROWN, Nancy Ann	Spouse of fourth great grandson
BROWN, Unk	Spouse of eleventh great granddaughter
BURKS, Mabel Elzora	Spouse of ninth great grandson
BURNETT	Spouse of ninth great granddaughter
BURRELL, Malinda Irene	Spouse of eighth great grandson
BURTRAM, Clayton	Spouse of ninth great granddaughter
BUSE, James Elbert	Spouse of ninth great granddaughter
BUSSEY, Addie	Ninth great granddaughter
BUSSEY, Adra "Addie"	Eighth great granddaughter
BUSSEY, Alice	Ninth great granddaughter
BUSSEY, Alma Eudora	Ninth great granddaughter
BUSSEY, Amanda	Ninth great granddaughter
BUSSEY, Anna	Eighth great granddaughter
BUSSEY, Annie	Ninth great granddaughter
BUSSEY, Baby Girl #1	Ninth great granddaughter
BUSSEY, Baby Girl #2	Ninth great granddaughter
BUSSEY, Barbara	Eleventh great granddaughter

Kinship List - Chief Wahunsonacock Powhatan

26 January 2012

Relative	Relationship
BUSSEY, Barbara Jean	Eleventh great granddaughter
BUSSEY, Beatrice	Eleventh great granddaughter
BUSSEY, Benjamin Harm Jr.	Eighth great grandson
BUSSEY, Benjamin Harmon (Harm) Sr.	Seventh great grandson
BUSSEY, Bennie Lou	Eleventh great grandchild
BUSSEY, Bennie Lucas	Tenth great grandson
BUSSEY, Bethany Claire	Twelfth great granddaughter
BUSSEY, Betty	Eleventh great granddaughter
BUSSEY, Bianca Malina	Twelfth great granddaughter
BUSSEY, Billie	Tenth great grandchild
BUSSEY, Billy Wayne	Eleventh great grandson
BUSSEY, Blanche Mae	Tenth great granddaughter
BUSSEY, Bobby	Tenth great grandson
BUSSEY, Brandi	Eleventh great granddaughter
BUSSEY, Brenda Jean	Eleventh great granddaughter
BUSSEY, Carl	Eleventh great grandson
BUSSEY, Carolyn	Tenth great granddaughter
BUSSEY, Carolyn Ann	Eleventh great granddaughter
BUSSEY, Carolyn Sue	Eleventh great granddaughter
BUSSEY, Catherine	Tenth great granddaughter
BUSSEY, Charles	Tenth great grandson
BUSSEY, Charles	Ninth great grandson
BUSSEY, Charles Drennen	Ninth great grandson
BUSSEY, Charles Freddie	Eleventh great grandson
BUSSEY, Charles Marshall	Tenth great grandson
BUSSEY, Charlie	Ninth great grandson
BUSSEY, Charlotte Loretta	Tenth great granddaughter
BUSSEY, Christina	Tenth great granddaughter
BUSSEY, Clary	Eighth great granddaughter
BUSSEY, Clifford	Ninth great grandson
BUSSEY, Clovus Alvon Alvin	Ninth great grandson
BUSSEY, Clyde	Ninth great granddaughter
BUSSEY, Clyde Thomas?	Tenth great grandson
BUSSEY, Daisy	Tenth great granddaughter
BUSSEY, Daisy Wonnell	Eleventh great granddaughter
BUSSEY, David Clarence	Tenth great grandson
BUSSEY, Dawson Ellard	Tenth great grandson
BUSSEY, Deborah Jean	Eleventh great granddaughter
BUSSEY, Delora	Tenth great granddaughter
BUSSEY, Delora Joan	Eleventh great granddaughter
BUSSEY, Dempsey (Demcey)	Eighth great grandson
BUSSEY, Dempsey C.	Seventh great grandson
BUSSEY, Don Thomas	Eleventh great grandson
BUSSEY, Donna Gaylene	Eleventh great granddaughter
BUSSEY, Donnis	Ninth great granddaughter
BUSSEY, Dora Oliver	Tenth great grandson
BUSSEY, Earlene	Eleventh great granddaughter
BUSSEY, Edmund Moody	Eighth great grandson
BUSSEY, Edward "Ed"	Ninth great grandson
BUSSEY, Edward "Eddie" H.	Eighth great grandson
BUSSEY, Edward Junior	Tenth great grandson
BUSSEY, Edward Moody	Spouse of sixth great granddaughter
BUSSEY, Edward Moody, Jr.	Seventh great grandson
BUSSEY, Elizabeth "Lizzie Beth"	Ninth great granddaughter

Kinship List - Chief Wahunsonacock Powhatan

26 January 2012

Relative | **Relationship**

Relative	Relationship
BUSSEY, Elizabeth Francis	Thirteenth great granddaughter
BUSSEY, Elizabeth M. "Lizzie"	Eighth great granddaughter
BUSSEY, Emma Ollie	Ninth great granddaughter
BUSSEY, Emmy Sue	Tenth great granddaughter
BUSSEY, Ernest Eugene	Tenth great grandson
BUSSEY, Euell	Ninth great grandson
BUSSEY, Eugene	Tenth great grandson
BUSSEY, Eula	Eighth great granddaughter
BUSSEY, Felix Hobson	Tenth great grandson
BUSSEY, Flora	Tenth great granddaughter
BUSSEY, Floyd	Eleventh great grandson
BUSSEY, Floyd Francis	Tenth great grandson
BUSSEY, Frances Maud	Eighth great granddaughter
BUSSEY, Frank	Ninth great grandson
BUSSEY, Frankie	Eleventh great grandchild
BUSSEY, Gary	Tenth great grandson
BUSSEY, Gayle	Eleventh great granddaughter
BUSSEY, George Washington	Ninth great grandson
BUSSEY, Georgell	Tenth great grandson
BUSSEY, Gertrude	Ninth great granddaughter
BUSSEY, Gladys Lula	Tenth great granddaughter
BUSSEY, Gladys Sue	Tenth great granddaughter
BUSSEY, Gwendolyn	Tenth great granddaughter
BUSSEY, Gwendolyn Joan	Tenth great granddaughter
BUSSEY, Hazel	Eleventh great granddaughter
BUSSEY, Hazel	Tenth great granddaughter
BUSSEY, Hezekiah	Seventh great grandson
BUSSEY, Dr. J. Everette	Ninth great grandson
BUSSEY, James	Eleventh great grandson
BUSSEY, James "Jimmy" David	Ninth great grandson
BUSSEY, James Arnold	Eleventh great grandson
BUSSEY, James Edward	Tenth great grandson
BUSSEY, James Howard	Twelfth great grandson
BUSSEY, James W.	Eighth great grandson
BUSSEY, Jason	Eleventh great grandson
BUSSEY, Jason Clark	Twelfth great grandson
BUSSEY, Jennifer	Thirteenth great granddaughter
BUSSEY, Jerry Wayne	Eleventh great grandson
BUSSEY, Jimmy Jr.	Eleventh great grandson
BUSSEY, Jimmy Carroll	Tenth great grandson
BUSSEY, Jimmy Eugene	Eleventh great grandson
BUSSEY, Jimmy Ray	Tenth great grandson
BUSSEY, JoAnn	Eleventh great granddaughter
BUSSEY, Joe	Eleventh great grandson
BUSSEY, Joe	Eleventh great grandson
BUSSEY, Joe Raymond	Tenth great grandson
BUSSEY, Joey Lemer	Eleventh great grandson
BUSSEY, John L.	Seventh great grandson
BUSSEY, John Rufus	Eleventh great grandson
BUSSEY, Johnny	Eleventh great grandson
BUSSEY, Johnny	Ninth great grandson
BUSSEY, Johnny Bruce	Twelfth great grandson
BUSSEY, Joseph	Seventh great grandson
BUSSEY, Judith Sharon	Eleventh great granddaughter

Kinship List - Chief Wahunsonacock Powhatan

26 January 2012

Relative	Relationship
BUSSEY, Judy	Eleventh great granddaughter
BUSSEY, Julia	Eighth great granddaughter
BUSSEY, Kandle Melissa	Twelfth great granddaughter
BUSSEY, Karen Rae	Eleventh great granddaughter
BUSSEY, Kaye	Tenth great granddaughter
BUSSEY, Kelly Anne	Twelfth great granddaughter
BUSSEY, Kerry Marshall	Eleventh great grandson
BUSSEY, Kimberly Adams	Twelfth great granddaughter
BUSSEY, Kimberly Kay	Eleventh great granddaughter
BUSSEY, Larry	Eleventh great grandson
BUSSEY, Lavora	Tenth great granddaughter
BUSSEY, Lela	Eighth great granddaughter
BUSSEY, Leo R.	Eighth great grandson
BUSSEY, Leon	Eleventh great grandson
BUSSEY, Letitia	Seventh great granddaughter
BUSSEY, Levicy	Eleventh great granddaughter
BUSSEY, Lillian (Lillie) Chester	Ninth great granddaughter
BUSSEY, Lillian B.	Ninth great granddaughter
BUSSEY, Lon A.	Ninth great grandson
BUSSEY, Louis	Ninth great grandson
BUSSEY, Luanna	Ninth great granddaughter
BUSSEY, Lucy	Tenth great granddaughter
BUSSEY, Lula	Ninth great granddaughter
BUSSEY, Lynn	Tenth great granddaughter
BUSSEY, Lynne	Eleventh great granddaughter
BUSSEY, Mable Ellen	Tenth great granddaughter
BUSSEY, Mack	Ninth great grandson
BUSSEY, Mai	Eighth great granddaughter
BUSSEY, Marilyn	Eleventh great granddaughter
BUSSEY, Marion Edward "Fat"	Tenth great grandson
BUSSEY, Marshall	Tenth great grandson
BUSSEY, Martha	Eighth great granddaughter
BUSSEY, Mary	Seventh great granddaughter
BUSSEY, Mary	Eighth great granddaughter
BUSSEY, Mary Elizabeth	Ninth great granddaughter
BUSSEY, Mary Elizabeth (Eliza)	Eighth great granddaughter
BUSSEY, Mary Ellen	Ninth great granddaughter
BUSSEY, Mary Ellen	Tenth great granddaughter
BUSSEY, Mary Ena	Tenth great grandchild
BUSSEY, Mary L.	Eleventh great granddaughter
BUSSEY, Mary Leonah "Molly"	Eighth great granddaughter
BUSSEY, Mary Lou Tassie	Seventh great granddaughter
BUSSEY, Mary Matilda	Spouse of seventh great grandson
BUSSEY, Mary Ruth	Tenth great granddaughter
BUSSEY, Mary Sue	Eleventh great granddaughter
BUSSEY, Mattie Marie	Tenth great granddaughter
BUSSEY, Mattie Marie "Sweetie"	Ninth great granddaughter
BUSSEY, Maudine	Eleventh great granddaughter
BUSSEY, Mell	Ninth great grandchild
BUSSEY, Mildred Ethel	Tenth great granddaughter
BUSSEY, Milton Travis	Ninth great grandson
BUSSEY, Minnie Malinda	Ninth great granddaughter
BUSSEY, Mitchell Lee	Tenth great grandson
BUSSEY, Myrtle Belle	Eleventh great granddaughter

Kinship List - Chief Wahunsonacock Powhatan

Relative | **Relationship**

Relative	Relationship
BUSSEY, Myrtle Katherine	Ninth great granddaughter
BUSSEY, Naoma "Naomi"	Tenth great granddaughter
BUSSEY, Nettie C.	Tenth great granddaughter
BUSSEY, Oral Lee	Tenth great granddaughter
BUSSEY, Oscar	Ninth great grandson
BUSSEY, Otis Howard	Tenth great grandson
BUSSEY, Pearly	Ninth great granddaughter
BUSSEY, Peggy Jean	Eleventh great granddaughter
BUSSEY, Richmond Hobson Pearson	Ninth great grandson
BUSSEY, Robert	Seventh great grandson
BUSSEY, Rodney Clark	Eleventh great grandson
BUSSEY, Ronald David	Eleventh great grandson
BUSSEY, Ronnie	Tenth great grandson
BUSSEY, Roxann	Tenth great granddaughter
BUSSEY, Roy Charles	Tenth great grandson
BUSSEY, Ruby Elizabeth	Tenth great granddaughter
BUSSEY, Ruby Lee	Ninth great granddaughter
BUSSEY, Rufus Terry	Tenth great grandson
BUSSEY, Rufus Thomas	Ninth great grandson
BUSSEY, Sallie Levert	Ninth great granddaughter
BUSSEY, Sandra "Sandy)	Tenth great granddaughter
BUSSEY, Sara	Eleventh great granddaughter
BUSSEY, Sarah Ann	Seventh great granddaughter
BUSSEY, Scott	Eleventh great grandson
BUSSEY, Sharon Faye	Eleventh great granddaughter
BUSSEY, Sheila Ann	Eleventh great granddaughter
BUSSEY, Sheila Faye	Tenth great granddaughter
BUSSEY, Steve	Eleventh great grandson
BUSSEY, Sue	Tenth great granddaughter
BUSSEY, Susan	Eighth great granddaughter
BUSSEY, Taylor Elizabeth Hope	Thirteenth great granddaughter
BUSSEY, Toby Ann	Eleventh great granddaughter
BUSSEY, Tommie Lee	Tenth great granddaughter
BUSSEY, Tommy	Eleventh great grandson
BUSSEY, Velma Leona	Tenth great granddaughter
BUSSEY, Virginia	Tenth great granddaughter
BUSSEY, Virginia	Tenth great granddaughter
BUSSEY, Walter	Ninth great grandson
BUSSEY, Walter Edwin	Tenth great grandson
BUSSEY, Wanda Lee	Eleventh great granddaughter
BUSSEY, Willard Van	Tenth great grandson
BUSSEY, William	Ninth great grandson
BUSSEY, William "Willie"	Ninth great grandson
BUSSEY, William C.	Tenth great grandson
BUSSEY, William J.	Seventh great grandson
BUSSEY, William Lafayette "Willie"	Eighth great grandson
BUSSEY, William M. (Will)	Eighth great grandson
BUSSEY, William Thomas	Eleventh great grandson
BUSSEY, William Thomas, Jr.	Twelfth great grandson
BUSSEY, Willie Benjamin "Will"	Ninth great grandson
BUSSEY, Willie Everette	Tenth great grandson
BUSSEY, Winifred	Eleventh great granddaughter
BUSSEY, Wonnell (Nell)	Tenth great granddaughter
BUSSEY, Zackery James Bryan	Twelfth great grandson

Kinship List - Chief Wahunsonacock Powhatan

Relative	**Relationship**
BUTLER	Spouse of eleventh great granddaughter
BYARS	Spouse of ninth great grandson
BYINGTON, Esther M.	Spouse of tenth great grandson
BYRD, Hobart Garet	Spouse of ninth great granddaughter
BYRD, William McKinley	Spouse of ninth great granddaughter
CADMANN, John	Spouse of eleventh great granddaughter
CAMPBELL, David	Thirteenth great grandson
CAMPBELL, David Morton	Spouse of twelfth great granddaughter
CAMPBELL, Lori Rae	Thirteenth great granddaughter
CAMPBELL, Michael	Spouse of tenth great granddaughter
CAMPBELL, Stacy	Eleventh great granddaughter
CAPLE, Jerry Thomas	Spouse of eleventh great granddaughter
CAPPS, David	Spouse of tenth great granddaughter
CAPPS, Mike	Eleventh great grandson
CAPPS, Scott	Eleventh great grandson
CAPPS, Tracy	Eleventh great granddaughter
CAREY, Esther	Ninth great granddaughter
CAREY, Thomas	Spouse of eighth great granddaughter
CARPENTER, Savannah Tom	Second great grandson
CARPENTER, Trader Tom	Spouse of great granddaughter
CARR, Diza M.	Spouse of seventh great grandson
CARR, Rebecca	Spouse of seventh great grandson
CARTER, Florence	Spouse of eighth great grandson
CASSIDY	Spouse of ninth great granddaughter
CHANDLER, Redora Vianna	Spouse of ninth great grandson
CHAVIS, Robert	Spouse of eleventh great granddaughter
CHEROKEE, Blue Holly	Spouse of second great granddaughter
CHEROKEE WOMAN	Spouse of second great grandson
CHESTER, Ann	Spouse of eighth great grandson
CHRESTMAN, Mary Amy Bell	Spouse of ninth great grandson
CLARK, Bill	Spouse of tenth great granddaughter
CLARK, Luried Navada	Spouse of ninth great grandson
CLEVELAND, Mary	Spouse of sixth great grandson
CLICK, Cecil Leon	Spouse of twelfth great granddaughter
CLICK, Teri Jeanette	Thirteenth great granddaughter
CLINE, Uldeen	Spouse of eleventh great grandson
CLOUD, Martin	Spouse of fifth great granddaughter
COALTER, Alton Bayne, Jr.	Twelfth great grandson
COALTER, Alton Boman	Spouse of eleventh great granddaughter
COALTER, Beverly Carolann	Twelfth great granddaughter
COALTER, David Andrew	Twelfth great grandson
COALTER, Elizabeth Jo	Twelfth great granddaughter
COALTER, Emily Jennette	Thirteenth great granddaughter
COALTER, Terry Michael	Twelfth great grandson
COBB, Walker Isaiah	Spouse of eighth great granddaughter
COKER, Bee	Spouse of tenth great granddaughter
COLE, George Washington	Spouse of eighth great granddaughter
COLE, Maude Lillie	Spouse of eighth great grandson
COLEMAN, Mildred Joy	Spouse of eleventh great grandson
COLLARD	Spouse of ninth great granddaughter
COLLINS, Helen	Spouse of tenth great grandson
COLLINS, Jerra Rae	Twelfth great granddaughter
COLLINS, Margaret Elizabeth	Twelfth great granddaughter
COLLINS, William Ray	Spouse of eleventh great granddaughter

Kinship List - Chief Wahunsonacock Powhatan

26 January 2012

Relative	Relationship
CONLEY, Bruce	Spouse of tenth great granddaughter
CONLEY, Christopher Gregory	Twelfth great grandson
CONLEY, Ethan Andrew	Twelfth great grandson
CONLEY, Gregory Christopher	Eleventh great grandson
CONLEY, Heidi Go	Twelfth great granddaughter
CONLEY, Henry Thomas	Eleventh great grandson
CONLEY, Holly Sue	Twelfth great granddaughter
CONLEY, Ivan Duell	Eleventh great grandson
CONLEY, Ivan Duell, Jr.	Twelfth great grandson
CONLEY, James Evans	Twelfth great grandson
CONLEY, Jeffrey Lynn	Eleventh great grandson
CONLEY, Jonathan William	Twelfth great grandson
CONLEY, Kerra Brienne	Twelfth great grandchild
CONLEY, Kiersten	Twelfth great grandchild
CONLEY, Louvinda Adiar	Twelfth great granddaughter
CONLEY, Lovinda Adiar	Twelfth great granddaughter
CONLEY, Mark David	Twelfth great grandson
CONLEY, Michael Adam	Twelfth great grandson
CONLEY, Michael Patrick	Twelfth great grandson
CONLEY, Navada Ann	Eleventh great granddaughter
CONLEY, Patrick Edward	Twelfth great grandson
CONLEY, Rhonda Yvette	Twelfth great granddaughter
CONLEY, Timothy Bruce	Eleventh great grandson
CONLEY, Timothy Devin	Twelfth great grandson
CONLEY, Timothy Lee	Eleventh great grandson
CONLEY, Timothy Paul	Twelfth great grandson
CONLEY, William Brian	Twelfth great grandson
CONLEY, William Hollie	Spouse of tenth great granddaughter
CONLEY, William Hollie "Bill", Jr.	Eleventh great grandson
CONNER, Mims Howard IV	Thirteenth great grandson
COOK	Spouse of ninth great granddaughter
COOK, Charles	Tenth great grandson
COOK, Jack A.	Tenth great grandson
COOK, William	Tenth great grandson
CORDELL, Karen	Spouse of twelfth great grandson
CORK, James Earl (Jim)	Twelfth great grandson
CORK, James Vernon	Spouse of eleventh great granddaughter
CORK, Rose Diane	Twelfth great granddaughter
CORKIN, Tommy	Spouse of tenth great granddaughter
CORNSTALK, Big Turkey Hop	Great grandson
CORNSTALK, Hokolesqua Opechan	Grandson
CORNSTALK, Little Turkey	Great grandson
CORNSTALK, Nancy Turkey	Great granddaughter
CORNSTALK, Nonoma	Spouse
CORNSTALK, Sister Turkey	Great granddaughter
CORSENTINO, Charles	Spouse of tenth great granddaughter
COSTEN, Thelma	Spouse of eighth great grandson
COTHERN, Andrew Jackson	Spouse of sixth great granddaughter
COTHERN, Bobby Nell	Eighth great granddaughter
COTHERN, Doris Loraine	Eighth great granddaughter
COTHERN, Edd Pickens	Seventh great grandson
COTHERN, Emma Hawkins	Seventh great granddaughter
COTHERN, Farrie	Eighth great granddaughter
COTHERN, Filo Knox	Eighth great grandson

Kinship List - Chief Wahunsonacock Powhatan

26 January 2012

Relative	Relationship
COTHERN, Frances	Spouse of eighth great grandson
COTHERN, John Emery	Eighth great grandson
COTHERN, Letha Lovie	Eighth great granddaughter
COTHERN, Mary Lavisa	Seventh great granddaughter
COTHERN, Murriel	Eighth great granddaughter
COTHERN, Nancy Carlida	Seventh great granddaughter
COTHERN, Nannie	Eighth great granddaughter
COTHERN, Ruby Gayle	Eighth great granddaughter
COTHERN, Vevi Vann	Seventh great grandson
COTHERN, Walter	Seventh great grandson
COTHERN, Walter James	Eighth great grandson
COTHERN, Willa Augusta	Eighth great granddaughter
COTHERN, William	Seventh great grandson
COTHERN, Willie Jewell	Eighth great granddaughter
COTTON	Spouse of sixth great granddaughter
COTTONHAM, Adeline	Spouse of seventh great grandson
COUCH, Anita	Tenth great granddaughter
COUCH, Betty Jo	Tenth great granddaughter
COUCH, Dawson	Tenth great grandson
COUCH, John W.	Spouse of ninth great granddaughter
COUCH, Johnnie Lou	Tenth great granddaughter
COUCH, Myrtle	Tenth great granddaughter
COX, Leslie P. "Pete"	Spouse of eleventh great granddaughter
COX, Marina	Twelfth great granddaughter
CRAIG, Arthur Winford	Spouse of eleventh great granddaughter
CRAIG, Fenton	Spouse of ninth great granddaughter
CRAIG, Hallie Michelle	Twelfth great granddaughter
CRANE, George Melvin	Spouse of ninth great granddaughter
CRANE, Wanda Glenn	Spouse of tenth great grandson
CRAUSWELL, Amy	Ninth great granddaughter
CRAUSWELL, Betty	Tenth great granddaughter
CRAUSWELL, Curby Brack	Spouse of eighth great granddaughter
CRAUSWELL, Dorothy	Tenth great granddaughter
CRAUSWELL, Jack	Tenth great grandson
CRAUSWELL, Spencer Avis "Skinny"	Ninth great grandson
CRAUSWELL, Trixie Ethelyn	Ninth great granddaughter
CRAWFORD, Albert Abb	Spouse of tenth great granddaughter
CRAWFORD, Arnold Wayne	Eleventh great grandson
CRAWFORD, Bobby	Eleventh great grandson
CRAWFORD, Carland	Eleventh great grandchild
CRAWFORD, John	Eleventh great grandson
CREW, Gilbert	Tenth great grandson
CREW, Tidie	Spouse of ninth great granddaughter
CUMMINGS, Norman J.	Spouse of eleventh great granddaughter
DANIEL, Arthur Leonard	Spouse of ninth great granddaughter
DANIELS, Winna	Spouse of sixth great grandson
DAUGHTER OF SHAWANO CHIEF	Great grandmother
DAVIS, Bob	Spouse of eleventh great granddaughter
DAVIS, Darlene Ann	Spouse of twelfth great grandson
DAVIS, Donna Rene	Twelfth great granddaughter
DAVIS, Emily	Thirteenth great granddaughter
DAVIS, Madison	Thirteenth great granddaughter
DAVIS, Michael Ray	Twelfth great grandson
DAVIS, Sarah	Spouse of seventh great grandson

Kinship List - Chief Wahunsonacock Powhatan

26 January 2012

Relative	Relationship
DAVIS, Sarah Ann	Spouse of seventh great grandson
DAVIS, Tracy	Spouse of eighth great grandson
DAWNEE	Spouse of fourth great grandson
DAY, Cora M.	Spouse of eighth great grandson
DEAN, Terraso	Spouse of seventh great grandson
DEAR, Eva Mae	Spouse of eighth great grandson
DEAR, William Bruce	Spouse of eighth great granddaughter
DEATON, Eddie	Spouse of eleventh great granddaughter
DECKER, Dana	Spouse of twelfth great grandson
DENTON, Martha	Spouse of fifth great grandson
DETURK, Kay	Spouse of eleventh great grandson
DICKARD, Claudia	Tenth great granddaughter
DICKARD, Leon Hall	Eleventh great grandson
DICKARD, Leon Hill	Spouse of ninth great granddaughter
DICKARD, Leon Hill Jr.	Tenth great grandson
DICKARD, Robert Dale	Eleventh great grandson
DICKARD, Ruth Waudell	Tenth great granddaughter
DICKENS, Mary Lil	Spouse of tenth great grandson
DICKINSON, Virginia	Spouse of twelfth great grandson
DOSS, Ranzy	Spouse of ninth great granddaughter
DUNCAN, Teri	Spouse of twelfth great grandson
DURBIN, Curtis	Thirteenth great grandson
DURBIN, Daniel	Thirteenth great grandson
DURBIN, Lonnie	Spouse of twelfth great granddaughter
DURBIN, Mitchell	Thirteenth great granddaughter
DURBIN, Tim	Thirteenth great grandson
DUTTON, Lorene	Spouse of tenth great grandson
EAGEN, Connie Francis	Spouse of twelfth great grandson
EATON, Eula	Ninth great granddaughter
EATON, George	Ninth great grandson
EATON, Grover	Ninth great grandson
EATON, Infant	Ninth great grandchild
EATON, Mary Lou	Ninth great granddaughter
EATON, Stella	Ninth great granddaughter
EATON, Will	Ninth great grandson
EATON, William Jackson	Spouse of eighth great granddaughter
EDWARD, Adam Kelly	Spouse of twelfth great granddaughter
EITSON, Lucy	Spouse of ninth great grandson
ELLISON, Betty Marie	Thirteenth great granddaughter
ELLISON, Roger Dale	Spouse of twelfth great granddaughter
ENGLAND, Amanda Lee	Twelfth great granddaughter
ENGLAND, Cynthia Lynn	Twelfth great granddaughter
ENGLAND, James David	Spouse of eleventh great granddaughter
ENGLAND, Michelle	Spouse of twelfth great grandson
ERSKINE, Albert R.	Spouse of ninth great granddaughter
EVANS, Andrew Blake	Thirteenth great grandson
EVANS, Austin Clay	Thirteenth great grandson
EVANS, Howard Clay	Spouse of twelfth great granddaughter
EVERITT, Mary Eleven	Spouse of tenth great grandson
EZELL, Luvicie Luice	Spouse of seventh great grandson
FALGOUT, Frank Julius	Spouse of tenth great granddaughter
FALGOUT, Winfred Marie	Eleventh great granddaughter
FANNIN, Abraham	Spouse of seventh great granddaughter
FARRIS, Gomer	Spouse of eighth great granddaughter

Kinship List - Chief Wahunsonacock Powhatan

Relative	Relationship
FINCHER, Corey Isaac	Thirteenth great grandson
FINCHER, Frank Newton	Spouse of twelfth great granddaughter
FLEMING, Sharon Elizabeth	Spouse of twelfth great grandson
FLOWER, Morning	Aunt
FOLSOM, Sophia	Spouse of seventh great grandson
FORD, J.P.	Spouse of ninth great granddaughter
FOSTER, Annawake	Spouse of fifth great grandson
FOSTER, Jennie	Spouse of fourth great grandson
FOX-TAYLOR	Spouse of fifth great granddaughter
FRANKS, Leona	Spouse of tenth great grandson
FREEMAN, Betty J.	Tenth great granddaughter
FREEMAN, Cora Lee	Tenth great granddaughter
FREEMAN, Joanna	Spouse of seventh great grandson
FREEMAN, Louie Edgar	Spouse of ninth great granddaughter
FREEMAN, Peggy	Tenth great granddaughter
FRIDDLE, Maxine	Spouse of eleventh great grandson
GAFFORD, Stepehn C.	Spouse of seventh great granddaughter
GALLO, Pierina	Spouse of twelfth great grandson
GARRISON	Spouse of eleventh great granddaughter
GAY, Benjamin Patrick Bussey	Thirteenth great grandson
GAY, Braeden Harding	Thirteenth great grandson
GAY, Patrick Benjamin	Spouse of twelfth great granddaughter
GAYLER, Gladys Lou	Spouse of tenth great grandson
GEE, Elbert J.	Ninth great grandson
GEE, Frances	Tenth great granddaughter
GEE, Lucile	Tenth great granddaughter
GEE, Lucille	Ninth great granddaughter
GEE, Robert	Tenth great grandson
GEE, Robert M.	Spouse of eighth great granddaughter
GIGANTI, Catherine Ann	Eleventh great granddaughter
GIGANTI, Charles Francesco	Twelfth great grandson
GIGANTI, Charles J.	Spouse of tenth great granddaughter
GIGANTI, Frank Charles	Eleventh great grandson
GIGANTI, Joseph	Twelfth great grandson
GIGANTI, Kate	Twelfth great granddaughter
GILBREATH, Gill	Spouse of ninth great granddaughter
GILLESPIE, Amy Elizabeth	Twelfth great granddaughter
GILLESPIE, Nancy Maureen	Twelfth great granddaughter
GILLESPIE, Robert	Spouse of eleventh great granddaughter
GLOVER	Spouse of tenth great granddaughter
GODSEY, Cheryl Lynn	Twelfth great granddaughter
GODSEY, Garland D.	Spouse of eleventh great granddaughter
GODSEY, Linda Lorene	Twelfth great granddaughter
GODSEY, Nancy	Twelfth great granddaughter
GOODMAN, John Charles	Spouse of eighth great granddaughter
GOODSON, William	Spouse of seventh great granddaughter
GOODWIN, Martha Nan	Spouse of ninth great grandson
GOOLSBY, Charles	Spouse of eleventh great granddaughter
GOOLSBY, Craig	Twelfth great grandson
GOOLSBY, Whit	Spouse of eleventh great granddaughter
GOSSETT	Spouse of tenth great grandson
GRAY, Caroline	Spouse of seventh great grandson
GRIFFITH, Marion	Spouse of ninth great grandson
GRIGSBY, Emer Mildred	Spouse of ninth great grandson

Kinship List - Chief Wahunsonacock Powhatan

Relative | **Relationship**

Relative	Relationship
GRISSOM	Spouse of tenth great granddaughter
GUTHERIE, Helen	Spouse of ninth great grandson
GUYTON, Carolyn Sue	Eleventh great granddaughter
GUYTON, Dewey	Tenth great grandson
GUYTON, Erin Nicole	Twelfth great granddaughter
GUYTON, Ernest Paul	Tenth great grandson
GUYTON, Eula Mae	Spouse of eighth great grandson
GUYTON, Grady Benton	Eleventh great grandson
GUYTON, Helen Faye	Eleventh great granddaughter
GUYTON, Kelley Jo	Twelfth great granddaughter
GUYTON, Lonnie Alonzo	Spouse of ninth great granddaughter
GUYTON, Marie Cardell	Twelfth great granddaughter
GUYTON, Patricia Anne	Eleventh great granddaughter
GUYTON, Raymond Paul	Eleventh great grandson
GUYTON, Roger Dale	Eleventh great grandson
GUYTON, Roger Dale II	Twelfth great grandson
GUYTON, Todd	Twelfth great grandson
GUYTON, Tommy T.	Tenth great grandson
GUYTON, Willie Atmus	Tenth great grandson
GUYTON, Willie C.	Eleventh great grandson
HALL, Clara Alice	Spouse of tenth great grandson
HALL, Frances Michelle	Eleventh great granddaughter
HALL, Maurice E.	Spouse of tenth great granddaughter
HALL, Patricia	Eleventh great granddaughter
HAMBLEY, Tommie Lucille	Spouse of tenth great grandson
HAMILTON, Arthur Lee "Pete"	Spouse of tenth great granddaughter
HAMILTON, Betty Lou	Eleventh great granddaughter
HAMILTON, Lindsay Hannah	Thirteenth great grandchild
HAMILTON, Ronnie Lee	Eleventh great grandson
HAMILTON, Ronnie Todd	Twelfth great grandson
HAMILTON, Russell Allen	Twelfth great grandson
HAMILTON, Will	Thirteenth great grandson
HANNAH, Angela Faye	Thirteenth great granddaughter
HANNAH, Jeffery Lawrence	Twelfth great grandson
HANNAH, Jennifer	Thirteenth great granddaughter
HANNAH, Jessica Marie	Thirteenth great granddaughter
HANNAH, Matthew	Thirteenth great grandson
HANNAH, Michael Lester	Twelfth great grandson
HANNAH, Robert	Spouse of eleventh great granddaughter
HANNAH, Robert Bradley	Twelfth great grandson
HANNAH, Stacey Leigh	Thirteenth great granddaughter
HANNAH, Wanda Faye	Spouse of eleventh great grandson
HARDING, Nora Josephine	Spouse of eighth great grandson
HARMS, David	Spouse of twelfth great granddaughter
HARMS, Mackenzie Rose	Thirteenth great granddaughter
HARRIS, Daisy Cardell	Spouse of tenth great grandson
HARRIS, Dallvore "Dolly" Frances	Spouse of ninth great grandson
HARRISON, Audoline	Eleventh great granddaughter
HARRISON, John T.	Eleventh great grandson
HARRISON, Robert Earl	Eleventh great grandson
HARRISON, Thomas	Spouse of tenth great granddaughter
HARTSHORN, Lewis	Spouse of tenth great granddaughter
HATCHER, Louise	Spouse of ninth great grandson
HAWKINS, George Lewis	Spouse of eleventh great granddaughter

Kinship List - Chief Wahunsonacock Powhatan

26 January 2012

Relative	Relationship
HAWKINS, Grayson	Thirteenth great grandchild
HAYES, Kathleen	Spouse of tenth great grandson
HAYGOOD	Spouse of eighth great granddaughter
HEATHERLY, Lillie Myrtle	Spouse of tenth great grandson
HENDERSON	Spouse of ninth great granddaughter
HENIGAN, Bernice	Spouse of tenth great grandson
HIBDON, Joanne	Eleventh great granddaughter
HIBDON, Lawrence	Spouse of tenth great granddaughter
HIBDON, Louise	Eleventh great granddaughter
HICKEY, Alfred Hill	Eleventh great grandson
HICKEY, Hiram Bewitt	Spouse of tenth great granddaughter
HICKEY, Hiram Dewitt	Eleventh great grandson
HICKMAN, Ann Thompson	Spouse of sixth great grandson
HICKS, Nova Jean	Spouse of tenth great grandson
HILL, Bill	Spouse of eleventh great granddaughter
HILL, Billie	Eleventh great grandchild
HILL, Bruce	Spouse of tenth great granddaughter
HILL, Delvin Fat	Spouse of tenth great granddaughter
HILL, Elsie Ruth	Eleventh great granddaughter
HILL, Jennifer	Eleventh great granddaughter
HILL, Katy	Spouse of ninth great grandson
HILL, Lindsay Hyche	Twelfth great granddaughter
HILL, Mary Hyche	Twelfth great granddaughter
HINCHMAN, Alda W. M.D.	Spouse of tenth great granddaughter
HINCHMAN, Sally Darlene	Twelfth great granddaughter
HINCHMAN, Warren	Eleventh great grandson
HINTON, Rebecca	Spouse of sixth great grandson
HITT, Margaret	Spouse of eleventh great grandson
HODGES, Addie Mae	Spouse of eighth great grandson
HODGES, Mary Appie	Spouse of eighth great grandson
HOFFMAN, Joe	Spouse of tenth great granddaughter
HOLDEN, Vickie	Spouse of twelfth great grandson
HOLLIS, Aileen	Tenth great granddaughter
HOLLIS, Charlie E.	Spouse of ninth great granddaughter
HOLMES, Guy	Spouse of eighth great granddaughter
HOLMES, Guy	Ninth great grandson
HOLMES, Lilac	Ninth great granddaughter
HOLMES, Lois	Ninth great granddaughter
HOLMES, Nancy	Spouse of sixth great grandson
HOLMES, Ned Evans	Ninth great grandson
HORN, Hazel	Spouse of tenth great grandson
HORTON	Spouse of ninth great granddaughter
HOSCH, Arvel Parks	Spouse of tenth great granddaughter
HOWARD, Adra	Spouse of sixth great grandson
HOWARD, Bruce Lewis	Spouse of eleventh great granddaughter
HOWARD, Elizabeth Rae	Twelfth great granddaughter
HOWARD, Maggie Ann	Thirteenth great granddaughter
HOWARD, Melissa Ann	Twelfth great granddaughter
HOWARD, Robert Bruce	Twelfth great grandson
HOWTON, Annie	Spouse of tenth great grandson
HUBBARD, Harold "Buddy"	Spouse of eleventh great granddaughter
HUFFMAN, Ira Annie	Spouse of tenth great grandson
HUFFMAN, Martha Ellen	Spouse of eighth great grandson
HUGHES, Dennis	Spouse of ninth great granddaughter

Kinship List - Chief Wahunsonacock Powhatan

26 January 2012

Relative	Relationship
HUGHES, Emily	Thirteenth great granddaughter
HUGHES, John David "JD"	Spouse of twelfth great granddaughter
HUGHES, John Rice	Spouse of granddaughter
HYDEN, Ballard	Spouse of twelfth great granddaughter
HYDEN, Nova Peggy	Fourteenth great granddaughter
HYDEN, Nova Rebecca	Thirteenth great granddaughter
INGRAM, Marew	Spouse of eighth great granddaughter
ITOYATIN	Spouse
JACKS	Spouse of ninth great granddaughter
JACKS, Douglas E.	Tenth great grandson
JACKS, Helen	Tenth great granddaughter
JACOBS, Minnie E.	Spouse of eighth great grandson
JAFFE, Jennifer Lea	Twelfth great granddaughter
JAFFE, Kenneth Lewis	Spouse of eleventh great granddaughter
JAFFE, Kevin Eric	Twelfth great grandson
JEFFERIES, Louise	Spouse of tenth great grandson
JERNIGAN, Benjamin	Spouse of fifth great granddaughter
JERNIGAN, Benjamin Lomax	Eighth great grandson
JERNIGAN, Benjamin W.	Sixth great grandson
JERNIGAN, Cary	Sixth great grandson
JERNIGAN, Curtis LeRoy	Eighth great grandson
JERNIGAN, Dizzy M.	Eighth great grandson
JERNIGAN, Edith	Sixth great granddaughter
JERNIGAN, Edward	Sixth great grandson
JERNIGAN, Ernest Edwin	Eighth great grandson
JERNIGAN, Fennig	Seventh great grandson
JERNIGAN, George Washington	Seventh great grandson
JERNIGAN, Henry	Seventh great grandson
JERNIGAN, Ida Evelyn	Eighth great granddaughter
JERNIGAN, James W.	Seventh great grandson
JERNIGAN, Joseph Jefferson	Sixth great grandson
JERNIGAN, Josephine M.	Seventh great granddaughter
JERNIGAN, Laura A.	Seventh great granddaughter
JERNIGAN, Martha Lulu	Eighth great granddaughter
JERNIGAN, Mary	Sixth great granddaughter
JERNIGAN, Nancy	Sixth great granddaughter
JERNIGAN, Nancy V.	Seventh great granddaughter
JERNIGAN, Richard Call	Seventh great grandson
JERNIGAN, Robert Henry	Eighth great grandson
JERNIGAN, Susan	Sixth great granddaughter
JERNIGAN, Thomas Jefferson	Seventh great grandson
JERNIGAN, Van Stallworth	Eighth great grandson
JERNIGAN, William	Sixth great grandson
JERNIGAN, William	Seventh great grandson
JERNIGAN, William Wiley	Eighth great grandson
JEWEL, Marla	Spouse of eleventh great grandson
JOHNSON, Aaron M.	Thirteenth great grandson
JOHNSON, Crystal L.	Thirteenth great granddaughter
JOHNSON, George	Spouse of ninth great granddaughter
JOHNSON, James W.	Twelfth great grandson
JOHNSON, Janice L.	Twelfth great granddaughter
JOHNSON, Jess Willard	Spouse of eleventh great granddaughter
JOHNSON, Jesse H.	Twelfth great grandson
JOHNSON, Larry Jim	Twelfth great grandson

Kinship List - Chief Wahunsonacock Powhatan

Relative	Relationship
JOHNSON, Melanie A.	Thirteenth great granddaughter
JOHNSON, Oliver	Spouse of tenth great granddaughter
JOHNSON, Phillip Michael	Twelfth great grandson
JOHNSON, Vivia June	Twelfth great granddaughter
JONES, Beth	Spouse of eighth great grandson
JONES, Doyle Daphney	Spouse of eleventh great granddaughter
JONES, Eric Allan	Spouse of tenth great granddaughter
JONES, Gary Dean	Spouse of twelfth great granddaughter
JONES, Keene	Spouse of twelfth great granddaughter
JONES, Mary Susanna	Spouse of seventh great grandson
JONES, Phillip Wayne	Twelfth great grandson
JONES, Sherry Lou	Spouse of twelfth great grandson
JONES, Susan Marie	Twelfth great granddaughter
JORDAN, Mary Frances	Spouse of eleventh great grandson
JOYCE, Kelly	Spouse of eleventh great grandson
KELLEY, Lana	Spouse of eleventh great grandson
KELLOGG, Georgia	Spouse of tenth great grandson
KELLY, Pamela Joyce	Spouse of twelfth great grandson
KENNEDY, Alexandra Charles	Twelfth great grandson
KENNEDY, Madison Wynn	Twelfth great grandson
KENNEDY, Robert Eric	Spouse of eleventh great granddaughter
KENNEDY, Robert Jacque	Twelfth great grandson
KEY	Spouse of tenth great granddaughter
KEY, Michael	Spouse of tenth great granddaughter
KILLINGSWORTH, James	Eighth great grandson
KILLINGSWORTH, Lee Levy R.	Eighth great grandson
KILLINGSWORTH, Mary Mollie Antoniette	Eighth great granddaughter
KILLINGSWORTH, Mattie	Eighth great granddaughter
KILLINGSWORTH, Thomas Abney	Spouse of seventh great granddaughter
KILPATRICK, Betty Ruth	Eleventh great granddaughter
KILPATRICK, Clyde H.	Spouse of tenth great granddaughter
KILPATRICK, David	Eleventh great grandson
KILPATRICK, Doris Marie	Eleventh great granddaughter
KING, Buford	Eleventh great grandson
KING, Helen	Eleventh great granddaughter
KING, Mary	Spouse of fourth great grandson
KING, Merlin	Spouse of tenth great granddaughter
KING, Mildred	Eleventh great granddaughter
KING, Pauline	Eleventh great granddaughter
KNIGHT, Earlene	Spouse of tenth great grandson
KNIGHT, Lillian	Spouse of eleventh great grandson
KNOX, Sallie Emma	Spouse of seventh great grandson
KNOX, Stanford	Spouse of ninth great granddaughter
KOBLECHECK, Betty	Spouse of tenth great grandson
KOYL, Ben Wynn	Twelfth great grandson
KOYL, Glenn	Spouse of eleventh great granddaughter
KOYL, Glenn Wynn	Twelfth great grandson
KOYL, Sam Wynn	Twelfth great grandson
KYKER, Nell Hortnese	Spouse of eighth great grandson
LAFFOOD, Frank	Spouse of tenth great granddaughter
LAMAR, James	Spouse of fifth great granddaughter
LARKIN, Child	Thirteenth great grandchild
LARKIN, Edward Steven	Spouse of twelfth great granddaughter
LARU	Spouse of tenth great granddaughter

Kinship List - Chief Wahunsonacock Powhatan

26 January 2012

Relative	Relationship
LARU, Elizabeth J.	Eleventh great granddaughter
LATTA, John Guthrie	Spouse of eighth great granddaughter
LATTA, Leslie Virginia	Ninth great granddaughter
LAWRENCE, Bob	Eleventh great grandson
LAWRENCE, Floyd	Spouse of tenth great granddaughter
LAWRENCE, William	Eleventh great grandson
LAWSON, Lorene	Spouse of tenth great grandson
LAWSON, Michael	Twelfth great grandson
LAWSON, Robert	Twelfth great grandson
LAWSON, Robert	Spouse of eleventh great granddaughter
LAYMAN, Nannie	Spouse of seventh great grandson
LE, David	Spouse of twelfth great granddaughter
LE, Noah	Thirteenth great grandson
LEMONS, Coy	Spouse of eighth great granddaughter
LESLIE, Darrell Blake	Thirteenth great grandson
LESLIE, Darrell Keith	Spouse of twelfth great granddaughter
LESLIE, Jonathan Keith	Thirteenth great grandson
LIGHT, Eloise	Spouse of tenth great grandson
LINDSAY, Dorothy	Spouse of tenth great grandson
LINXWITER, Mary M.	Spouse of tenth great grandson
LOCKHART, Jackie Edins	Spouse of tenth great grandson
LOGAN, Mamie	Spouse of seventh great grandson
LOLLAR, Lehman	Spouse of tenth great granddaughter
LOLLAR, Melinda	Eleventh great granddaughter
LOLLAR, Michael	Eleventh great grandson
LONG	Spouse of sixth great granddaughter
LONG, Arlene	Spouse of tenth great grandson
LONG, Chad Mikel	Thirteenth great grandson
LONG, Joseph Gordon	Spouse of twelfth great granddaughter
LOVELACE, Katie	Spouse of tenth great grandson
LOVELACE, Sue	Spouse of ninth great grandson
LOVVORN, Farrell	Spouse of eleventh great granddaughter
LOVVORN, Scott	Twelfth great grandson
LOVVORN, Sean	Twelfth great grandson
LOVVORN, Shannon	Twelfth great grandchild
LOWERY, Billy Ralph	Eleventh great grandson
LOWERY, Clarence Howard	Tenth great grandson
LOWERY, Cory	Eleventh great grandson
LOWERY, Howard Keith	Eleventh great grandson
LOWERY, Jenny	Eleventh great granddaughter
LOWERY, Joe Stanley	Tenth great grandson
LOWERY, John William "Billy"	Tenth great grandson
LOWERY, Kelly	Eleventh great grandchild
LOWERY, Lois Christine	Tenth great granddaughter
LOWERY, Margaret Ruth	Tenth great granddaughter
LOWERY, Mary Louise	Tenth great granddaughter
LOWERY, Mattie Bee	Tenth great granddaughter
LOWERY, Rose Marie	Eleventh great granddaughter
LOWERY, Thomas Earl	Spouse of ninth great granddaughter
LOWERY, Thomas Harold	Tenth great grandson
LOWERY, Thomas Howard Jr.	Eleventh great grandson
LYKINS, Diana Hope	Spouse of eleventh great grandson
LYONS, Annie Mae	Ninth great granddaughter
LYONS, Earl Monroe	Spouse of eighth great granddaughter

Kinship List - Chief Wahunsonacock Powhatan

26 January 2012

Relative	Relationship
MANDOLINI, Ann Elizabeth	Eleventh great granddaughter
MANDOLINI, Carl Chester	Eleventh great grandson
MANDOLINI, Carla	Twelfth great granddaughter
MANDOLINI, Merico Cesare "Mike Chester"	Spouse of tenth great granddaughter
MANGOPEESOMON, Nonoma	Spouse
MANSFIELD, Pamela Sue	Spouse of eleventh great grandson
MARLEY, Hampton Oscar	Spouse of tenth great granddaughter
MARTIN	Spouse of tenth great granddaughter
MARTIN, Joshua	Thirteenth great grandson
MARTIN, Michael	Spouse of twelfth great granddaughter
MARTIN, Robbie	Thirteenth great grandchild
MARTIN, Rose Marie	Spouse of eleventh great grandson
MASSIE, Mark Lincoln	Spouse of twelfth great granddaughter
MASSIE, Savannah Marie	Thirteenth great granddaughter
MATHEWS, Ethel	Spouse of tenth great grandson
MATHEWS, John	Spouse of seventh great granddaughter
MAYS, Florence	Spouse of tenth great grandson
MAYS, Unk	Spouse of eleventh great granddaughter
MCANULTY, Jerry Duaine	Spouse of twelfth great granddaughter
MCANULTY, Lisa Darlene	Thirteenth great granddaughter
MCCANDLISH, Alexandra Marie	Fourteenth great granddaughter
MCCANDLISH, John Pierce	Spouse of thirteenth great granddaughter
MCCASLIN, Florence Maggie	Ninth great granddaughter
MCCASLIN, Grace Loyce	Ninth great granddaughter
MCCASLIN, John Sheridan	Spouse of eighth great granddaughter
MCCASLIN, John Sheridan	Ninth great grandson
MCCASLIN, Kenneth Van	Ninth great grandson
MCCASLIN, Ron Lee	Ninth great grandson
MCCAUGHREN, Theresa	Spouse of twelfth great grandson
MCCOMBS, Billie	Spouse of ninth great grandson
MCCOMBS, Jackie	Spouse of ninth great grandson
MCCOMBS, Linda	Tenth great granddaughter
MCCOMBS, Wiley Mason	Spouse of ninth great granddaughter
MCCOMBS, Wiley Michael	Tenth great grandson
MCCRARY, Billy Douglas	Eleventh great grandson
MCCRARY, Charles Dennis	Thirteenth great grandson
MCCRARY, Charles William	Twelfth great grandson
MCCRARY, Debbie	Eleventh great granddaughter
MCCRARY, Jesse B.	Spouse of tenth great granddaughter
MCCRARY, Ollie William	Spouse of eleventh great granddaughter
MCCRARY, Rodney Wayne	Eleventh great grandson
MCCURRY, Ollie Lee	Spouse of ninth great granddaughter
MCDONALD, Dennis	Spouse of eleventh great granddaughter
MCFARLAND, Albert	Ninth great grandson
MCFARLAND, Edith	Tenth great granddaughter
MCFARLAND, Fannie Antoniette	Ninth great granddaughter
MCFARLAND, Fred	Ninth great grandson
MCFARLAND, Harold	Tenth great grandson
MCFARLAND, James Alford	Ninth great grandson
MCFARLAND, James William	Spouse of eighth great granddaughter
MCFARLAND, Lottie	Ninth great granddaughter
MCFARLAND, Myrtle	Ninth great granddaughter
MCFARLAND, Ruth	Tenth great granddaughter
MCFARLAND, Ruth Mae	Ninth great granddaughter

Kinship List - Chief Wahunsonacock Powhatan

26 January 2012

Relative	Relationship
MCFARLAND, Tessie	Ninth great granddaughter
MCFARLAND, Thomas Leo	Ninth great grandson
MCFARLAND, William "Billy"	Tenth great grandson
MCKENLEY, J.R. Bob Jr.	Spouse of tenth great granddaughter
MCKENLEY, Lande	Eleventh great grandchild
MCKENLEY, Rob	Eleventh great grandson
MCKENLEY, Steve	Eleventh great grandson
MCKINNEY, Adrian O'Neal	Spouse of tenth great granddaughter
MCKINNEY, Peggy	Eleventh great granddaughter
MCKINNEY, Sandra	Eleventh great granddaughter
MCKINNEY, Teresa	Eleventh great granddaughter
MCMILLEN, Bettie H.	Seventh great granddaughter
MCMILLEN, James	Spouse of sixth great granddaughter
MCMILLEN, John H.	Seventh great grandson
MCMILLEN, Mahalia	Seventh great granddaughter
MCMILLEN, Sophia	Spouse of sixth great grandson
MCNAIR, Captain David	Spouse of fifth great granddaughter
MCNEARNY, Joyce Lynn	Spouse of eleventh great grandson
MCNEICE	Spouse of ninth great granddaughter
MELIORISOVA, Slavomira	Spouse of twelfth great grandson
MELTON, Juanita	Spouse of tenth great grandson
MILLER, Clara	Spouse of tenth great grandson
MILLIGAN	Spouse of tenth great granddaughter
MIMS, Kayla Lynn	Fourteenth great granddaughter
MIMS, Shannon	Spouse of thirteenth great granddaughter
MITCHELL, Bonnie Grace	Ninth great granddaughter
MITCHELL, Edith	Ninth great granddaughter
MITCHELL, Fay	Ninth great granddaughter
MITCHELL, Gladys	Ninth great granddaughter
MITCHELL, Gus	Spouse of eighth great granddaughter
MITCHELL, Ray	Ninth great grandson
MITCHELL, Rebedda	Ninth great granddaughter
MONCRIEF, James	Spouse of seventh great granddaughter
MONCRIEF, Peneloupe "Penny"	Eighth great granddaughter
MONKUS, Mattie	Spouse of ninth great grandson
MOORE, Albert Roy	Tenth great grandson
MOORE, Alfred Lamar "Al"	Eleventh great grandson
MOORE, Alta	Spouse of tenth great grandson
MOORE, Annie Jewel	Eleventh great granddaughter
MOORE, Annie Louvenia Lou	Ninth great granddaughter
MOORE, Aralree Elna Bussey	Tenth great granddaughter
MOORE, Bobbie	Eleventh great grandchild
MOORE, Bobby Glynda	Eleventh great grandchild
MOORE, Charles Samuel Jr.	Spouse of twelfth great granddaughter
MOORE, Charles Vernon	Eleventh great grandson
MOORE, Clarence William	Tenth great grandson
MOORE, Clarence William "Billy"	Eleventh great grandson
MOORE, Cristy Diane	Thirteenth great granddaughter
MOORE, Donald E.	Eleventh great grandson
MOORE, Drue Milton	Ninth great grandson
MOORE, Edith Mozelle	Tenth great granddaughter
MOORE, Emery L.	Tenth great grandson
MOORE, Estelle	Tenth great granddaughter
MOORE, Eunice Mae	Tenth great granddaughter

Kinship List - Chief Wahunsonacock Powhatan

26 January 2012

Relative	Relationship
MOORE, Floyd Enice	Tenth great grandson
MOORE, Gus Lewis	Ninth great grandson
MOORE, Guy Ellis	Ninth great grandson
MOORE, Harold Gusse	Tenth great grandson
MOORE, Henry Chester	Tenth great grandson
MOORE, Hubert Lewis	Tenth great grandson
MOORE, James Derrick	Thirteenth great grandson
MOORE, Janet Dall	Eleventh great granddaughter
MOORE, Jasmine Alexis	Fourteenth great granddaughter
MOORE, Jerry	Eleventh great grandson
MOORE, Jesse Daine	Eleventh great grandson
MOORE, Jesse Marion	Eleventh great grandson
MOORE, Jesse Milton	Tenth great grandson
MOORE, Jesse Monroe	Spouse of ninth great granddaughter
MOORE, John Molton	Spouse of eighth great granddaughter
MOORE, John Wilbur	Eleventh great grandson
MOORE, John Wilson Bill	Tenth great grandson
MOORE, Johnnie	Ninth great granddaughter
MOORE, June	Eleventh great granddaughter
MOORE, Kesley Earil	Eleventh great grandchild
MOORE, Lillie Mande	Ninth great granddaughter
MOORE, Linda M.	Eleventh great granddaughter
MOORE, Marton	Tenth great grandson
MOORE, Mary	Eleventh great granddaughter
MOORE, Mary Eleven	Eleventh great granddaughter
MOORE, Mary Louise	Eleventh great granddaughter
MOORE, Mildred	Eleventh great granddaughter
MOORE, Milton Earl	Tenth great grandson
MOORE, Murrah Lee	Tenth great grandson
MOORE, Murrah Lee Moe	Eleventh great grandson
MOORE, Nance	Eleventh great grandson
MOORE, Nelwyn Marie	Eleventh great granddaughter
MOORE, Orvele	Tenth great grandson
MOORE, Philip Dennis	Eleventh great grandson
MOORE, Philip Morton	Tenth great grandson
MOORE, Robben	Eleventh great grandchild
MOORE, Ronald C.	Eleventh great grandson
MOORE, Roy Albert	Eleventh great grandson
MOORE, Samuel David	Eleventh great grandson
MOORE, Sible	Tenth great granddaughter
MOORE, Sible Gale	Eleventh great granddaughter
MOORE, Susan Marie	Eleventh great granddaughter
MOORE, Thomas K.	Eleventh great grandson
MOORE, Vernon Odell	Tenth great grandson
MOORE, Winnie Easter	Tenth great granddaughter
MORGAN, James Franklin	Spouse of ninth great granddaughter
MORRIS	Spouse of sixth great granddaughter
MORRIS, June Rose	Spouse of tenth great grandson
MORROW, Jess	Spouse of eighth great granddaughter
MOSELEY, Adam	Seventh great grandson
MOSELEY, Adra Howard	Seventh great grandchild
MOSELEY, Albert P.	Seventh great grandson
MOSELEY, Benjamin	Sixth great grandson
MOSELEY, Clement T.	Sixth great grandson

Kinship List - Chief Wahunsonacock Powhatan

26 January 2012

Relative	**Relationship**
MOSELEY, Daniel	Sixth great grandson
MOSELEY, Daniel	Seventh great grandson
MOSELEY, Eliaha Anne	Eighth great granddaughter
MOSELEY, Elisha Sr.	Sixth great grandson
MOSELEY, Elisha Jr.	Seventh great grandson
MOSELEY, Elizabeth	Seventh great granddaughter
MOSELEY, George	Sixth great grandson
MOSELEY, George Washington	Seventh great grandson
MOSELEY, Hannah	Sixth great granddaughter
MOSELEY, Hiram	Seventh great grandson
MOSELEY, Huldah Lewis	Seventh great grandchild
MOSELEY, Jesse	Seventh great grandson
MOSELEY, John Albert	Eighth great grandson
MOSELEY, Joseph Sr.	Sixth great grandson
MOSELEY, Lucinda E.	Seventh great granddaughter
MOSELEY, Lydia	Spouse of sixth great grandson
MOSELEY, Lydia	Seventh great granddaughter
MOSELEY, Lydia F.	Eighth great granddaughter
MOSELEY, Mahulda Hulda	Sixth great granddaughter
MOSELEY, Margaret E.	Seventh great granddaughter
MOSELEY, Margaret Salena	Seventh great granddaughter
MOSELEY, Margaret Vann	Sixth great granddaughter
MOSELEY, Martha (Malinda)	Spouse of seventh great grandson
MOSELEY, Mary	Seventh great granddaughter
MOSELEY, Mary Ann	Sixth great granddaughter
MOSELEY, Mason	Sixth great grandson
MOSELEY, Mildred	Seventh great granddaughter
MOSELEY, Nancy Naomi	Sixth great granddaughter
MOSELEY, Robert	Seventh great grandson
MOSELEY, Robert	Seventh great grandson
MOSELEY, Robert "Robin" Jr.	Sixth great grandson
MOSELEY, Robert D. Sr.	Spouse of fifth great granddaughter
MOSELEY, Tabitha	Seventh great granddaughter
MOSELEY, Texaner	Eighth great grandchild
MOSELEY, Virginia	Eighth great granddaughter
MOSELEY, William Brantley Sr.	Sixth great grandson
MOSELEY, William Henry	Spouse of seventh great granddaughter
MOSELEY, Zelphia	Sixth great granddaughter
MOSLEY, Adrin Bethiah	Eighth great granddaughter
MOSLEY, Alabama	Eighth great granddaughter
MOSLEY, Alice Mae	Ninth great granddaughter
MOSLEY, Ann	Eighth great granddaughter
MOSLEY, Annie	Ninth great granddaughter
MOSLEY, Ashley Nell	Tenth great granddaughter
MOSLEY, Barbara	Tenth great granddaughter
MOSLEY, Barry Michael	Tenth great grandson
MOSLEY, Beaulta	Ninth great granddaughter
MOSLEY, Benjamin Milton	Eighth great grandson
MOSLEY, Benjamin Milton Jr.	Ninth great grandson
MOSLEY, Bessie	Ninth great granddaughter
MOSLEY, Bethia	Ninth great granddaughter
MOSLEY, Betty	Tenth great granddaughter
MOSLEY, Billy	Tenth great grandson
MOSLEY, Bobby Edward	Tenth great grandson

Kinship List - Chief Wahunsonacock Powhatan

26 January 2012

Relative	Relationship
MOSLEY, Celeste	Ninth great granddaughter
MOSLEY, Charles Ray	Tenth great grandson
MOSLEY, Christine	Ninth great granddaughter
MOSLEY, Clarence Lee	Ninth great grandson
MOSLEY, Clyde Herman	Tenth great grandson
MOSLEY, Colleen	Ninth great granddaughter
MOSLEY, Dan Wilson	Tenth great grandson
MOSLEY, Daniel	Tenth great grandson
MOSLEY, Daphne	Ninth great granddaughter
MOSLEY, Douglas McArthur	Tenth great grandson
MOSLEY, Dovie Lorene	Ninth great granddaughter
MOSLEY, Earl Frank	Tenth great grandson
MOSLEY, Earnest	Ninth great grandson
MOSLEY, Earsie	Ninth great grandchild
MOSLEY, Edward Neely	Tenth great grandson
MOSLEY, Eleanora	Ninth great granddaughter
MOSLEY, Elizabeth Crane	Eleventh great granddaughter
MOSLEY, Etta	Ninth great granddaughter
MOSLEY, Eugene Nolan	Tenth great grandson
MOSLEY, Evelyn Eleanor	Tenth great granddaughter
MOSLEY, Fannie Sue	Ninth great granddaughter
MOSLEY, Ferrolyn	Tenth great granddaughter
MOSLEY, Florence	Tenth great granddaughter
MOSLEY, Frank Hiram	Tenth great grandson
MOSLEY, George	Eighth great grandson
MOSLEY, George Benjamin Alexander	Seventh great grandson
MOSLEY, George Sylvester	Ninth great grandson
MOSLEY, George W.	Eighth great grandson
MOSLEY, Gerald Olaf	Ninth great grandson
MOSLEY, Gregory	Tenth great grandson
MOSLEY, Grover Cecil	Ninth great grandson
MOSLEY, Hiram A.	Eighth great grandson
MOSLEY, Hiram Mace	Eighth great grandson
MOSLEY, J.D.	Ninth great grandson
MOSLEY, James Augusta	Eighth great grandson
MOSLEY, James Earl	Ninth great grandson
MOSLEY, Jeffery Terence	Ninth great grandson
MOSLEY, Jennie Inez	Tenth great granddaughter
MOSLEY, Jerri Leigh	Tenth great granddaughter
MOSLEY, Jill Stone	Tenth great granddaughter
MOSLEY, Joe	Tenth great grandson
MOSLEY, John Edythe "Edie"	Tenth great granddaughter
MOSLEY, John Erskine	Ninth great grandson
MOSLEY, John M.	Ninth great grandson
MOSLEY, John Wesley	Tenth great grandson
MOSLEY, Karen	Tenth great granddaughter
MOSLEY, Karen S.	Tenth great granddaughter
MOSLEY, Kathleen	Ninth great granddaughter
MOSLEY, Keith Alan	Tenth great grandson
MOSLEY, Leon Wayne	Tenth great grandson
MOSLEY, Linda	Eleventh great granddaughter
MOSLEY, Lizzie Irene	Ninth great granddaughter
MOSLEY, Lousana	Eighth great granddaughter
MOSLEY, Mark Duane	Tenth great grandson

Kinship List - Chief Wahunsonacock Powhatan

Relative | **Relationship**

Relative	Relationship
MOSLEY, Martha Louise	Tenth great granddaughter
MOSLEY, Matilda	Ninth great granddaughter
MOSLEY, Michael Frank	Eleventh great grandson
MOSLEY, Michael Royce	Tenth great grandson
MOSLEY, Minnie Pearl	Ninth great granddaughter
MOSLEY, Myrtle Addie	Eighth great granddaughter
MOSLEY, Myrtle Lucile	Ninth great granddaughter
MOSLEY, Nancy Lee	Tenth great granddaughter
MOSLEY, Opal Mae	Ninth great granddaughter
MOSLEY, Oscar Newton "Junior"	Tenth great grandson
MOSLEY, Pamela Sue	Tenth great granddaughter
MOSLEY, Patricia Diane	Eleventh great granddaughter
MOSLEY, Robert Elisha	Eighth great grandson
MOSLEY, Robert Herman	Ninth great grandson
MOSLEY, Royce George	Ninth great grandson
MOSLEY, Ruby Estelle	Ninth great granddaughter
MOSLEY, Ruth Stone	Ninth great granddaughter
MOSLEY, S.E.	Ninth great granddaughter
MOSLEY, Sandra	Eleventh great granddaughter
MOSLEY, Sarah Pauline	Tenth great granddaughter
MOSLEY, Savannah	Ninth great granddaughter
MOSLEY, Sherwin Anita	Tenth great granddaughter
MOSLEY, Sudie "Sue"	Tenth great granddaughter
MOSLEY, Susan Leigh	Eleventh great granddaughter
MOSLEY, Thelma Mae	Ninth great granddaughter
MOSLEY, Thomas Lee	Tenth great grandson
MOSLEY, Thomas Samuel	Ninth great grandson
MOSLEY, Travis Forrest Sr.	Ninth great grandson
MOSLEY, Travis Forrest Jr.	Tenth great grandson
MOSLEY, William Alexander (Oscar)	Ninth great grandson
MOSLEY, William Alexander Newton	Eighth great grandson
MOSLEY, William Lafayette	Seventh great grandson
MOSLEY, William Lee	Eighth great grandson
MOSLEY, Willie	Ninth great grandson
MOUNCE, Unk	Spouse of eleventh great granddaughter
MURPHY, Unk	Spouse of eleventh great granddaughter
MUSKRAT, Oshaqua	Spouse of second great granddaughter
MYERS, Catherine	Spouse of fifth great grandson
NASH, William Newton	Spouse of ninth great granddaughter
NAVE, Alexander	Spouse of fifth great granddaughter
NEELY, Sharon	Spouse of tenth great grandson
NEFF, Calvin Wayne	Spouse of twelfth great granddaughter
NEFF, Charity Elizabeth	Thirteenth great granddaughter
NEFF, Issac Eugene	Thirteenth great grandson
NEWCOMBE, Mrytle	Spouse of eighth great grandson
NICHOLSON, Evan	Spouse of fifth great granddaughter
NORTHCUTT, Juanita	Eleventh great granddaughter
NORTHCUTT, Ladona	Eleventh great granddaughter
NORTHCUTT, Louie Dean	Eleventh great grandson
NORTHCUTT, Maurine	Eleventh great granddaughter
NORTHCUTT, Paul	Spouse of tenth great granddaughter
NORTON, Rhonda	Spouse of twelfth great grandson
NOWELL, Martha E. Mattie	Spouse of eighth great grandson
NUNCIO, Fred	Spouse of ninth great granddaughter

Kinship List - Chief Wahunsonacock Powhatan

26 January 2012

Relative	Relationship
O'NEAL, William A.	Spouse of ninth great granddaughter
O'ROURKE, Amy Katherine	Twelfth great granddaughter
O'ROURKE, Daniel Thomas	Twelfth great grandson
O'ROURKE, Kelly Jane	Twelfth great granddaughter
O'ROURKE, Thomas John	Spouse of eleventh great granddaughter
OFFETT	Spouse of eighth great granddaughter
OFFETT, Nell	Ninth great granddaughter
OGLETREE, Tommie Pierce	Spouse of ninth great granddaughter
OHOLASE, Quiquocohannock	Spouse
ONEY, Clara Lucile	Spouse of ninth great grandson
OPECHAN, Nicketti	Granddaughter
OPECHAN, Nonoma	Spouse
OPIRHAPAN, Itoyah-Sasawpen	Spouse
ORTOUGHNOISKE	Spouse
OSHASQUA, Muskrat	Spouse of great granddaughter
OTTERMISKE, Ottachugh	Spouse
OTTOPOMTACKE, Potomac	Spouse
OWENS, Henry	Spouse of ninth great granddaughter
OWEROUGHWOUGH, Werawahon	Spouse
PALMER, Anna Lee	Thirteenth great granddaughter
PALMER, Brady	Thirteenth great grandson
PALMER, Gene	Eleventh great grandson
PALMER, James Walter	Eleventh great grandson
PALMER, Jon Randle "Randy"	Twelfth great grandson
PALMER, Lauren Elizabeth	Thirteenth great granddaughter
PALMER, Mark Dexter	Twelfth great grandson
PALMER, Mary Sue	Eleventh great granddaughter
PALMER, Paul Greg	Twelfth great grandson
PALMER, Troy William	Spouse of tenth great granddaughter
PALMER, William Andrew (Bill)	Twelfth great grandson
PAMUKEY WOMAN	Spouse of first cousin
PARKER	Spouse of tenth great granddaughter
PARKER, Doris	Spouse of tenth great grandson
PARKER, Oscar Harry	Spouse of eleventh great granddaughter
PARKER, Sarah Jane	Spouse of eighth great grandson
PARMER, Josiah	Spouse of sixth great granddaughter
PARR, Iva Jean	Tenth great granddaughter
PARR, James	Eleventh great grandson
PARR, James Thomas	Tenth great grandson
PARR, Lawrence Ray	Tenth great grandson
PARR, Linda	Spouse of tenth great grandson
PARR, Thomas Clarence	Spouse of ninth great granddaughter
PARR, William Wilford	Tenth great grandson
PARSONS, Kathryn	Spouse of eleventh great grandson
PATRICK, John K. Clinton	Spouse of eighth great granddaughter
PATTERSON, Dorothy	Spouse of ninth great grandson
PAWSON	Spouse of tenth great granddaughter
PEARSON, Jane Lynn	Spouse of eleventh great grandson
PECK, Jeffrey Oran	Spouse of twelfth great granddaughter
PECK, Jesse Ray	Thirteenth great grandson
PECK, Jodi Kathryn	Thirteenth great granddaughter
PECK, Joshua Howard	Thirteenth great grandson
PICKETT, David	Spouse of ninth great granddaughter
PITTS, Leland	Tenth great grandson

Kinship List - Chief Wahunsonacock Powhatan

26 January 2012

Relative	Relationship
PITTS, Ross	Spouse of ninth great granddaughter
POLAND, C.L.	Eighth great grandchild
POLAND, Daniel Grigsby	Tenth great grandson
POLAND, Elvira	Seventh great granddaughter
POLAND, John Stratton	Seventh great grandson
POLAND, Lenora Lee	Eighth great granddaughter
POLAND, Lucy	Ninth great granddaughter
POLAND, Mary A.	Eighth great granddaughter
POLAND, Nelson	Spouse of sixth great granddaughter
POLAND, Raymond	Ninth great grandson
POLAND, Robert Pytchlynn	Ninth great grandson
POLAND, Sarah Ann	Seventh great granddaughter
POLAND, Sarah Ann E.	Seventh great granddaughter
POLAND, Thomas	Spouse of sixth great granddaughter
POLAND, Thomas	Seventh great grandson
POLAND, Virginia "Jenny"	Eighth great granddaughter
POLAND, Walter Henry	Eighth great grandson
POLAND, William Henry	Seventh great grandson
POLAND, William Pytchlynn	Eighth great grandson
PONNOISKE, Quiquocohannock	Spouse
PORTER, Hurbert	Spouse of tenth great granddaughter
PORTER, Judy	Eleventh great granddaughter
POWELL, Danny Everette	Eleventh great grandson
POWELL, Danny Ray	Spouse of tenth great granddaughter
POWELL, Kenneth Ray	Eleventh great grandson
POWELL, Mike Eugene	Eleventh great grandson
POWELL, Stacey Don	Eleventh great grandson
POWHATAN, Apachano	Spouse of first cousin
POWHATAN, Cleopatra the Shawano	Spouse of first cousin
POWHATAN, Ensenor	Father
POWHATAN, Itoyatin	Brother
POWHATAN, Kekataugh	Brother
POWHATAN, Mangopeesomon	Brother
POWHATAN, Matoaka-Pocahontas	Daughter
POWHATAN, Nantaquas the Shawano	Daughter
POWHATAN, Parahunt the Shawano	Son
POWHATAN, Pochins the Shawano	Son
POWHATAN, Tatacoope the Shawano	Son
POWHATAN, Taux the Shawano	Son
POWHATAN, Chief Wahunsonacock	Self
POWHATAN, Winsonocock	Brother
POYTHRESS, Jane	Spouse of grandson
PRESCOTT, Dewey	Spouse of tenth great granddaughter
PRESTON, Michael Dean	Spouse of twelfth great granddaughter
PYTCHLYNN, Kezzie	Spouse of seventh great grandson
RAGER, Kathlee	Spouse of eleventh great grandson
RAINES, Mollie	Spouse of seventh great grandson
RAINMAKER, Sugi	Spouse of second great grandson
RASCO	Spouse of ninth great granddaughter
RAY, Bill	Eleventh great grandson
RAY, Carole	Eleventh great granddaughter
RAY, Cathy	Eleventh great granddaughter
RAY, John M.	Spouse of tenth great granddaughter
RAY, Johnny	Eleventh great grandson

Kinship List - Chief Wahunsonacock Powhatan

Relative | **Relationship**

Relative	Relationship
REED, Gertrude Lenora	Spouse of ninth great grandson
REEVES, Dan	Spouse of ninth great granddaughter
REEVES, John	Spouse of ninth great granddaughter
RHULE, Elmer	Spouse of eleventh great granddaughter
RICE, Dorothy Renee	Spouse of tenth great grandson
RICH, Unk	Spouse of eleventh great granddaughter
RICHARDS, M.	Spouse of tenth great granddaughter
RICHARDSON	Spouse of tenth great granddaughter
RICHARDSON, Alexandria Raine	Fourteenth great granddaughter
RICHARDSON, Annie Mae	Spouse of eighth great grandson
RICHARDSON, Matthew Cash	Fourteenth great grandson
RICHARDSON, Matthew Scott	Spouse of thirteenth great granddaughter
RIDDER, George	Spouse of tenth great granddaughter
RIDDER, Wavey	Spouse of ninth great grandson
RIFFIE, Eugene	Spouse of eleventh great granddaughter
RILEY, Andrew Jackson Sr.	Spouse of seventh great granddaughter
RILEY, Andrew Lawrence	Ninth great grandson
RILEY, Andrew Leonard	Eighth great grandson
RILEY, Arthur Leonard	Ninth great grandson
RILEY, Carrie Velma	Eighth great granddaughter
RILEY, Charles Robert	Eighth great grandson
RILEY, Chessie Grace	Eighth great granddaughter
RILEY, Clarence	Ninth great grandson
RILEY, Dora	Ninth great granddaughter
RILEY, Joseph Arthur	Eighth great grandson
RILEY, Letty Annety	Eighth great granddaughter
RILEY, Levi Lavan	Eighth great grandson
RILEY, Lewis	Ninth great grandson
RILEY, Mary Louise	Ninth great granddaughter
RILEY, Sidney Alfred	Eighth great grandson
RILEY, Thomas Jefferson	Ninth great grandson
RILEY, Virgil Guy	Eighth great grandson
RILEY, Willey Price	Eighth great granddaughter
RILEY, William Leon	Ninth great grandson
ROBERTSON, Martha A.	Spouse of seventh great grandson
ROBINSON, Lillian Tolbert	Spouse of ninth great grandson
ROBINSON, Ruth	Spouse of ninth great grandson
RODEN, JoAnn	Spouse of eleventh great grandson
ROGERS, Ella Mae	Tenth great granddaughter
ROGERS, John William	Spouse of ninth great granddaughter
ROLFE, Jane	Great granddaughter
ROLFE, John	Son In Law
ROLFE, Thomas	Grandson
ROLLO, Mary Frances "Missy"	Spouse of eighth great grandson
ROLLO, Susan Emoley (Lee) (Sudie)	Spouse of eighth great grandson
ROPER, Phillip Anthony	Spouse of eleventh great granddaughter
ROPER, Teresa Michelle	Twelfth great granddaughter
ROSE, Frank A. Jr.	Spouse of ninth great granddaughter
ROSE, Sr. Frank Alexander	Spouse of ninth great granddaughter
ROSE, Frank Howard	Tenth great grandson
ROSE, Mattie Lula	Spouse of ninth great grandson
ROSE, Robert	Tenth great grandson
ROSE, Unk	Tenth great grandchild
ROSSOW, Sue Dorothy	Spouse of twelfth great grandson

Kinship List - Chief Wahunsonacock Powhatan

26 January 2012

Relative	Relationship
ROWCLIFF, James Mikel	Spouse of tenth great granddaughter
ROWCLIFF, James Mikel, III	Twelfth great grandson
ROWCLIFF, James Mikel, Jr.	Eleventh great grandson
RUHMANN, James Meece	Spouse of eleventh great granddaughter
RUHMANN, Latta Lillian	Twelfth great granddaughter
RUHMANN, Nance Ann	Twelfth great granddaughter
RUSSELL, Fletcher T.	Spouse of ninth great granddaughter
RUSSELL, L.C.	Tenth great grandson
RUSSELL, Thomas S.	Tenth great grandson
SADLER, Bertha	Eighth great granddaughter
SADLER, Christopher Cornelius	Spouse of seventh great granddaughter
SADLER, Earl	Eighth great grandson
SADLER, Ed	Eighth great grandson
SADLER, Ethel	Eighth great granddaughter
SADLER, Ira Melbert	Eighth great grandson
SADLER, Limmie	Eighth great grandchild
SADLER, Lizzie	Eighth great granddaughter
SADLER, Lulu	Eighth great granddaughter
SADLER, Melvin	Eighth great grandson
SADLER, Minnie Myrtle	Eighth great granddaughter
SANDERS, Pauline	Spouse of ninth great grandson
SANFORD, Imogene	Eleventh great granddaughter
SANFORD, James Leslie	Spouse of tenth great granddaughter
SANFORD, Nina	Eleventh great granddaughter
SANFORD, Octavia	Spouse of ninth great grandson
SANFORD, Ora Lorien	Spouse of tenth great grandson
SAVAGE, Leslie Eugene	Spouse of ninth great granddaughter
SAWYER, Dennis	Spouse of eleventh great granddaughter
SCHALSKI, Louella	Spouse of tenth great grandson
SCOTT, Elizabeth	Spouse of fourth great grandson
SCOTT, Mary	Spouse of fourth great grandson
SCOTT, Sonjia	Spouse of twelfth great grandson
SELF, James Ernest	Spouse of ninth great granddaughter
SELF, Nora Louise	Tenth great granddaughter
SELLERS, Flora Mae	Spouse of ninth great grandson
SELLERS, Frank	Spouse of tenth great granddaughter
SHARP, Stephanie	Spouse of twelfth great grandson
SHAW, Jane	Spouse of fifth great grandson
SHAW, Joyce	Spouse of twelfth great grandson
SHAWANO, Amopotoiske	Spouse
SHAWANO, Ioutegaoan	Brother
SHAWANO, Kecatough	Brother
SHAWANO, Opachisco	Brother
SHAWANO, Opitchapan	Brother
SHAWANO, Powtianan	Brother
SHAWANO, Wahunsonacock	Brother
SHEARER, Dora Frances	Eleventh great granddaughter
SHEARER, Edmund	Eleventh great grandson
SHEARER, Glenn	Spouse of tenth great granddaughter
SHEARER, Hazel Valerie	Eleventh great granddaughter
SHEARER, Joyce Glenda	Eleventh great granddaughter
SHEARER, Lola Faye	Eleventh great granddaughter
SHEARER, Norman	Eleventh great grandson
SHEARER, Patricia Ann	Eleventh great granddaughter

Kinship List - Chief Wahunsonacock Powhatan

Relative	Relationship
SHEARER, Pauline Mildred	Eleventh great granddaughter
SHEARER, Robert Lee	Eleventh great grandson
SHEARER, William Verlan	Eleventh great grandson
SHELNUTT, Christopher Alan	Spouse of twelfth great granddaughter
SHELNUTT, Christopher Michael	Thirteenth great grandson
SHELNUTT, Elizabeth Jane	Thirteenth great granddaughter
SHELNUTT, Jonathan Thomas	Thirteenth great grandson
SHELNUTT, Joseph Matthew	Thirteenth great grandson
SHEPPARD, Levinia Mildred	Spouse of sixth great grandson
SIDES, Fred	Spouse of eleventh great granddaughter
SIMMONS, Elizabeth Marthina	Spouse of fifth great grandson
SIMMONS, William I.	Spouse of sixth great granddaughter
SLASHRE, Carman Balbee	Spouse of tenth great grandson
SLATER, Mary Ann	Spouse of sixth great grandson
SMITH, Ann	Spouse of eleventh great grandson
SMITH, Asbury Waskom	Tenth great grandson
SMITH, Charles Edwin	Eleventh great grandson
SMITH, Daniel K	Spouse of eighth great granddaughter
SMITH, Dawson Oliver Reed	Thirteenth great grandson
SMITH, Dorothy Lee	Eleventh great granddaughter
SMITH, Edward	Tenth great grandson
SMITH, Ella Virginia "Dubba"	Ninth great granddaughter
SMITH, Henry Arlington	Eleventh great grandson
SMITH, Infant	Ninth great granddaughter
SMITH, Infant	Ninth great grandson
SMITH, Infnat	Ninth great grandson
SMITH, James Allen	Spouse of tenth great granddaughter
SMITH, Kenneth	Spouse of tenth great granddaughter
SMITH, Kimberly	Eleventh great granddaughter
SMITH, Lillian	Eleventh great granddaughter
SMITH, Lorena S. "Lola"	Spouse of ninth great grandson
SMITH, Louella	Tenth great granddaughter
SMITH, Marton	Spouse of ninth great granddaughter
SMITH, Mary Belle	Eleventh great granddaughter
SMITH, Mattie Sue	Spouse of ninth great grandson
SMITH, Peggy	Eleventh great granddaughter
SMITH, Sandra Gayle	Twelfth great granddaughter
SMITH, Steve	Eleventh great grandson
SMITH, Thomas Benton	Spouse of eleventh great granddaughter
SMITH, Thomas Benton, Jr.	Twelfth great grandson
SMITH, Thomas Poland	Ninth great grandson
SMITH, Thomas Pollard, Jr.	Tenth great grandson
SMITH, Unk	Spouse of eleventh great granddaughter
SMITH, Wynonia	Spouse of eleventh great grandson
SMOCK, Ruth	Spouse of tenth great grandson
SNOWDEN, Lucy Ann	Spouse of sixth great grandson
SOLIS, Maria Alberta	Spouse of eleventh great grandson
SPRAKER, Chad E.	Spouse of thirteenth great granddaughter
SPRAKER, Lauren M.	Fourteenth great granddaughter
SPRINGSTON, Gennie	Spouse of fifth great grandson
STACEY, Lenora	Spouse of seventh great grandson
STAFFORD, Thomas	Spouse of tenth great granddaughter
STANLEY, Mark	Spouse of eleventh great granddaughter
STEAGER, Linda	Spouse of tenth great grandson

Kinship List - Chief Wahunsonacock Powhatan

26 January 2012

Relative	Relationship
STEPHENSON, Donley Randall	Spouse of twelfth great granddaughter
STEVENS, Kathrine	Spouse of tenth great grandson
STEWART, Fleta	Spouse of tenth great grandson
STIDHAM, John	Spouse of fifth great granddaughter
STINSON, Gregory Weylan	Eleventh great grandson
STINSON, Jama Chernault	Twelfth great granddaughter
STINSON, Rae Evelyn	Eleventh great granddaughter
STINSON, Rebecca Louise	Eleventh great granddaughter
STINSON, Sue Angela	Eleventh great granddaughter
STINSON, Walter Lafayette Jr.	Spouse of tenth great granddaughter
STORM	Spouse of eleventh great granddaughter
STORM, Joseph Erik	Twelfth great grandson
STOTTS, Howard	Spouse of ninth great granddaughter
STOYANOSKI, Anna	Twelfth great granddaughter
STOYANOSKI, Stanley Theodore	Spouse of eleventh great granddaughter
STOYANOSKI, Vincent	Twelfth great grandson
STREAM, Dashing	Grandfather
STREAM, Katataugh	First cousin
STREAM, Opechan	Brother In Law
STREAM, Opitchapam	First cousin
STREAM, Chief Rippling	Great grandfather
STREAM, Running	Uncle
STREAM, Scent Flower	Mother
STUART, Barbara	Spouse of eleventh great grandson
STYLES, Mabrie	Spouse of ninth great granddaughter
SUDDETH, Lena Deloys	Spouse of eighth great grandson
SUGGS, Martha A. (Mattie R.)	Spouse of eighth great grandson
TAYLOR, B.B.	Spouse of seventh great grandson
TAYLOR, Blanche Eloise	Spouse of ninth great grandson
TAYLOR, Mary	Spouse of seventh great grandson
THEEL, Norman	Spouse of ninth great granddaughter
THOMAS, Pat	Spouse of twelfth great grandson
THOMPSON, Ann	Eleventh great granddaughter
THOMPSON, Evaughna	Spouse of tenth great grandson
THOMPSON, Freeda Darlene	Spouse of eleventh great grandson
THOMPSON, Gerald	Eleventh great grandson
THOMPSON, Luther	Spouse of tenth great granddaughter
THOMPSON, Mary	Eleventh great granddaughter
TITTLE, Barbara	Eleventh great granddaughter
TITTLE, Donna	Eleventh great granddaughter
TITTLE, Joann	Eleventh great granddaughter
TITTLE, Roak	Spouse of tenth great granddaughter
TITTLE, Timothy	Eleventh great grandson
TORGENSON, Carson Joseph	Spouse of thirteenth great granddaughter
TRAVIS, Martha Jane	Spouse of seventh great grandson
TRUELOVE, Bobby	Spouse of tenth great granddaughter
TSULA FOX, Smallpox Conjurer	Spouse of second great granddaughter
TUCKER, Bertie	Spouse of ninth great grandson
TUCKER, Rochelle	Spouse of tenth great grandson
TURKEY, Aganunitsi-Wild Potato Hop	Second great granddaughter
TURKEY, April-Tkikami Hop	Second great granddaughter
TURKEY, Ghigoneli Hop	Second great granddaughter
TURKEY, Oolootah-Ulutse Hop	Second great granddaughter
TURKEY, Quatsis Hop	Second great granddaughter

Kinship List - Chief Wahunsonacock Powhatan

26 January 2012

Relative	Relationship
TURKEY, Raven Moytoy	Second great grandson
TURKEY, Standing Old Hop	Second great grandson
TURKEY, Swan-Wapehti Hop	Second great granddaughter
TWITCHELL, Dale	Spouse of tenth great granddaughter
TWITCHELL, Dale Carlton	Eleventh great grandson
TWITCHELL, Michael Lee	Eleventh great grandson
TWITCHELL, Pamela Ellen	Eleventh great granddaughter
TWITCHELL, Roger Bruce	Eleventh great grandson
TWITCHELL, Vickie Sue	Eleventh great granddaughter
UNK	Spouse of seventh great grandson
UNK	Spouse of eighth great grandson
UNK	Spouse of ninth great grandson
UNK, Amy	Spouse of twelfth great grandson
UNK, Frances R.	Spouse of sixth great grandson
UNK, Judy	Spouse of tenth great grandson
UNK, Mary	Spouse of sixth great grandson
UNK, Sandra	Spouse of twelfth great grandson
URBAN, Wayne	Spouse of eleventh great granddaughter
UTTOPOMTACKE, Uttamussamacoma	Spouse
VANN	Ninth great granddaughter
VANN, Anna	Seventh great granddaughter
VANN, Avery	Fourth great grandson
VANN, Cynthia	Sixth great granddaughter
VANN, Delilah Amelia	Fifth great granddaughter
VANN, Edith	Fourth great granddaughter
VANN, Edith B.	Fifth great granddaughter
VANN, Edward III	Fifth great grandson
VANN, Edward	Sixth great grandson
VANN, Edward Ned	Spouse of third great granddaughter
VANN, Edward Ned Jr.	Fourth great grandson
VANN, Elizabeth Jane	Sixth great granddaughter
VANN, Eva Lou	Eighth great granddaughter
VANN, Harvey	Ninth great grandson
VANN, Homer	Ninth great grandson
VANN, Howard	Ninth great grandson
VANN, James	Fifth great grandson
VANN, James Albert	Eighth great grandson
VANN, James Clement	Fourth great grandson
VANN, James Mason	Seventh great grandson
VANN, Jenny	Fourth great granddaughter
VANN, Jesse	Fifth great grandson
VANN, John	Fifth great grandson
VANN, John David	Eighth great grandson
VANN, John Joseph	Fourth great grandson
VANN, Joseph	Ninth great grandson
VANN, Joseph	Fifth great grandson
VANN, Joseph	Sixth great grandson
VANN, Katie	Eighth great granddaughter
VANN, Lavica Jane	Sixth great granddaughter
VANN, Lois Mae	Ninth great granddaughter
VANN, Luther	Ninth great grandson
VANN, Maggie	Eighth great granddaughter
VANN, Margaret	Fifth great granddaughter
VANN, Martha M.	Sixth great granddaughter

Kinship List - Chief Wahunsonacock Powhatan

Relative	Relationship
VANN, Mary	Fifth great granddaughter
VANN, Mary Ann	Sixth great granddaughter
VANN, Mary Ann	Eighth great granddaughter
VANN, Mason M.	Fifth great grandson
VANN, Mason M.	Sixth great grandson
VANN, Melvin	Ninth great grandson
VANN, Nancy	Seventh great granddaughter
VANN, Pauline	Ninth great granddaughter
VANN, Robert	Sixth great grandson
VANN, Robert	Eighth great grandson
VANN, Robert B.	Fifth great grandson
VANN, Sally	Fifth great granddaughter
VANN, Sarah	Eighth great granddaughter
VANN, Susanna	Fourth great granddaughter
VANN, Thomas	Fourth great grandson
VANN, Thomas	Eighth great grandson
VANN, Vashti	Fifth great granddaughter
VANN, Vernon	Ninth great grandson
VANN, William	Fifth great grandson
VANN, William	Sixth great grandson
VANN, William Green Jr.	Ninth great grandson
VANN, William Green	Eighth great grandson
VELASCO, Cleopatra	Sister
VELASCO, Don Luis	Spouse of mother
VELASCO, Oppechancino	Brother
VELASCO, Wereowance	Brother
VELASCO, Winsonocock	Brother
WADSWORTH, Elizabeth	Spouse of eleventh great grandson
WAH-LI-OTTERLIFTER	Spouse of fourth great grandson
WAHUNSEEACAWH, Secacawoni	Spouse
WALKER, Bill	Eleventh great grandson
WALKER, Eugene	Eleventh great grandson
WALKER, Robert	Eleventh great grandson
WALKER, Thad	Eleventh great grandson
WALKER, Thaddeus	Spouse of tenth great granddaughter
WALLS, Elizabeth	Spouse of fifth great grandson
WALTERS, Sarah	Spouse of seventh great grandson
WARD, Ruby	Spouse of ninth great grandson
WARREN, Ruby Lee	Spouse of tenth great grandson
WASHINGTON, Agnes	Eleventh great granddaughter
WASHINGTON, Earl	Tenth great grandson
WASHINGTON, Earline	Eleventh great granddaughter
WASHINGTON, Edward Moody	Tenth great grandson
WASHINGTON, Helen	Tenth great granddaughter
WASHINGTON, John Edward	Eleventh great grandson
WASHINGTON, John T.	Spouse of ninth great granddaughter
WASHINGTON, Lester	Tenth great grandson
WASHINGTON, Peggy Sue	Eleventh great granddaughter
WASHINGTON, Roy	Tenth great grandson
WASHINGTON, Tee Ester	Tenth great granddaughter
WASHINGTON, Thomas Anders	Eleventh great grandson
WASHINGTON, Tressie Olene	Tenth great granddaughter
WASKOM	Spouse of ninth great grandson
WATERS, Sarah	Spouse of sixth great grandson

Kinship List - Chief Wahunsonacock Powhatan

26 January 2012

Relative	Relationship
WATKINS, Flay Latta	Tenth great granddaughter
WATKINS, Harry Beaumont	Spouse of ninth great granddaughter
WATKINS, Nelle	Tenth great granddaughter
WATSON, Vernon	Spouse of ninth great granddaughter
WATTS, Donna	Spouse of twelfth great grandson
WEBBER, William	Spouse of second great granddaughter
WEEKS, Allison	Twelfth great granddaughter
WEEKS, Bobbie Jo	Eleventh great granddaughter
WEEKS, Catherine Marie	Twelfth great granddaughter
WEEKS, Christopher Benson	Twelfth great grandson
WEEKS, Cullen Dexter	Tenth great grandson
WEEKS, Cynthia Diane	Twelfth great granddaughter
WEEKS, David Earl	Twelfth great grandson
WEEKS, Donald Wayne	Twelfth great grandson
WEEKS, Edmund Douglas	Thirteenth great grandson
WEEKS, Era Earl	Tenth great grandson
WEEKS, Hugh Middleton	Thirteenth great grandson
WEEKS, J.D.	Eleventh great grandson
WEEKS, James Martin	Spouse of ninth great granddaughter
WEEKS, Jason	Thirteenth great grandson
WEEKS, Jennifer Lynn	Twelfth great granddaughter
WEEKS, Jerry Earl	Eleventh great grandson
WEEKS, Lisa Anne	Twelfth great granddaughter
WEEKS, Marvin Benson	Tenth great grandson
WEEKS, Richard Pearson	Thirteenth great grandson
WEEKS, Stephen Douglas	Twelfth great grandson
WEEKS, Stephen Middleton	Thirteenth great grandson
WEEKS, Venice Myrtle	Tenth great granddaughter
WEEKS, Verda Louise	Tenth great granddaughter
WEEKS, Wanda Gay	Eleventh great granddaughter
WEEKS, Wayne Martin	Eleventh great grandson
WEEKS, Willard Earnest	Tenth great grandson
WELCH, Clarence	Spouse of tenth great granddaughter
WELCH, Dorothy	Eleventh great granddaughter
WELCH, Illa Mae	Eleventh great granddaughter
WELCH, Velma A.	Spouse of tenth great grandson
WHISENANT, Adolphus	Spouse of eighth great granddaughter
WHISENANT, Clyde Earl Jr.	Tenth great grandson
WHISENANT, Clyde Earl	Ninth great grandson
WHISENANT, Mary Louise	Ninth great granddaughter
WHISENANT, Nightie Mae	Ninth great granddaughter
WHISENANT, Olive Inez	Ninth great granddaughter
WHISENANT, Roland Johnnie	Ninth great grandson
WHISENANT, Stella	Spouse of eighth great grandson
WHISENANT, Trudy Sylvia	Ninth great granddaughter
WHISENANT, William	Tenth great grandson
WHITE, Emily Elizabeth	Fourteenth great granddaughter
WHITE, Philip Wayne Jr.	Spouse of thirteenth great granddaughter
WHITMIRE, William	Spouse of sixth great granddaughter
WIEBERDINK, Unk	Spouse of eleventh great granddaughter
WILKINSON, George Allen	Spouse of twelfth great granddaughter
WILKINSON, Jana Marie	Thirteenth great granddaughter
WILLIAMS, Mary Jane	Spouse of seventh great grandson
WILLIAMSON, Peter Nathan	Spouse of thirteenth great granddaughter

Kinship List - Chief Wahunsonacock Powhatan

26 January 2012

Relative	Relationship
WINGANUSKE, Matatiske	Spouse
WINGANUSKE, Nonoma	Spouse
WINGANUSKE, Queen	Spouse
WINNETT, Lonnie	Spouse of ninth great granddaughter
WINSTANLEY	Spouse of ninth great granddaughter
WOLF, Mildred	Spouse of tenth great grandson
WOLFORD, Mavis	Spouse of ninth great grandson
WOOD, Tammie Lynne	Eleventh great granddaughter
WOOD, William Cuthbert	Spouse of tenth great granddaughter
WOODSON	Spouse of tenth great granddaughter
WOODSON, Richard Sible	Eleventh great grandson
WORTHAM, Christina	Spouse of tenth great grandson
WOWINCHO, Nonoma	Spouse
WRIGHT, John Edward	Spouse of eighth great granddaughter
WRIGHT, Troy Lee	Spouse of eighth great granddaughter
WYNN, Cynthia Beth	Eleventh great granddaughter
WYNN, Jacque Leonard	Spouse of tenth great granddaughter
WYNN, Jacqueline	Eleventh great granddaughter
WYNN, Nancy	Eleventh great granddaughter
WYNN, Susan	Eleventh great granddaughter
YEAMAN, Susan	Spouse of eleventh great grandson
YIELDING, Dale	Spouse of twelfth great granddaughter
YIELDING, Jared	Thirteenth great grandson
YIELDING, Rachael	Thirteenth great granddaughter
YOUNG, Adalyn J.	Spouse of tenth great grandson
YOUNG RAINMAKER	Spouse of second great granddaughter
ZIEGLER, Annie	Spouse of eighth great grandson
ZOULA	Spouse of seventh great grandson

Preparer:
JD Weeks
1636 Magnolia Street
Gardendale, AL 35071
jd@jdweeks.com

Made in the USA
Columbia, SC
07 January 2022